MW00769478

Martin Heidegger is one of the twentieth century's most influential, but also most cryptic and controversial philosophers. His early fusion of phenomenology with existentialism inspired Sartre and many others, and his later critique of modern rationality inspired Derrida and still others. This introduction covers the whole of Heidegger's thought and is ideal for anyone coming to his work for the first time.

John Richardson centers his account on Heidegger's persistent effort to change the very kind of understanding or truth we seek. Beginning with an overview of Heidegger's life and work, he sketches the development of Heidegger's thought up to the publication of *Being and Time*. He shows how that book takes up Husserl's method of phenomenology and adapts it. He then introduces and assesses the key arguments of *Being and Time* under three headings—pragmatism, existentialism, and temporality—its three levels of analysis of human experience.

Subsequent chapters introduce Heidegger's later philosophy, including his turn towards a historical account of being, and new ideas about how we need to 'think' to get the truth about it; his influential writings on language, art, and poetry, and their role in the Western history of being; and his claim that this history has culminated in a technological relation to things that is deeply problematic, above all in the way it excludes the divine. The final chapter looks at Heidegger's profound influence on several intellectual movements ranging from phenomenology to existentialism to postmodernism.

A much-needed and refreshing introduction to this major figure, *Heidegger* is ideal reading for anyone coming to his work for the first time and will interest and stimulate students and scholars alike.

John Richardson is Professor of Philosophy at New York University, USA. He is the author of *Existential Epistemology; A Heideggerian Critique of the Cartesian Project* (1986), *Nietzsche's System* (1996), and *Nietzsche's New Darwinism* (2004). He is a co-editor of *Nietzsche* (2001) in the series *Oxford Readings in Philosophy*.

Routledge Philosophers

Edited by Brian Leiter

University of Chicago

Routledge Philosophers is a major series of introductions to the great Western philosophers. Each book places a major philosopher or thinker in historical context, explains and assesses their key arguments, and considers their legacy. Additional features include a chronology of major dates and events, chapter summaries, annotated suggestions for further reading and a glossary of technical terms.

An ideal starting point for those new to philosophy, they are also essential reading for those interested in the subject at any level.

Hobbes
A. P. Martinich

Leibniz
Nicholas Jolley

Locke
E. J. Lowe

Hegel
Frederick Beiser

Rousseau
Nicholas Dent

Schopenhauer
Julian Young

Freud
Jonathan Lear

Kant
Paul Guyer

Husserl
David Woodruff Smith

Darwin
Tim Lewens

Aristotle
Christopher Shields

Rawls
Samuel Freeman

Spinoza
Michael Della Rocca

Merleau-Ponty
Taylor Carman

Russell
Gregory Landini

Wittgenstein
William Child

Forthcoming:

Adorno
Brian O'Connor

Plato
Constance Meinwald

Hume
Don Garrett

Dewey
Steven Fesmire

Habermas
Kenneth Baynes

Smith
Eric Schliesser

Mill
Daniel Jacobson

John Richardson

Heidegger

Routledge
Taylor & Francis Group

LONDON AND NEW YORK

First published 2012
by Routledge
2 Park Square, Milton Park, Abingdon, Oxon, OX14 4RN

Simultaneously published in the USA and Canada
by Routledge
711 Third Avenue, New York, NY 10017

*Routledge is an imprint of the Taylor & Francis Group, an
informa business*

© 2012 John Richardson

All rights reserved. No part of this book may be reprinted or
reproduced or utilised in any form or by any electronic,
mechanical, or other means, now known or hereafter
invented, including photocopying and recording, or in any
information storage or retrieval system, without permission
in writing from the publishers.

Trademark notice: Product or corporate names may be
trademarks or registered trademarks, and are used only for
identification and explanation without intent to infringe.

British Library Cataloguing in Publication Data

A catalogue record for this book is available from the British
Library

Library of Congress Cataloging in Publication Data
Richardson, John, 1951-
Heidegger / by John Richardson.
p. cm. -- (The Routledge philosophers)
Includes bibliographical references and index.
1. Heidegger, Martin, 1889-1976. I. Title.
B3279.H49R495 2012
193--dc23
2011034785

ISBN: 978-0-415-35070-9 (hbk)
ISBN: 978-0-415-35071-6 (pbk)
ISBN: 978-0-203-12710-0 (ebk)

Typeset in Joanna and DINOT
by Taylor & Francis Books

To Hubert Dreyfus

Contents

Acknowledgments

My founding debt is to Bert Dreyfus, who brought Heidegger to life for me when I was his graduate student at Berkeley. He is also the first cause of my second debt, to the meetings at Asilomar held every summer by (mainly) his former students and influencees. Here I profited from friendly interaction with the many regular attenders of these meetings, too many to name; my great debts to their individual writing are shown in this book. I am further grateful to those who read and gave valuable reactions to drafts: Jeff Sebo, Tito Magri, Paul Lodge, and (especially) Lee Braver.

A note on translations

Although I cite texts by English language editions, I have revised the translations for the sake of consistency; this is especially important with his later vocabulary, which is translated in a confusing variety of ways in those editions. I have also aimed at simpler and more literal renderings of Heidegger's German. In a few cases (*Dasein*, *das Man*, *Ereignis*) I have mainly kept the German. I list some of my translations in the Glossary at the back. But let me mention here one most important case: I translate Heidegger's *Sein* by "being" and *Seiendes* by "entity"; more usually these are both rendered "being," relying on context (or by pluralizing *Seiendes* as "beings," or by capitalizing *Sein* as "Being") to distinguish them. Since the difference between these is so crucial to Heidegger's thinking, I think a sharper distinction is appropriate.

Abbreviations for Heidegger's works

Abbreviations are based on my own translations of Heidegger's titles, given below; these sometimes differ from the cited editions' titles. For each work I also give the German title, the year of initial composition (many pieces he later reworked), the kind of piece it began as (e.g. lecture or lecture-course), and its volume number in the standard edition of Heidegger's works, the *Gesamtausgabe* (*GA*) published by Vittorio Klostermann. The next line gives first the English edition whose page numbers I cite (though I have often revised the translation), then any other English editions that contain the piece. Volume titles are italicized.

A   "Alêtheia (Heraclitus, Fragment B16)"
"Alêtheia (Heraclit, Fragment 16)"; 1951, lecture; in *GA* 7; tr. by D. Krell & F. Capuzzi in *EGT*.

AM   *Aristotle, Metaphysics Theta 1–3: On the Essence and Actuality of Force*
Aristoteles, Metaphysik Theta 1–3: Von Wesen und Wirklichkeit der Kraft; 1931, lecture-course; *GA* 33; tr. by W. Brogan & P. Warnek, Bloomington: Indiana University Press, 1995.

AS   "Anaximander's Saying"
"Der Spruch des Anaximander"; 1946, essay; in *GA* 5; tr. by J. Young & K. Haynes in *W*; also tr. as "The Anaximander Fragment" by D. Krell & F. Capuzzi in *EGT*.

AWP   "The Age of the World Picture"
"Die Zeit des Weltbildes"; 1938, lecture; in *GA* 5; tr. by J. Young & K. Haynes in *W*; also tr. by W. Lovitt in *QTE*.

AWH "'As When on a Holiday ... '"
"'Wie Wenn am Feiertage ... '"; 1939, lecture; in *GA* 4; tr. by K. Hoeller in *EHP*.

AWM "Afterword to 'What Is Metaphysics?'"
"Nachwort zu 'Was ist Metaphysik?'"; 1943, later addition to WM; in *GA* 9; tr. as "Postscript to ..." by W. McNeill in *P*.

BC *Basic Concepts*
Grundbegriffe; 1941, lecture-course; *GA* 51; tr. by G. Aylesworth, Bloomington: Indiana University Press, 1993.

BCA *Basic Concepts of Aristotelian Philosophy*
Grundbegriffe der aristotelischen Philosophie; 1924, lecture-course; *GA* 18; tr. by R. Metcalf & M. Tanzer, Bloomington: Indiana University Press, 2009.

BCM *The Basic Concepts of Metaphysics: World, Finitude, Solitude*
Die Grundbegriffe der Metaphysik. Welt—Endlichkeit—Einsamkeit; 1929–30; lecture-course; *GA* 29/30; tr. as *The Fundamental Concepts of Metaphysics* ... by W. McNeill & N. Walker, Bloomington: Indiana University Press, 1995.

BDT "Building Dwelling Thinking"
"Bauen Wohnen Denken"; 1951, lecture; in *GA* 7; tr. by A. Hofstadter in *BW*; also in *PLT*.

BP *The Basic Problems of Phenomenology*
Die Grundprobleme der Phänomenologie; 1927, lecture-course; *GA* 2; tr. by A. Hofstadter, Bloomington: Indiana University Press, 1982.

BT *Being and Time*
Sein und Zeit; 1927, book; *GA* 2; tr. by J. Macquarrie & E. Robinson, New York: Harper & Row, 1962; also tr. by J. Stambaugh, Albany: SUNY Press 1996; cited by pagination in the German first edition, given marginally in both English translations (and in *GA* 2).

BW *Basic Writings*
Selected essays ed. by D. Krell, Rev. Edition, San Francisco: HarperCollins Publishers, 1993.

CL "Creative Landscape: Why Do We Stay in the Provinces?"
"Schöpferische Landschaft: Warum bleiben wir in der Provinz?"; 1933, radio talk; in *GA* 13; tr. as "Why Do I Stay in the Provinces?" by T. Sheehan in *Heidegger: The Man and the Thinker*, Chicago: Precedent Press, 1981.

CP *Contributions to Philosophy (From Ereignis)*
Beiträge zur Philosophie (Vom Ereignis); 1936–38, book draft; *GA* 65tr. as *Contributions to Philosophy (From Enowning)* by P. Emad & K. Maly, Bloomington: Indiana University Press, 1999.

CPC "Conclusion: The Problem of the Categories"
"Schluss. Die Kategorienproblem"; 1916, afterword to DC; in *GA* 1; tr. by R. Stewart & J. van Buren in *S*.

CT   "The Concept of Time"
Der Begriff der Zeit; 1924, lecture; in *GA* 64; tr. as *The Concept of Time* by W. McNeill, Oxford: Blackwell Publishing, 1992.

CTS   "The Concept of Time in the Science of History"
"Die Zeitbegriff in der Geschichtswissenschaft"; 1916, article; in *GA* 1; tr. by H. Taylor *et al.* in *S*.

DC   "The Doctrine of Categories and Meaning of Duns Scotus"
"Die Kategorien- und Bedeutungslehre des Duns Scotus"; 1915, postdoctoral dissertation; in *GA* 1.

DL   "From a Dialogue on Language"
"Aus einem Gespräch von der Sprache"; 1953–54, dialogue; in *GA* 12; tr. by P. Hertz in *UL*.

DP   *Towards the Definition of Philosophy*
Zur Bestimmung der Philosophie; 1919, two lecture-courses; *GA* 56/57; tr. by T. Sadler, London: Continuum, 2008.

DR   "Towards Discussion of Releasement; From a Fieldpath-Conversation on Thinking"
"Zur Erörterung der Gelassenheit; Aus einem Feldweggespräch über das Denken"; 1944–45, extract from FC; in *GA* 13; tr. as "Conversation on a Country Path" by J. Anderson & E. Freund in *DT*.

DS   *Der Spiegel* Interview
"Spiegel-Gespräch mit Martin Heidegger"; 1966, interview; in *GA* 16; tr. by R. Wolin in *The Heidegger Controversy: A Critical Reader*, Cambridge, MA: MIT Press.

DT   *Discourse on Thinking*
Contains Rel & DR, tr. by J. Anderson & E. Freund, New York: Harper & Row, 1966.

EC   "On the Essence and Concept of *Phusis* in Aristotle's *Physics* B, 1"
"Vom Wesen und Begriff der *Phusis*. Aristoteles, Physik B, 1"; 1939, treatise; in *GA* 9; tr. by T. Sheehan in *P*.

EG   "On the Essence of Ground"
"Vom Wesen des Grundes"; 1929, essay; in *GA* 9; tr. by W. McNeill in *P*; also tr. as *The Essence of Reasons* by T. Malick, Evanston: Northwestern University Press, 1969.

EGT   *Early Greek Thinking*
Selected essays tr. by D. Krell & F. Capuzzi, New York: Harper & Row, 1975.

EHP   *Elucidations of Hölderlin's Poetry*
Erläuterungen zu Hölderlins Dichtung; 1944 and after, essay collection; *GA* 4; tr. by K. Hoeller, Amherst, NY: Humanity Books, 2000.

EL   "The Essence of Language"
"Das Wesen der Sprache"; 1957, three lectures; in *GA* 12; tr. as "The Nature of Language" by P. Hertz in *UL*.

EN   "European Nihilism"
"Der europäische Nihilismus"; 1940, lecture-course; in *GA* 6.2; tr. by F. Capuzzi in *N*, vol. 4.

EP   "The End of Philosophy and the Task of Thinking"
"Das Ende der Philosophie und die Aufgabe des Denkens"; 1964, lecture; in *GA* 14; tr. by J. Stambaugh in *BW*; also in *OTB*.

ERW   "The Eternal Return of the Same and the Will to Power"
"Die ewige Wiederkehr des Gleichen und die Wille zur Macht"; 1939, lectures; in *GA* 6.2; tr. as "The Eternal Recurrence ... " by J. Stambaugh *et al.* in *N*, vol. 3.

ET   "On the Essence of Truth"
"Vom Wesen der Wahrheit"; 1930, lecture; in *GA* 9; tr. by J. Sallis in *P*; also in *BW*.

ETP   *On the Essence of Truth: On Plato's Cave Allegory and Theaetetus*
Vom Wesen der Wahrheit: zu Platons Höhlengleichnis und Theätet; 1931–32, lecture-course; *GA* 34; tr. by T. Sadler, London: Continuum, 2002.

FC   *Fieldpath Conversations*
Feldweg-Gespräche; 1944–45, three dialogues; *GA* 77; tr. as *Country Path Conversations* by B. Davis, Bloomington: Indiana University Press, 2010.

FS   "Four Seminars"
"Vier Seminare. Le Thor 1966, 1968, 1969 – Zähringen 1973"; 1966, 1968, 1969, 1973, seminars; in *GA* 15; tr. as *Four Seminars* by A. Mitchell & F. Raffoul, Bloomington: Indiana University Press, 2003.

GA   *Gesamtausgabe*
Frankfurt am Main: Vittorio Klostermann. [Cited by volume number in this standard edition, projected to contain about 100 volumes.]

HC   "Hegel's Concept of Experience"
"Hegels Begriff der Erfahrung"; 1942–43, treatise; in *GA* 5; tr. as HC by J. Young & K. Haynes in *W*.

HE   "Hölderlin and the Essence of Poetry"
"Hölderlin und das Wesen der Dichtung"; 1936, lecture; in *GA* 4; tr. by K. Hoeller in *EHP*.

HG   "Hegel and the Greeks"
"Hegel und die Griechen"; 1958, lecture; in *GA* 9; tr. by R. Metcalf in *P*.

HHI   *Hölderlin's Hymn "The Ister"*
Hölderlins Hymne "Der Ister"; 1942, lecture-course; *GA* 53; tr. by W. McNeill & J. Davis, Bloomington: Indiana University Press, 1996.

HK "'Homecoming/To Kindred Ones'"
"'Heimkunft/An die Verwandten'"; 1943, lecture; in *GA* 4; tr. by K. Hoeller in *EHP*.

ID *Identity and Difference*
Identität und Differenz; 1957, lectures; *GA* 11; tr. by J. Stambaugh, New York: Harper & Row, 1969.

IM *Introduction to Metaphysics*
Einführung in die Metaphysik; 1935, lecture-course; *GA* 40; tr. by G. Fried & R. Polt, New Haven: Yale University Press, 2000.

IP *Introduction to Philosophy: Thinking and Poeming*
Einleitung in die Philosophie: Denken und Dichten; 1944–45, lecture-course; in *GA* 50; tr. as *Introduction to Philosophy—Thinking and Poetizing* by P. Braunstein, Bloomington: Indiana University Press, 2011.

IPR *Introduction to Phenomenological Research*
Einführung in die phänomenologische Forschung; 1923–24, lecture-course; *GA* 17; tr. by D. Dahlstrom, Bloomington: Indiana University Press, 2005.

IWM "Introduction to 'What Is Metaphysics?'"
"Einleitung zu 'Was ist Metaphysik?'"; 1949, later addition to *WM*; in *GA* 9; tr. by W. Kaufmann in *P*.

KJ "Comments on Karl Jaspers's *Psychology of Worldviews*"
"Anmerkungen zu Karl Jaspers *Psychologie der Weltanschauungen*"; 1919–21; in *GA* 9; tr. by J. van Buren in *P*; also in *S*.

KP *Kant and the Problem of Metaphysics*
Kant und das Problem der Metaphysik; 1929, book; *GA* 3; tr. by R. Taft, Fifth Edition, Bloomington: Indiana University Press 1997.

KT "Kant's Thesis about Being"
"Kants These über das Sein"; 1961, lecture; in *GA* 9; tr. by T. Klein & W. Pohl in *P*.

LH "Letter on 'Humanism'"
"Brief über den Humanismus"; 1946; in *GA* 9; tr. by F. Capuzzi in *P*; also in *BW*.

Lo "Logos (Heraclitus, Fragment B50)"
"Logos (Heraklit, Fragment 50)"; 1951, lecture; in *GA* 7; tr. as Lo by D. Krell & F. Capuzzi in *EGT*.

LP "Language in the Poem: A Discussion on Georg Trakl's Poetic Work"
"Die Sprache im Gedicht. Eine Erörterung von Georg Trakls Gedicht"; 1953, essay; in *GA* 12; tr. by P. Hertz in *UL*.

LQ *Logic as the Question Concerning the Essence of Language*
Logik als die Frage nach dem Wesen der Sprache; 1934, lecture-course; *GA* 38; tr. by W. Gregory & Y. Unna, Albany: SUNY Press, 2009.

M Mindfulness
   Besinnung; 1938–39, book draft; GA 66; tr. by P. Emad & T. Kalary, London: Continuum, 2006.

MF The Metaphysical Foundations of Logic Starting from Leibniz
    Metaphysische Anfangsgründe der Logik im Ausgang vom Leibniz; 1928, lecture-course; GA 26; tr. The Metaphysical Foundations of Logic by M. Heim, Bloomington: Indiana University Press, 1984.

Mo "Moira (Parmenides, Fragment 8)"
    "Moira (Parmenides, Fragment 8)"; 1951–52, lecture; in GA 7; tr. as Mo by D. Krell & F. Capuzzi in EGT.

N Nietzsche
   Nietzsche; 1936–53, collected lecture-courses, lectures, essays; GA 6.1 & 6.2; tr. (omitting several pieces) by D. Krell et al. as Nietzsche, vols. 1–4, New York: Harper & Row, 1979–87.

ND "Nihilism as Determined by the History of Being"
    "Die seinsgeschichtliche Bestimmung des Nihilismus"; 1944–46, essay; in GA 6.2; tr. by F. Capuzzi in N, vol. 4.

NM "Nietzsche's Metaphysics"
    "Nietzsches Metaphysik"; 1940, treatise; in GA 6.2; tr. by J. Stambaugh et al. in N, vol. 3.

NW "Nietzsche's Word: 'God Is Dead'"
    "Nietzsches Wort 'Gott ist tot'"; 1943, lecture; in GA 5; tr. by J. Young & K. Haynes in W; also tr. as "The Word of Nietzsche ... " by W. Lovitt in QTE.

OA "The Origin of the Artwork"
    "Die Ursprung des Kunstwerkes"; 1935–36, lectures; in GA 5; tr. as "The Origin of the Work of Art" by J. Young & K. Haynes in W; also tr. by A. Hofstadter in BW, PLT.

OTB On Time and Being
     Selected essays tr. by J. Stambaugh, New York: Harper & Row, 1972.

P Pathmarks
   Wegmarken; 1967, essay collection; GA 9; ed. by W. McNeill, Cambridge, UK: Cambridge University Press, 1998.

Par Parmenides
     Parmenides; 1942–43, lecture-course; GA 54; tr. by A. Schuwer & R. Rojcewicz, Bloomington: Indiana University Press, 1992.

PD "Plato's Doctrine of Truth"
    "Platons Lehre von der Wahrheit"; 1931–32, 1940, essay derived from ET; in GA 9; tr. by T. Sheehan in P.

PG The Principle of Ground
    Der Satz vom Grund; 1955–56, lecture-course; GA 10; tr. as The Principle of Reason by R. Lilly, Bloomington: Indiana University Press, 1991.

PH   Prolegomena to the History of the Concept of Time
      Prolegomena zur Geschichte des Zeitbegriffs; 1925, lecture-course; GA 2; tr. as
      History of the Concept of Time: Prolegomena by T. Kisiel, Bloomington: Indiana
      University Press, 1985.

PIE   Phenomenology of Intuition and Expression
      Phänomenologie der Anschauung und des Ausdrucks; 1920; lecture-course; GA 59;
      tr. by T. Colony, London: Continuum, 2010.

PL   "The Path to Language"
      "Der Weg zur Sprache"; 1959, lecture; in GA 12; tr. as "The Way to
      Language" by P. Hertz in UL; also tr. by D. Krell in BW.

PLT   Poetry, Language, Thought
      Selected essays tr. by A. Hofstadter, New York: Harper & Row, 1971.

PR   Phenomenology of Religious Life
      Phänomenologie des religiösen Lebens; 1920–21, lecture-course; GA 60; tr. by
      M. Fritsch & J. Gosetti-Ferencei, Bloomington: Indiana University Press,
      2004.

QB   "On the Question of Being"
      "Zur Seinsfrage"; 1955, essay; in GA 9; tr. by W. McNeill in P.

QT   "The Question about Technology"
      "Die Frage nach der Technik"; 1949, lecture; in GA 7; tr. as "The
      Question Concerning Technology" by W. Lovitt in BW; also in QTE.

QTE   The Question Concerning Technology and Other Essays
      Selected essays tr. by W. Lovitt, New York: Harper & Row, 1977.

Rel   "Releasement"
      "Gelassenheit"; 1955, lecture; in GA 16; tr. as "Memorial Address" by
      J. Anderson & E. Freund in DT.

Rem   "'Remembrance'"
      "'Andenken'"; 1943, essay; in GA 4; tr. by K. Hoeller in EHP.

S   Supplements: From the Earliest Essays to Being and Time and Beyond
      Selected essays etc. ed. by J. van Buren, Albany: SUNY Press, 2002.

SA   "The Self-Assertion of the German University"
      "Die Selbstbehauptung der deutschen Universität"; 1933, speech; in GA
      16; tr. by R. Wolin in The Heidegger Controversy: A Critical Reader, Cambridge,
      MA: MIT Press.

Soj   "Sojourns"
      "Aufenthalte"; 1962, travel memoir; in GA 75; tr. as Sojourns by J. Manoussakis,
      Albany: SUNY Press, 2005.

SR   "Science and Reflection"
      "Wissenschaft und Besinnung"; 1954, lecture; in GA 7; tr. by W. Lovitt
      in QTE.

TB   "Time and Being"
"Zeit und Sein"; 1962, lecture; in *GA* 14; tr. by J. Stambaugh in *OTB*.

Tu   "The Turning"
"Die Kehre"; 1949, lecture; in *GA* 79; tr. by W. Lovitt in *QTE*.

UL   *Underway to Language*
Unterwegs zur Sprache; 1959, essay collection; *GA* 12 tr. (omitting one essay) as *On the Way to Language* by P. Hertz, New York: Harper & Row, 1971.

W   *Woodpaths*
Holzwege; 1950, essay collection; *GA* 5; tr. as *Off the Beaten Track* by J. Young & K. Haynes, Cambridge, UK: Cambridge University Press, 2002.

WCT   *What Is Called Thinking?*
Was heisst Denken?; 1951–52, lecture-course; *GA* 8; tr. by F. Wieck & J. Gray, New York: Harper & Row, 1968.

WM   "What Is Metaphysics?"
"Was ist Metaphysik?"; 1929, lecture; in *GA* 9; tr. by D. Krell in *P*; also in *BW*.

WN   "Who Is Nietzsche's Zarathustra?"
"Wer ist Nietzsches Zarathustra?"; 1953, lecture; in *GA* 7; tr. by D. Krell in *N*, vol. 2.

Wo   "The Word"
"Das Wort"; 1958, lecture; in *GA* 12; tr. as "Words" by P. Hertz in *UL*.

WP   "Why Poets?"
"Wozu Dichter?"; 1946, lecture; in *GA* 5; tr. by J. Young & K. Haynes in *W*; also tr. as "What Are Poets for?" by A. Hofstadter in *PLT*.

WPA   "The Will to Power as Art"
"Der Wille zur Macht als Kunst"; 1936–37, lecture-course; in *GA* 6.1; tr. by D. Krell as *N*, vol. 1.

WPK   "The Will to Power as Knowledge"
"Die Wille zur Macht als Erkenntnis"; 1939, lecture-course; in *GA* 6.1; tr. by J. Stambaugh et al. in *N*, vol. 3.

Z   *Zollikon Seminars*
Zollikoner Seminare; 1959–69, seminars, conversations, letters; *GA* 89; tr. as *Zollikon Seminars: Protocols—Conversations—Letters* by F. Mayr & R. Askay, Evanston: Northwestern University Press, 2001.

Chronology

1889	Born September 26 in Messkirch, a town in Baden, SW Germany.
1895	Begins at local schools in Messkirch.
1903	Supported by a grant from the Catholic Church, goes away to school in Konstanz.
1906	On another Church grant, begins study in Berthold Gymnasium in Freiburg.
1909	Enters Society of Jesus as a novice, but is dismissed with heart pains after two weeks. Enters Freiburg Theological Seminary.
1911	Leaves the seminary after recurring heart problems. Begins in the Department of Natural Science and Mathematics at the University of Freiburg.
1913	Completes doctoral dissertation on "The Doctrine of Judgment in Psychologism." Moves to the Department of Philosophy at Freiburg.
1915	Completes qualifying dissertation on "The Doctrine of Categories and Meaning in Duns Scotus." Begins teaching as a *Privatdozent* at Freiburg. Is called for military service but released for health reasons.
1916	Is passed over for the chair in Catholic philosophy he had aimed at. Husserl arrives in Freiburg.

1917	Marries Elfride Petri, who had been a student in his first class.
1918	After meteorological training, serves the last few months of the war in a weather station near the front lines.
1919	Son Jörg is born. With Husserl's support, obtains a paid teaching position at Freiburg. Announces that he no longer accepts Catholic doctrine.
1920	Son Hermann is born.
1922	By Elfride's arrangement, cabin in Todtnauberg is built.
1923	Again with Husserl's help, is appointed associate professor at Marburg.
1924	Begins affair with Hannah Arendt, recently arrived as a student in Marburg.
1927	Publishes *Being and Time*. Promoted to full professor at Marburg.
1928	Returns to Freiburg as professor, receiving Husserl's former chair.
1929	Publishes *Kant and the Problem of Metaphysics*. Presents "What Is Metaphysics?" as inaugural lecture at Freiburg.
1933	Elected Rector of Freiburg on April 21. Joins National Socialist Party in May. Delivers inaugural address "The Self-Assertion of the German University." Declines offers of chairs at Berlin and Munich. Organizes "science camp" in Todtnauberg.
1934	Resigns Rectorship of Freiburg on April 23.
1935	Gives lecture-course later published as *Introduction to Metaphysics*.
1936	Gives lecture "The Origin of the Artwork." Begins *Contributions to Philosophy*, articulating his "turning." Begins lecturing on Nietzsche.
1939	Sons Jörg and Hermann enter the military.

1944	Publishes first edition of essay collection *Elucidations of Hölderlin's Poetry*. Is conscripted into the militia to dig trenches. On release, leaves Freiburg for Messkirch.
1945	Teaches an informal spring term at Castle Wildenstein near Messkirch. Sons are missing on the Eastern Front. Returns to Freiburg to defend himself in denazification proceedings.
1946	After nervous breakdown spends several weeks in a sanatorium. Is prohibited from teaching by French military authorities, but allowed to keep his pension. Writes "Letter on 'Humanism'" to Jean Beaufret.
1949	Begins lecturing in Bremen and Bühlerhöhe.
1950	Visited by Hannah Arendt. Publishes essay collection *Woodpaths*.
1951	Resumes teaching at Freiburg.
1954	Publishes collection *Lectures and Essays*. Publishes *What Is Called Thinking?*
1959	Publishes essay collection *Underway to Language*. Gives first seminar in Zollikon.
1961	Publishes *Nietzsche*, a two-volume collection of lectures and essays.
1962	Makes first trip to Greece.
1966	Gives first seminar in Le Thor. Interviewed by *Der Spiegel*. With Eugen Fink, gives seminar in Freiburg on Heraclitus.
1967	Publishes essay collection *Pathmarks*.
1970	Suffers stroke.
1974	Ceases teaching.
1976	Dies May 26. Is buried in Messkirch in a Catholic service.

Introduction

Heidegger is a philosopher with a difference, a difference that makes him easier and harder to introduce. He sets unusual goals for philosophy, and by this change in aim he both invites and resists our understanding him. For he promises us a new kind of truth, but—inevitably—requires that we think this truth in a new and difficult way.

That Heidegger invites readers is evident in the great appeal he has had, and in particular in its unusual breadth: although his influence on (many) philosophers has been huge, he has also appealed to very many readers outside the discipline, not trained or experienced in philosophy. He is a philosopher many dip into philosophy for, whether from other academic fields, or from everyday life. He seems to say: you don't need to know a lot of other philosophy in order to read me.

In fact Heidegger appeals to many of these readers in pointed contrast with academic philosophy: he strikes them as addressing issues crucial to their own disciplines, or to their personal and human concerns, but issues which much other philosophy seems (to them) to have lost sight of. Many readers gather this sense of importance at once from the writings, which persuade them that he has deep truths, and a rare authority in teaching them.

This holds true, I think, of both of the periods of Heidegger's philosophy. For, like most philosophers', his views changed through the years, and, like some others', his views are usually divided into two main stages or phases. The first is crystallized in the magnum opus *Being and Time*, published in 1927. The latter is represented in no one dominant work, but in a developing series of books and (especially) essays, published from the mid-1930s on. Famously he calls his shift between these two viewpoints his "turning," the same name he also gives to the culture-wide redemption he thinks we must hope for. Between these two phases of his thinking there are differences not only in content but in style—but both have attracted that unusual breadth of readers.

Nevertheless, Heidegger has drawn this audience despite serious obstacles or hurdles he also poses to his readers—and to us as we start into him. There are concrete and obvious ways in which his writing resists our effort to "grasp" him. Several specific challenges are, I think, fairly readily coped with. However, there is also a more fundamental and less conspicuous problem he poses, which will be an issue for us throughout.

(a) A first evident problem is his *historicality*. He has, of the "major philosophers"—among whom he blatantly counts himself—a quite exceptional interest in the history of philosophy. Indeed he thinks this history of philosophy *matters* to a degree that would surprise even most historians of philosophy. So to get to his own views we have to go through some philosophical history. He is interested especially in those major, landmarking figures in that history—the ones before him.

His view of history's importance is reflected in his practice. Much of his own writing is interpretive: readings and analyses of these great dead figures, especially Aristotle, Kant, and Nietzsche. For the most part his own views emerge only eventually within these readings, coming gradually into focus as part of a diagnosis and critique of his predecessors' views. So much of the time he presents his own position in terms of theirs, in contrast with theirs, and as part of a critique of theirs. This puts him hugely at odds with our own dominant philosophical practice, which makes history an adjunct to the main business. It also sets a hurdle in front of his readers, a scholarly task which seems at odds with the populist appeal I noted: we need to know his history of thinkers before we can know what he thinks.

If Heidegger's many readers are not dissuaded, it is because his histories can have a distinctive attraction or power. He has a rare ability to revive the philosophies he examines: he puts life back into their concepts and claims. And he does so precisely by bringing them—and us—into better relation with philosophical issues themselves; proper history needs this attention to "the problems themselves," he insists. A common objection to his histories will be, indeed, that they have too much of Heidegger's own thinking in them.

(b) A second concrete challenge Heidegger poses to new readers is the elaborate new *jargon* he devises to state his views. The intricate and idiosyncratic terminology in which *Being and Time* is presented is famous, but his later works pose, in this regard, even greater difficulties. For in them the new terms have a strong poetic and allusive cast, and are far less susceptible to definition or clear explication than the earlier vocabulary. What, for example, should we make of his (late) assertion that "language is the house of being"?

Heidegger makes new terms with a vengeance. He is convinced that the terms in the current debates are all unapt and misleading, even corrupt. He eventually argues that it is the prime business of philosophy to make new words—this is how it changes our world. We observe through his career a steady casting-off of terms he once deemed adequate, and ever new coinages. So you can't hear about Heidegger without learning some jargon.

However, there's a second problem here, even worse, over how to *translate* these new terms into (in our case) English. Heidegger is famously hard to translate. And since there's often not even a clear most-nearly-best English word to match one of his special terms, different translators render even very central terms in a confusing variety of ways. It can be very hard to connect the ideas in two of Heidegger's later essays if one has read them in different translations.

He is especially hard to translate because of the way he "plays" with his new terms. He builds clusters of terms on shared stems, and makes a web of apparently punning connections among them. He inflects these words by marking etymologies and dialects that will mean little to us without study. Beyond this, his later writing often takes a self-consciously "poetic" character. The ways the (mere) sound of his German words connects them is important to him, and is very hard to reflect in translation.

Finally, along with all of these difficulties with his terminology there also lurks a temptation and danger: it's easy to feel that getting a grip on this complex vocabulary is the point. It's so hard to learn to speak his language that doing so has seemed to many readers to be enough—a high achievement. But Heidegger himself, we'll see, stresses over and again that it is *not* enough.

And yet his jargon, like his historicality, also has redeeming features. Many terms have struck readers as unusually apt (one reason speaking Heideggerian is enticing). As he persuades us to his views he'll persuade us of the need for new words—whether or not precisely his own. In addition we can artificially reduce the weight of new vocabulary for our purposes here. I will try to be frugal in how many of his terms I introduce, to make a handful as clear and vivid as I can.[1]

I won't follow Heidegger's neologies across the board—which means that I'll keep some customary terms that he casts off. These will generally be terms of prevailing debates, for we do want to see how Heidegger speaks to these. So I'll use terms that he disavows, such as "pragmatism," "intentionality," and even "truth." In all these cases he is (I claim) still "in the neighborhood" of how these terms are debated—and we can cross the remaining ground by stipulation. I'll try to say clearly how we need to rehear "truth," in particular, if we're to use it for Heidegger's point.

(c) There's another way Heidegger challenges his readers: he constantly stresses that the truth he has in view is extraordinarily difficult and rare (rarely achieved); I'll call this his *esotericism*. He insists that this truth is not at all easily taught or conveyed, and that his words, even the new words formed for this truth, can state it only enigmatically or obscurely. He warns that the reader needs to catch or process what he says in a specific and special way, to get the point—it can't just be read off from his sentences. In his latest book *What is Called Thinking?*:

> World opinion today cherishes the notion that the thinking of thinkers must let itself be understood in the same manner as one reads the newspaper. That not everybody can follow the thought processes of modern theoretical physics one finds quite in order. But to learn the thinking of the thinker is essentially harder, not because this thinking is more involved but because it is simple, too simple for the fluency of common representing.
>
> [*WCT* 238–39][2]

And, indeed, his writing—where he comes to his gist, his key points—is very often obscure. Gilbert Ryle makes a famous early statement of this judgment, in his 1929 review of *Being and Time* in *Mind*: "But here, for the reviewer at any rate, the fog becomes too thick; and the results of the analyses of our intrinsic temporality, of the several concepts of time, historical becoming, history, and the criticisms of the theories of Dilthey and Hegel must go unexpounded" [1929 367]. So Ryle forgoes treating most of the book's second half. And I do think he was *trying* to understand it.

Heidegger's obscurity can seem willful. "Making itself intelligible is suicide for philosophy," he says [CP 307]. He can strike us as simply not trying to explain himself—in not taking the fairly simple steps we expect from anyone (not to mention a philosopher) to clarify his/her meanings. He offers an egregious sparseness of concrete examples to illustrate his points, and seldom defines his terms—at least in words we already understand. He seems not to "state his points clearly." It is easy to attribute some of this reticence to self-indulgence or arrogance.

Even this esotericism, however, is friendly and inviting in some ways. We've seen how *WCT*, in describing the difficulty of access, still gives hope to general readers: his truth is hard because it's *simple*. So too in the "Letter on 'Humanism'": "The strangeness in this thinking of being is its simplicity. Precisely this keeps us from it" [LH (P 275)]. So it's not at all a matter of controlling a complex system of concepts and claims, nor of knowing the right arguments to justify these claims. Such skills cultivated in philosophy courses are not germane. For "the difficulty does not lie in engaging in an unusual profundity and building involved concepts" [LH (P 261)].[3]

Indeed, this simple truth is supposed to be something that we have "known all along," though somehow defectively or inadequately. So it is not something altogether novel and unfamiliar. It escapes us by its very obviousness. It is, as it were, beneath our regard rather than above it, and hence looks more accessible. So here again, even in stressing the great difficulty of his ideas, Heidegger shows an encouraging "populist" bent. He presents himself as trying to remind us, against all theory and expertise, of common truths. And this is linked with a plainness in some of his writing, a plainness and down-to-earthness even in his new vocabulary.

This idea that we might already understand his truths *in a way*, yet also find it extremely difficult to understand them in a certain other, really requisite way, brings us to what I have called the deeper problem of access Heidegger poses. The ultimate reason he is hard, the reason that underlies all the others, is that he wants, he preaches, a *different kind of understanding* than the sort or sorts we're used to. His historicality, his jargon, and his esotericism are all consequences of this.

I will argue that this is Heidegger's most important philosophical aim. It will be the central theme of this book, and I want to give a strong sense of it next, in section 1. In section 2 I'll preview some of the topics about which Heidegger will pursue this new kind of truth.

1. Truth

How do we think we come to "have" truths? We discover which propositions are true, and add them to our stock of beliefs, which we then express or employ in thinking, speaking, and acting. We constantly judge and amend these beliefs when we find them in conflict with experience, or one another. So it seems that if someone is going to give us truth, it would be by giving us new beliefs, with repercussions to amend existing beliefs.

But this is very much not the way Heidegger hopes we will acquire his truth. Instead of adding to our beliefs, to our collection of truths or facts, he wants to change our relation to truths we already have. Instead of inducing us to stop believing x, y, z and to start believing a, b, c, he tries to show us a different relation to truths than that of "belief," a different way of "having" or "being in" the truth. As I'll say, he has a different truth-aim. So his writings are pitched to reorient our (philosophical and personal) effort to understand—jostling it out of a rut he claims it has always been in. I think this new aim is at once the most perplexing and the most exciting thing about Heidegger.

This stress on the "how" of understanding takes up a famous idea of Kierkegaard, that "truth is subjectivity." "When the question about truth is asked subjectively, the individual's relation is reflected upon subjectively. If only the how of this relation is in truth, the individual is in truth, even if he in this way were to relate himself to untruth" [1992 199; also 202]. What counts is the right subjective relation to the content, more than the content itself. Kierkegaard thinks that ethical and religious truths need to be grasped in this special relation; Heidegger transfers the idea to truths about being.

His focus on truth's how is reflected in his insistence that we're already acquainted with truth's what. We already understand the content, just defectively or deficiently. It has been half-grasped all along; we just haven't paid the right kind of attention to it. So when we experience these truths properly, we will recognize them as things we have always known, in a way. There will be no real surprises.

Heidegger's eventual name for his special way of being in the truth is "thinking." None of what we commonly do, he says, not our philosophy, not our science, not our common sense, "thinks" in this special sense. So, at the opening of WCT, he insists "we must be ready to learn thinking," which involves admitting "that we are not yet capable of thinking" [3]. A bit later: "science itself does not think and cannot think" [8]. Nor, he makes clear, do we in our everyday lives.

In this new truth-aim Heidegger believes he makes a *radical* break from his predecessors—to be more different from the philosophers before him, including (finally) Nietzsche, than they were from one another.[4] And this claim at radicalness itself becomes more radical as he goes on. We find him casting off a succession of labels and affinities: metaphysics, philosophy, truth, being. All of these terms philosophers—and he himself—have used to define themselves he eventually renounces, as too likely to mislead, or not quite right for what he has in mind.

Against them all, he promotes his new truth-aim with prophetic fervor. He thinks our fate as humans depends on this *awakening*—on *Ereignis*, as he eventually calls it. The one thing we need is to learn how to think "justly to essence" [WCT 157]. He thinks this should be the point of studying him, and if we don't get it, (he tells his students) we should "destroy even the most precise notes of this lecture, better today than tomorrow" [158].

I think this new truth-aim is the deepest reason for the opposites I started with—why Heidegger is both so easy and so hard to read.

He wins his readers by their feeling that what he offers, under all, is not a new theory, a new system of beliefs and arguments, but a kind of adjustment in our stance, simple if we can only catch a view (or get the knack) of it. There's strong appeal in this promise. But this different truth-aim is also what most makes him so hard. His historicality, his jargon, and his esotericism all reflect the difficulty of shifting not what but how we think. Supplying a new content for us to believe, a new set of truths and justifications, would be straightforward, compared with changing the deep habit in how we understand.

This new truth-aim also explains another striking fact about Heidegger's reception, which I have so far kept to the side, though all are aware of it. This is the extreme division and divergence of opinion about him. His appeal, while broad, is also (as it were) patchy: there are kinds of readers to whom it definitely does not extend. He provokes extreme reactions. To some he is rather obviously the most important philosopher of the twentieth century. To others he is not a philosopher at all, but a mystifier and charlatan. I think the main roots of both judgments are the judgers' different responses to his new truth-aim.

Heidegger is, indeed, a great polarizing figure, who more than anyone else (except Nietzsche?) is responsible for opening and widening the famous divide between "Continental" and "analytic" philosophy. He did this both in himself, and by his huge influence on two waves of French philosophy—the existential-phenomenological, and the deconstructive—each of which analytic philosophers have so often viewed as an alien other, a non-philosophy, or as a soft, unrigorous, and self-indulgent way of doing philosophy, of doing it poorly. Heidegger was so appraised and dismissed by analytics from early on.[5] And he is for the most part now confined to ghetto status in the Anglo-American world.

For those taken with Heidegger, including those two waves of French responders, and his sympathetic readers in English today, I think it's usually this aspiration towards a new kind of truth that

counts most—or most deeply—in his favor. It's responsible for
Heidegger's reception and influence in literature departments, and
other academic locales outside philosophy. They sense that he wants
a kind of insight closer to (or the same as) the kind one might get
from literature or art. And I think even scientists, when drawn to
Heidegger, are drawn by their deference to those arts, as holding
truths they don't find in science.

These non-philosophers notice how predictably philosophers
hold that real truth, important truth, lies in the very sort of thing
that professional philosophers do. This looks like occupational
chauvinism to many, elsewhere in the humanities especially. They
want (to be able to have or aspire to) another, no less truthful
truth, and no less valuable. Heidegger looks refreshingly free of that
chauvinism. His vital truth is not the kind achieved in technical
philosophy, but has some kind of poetic component.

Likewise (and oppositely), for those hostile to Heidegger, I think
it's his aim at a new kind of truth, gathered from every aspect of
his writing, including its style and mannerisms, that is the really
damning offense. His claims seem not just unsupported but
obscure, stated in a personal jargon that seems designed not to be
clear and available for inspection. All of this suggests that he
doesn't care about the kind of truth we pursue by science, logic,
and reason. And it even expresses, such readers feel, character
faults: Heidegger dispenses with arguments because he lacks them,
and he cultivates obscurity as a way to avoid close scrutiny.

So Heidegger provokes this polarized response, from these
opposite sides. But now, as we make our way into his ideas ourselves, where shall we stand on this dispute? I of course think
that he is worth introducing, and so in that all-important respect
I fall on the former side. But I also think that we should resist
this monolithic either/or. I think we all share in the motives and
values that prompt both judgments, opposite as they are. And
I would like to bring out both strengths and weaknesses. So I hope
that I can help Heidegger's devotees to notice problems, and his

detractors to feel strengths. But on the whole my aim is to build a positive case that acknowledges, and responds to, the problems felt against him.

As a way to pose the challenges I will address, let me dwell a little further on these problems—the worries I think we all should have about Heidegger's attitude towards truth. Let's revisit some of the points we've noted as "obstacles" to understanding him, and view them in a more damning light: not as barriers to a (perhaps) valuable truth, but as signs or evidence that he has no such truth. I think it's important to make these doubts and reservations explicit from the beginning, since they so dominate the general view of him. So I will say what I think these doubts are, and give a first sense how Heidegger will reply to them.

Bernard Williams [2002] has called accuracy and sincerity "the virtues of truth," and Heidegger may seem to show little of either—this is perhaps the crux.

With respect to *accuracy* (proper care and method in arriving at one's opinions): he may well seem too "loose" in his beliefs, too "speculative," in the bad sense of jumping to them without adequate grounds. We have reason to trust in the accuracy of his thinking insofar as he gives us his reasons—reasons that therefore should not be purely private, but that we can acquire as well. But he appears, to many, not to give such grounds; real arguments look sparse in him. He has an air of resting his case on his own authority, as entitled by his own intuitions. But we don't, perhaps, share these intuitions, and have no reason to trust them in him. His new conception of truth seems just a lure to credit such private revelations, and to cultivate a disregard for accuracy and reasons.

And regarding *sincerity* (saying what one really thinks): we may well suspect him of disingenuousness as well. Many judge that he mystifies in order to escape close analysis—that he himself knows he has no real case, and writes to hide this.[6] So he has struck some as an outright charlatan, who means to trick or seduce us—and with this aim undermines our value of a reasoned and defendable truth. Moreover, his honesty is in question on famous biographical grounds: his unreliable recountings of his National Socialism. His philosophical procedure may look continuous with this.

Read so, there is something off-putting in his very manner—in his prophetic air, and the grand claims he implicitly makes for himself.[7] I think even the analytic philosophers who take an interest in him find this air grating. He shares with Nietzsche a mien—an expressed persona—of great self-importance, as a world-historical philosopher. He engages the ideas not of any (mere) contemporaries, but of the line of great philosophers. He speaks as a prophet calling out against the main trend of the whole age. But Nietzsche is more witty and bearable in the role than Heidegger, who carries it less happily in his humorlessness.[8]

This runs contrary to the collegial and corporate character of academic philosophy, in which each contributes a part or a push in a great joint effort. Even the analytic thinkers who have played the largest parts, and had the greatest influence, haven't set themselves up as world-historical in Heidegger's way. And this difference too is really about kinds of truth. Analytics want truths that hold up under professional inspection, that are assimilated into the collective viewpoint. Any one member's claims, even if successful, get modified under that inspection, as arguments and reasons are refined in the common debate. Heidegger seems to claim a kind of truth that exempts his claims from subjection to this inspection, and that can't be appropriated into any shared knowledge.

Heidegger's deficit in accuracy and/or sincerity seems also to show in those unwelcome changes in procedure. He criticizes the effort to define terms, which seems to us such a crucial clarifying tool: "Academic philosophy has done its share to stunt the word, from which is to be gathered, that conceptual definitions of words, though technologically-scientifically necessary, are for themselves not suited to protect or to advance the flourishing of language, as one supposes" [*WCT* 139–40].

We've noted how he often dispenses with (anything we can recognize as) argument. Instead he says elusively that thinking is a matter of "taking a path"—a path that doesn't reach a conclusion, as arguments do. "Thinking itself is a path. We accord with the path [*Weg*] only by remaining underway [*unterwegs*]" [WCT 168–69]. Moreover, it won't be reason that guides us on this path: "Thinking first begins when we have experienced, that the reason that has been celebrated for centuries is the most stubborn opponent of thinking" [NW (*W* 199)].

I hope that by now I have articulated the crucial qualms against Heidegger, and given a sense why he is controversial. His dis-allegiance to the kind of truth we care about seems an ultimate and unforgiveable error in a philosopher. This book as a whole tries to give a response to these doubts, by elaborating how and why Heidegger criticizes our kind of truth, and promotes his own. I'll very quickly sketch here his strategy.

First, he will elaborate a critique of our existing truth-aims—against the prevailing scientific and academic culture. This critique includes a diagnosis of these aims, which tries to discredit and defuse the complaints they make against him. He thinks that when we better understand why this culture dominates, and why it has these epistemic standards, we'll lose faith in them.

This critique of science becomes most pointed in his later years. He comes to see modern science as an adjunct to modernity's deeper "technological" stance, by which we are driven to "enframe" all things, setting them in a framework that makes them maximally useful to us, or brings them under our maximal control. Science is one form of this control; it ferrets out all the secrets of a thing it studies, and fixes it within its theoretical system. Really thinking about a thing requires, Heidegger insists, a different attitude altogether.

He is not opposed to using science for thinking, indeed he even requires it. "Science does not think in the sense in which thinkers think. Still, it does not at all follow that thinking need pay no attention to the sciences" [WCT 134]. But he is critical of a "scientific philosophy" [CP 26], a philosophy which is taken over by the scientific stance, by that truth-aim. "Even more shortsighted is the alignment of philosophy towards the 'sciences', which has become customary—and not accidentally—since the beginning of modernity. This direction of inquiry—and not just the explicit 'science-theoretical' kind—must be given up completely" [CP 31].

It seems pretty clear that this critique would apply to analytic philosophy. The latter is perhaps the "logistics" he predicts will be dominant in America:

> In many places, above all in the Anglo-Saxon countries, logistics is now counted the only possible form of strict philosophy, because its result and procedures yield a sure use for constructing the technological world. In America and elsewhere logistics is beginning today to seize mastery over the spirit, as the authentic philosophy of the future.
>
> [WCT 21][9]

As I've hinted, Heidegger replaces analytic and scientific methods with an appeal to the epistemic self-evidence of the experience of (his kind of) thinking, itself. The proof is supposed to lie in the special experience of being, Ereignis, which is claimed both necessary and sufficient to justify the claims Heidegger makes about being. "What has been seen can be demonstrated [ausweisen] only by being seen and seen again. What has been seen never lets itself be proved [beweisen] by adducing grounds and counter-grounds. Such a procedure forgets what is decisive, the looking" [WCT 233]. We will do this looking in a genuine thinking, different from science's, that we need to "leap into."[10]

These truths must be appropriated by our sharing in this experience, not by acquiring the propositions that describe or express them. Already in Being and Time Heidegger is worried that we will just learn to repeat his claims: "the answer to the question of being cannot lie in an isolated and blind proposition. The answer is not conceived in re-saying that which is asserted propositionally" [BT g19]. For such transmission is just a "mouthing" or "parroting" of the words.[11] He tries to pull the rug out from under all efforts to "capture" his views in propositions.

Now all of this poses a rather obvious challenge to my task in this very book. By assignment and by inclination, I aim to make his ideas as clear as I can, in the usual ways: by trying to define his terms and to map his claims and arguments. I will try to congeal his ideas in propositions that will let others understand them—and isn't this precisely how he says we should *not* pursue them? Isn't this an effort to control and "enframe" his ideas, in a package alongside the others in this series?

Well, I hope the book isn't just these things. Heidegger has the obvious faith, as a writer, that his sentences can be more than propositions we take over to believe. He thinks his words can occasion the experience of "looking," and the activity of thinking. It is incumbent on any interpreter of him to have an eye on this different ambition, and to write accordingly. His ideas need to reach us alive, not as formulae or positions, but in words that can provoke the kind of looking and thinking he wants. I'll do my best at this too.

2. Being

I've dwelt so long on the obstacles and problems with Heidegger's philosophy that it may have come to seem not worth the effort. In the rest of this introduction I'll try to restore interest by previewing some of the topics he will offer his (new kind of) truth about. In doing so I'll also outline the structure of this book.

Famously, there is one topic above all with which he is persistently obsessed: being [*Sein*]. He identified himself with this topic as few other philosophers have with a single issue. It is his constant lure to his readers, the all-important topic that they and he are always on the track of. He treats this topic with a vividness that gives it a powerful appeal.

Now the very fact that he has this favorite topic—and things to say about it—may seem at odds with my claim that he focuses on the how of truth rather than its what. Isn't being what his truth is about, and indeed very distinctively about? It appears that being and its features are the truth-content he means to convey to us.

Yet he also insists that being is an utterly different kind of topic than we deal with anywhere else. *All* of our other topics are entities, but being is decidedly not. Indeed the major challenge is to learn not to treat it as an entity [*ein Seiendes*].[12] The all-important difference between being and entities he will call the "ontological difference," and his life-long calling is to turn our attention to it—and to being itself.

It's this special topic that calls for a new truth-method, and even (as we've seen) a new truth-aim. It's being, above all, that we require the new kind of truth about. This is already Heidegger's view in *Being and Time*, where he crafts his method of *phenomenology* to handle the topic. I'll develop this famous method in Chapter 3. Heidegger learns a version of this method from Edmund Husserl, but modifies it so that it can get at being. He relies here, we'll see, on an ultimately Kantian argument, that pursues being by uncovering the "conditions of the possibility" of our experience. This will give us a good route to *Being and Time*'s conception of being.

But we'll see that Heidegger progressively raises the bar here—or that being is a receding target for him. The methods of Husserl and Kant come to seem less and less adequate for it. So phenomenology ramifies, in his later works, into an ever more radical method. He discovers more and more ways of missing that ontological difference between being and entities, or of failing to take adequate account of it. He eventually decides that his topic is not *Sein* but *Seyn*, or *Sein* "under erasure" (he writes *Sein* with an X through it). Or, his topic is not being "as the ground of entities," but "being without entities" [TB (OTB 2, 6)].

From first to last, however, he stresses how we need a different kind of access to being than to entities. Adopting the topic of being is not enough—one also needs to approach it in the special way appropriate to being. We need, as it were, to adjust our eyes, or our sense of what it is to understand something. Heidegger quotes Aristotle [*Met.* 993b] in making the point:

> "Just as bats' eyes react to the apparent light of day, so also the perception proper to our essence reacts to what for itself ... is the most apparent of all". ... The being of entities is the most apparent; and yet we ordinarily don't see it at all—and if [we do], then only with difficulty.
>
> [*WCT* 110]

Being and Time's route to being lies through what the book famously calls "Dasein," i.e. our human existence. Indeed, this, much more than being itself, is the topic of the book as published. It lays out a template for thinking about the overall or underlying structure of human experience, or rather of human "intentionality"— the way we "intend" both goals and meanings. This analysis, which has pragmatic, existential, and temporal parts, had enormous influence on later "existential phenomenologists," including Sartre and Merleau-Ponty. It struck and still strikes many readers as an unusually apt and helpful schema for thinking about ourselves.

This schema is both an account of how we (generally, basically) are, and of how we can be. Heidegger insists that his analysis of Dasein posits no "values"; he would not want to say that it says how we "should" be. Nevertheless, in laying out the deep structure of our directedness, he claims to uncover underlying aims. And he projects from these what their adequate (or ideal) fulfillment or achievement would be. This is authenticity, famously. I'll try to make concrete what this condition is, and also to show why Heidegger so insists that this is not a value, and not part of an ethics or morality.

I mentioned three main elements in *Being and Time*'s theory of us, pragmatic, existential, and temporal. These are the three main waves of that book's argument, and I'll treat them in turn in my Chapters 4–6. They overlap one another, and are not reflected in the book's part–chapter structure, but are the three stages in which Heidegger claims to dig down into us, each deeper than the one before.

The first several chapters of *Being and Time* introduce Heidegger's pragmatism—by which I mean his account of us as more basically doers than knowers. He thinks that a strong philosophical tradition, owing especially to Descartes, makes us think of ourselves as fundamentally subjects or thinkers or cognizers. Even common sense makes this mistake he thinks. The error is rooted in ways that our pragmatic, "concernful," directed intending tends to work best when it works implicitly. And it is hard to study or even to notice this stance from the very different stance of thinking, studying, knowing.

Heidegger develops this pragmatism under the general rubric of "being-in-the-world." Here my world is (roughly) all the networks of things I "know how to do": a field of opportunities (and dangers), a web of paths I know how, am poised and often eager, to follow (or avoid). So my world is this network of possibilities I project about myself, within and towards which I live. And my "being in" this world is the manner in which I am "towards" these possibilities—the structured way that I at once understand, feel, and express them. In laying out these structures of being-in and world Heidegger introduces an intricate new technical vocabulary, some of which has spread widely.

I'll lay out the main structures, with a ration of that vocabulary, but here too we must remember that Heidegger demands a different way of understanding from the mere acquisition of this content in beliefs. We need to achieve insight into this being-in-the-world within the very stance itself, and not just in a theoretical perspective upon it.

The book's second wave, its existentialism, begins in places within the pragmatic story, but reaches center stage in the opening chapters of Division II. This second story lays over the first—or, rather, under it—another set of structures, which includes such influential notions as falling, the "they-self," being-towards-death, and authenticity. Heidegger thinks that we discover these structures when we consider certain limits or boundaries to our pragmatic directedness.

That directedness is an engagement in a host of projects, but this projecting operates under the overall constraints of death and guilt—both of which Heidegger gives fascinating new sense to. We also discover, he thinks, that for the most part persons ignore these constraints or limits, and live and aim as if they weren't there (as if they weren't guilty, and mortal). Indeed, the motive of not facing these constraints explains pervasive features of our ordinary living. So these deeper structures set in new perspective the pragmatism laid out before.

But again the point is not to learn to believe these things—much less just to "parrot back" Heidegger's assertions. These truths too need to be comprehended somehow at the level in us which they concern. We acknowledge them in and by restructuring our own existential stance. We need to "become transparent" to ourselves in that stance itself. This means, in fact, that we need to become authentic.

The identification of authenticity leads Heidegger immediately down to the third level of *Being and Time*, for (he claims) it makes visible the temporal logic or structure of our intending, which underlies both the pragmatic and existential structures. It lets us restate the preceding analyses in ways that show the context and larger pattern in them. So our concern in our dealings has a particular temporal character, and this is its ultimate point or aim: we concern ourselves as a way to be in a certain kind of present, Heidegger thinks. By contrast authenticity turns out to be a way of stretching ourselves out beyond that present through all three "ecstases" of temporality.

By means of this account of Dasein's temporality, *Being and Time* intends to clarify time, and by that in turn to treat at last its ultimate topic, being. But Heidegger never wrote this part of the book. So we will need to infer just what lessons he intended to draw from the account of our temporality for the topics of time and being. I will offer a suggestion what that book might have ended up saying about being.

What *Being and Time* would have so concluded is most germane to the question how his views change after that book (and in particular in the mid-1930s). For being is very much the focal topic of the later writing, and the "turning" from *Being and Time*, to be so decisive, must lie mainly in some change concerning it. I will treat this famous turning in Chapter 7.

One chief idea in the later work is that Western history is typified by the understanding of being as "presence." Presence is the way being shows itself to us most basically and pervasively—and it has done so since the beginnings of Greek philosophy. Heidegger tries to show that all the stages in Western philosophy are different ways of interpreting that "presence." I'll develop how this "history of being as presence" arises out of the ideas of *Being and Time*, with differences. These changes are, we may presume, what made the book uncompleteable.

There are other important themes in the later writings that have less precedent in *Being and Time*. Poetry now plays the same role that philosophy does, of articulating and fixing the "understanding of being" that pervades and typifies a culture in a given historical epoch. Each such epochal understanding needs to be "housed" in language, and it is poets and thinkers who give the words for it. They use language "originarily," to inaugurate these epochs of being. The difference between the language of poetry and the language of thinking will be a large issue for us. His view of it will explain his spirit and strategy in writing in the more poetic or literary style he now adopts. I'll discuss this network of ideas, and Heidegger's striking new account of language, in Chapter 8.

Another new theme in Heidegger's later writing is technology, which he claims typifies our own age. In his epic story about the history of being, this is the upshot of its long logic. The pre-Socratics' initial uncovering of being as presence has been ever more fully realized or perfected through that history since. Technology, and our advanced scientific understanding of things, bring all entities to a fullest presence for us, in the maximal control we have over them, by having slotted each into place in a framework, practical and theoretical. This "enframing"—*Gestell*—thus realizes the aim built deeply into our history by that original Greek posit of presence as the basic way entities can be.

Heidegger takes Nietzsche to state the metaphysics of this culminating stage, in his ontological picture of the world as will to power. Power is above all control, by setting in order and making available—and these aims express the viewpoint of technology. Nietzsche's ideal of the overman is of a superlative level or degree of such power. This is also an ultimate refinement of the original understanding of being as presence, so that Nietzsche expresses the culmination or completion of Western cultural history. It's because elements of that Nietzschean metaphysic still remain in *Being and Time* that Heidegger works out his "turning" in relation to Nietzsche.

And yet, Heidegger further judges, this culmination exposes a decisive flaw in that basic posit of presence. It has, while bringing entities into sharper and sharper focus, hidden from us its own role as an understanding of being, and hence also being itself. Technology, as enframing, stunts a stance in us that is really essential, and gives us a world without kinds of meaning we need. Here Heidegger, most in his prophet's hat, addresses an age he takes to be deeply nihilistic, and appeals to it to look for the way out. We require a turning, out of enframing and into a new epoch of being. A key feature of this new understanding is that it will again make room for "gods." To outgrow our technological and scientific domination of the world we must reawaken a sense that this world has powers and meanings higher than our own, not fully accessible to us. My Chapter 9 will treat these linked topics of technology and the need for new gods.

Regarding these last ideas Heidegger again insists on the need for a special kind of appropriation. Indeed he is all the more emphatic about this in his later writings, which are often in a style that makes clear he wants us to hear him a different way. Grasping his ideas in our ordinary manner would be to enframe them, precluding the insight we need. He tries to help us to the special experiences we need. BCM 59: "Our basic task now consists in awakening a basic mood of our philosophizing." We will need to keep this different ambition near the front of our minds as we read him—and about him.

Summary

Heidegger's effort to aim us at a different kind of truth—and not just to convey to us a different set of truths—is crucial to his philosophical project. It explains both his unusual appeal and the several special challenges he poses to us his readers: his historicality, his elaborate and idiosyncratic terminology, and his esotericism. His revised truth-aim is also the main reason his thinking is so strongly polarizing, and viewed with such disdain by many analytic philosophers. So we appropriately center our attention on his new notion of truth, to try to make it as clear and concrete as we can, and with an eye to certain obvious worries and doubts against this epistemic change.

This new truth-aim is requisite, Heidegger claims, by virtue of what we above all need to understand: being, and not just entities. The discontinuity between being and entities, the great necessity that we think about the former, but our prevailing preoccupation with the latter, are his abiding themes. Being's great difference from entities demands that different kind of truth about it. Heidegger pursues this truth one way in his masterwork *Being and Time*, and another in the writings that follow the "turning" he made from its views.

In *Being and Time* his method is phenomenology, which approaches being by analyzing the structure of human (Dasein's) intentionality. This analysis uncovers three progressively deeper layers in this intentionality—pragmatic, existential, and temporal—each requiring to be "seen" in a special way quite unlike our usual theoretical grasp. The method, and those three layers of our intending, are the topics of Chapters 3–6.

Heidegger's later writings abandon phenomenology and much of its analysis, but remain in pursuit of being, still considered to require a special kind of truth. But now the route to this truth lies principally through history, in particular the history of metaphysics. We find being there by seeing how it has been "housed" in language, and above all in the formative language of metaphysics, as well as poetry. Finding being in history, we see our own age's basic character as technology, in which we suffer the absence of gods. Truth in history, language, and technology's exclusion of gods are the topics of Chapters 7–9.

Further reading

H. Dreyfus and M. Wrathall (eds.): *A Companion to Heidegger*. Oxford: Blackwell Publishers, 2005. [An excellent collection of analytic essays treating topics across the range of Heidegger's writing.]

H. Philipse: *Heidegger's Philosophy of Being; A Critical Interpretation*. Princeton: Princeton University Press, 1998. [A critical assessment trying to address Heidegger's thought as a whole.]

One

Life and works

Heidegger himself was little interested in philosophers' biographies or personalities. Near the beginning of a 1924 lecture-course on Aristotle he said: "About the personality of a philosopher only this has interest: He was born then and there, he worked and died. The character of the philosopher, and issues of that sort, will not be given here" [BCA 4]. He was relentlessly focused on philosophers' thinking, and not at all inclined to suppose that this would be illuminated by any attention to facts about their lives or persons.

Such a policy of ignoring biography might seem to favor him. For attention to parts of his own biography may make us less sympathetic and receptive to what he has to say. Many have found certain facts about his life and personality reasons to dislike him. So there's special risk in his case that biographical facts will spoil proper attention to his thinking. Of course those facts will only "spoil" this attention if it's not actually the case that they reveal flaws in his thinking. Heidegger's biography includes choices and actions which, to the extent that they "flow from" the ideas, may seem to discredit them. The central such fact is his embrace of Nazism in 1933, and for the moment I'll use this to stand for what we'll see is a much wider phenomenon. If his thinking caused this embrace, or expresses a personality or mentality that caused this embrace, does that not count against it? This is an easy application of one of our favorite and most effective reductios of positions, not to absurdity but *ad Nazism*.

The general question—a philosophical question—is whether we better understand a philosopher's thinking by seeing its involvement in his/her life. We may partition this involvement on two sides: the thinking may (1) express this individual human being's psychology, and/or (2) lead the individual to live and act in certain ways. Don't we better understand—and better judge—a philosophy by seeing its source and its effects? And don't we find these in the philosopher's own life? On both grounds (1) and (2), it seems Heidegger's Nazism should count strongly against his ideas.

Nietzsche, in contrast with Heidegger, famously insists on the relevance of "personal" factors. Indeed his most characteristic move is to shift our attention to them, so that we understand and judge Christian morality (e.g.) by the psychic set it expresses (*ressentiment*, according to Nietzsche). This psychological turn is perhaps the most constant lesson in his writings. Heidegger read Nietzsche intently—is he so unpersuaded by that pervasive point?[1]

We'll see that there are places where Heidegger agrees with Nietzsche on the importance of the personal and contingent in philosophical thinking. For example, *Being and Time* will claim that phenomenological insight is only attainable through the thinker's personal authenticity. And later, Heidegger will stress how his own thinking expresses his personal roots in his region and "soil." So here, in certain ways, the particular *is* germane.[2]

Nevertheless I think Heidegger does largely deny the relevance of such factors, and for his own strong reason, at deep odds with Nietzsche. What's crucial in philosophy is to have the special vision needed for its special topic, being, and for this all biographical facts are irrelevant. A philosopher's thinking—the genuine thinking that matters—reflects this special access, and not his/her idiosyncratic psychic or life situations.

It's not, however, as we might think is true of, e.g., the mathematician or logician, that the philosopher occupies a purely rational

and decontextualized viewpoint—a "view from nowhere," in
Nagel's expression [1986]. Rather, the philosopher has special
access to being because he/she is most deeply attuned to the historical moment. The philosopher thinks as *must* be thought, in his/
her age. He/she is uncommonly responsive to the "destiny of
being." So Heidegger has less a Nietzschean than a Hegelian diagnosis
of philosophers: their ideas reflect the "understanding of being"
that typifies their respective times. So they *are* to be understood "by
context," but only by their most general and cultural-historical
context.[3]

The upshot of all this is that if Heidegger can persuade us to his
idea of philosophical truth, we will be more likely to count his
biography irrelevant. But we shouldn't discount that relevance in
advance, while we're weighing his ideas. So I'll survey his biography here, including "his Nazism," and will briefly anticipate
what relations there do seem to be with his ideas themselves.

I'll start with a barebones account of the main events in his life,
focusing on his academic training and career, and on how economic and career considerations interacted with his intellectual
direction. (Since he lived most of his life on the academic calendar,
I use it in age-dating below.) I'll then locate particular topics against
this framework, and treat them further.

"He was born ... ": September 26, 1889 in Messkirch, a town
in the district of Baden of SW Germany, near the upper Danube,
and within the historical and cultural region of Swabia. His childhood and early education were here: from age 6 to 13 (1895–
1903) he attended local schools (the town's *Volks-* and *Bürgerschule*);
he began private lessons in Latin at 11, to prepare for seminary.
Heidegger recalled a happy childhood. The family was "lower
middle class," secure by the father's job, but with little to spare.

Due to his abilities, as well as his family's staunch Catholicism
and meager resources, he went away for further schooling through
the Church. From age 14 to 16 (1903–06) he was in Konstanz
(60 km south of Messkirch) on a Weiss Grant: he boarded at an

archdiocesan seminary (Studienhaus St. Konrad, or Konradihaus), and went to school in the state Heinrich-Suso-Gymnasium, where he and the other seminarians mixed uneasily with the urban, liberal, and often wealthier local students.

He then obtained an Eliner Grant to continue his studies in Freiburg (115 km west of Messkirch), and from age 17 to 19 (1906–09) he boarded at the archiepiscopal seminary (St. George) in Freiburg, and attended the state Berthold Gymnasium. Of this he recalled especially his work in mathematics, his discovery of Aristotle, and his strong side-interest in German literature. This "high school" education was designed to prepare him for Church service as a Jesuit, but when, at age 20 (1909), he entered the Society of Jesus as a novice (at Tisis near Feldkirch, in western Austria), he lasted only two weeks before being dismissed with heart pains.

He returned to Freiburg in time to enter the archdiocesan Freiburg Theological Seminary ("Sapienz"), and take classes in the Department of Theology at the University of Freiburg (officially Albert Ludwig University), still in preparation for a Church career as a priest; he did so from age 20 to 21 (1909–11). It was in this period that he began to study Husserl. But in early 1911 he left the seminary and returned home to Messkirch due to a recurrence of his heart problems; these were deemed to exclude him from future Church service.

He then moved to the Department of Natural Science and Mathematics, where he studied mathematics, the sciences, and philosophy from age 22 to 23 (1911–13), with the aid of a Grieshaber-Pino Grant that would be renewed until 1916. His philosophical studies were dominated by Husserl, and by the neo-Kantians Rickert and Lask. He earned his doctorate, *summa cum laude*, with a dissertation (in philosophy) on "The Doctrine of Judgment in Psychologism: A Critical-Positive Contribution to Logic."

He then completed his education with a further two years, age 24 to 25 (1913–15), in the Department of Philosophy (still in Freiburg), writing his qualifying dissertation [*Habilitationsschrift*] on

"The Doctrine of Categories and Meaning of Duns Scotus." It was in this period that his philosophical interest shifted from logic and philosophy of mathematics to history, and particularly medieval philosophy, which he aspired to relate to phenomenology; this shift may have been partly motivated by his hopes for the vacant chair in Catholic philosophy at Freiburg. He was supported in this work by the award of a Schäzler Grant designed for Thomistic philosophers.

He now entered upon his 30-year teaching career. He began as a *Privatdozent* at Freiburg, and taught there from age 26 to 33 (1915–23). He was called for military service in 1915, but his heart problems remanifested (they had also ended two brief periods of service in 1914), and he was assigned to home reserve work in the postal censorship office, where he worked 1915–18; in 1918 he was assigned to the meteorological service, and, after a training course in Berlin, served the last few months of the war at a weather station near the front lines in the Ardennes (weather predictions were needed for poison gas attacks). In 1916 he was disappointed not to get the chair in Catholic philosophy that he had seemed a strong candidate for. But Husserl arrived in Freiburg in that year, and Heidegger pursued him assiduously, with eventual success, so that by early 1919 Husserl was his strong advocate and secured for him a paid teaching post at Freiburg. (Heidegger had lost support from his wife's parents when they lost their fortune after the war.)

Again with Husserl's energetic support, he was offered an associate professorship (*Extraordinarius*) at Marburg (420 km north of Messkirch), and taught there from age 34 to 38 (1923–28). Here the noteworthy event was the publication of *Being and Time* in 1927, which soon made him internationally famous. On its basis (his publications had been sparse before) he was promoted to full professor (*Ordinarius*) at Marburg, but then offered Husserl's (former) chair back in Freiburg, where he returned to teach from age 39–55 (1928–44). He declined offers of chairs at Berlin (in 1930 and

1933) and Munich (1933). But the outstanding event in this period was his brief term in 1933–34 as Rector of the university, and his associated involvement in the Nazi party and movement (to which I'll return).

This long stretch of teaching ended when he was very briefly conscripted into the militia (the *Volkssturm*) in October 1944; on his release from this he left Freiburg (which had been devastated by bombing) for Messkirch. He obtained leave to do so on the ground that he needed to move his manuscripts to safety; in February 1945 he extended his absence from Freiburg with a medical exemption. As the war was ending he taught an informal spring term at Castle Wildenstein near Messkirch, to which most of the Freiburg faculty had by now fled.

After the war he was prohibited from teaching by a university committee and the military authorities. This ban remained in effect until 1951, and he never resumed lecturing at Freiburg with his former regularity. Instead he mainly turned in this period, age 56–84 (1945–73), to a different kind of outreach: talks to non-academic groups, seminars in a variety of less formal venues, as well as more intensive publication. Among the non-academic settings in which he repeatedly lectured—to businessmen, politicians, and intellectuals—were the Bremen city hall, the Bühlerhöhe spa above Baden-Baden, and the Bavarian Academy of Fine Arts in Munich. And he taught special seminars in Zollikon (Switzerland) and Le Thor (Provence), organized respectively by his friends Medard Boss and Jean Beaufret.

He ceased teaching in his last couple years, age 85–86 (1974–76), and now devoted himself to the preparation of his Collected Works. He died May 26, 1976 in Freiburg, and was buried May 28 in Messkirch, in the Catholic service he wanted.

This outline shows the great simplicity of his academic career: all of his higher education took place in Freiburg, and all of his formal teaching as well, with the exception of the five middle years at Marburg. But he also reached beyond academic settings in his

post-war lectures and seminars. Now let me add to this outline by
treating in turn a series of themes.

i. Places

It was by choice that Heidegger lived in so few places. He had
offers to teach elsewhere, including Berlin, but declined for reasons
he expressed in the little 1933 radio talk "Creative Landscape: Why
Do We Stay in the Provinces?" [CL]. These reasons ramify into his
very conception of philosophy, as we'll see. And "place" is an
abiding topic for him.[4]

His first home, around which he orbited all his life, was Messkirch,
a town of about 2,000 (in the late nineteenth century). His own
family roots went well back in the area, among farmers and craftsmen. On a plain above the narrow valley of the Upper Danube, it
later took for Heidegger the spiritual significance Hölderlin had
given to that river, as flowing back from modern Europe to its
beginnings in the East (Greece). He came back often to Messkirch,
to visit his parents and brother, and in periods of stress. Northwest
of Messkirch, in the valley itself, were two other places he would
return to: the Benedictine abbey in Beuron, by the river (where
he spent break weeks from Freiburg, in a monastic cell, and also
gave talks), and Castle Wildenstein, on a cliff edge overlooking the
valley. He identified all his life with Messkirch's rural simplicity in
contrast with city sophistications.

Still, he lived most of his life in Freiburg, a city of about
100,000 in the 1920s and 1930s. He and his wife bought land and
had a house built in the Zähringen district to the north of Freiburg,
at Rötebuckweg 47, in preparation for his return in Fall 1928.
Above the front door he put (where it remains today) Luther's
translation of Prov. 4:23: "Shelter your heart with all diligence; for
life flows out of it." He resided here until his death—in his last
years in a "retirement" apartment added in the back garden. The
house is now the home of his granddaughter and her family.

Heidegger's third crucial place was Todtnauberg, a village 30 km south of Freiburg, at about 1,000 m elevation. Heidegger owned a cabin (the "Hütte") on a slope above the village, built by his wife's arrangement in 1922, and which he traveled to even in the Marburg years. It was here he felt he thought and wrote best. (*Being and Time* was written in a room he rented in a farmhouse nearby, to escape family distractions.) In CL he describes writing in the cabin while a storm batters it. And he took from his walks in this area his primary image for thinking, naming works after "woodpaths," "fieldpaths," "pathmarks."

Outside of this home ground in southwest Germany, Heidegger had other special places afield, which he sought out or found by travel. Chief among these was Greece, cathected by his history of being (and reading of Hölderlin) as the site of the "first beginning." He made his first trip there in 1962 (at 72), after backing out of two previously planned ones. He visited, by ship and bus, many main sites; his strongest impressions were of Olympia, Mycenae, and especially Delos.[5] He returned to Greece in 1964 (when he spent two weeks on Aegina), 1966, and 1967.

ii. Childhood and family

Heidegger's parents both came from local families. His mother, née Johanna Kempf (1858–1927), came from a family of farmers on good property in nearby Göggingen, while his father, Friedrich Heidegger (1852–1924), was descended from local craftsmen and peasants. The father was a master cooper, and as a child Heidegger frequented his workshop. But his chief employment was as sexton of St. Martin's (Catholic) Church, and the family lived (with an interruption I mention on p. 32) in the sexton's house, which still faces the church across a small square.

Heidegger's grandparents all died before he was born. All the rest of his family were his two siblings, his sister Marie (1892–1956) and brother Fritz (1894–1980). Neither Heidegger nor his biographers have much to say about Marie. Fritz was a well known and liked character in Messkirch, where he lived all his life as a bank official; Heidegger kept up good relations with him.

iii. Religion

The region of Messkirch is strongly Catholic, and the family was all the more firmly so by the father's employment. The region's Catholic community was strongly divided in the 1880s and 1890s by the growth of the "Old Catholic" movement that resisted papal infallibility and aimed to liberalize and nationalize the Church. By contrast Heidegger's parents belonged to a conservative "Roman" faction, more broadly based in the rural population. When in 1875 the Old Catholics were allowed partial use of St. Martin's, the conservative group removed to worship in a nearby fruit barn, which was converted to a church with the help of Beuron monks. And Heidegger's parents removed to a small house (at 16 Kolpingstrasse, but since torn down), where Heidegger was born (and then baptized in the ex-barn). It was only in 1895 that the "Roman" Catholics were restored to sole use of St. Martin's, and the family moved back into the sexton's house on the square.

Heidegger kept through his life the anti-liberal and populist sentiment evinced in his family's religious stance. He did not, however, keep his Catholic faith, but very gradually and painfully separated from it by the time of his late twenties. His philosophical reasons will concern us in Chapter 2, but here we should notice the life-circumstances.[6]

His separation was difficult partly because his economic and professional prospects depended heavily on the Church. As we saw his education, from age 14 until he finished his post-doctoral thesis at 25, was underwritten by Church grants. The expectation behind this support was that he would enter Church service as a priest—or, when his health ruled this out, as a professor of Catholic philosophy. (E.g. the grant that supported him from 1913 to 1916 committed him to study "in the spirit of Thomist philosophy.") This economic dependence greatly complicated his intellectual engagement with religious issues. As his thinking pulled him away from Church doctrine, he concealed the widening gap because of these career considerations—and was perturbed over this.

While economic needs pulled him towards the Church, we've seen how his bodily health held him back. Chest pains prevented him from entering the Jesuit order at age 20, and a recurrence a year and a half later led him, on advice of the archiepiscopal authorities, to abandon hopes of a Church career. (To what extent these may have been psychosomatic or even feigned is open to question.) Nevertheless he still had the prospect of an academic career as a Catholic philosopher, and persisted in this aim even as his philosophical views shifted from orthodoxy. Let's look quickly at this shift.

His early allegiance was to a conservative and antimodernist strand of Catholic thinking. While in the Freiburg Department of Theology he was a member of the Gralbund (Society of the Grail), which dreamed of reorganizing Germany under a revived Catholic faith. And he was much affected by his favorite teacher, Carl Braig, a theologian whose critique of modern secularism is a clear ancestor to his much later attack on technology.

Heidegger's path out of Catholicism was not by liberalizing these early views, but by a kind of intensification of their conservative themes. He found in medieval mysticism—Meister Eckhart in particular—a return to a purist Christianity, unadulterated by the conceptual frameworks of Plato and Aristotle, whose views lie behind modernity. And he found a similar authentic return in Luther, read as preaching an unmediated relation to divinity, a personal religious experience.

This shift towards a more Protestant sensibility was already underway when, in 1916, he suffered the crushing disappointment of being passed over for the chair in Catholic philosophy, which he had long set his sights on. With this hope removed his shift accel-erated, and in early 1919 he wrote Engelbert Krebs, who had married him, to announce that his thinking about "historical knowledge" had made "the *system* of Catholicism problematic and unacceptable to me, but not Christianity and metaphysics—these, though, in a new sense" [S 69]. But he continued to view himself as a Christian thinker, and Husserl now recommended him for positions as a Protestant philosopher.

During the 1920s, however, he seems to have passed out of Christianity altogether. By now I think philosophical considerations become primary, and I'll come back to these in Chapter 2. By the late 1920s he has begun to adopt the Hölderlinian view that we live in a godless age, but must hope for the "return" of a god or gods. He held this religious but (it seems) non-Christian position the rest of his life, though it should be noted that by his own direction he was buried in a Christian service following the Catholic liturgy. But his (and his wife's) headstone bears a star, not the crosses on the flanking stones for his parents and for his brother (and his wife).

iv. Health and physicality

He was short—shorter than his wife—with black curly hair. He tanned easily and referred to himself in letters to his wife as "Little Blackamoor." He was unprepossessing, at least in his early years, and lacked urban polish, showing his rural and lower-middle-class roots. His student Löwith wrote that in conversation he didn't look one in the eye, and conveyed a personal discomfort. Yet in his teaching, we'll see, he was a magnetic presence; for this he dres-sed, very eccentrically, in lederhosen and a peasant-style coat, which some students called his "existential suit."

As we've seen, he suffered from heart problems that recurred at certain stressful moments; these prevented him from pursuing a Jesuit career, and also spared him from most military service (he spent four weeks in a military hospital in 1915). The problems are described as "a nervous heart condition," "of an asthmatic nature"; Heidegger says that this was "brought on by too much sport."

For he was also vigorously physical. He skied avidly, and was impressed by Sartre's philosophical treatment of skiing; he proposed in a letter that Sartre come to Todtnauberg so that they could ski and philosophize together. We've seen that he hiked, and will see that he valued "physical education" in the university. In his late years he watched soccer matches on a neighbor's TV, and became a great fan of the German star Beckenbauer.

In the wake of the war and his subjection to denazification processes he suffered a physical and mental breakdown in 1946, and went to the Haus Baden sanatorium in Badenweiler, just south of Freiburg. He suffered a stroke in 1970 in Augsburg, and was taken by ambulance to Freiburg, where he recovered at home.

v. Marriage and children

In 1915 Heidegger broke off a two-year engagement with a woman ("Margaret") from Strasbourg. It was in the same year that he met Elfride Petri, a student in the first class he taught. She was from Saxony, an economics student, an advocate of women's rights, and a Lutheran. They were married in a Catholic service in the university chapel of the Freiburg Cathedral in March 1917 (Heidegger was 27).

Elfride was an authoritative and capable woman. Unlike Heidegger, she embraced the racial and anti-Semitic aspect of Nazism—and the movement itself earlier and later than he did. As a Nazi activist, she alienated many by her harsh impressment of neighborhood women to dig trenches in late 1944. She was Heidegger's dedicated enabler and defender, who took care of his practical needs and facilitated his work. Their marriage lasted 59 years until Heidegger's death—and Elfride slept beside him in their bed the night after the morning he died.

The marriage was strong despite the stresses of affairs by both husband and wife. (Their granddaughter published a selection from over 1,000 letters and cards he wrote to Elfride.) They raised two sons, Jörg (b. 1919), and Hermann (b. 1920), but Hermann was the product of Elfride's affair with Friedel Caesar, a Freiburg doctor and old friend of hers. (Heidegger treated him as his own; Hermann was told by Elfride when he was 14.) In 1935 they brought into their home, from Brazil, an adoptive daughter, Erika Birle (b. 1921), whose parents had died (the mother was related to Elfride and had been Hermann's godmother).

The sons both served on the Eastern Front in the war, and Heidegger and his wife had no word from them towards the end. Both were held in Russian prisoner-of-war camps, not returning home until 1947 and 1949.[7]

vi. Friendships and affairs

Heidegger inspired strong personal attachments. He formed friendships, especially with teachers, colleagues, and students, right up to his later years. It does seem, however, that these connections were somewhat more than usually dependent on practical (career, political) or theoretical considerations. Heidegger also seems generally to have expected more to be done for him than by him. His confidence in his own preeminence—on the depth of his own truth—cast others into orbital roles. Many friendships expired around 1933 when they became inexpedient for his political advancement—and, later, security. The relation to Husserl was emblematic.

Heidegger had been impressed and influenced by Husserl's writings for some six years before the latter fortuitously moved to Freiburg, taking the philosophy chair, in 1916. Heidegger worked hard to come to Husserl's attention and eventually succeeded. Husserl came to regard him not only as his most outstanding student, but as his best friend; their wives were also close.

There were the usual complicating motives on both sides: Husserl wanted his student to bring his phenomenological method to glory; Heidegger wanted to pull himself up by Husserl's standing, the better to be something of his own that left Husserl behind. Perhaps it's inevitably the student, in this context, who looks more calculating, but Heidegger carries this far. He stressed their affinities in his dealings with Husserl, but was scathing and dismissive behind his back (e.g. in letters to Jaspers).[8]

Husserl was his greatest academic patron, securing him first a paid position at Freiburg, then an associate professorship at Marburg, and finally arranging for Heidegger to succeed him back in Freiburg in 1928. But within two months of taking the chair Heidegger began to avoid him, Husserl later reported, and their friendly relations ceased. It also became increasingly clear to Husserl that Heidegger was deeply opposed to him philosophically. By 1933 Husserl, a Jew, was also a political liability to Heidegger, who made no practical efforts or personal gestures towards him as Husserl suffered various insults under Nazi rule, nor in his long illness, nor to Husserl's wife after his death in 1938.

Heidegger apparently had numerous affairs, but by far the most important was that with Hannah Arendt,[9] which began soon after she arrived as a student in Marburg in 1924. She was 18 but already a remarkable, strong-willed woman; he was 35. The affair was passionate on both sides, but kept absolutely secret not only with an eye to Elfride's jealousy, but because Heidegger's job was at stake. Indeed it was to reduce this risk that he persuaded Arendt to transfer to Heidelberg to study with Jaspers in 1925. They continued to meet at points between, and the affair went on until Heidegger broke it off after he was appointed at Freiburg in 1928.

Heidegger was clearly energized by this brilliant young woman who he felt understood his thinking. He credited her as making *Being and Time* possible. And she felt a reverence and gratitude towards him that survived even "his Nazism," and the defects in him this exposed. Jewish, she had fled Germany in 1933 and eventually found her way to the United States to make her own academic reputation. She reestablished contact with Heidegger when she revisited Germany in 1950, and thereafter did him many large and small services. She was undissuaded by the hostility evinced towards her by Elfride, who had since learned that she "was once the passion of his life." She was also undissuaded by Heidegger's complete inability to regard her as a thinker in her own right.

vii. Teaching

Heidegger was becoming famous as a teacher well before he debuted with Being and Time. He had a powerful effect on his audiences, and attracted a remarkable number of talented students who went on to eminence themselves. Although many would later break drastically from Heidegger's central views, they caught from his lectures a philosophical spark which founded their later achievements, and which they always credited him for. His lectures brought concepts and problems to life, out of abstraction and routine.[10] Their overall trend was in a way Socratic: to show that we don't know the most basic things—but in a way that energizes us to try to find them out.[11] When he was barred from teaching after the war, this was not on purely punitive grounds, but in recognition of the strength of his pedagogic impact. The lectures he gave to non-academic audiences in these later years likewise generated great excitement.[12]

viii. Nazism

The "episode" in Heidegger's life that has tended to overshadow all the rest—or to give a central meaning by which the rest is judged—is his participation in the National Socialist party and movement in 1933–34. Or rather, it is this participation, and then Heidegger's very inadequate apologies or atonements for his involvement—and indeed his efforts to diminish its extent. It's the feeling that his favorable interpreters continue these efforts that explains the cyclically renewed campaigns by other scholars to show that the full scope of his Nazism has still not been faced.[13] I will present what seem to me the main facts.

It's not clear just how long before 1933 Heidegger's Nazi sympathies began. He seems to have been largely unpolitical, but with conservative sentiments that prepared him for conversion; this was a radical conservatism that hoped for a transforming spiritual renewal of Germany, which National Socialism seemed to him to promise. He viewed the party favorably by at least 1932. But he largely kept these sympathies out of his classes, and they were a surprise to his students.[14] A part of the movement's appeal to him was Hitler himself; Heidegger famously spoke to Jaspers of Hitler's "wonderful hands." He thought that Hitler would grow past the party and many of its doctrines.

In 1933 the Nazi regime began to consolidate its control by absorbing all other social organizations, including the universities (this was the Gleichschaltung). Several academics jockeyed for leadership in this, Heidegger among them. While he later depicted himself as persuaded to take the Rectorship of Freiburg in an emergency situation, he had been lobbying and negotiating for some time before. Already Germany's most famous philosopher, he aspired now to a national and social role; he had in particular a vision of pedagogic reform to effect.

He was elected Rector on April 21, 1933, by a faculty that had already been thinned by the suspension of its non-Aryan members. In early May he joined the party, and in late May delivered his inaugural address, "The Self-Assertion of the German University" [SA], at a ceremony at which, by his arrangement, the Horst-Wessel Lied was sung, and "Sieg Heil!" shouted. This speech and several others he gave in the period supply his pedagogic, political, and metaphysical grounds, which fit well with his practical steps as Rector.

His guiding idea is metaphysical: it concerns the relation to being. This sets these speeches at a level of abstraction that must have mystified most hearers. Proper relation to being depends on revolutionary moments of decision through which one "chooses oneself" and becomes authentic; we'll see how this idea was central to *Being and Time*. But in 1933–34 Heidegger applies the idea not to individuals but to the people [*Volk*]. He fuses it into a communitarianism in which it is the *Volk* that unifies itself by acts of authentic choice.[15] And the role of the university is to serve this national self-discovery and self-choice, not to abet the private insights of faculty or students, nor to pile up scientific or scholarly facts. (So the aim reaches all the way down to his different idea of truth, our theme.) The university needs to be shaken up and overhauled to play this proper role; it is mired in routine and complacency, Heidegger thinks, especially among its full professors. The urgency of working in this national service must be inculcated in its younger members.

Heidegger's speeches present these tasks in strongly martial terms, appropriated not just from the Nazis but from Nietzsche. The radical break requires an intensity of will and effort which is abetted by conceiving it as a "fight" and "struggle" requiring "courage." "[T]he German university can only attain form and power when the three forms of service—labor-, military-, and knowledge-service—come together originally into *one* formative force" [SA 37]. As Rector he furthered a military orientation of the university, requiring participation in sports; he organized paramilitary exercises and labor service. He also devised and led a "science camp" [*Wissenschaftslager*] in October 1933 in Todtnauberg, a philosophical retreat whose participants were (somehow) "fighting" for national ends.

His comportment towards Jewish colleagues and students changed during these years. He had had many Jewish students, including Arendt, Blochmann, and Karl Löwith, but began to hand his current ones off to other colleagues. He broke off personal contacts with Jewish colleagues. And in 1940 he acceded to pressure from his publishers to remove from *Being and Time* its dedication to Husserl.

This seems to have reflected political calculation rather than personal anti-Semitism, and in the same period he extended help to Jews in other ways: as Rector he defended two professors he was called to fire as Jews; he helped his personal assistant find employment in England. He never expresses anti-Semitism in his writing, and indeed is hostile to "biologism" of all sorts.[16] (And it may be added that he was hostile towards Christianity and Catholicism in particular in this period—as standing in the way of revolutionary change.)

Heidegger served as Rector of Freiburg University for almost exactly a year, submitting his resignation letter on April 23, 1934. He later claimed he resigned because unwilling to carry out an order from the Ministry of Education to dismiss two deans on political grounds. But it seems, rather, that he felt himself not adequately supported by this ministry in his radical vision for the university. He came to see National Socialism as betraying the revolution it had promised. And on the other side he was viewed by the real Nazi ideologists as a fraud and mystifier, whose speeches mimicked Nazi themes but with an unintelligible abstractness.

Although he remained a party member through the end of the war, he fell increasingly out of favor with the authorities and in 1937 was apparently put under surveillance. He felt himself to be making a public critique of the party, especially in his lectures on Nietzsche, so widely viewed as the Nazis' philosopher. In diagnosing Nietzsche as in fact subject to the nihilism he attacked, Heidegger meant to imply a similar critique of National Socialism. He saw it, from 1935 on, as an especially thorough application (along with Communism and "Americanism") of the technological understanding of being that became his principal target.

When he returned from Messkirch to Freiburg after the war he faced serious problems. He was identified by the French military authorities as a Nazi, and his house and library were at risk of being confiscated. A denazification commission (three faculty picked by the authorities) examined his case. At Heidegger's request they asked for an opinion from Jaspers, with whom he had had no contact since 1936. Jaspers wrote that "Heidegger's mode of thinking, which seems to me to be fundamentally unfree, dictatorial, and uncommunicative, would have a very damaging effect on students at the present time";[17] he recommended that he be prohibited from teaching, but allowed to keep his pension, and this was the upshot the French authorities eventually settled on. In addition people were billeted in his house, which drove him to spend much of 1946 in his Todtnauberg cabin.

In defending himself to this committee Heidegger set the pattern of disavowal that would so grate. He refused to acknowledge guilt, beyond brief political error. He depicted himself as "resisting" the regime by his lectures' critique of its metaphysical underpinnings. ("I claim no special credit for the spiritual resistance [Widerstand] I have rendered over the last eleven years," he says in a November 1945 letter to the rector's office [GA 16 404].) From his 1945 accounts of himself, right up to the Der Spiegel interview of 1966 (and published after his death [DS]), "Heidegger simply whitewashes himself," as Habermas puts it [1992 199].[18]

I've tried to state the main points concisely. Obviously I hope that readers will not take these to refute in advance the philosophical ideas the rest of this book will recount. My own view, very briefly, is that this "episode" certainly shows various flaws in Heidegger the man, but that the relevance to his ideas is complex and mixed. The "turning" into his later ideas really is, in important part, an effort to learn a deep lesson from Nazism—to correct, at the very bottom of his thinking, what had led him to embrace it.[19] But even the earlier views, of Being and Time, are not condemned by this connection, since it is mediated by that extension from individual to Volk just mentioned. I hope in what follows to give a clear enough picture of his philosophical thinking to enable readers to judge these relations for themselves.

ix. Works

His one-sentence biography of Aristotle stresses that "he worked," and Heidegger certainly did so himself, as we see from the roughly 100 volumes projected for his *Gesamtausgabe*. To be sure much of this writing consists in one-draft lecture notes, but it is very striking how many different such courses he taught, on how many different philosophers, and how little he reused material. We can classify his work under three main headings.

First are the 16 volumes of "published writings" that make up the first part of the *Gesamtausgabe*. These include, on the one hand, several books, including *Being and Time* [BT], *What Is Called Thinking?* [WCT], *The Principle of Ground* [PG], and *Identity and Difference* [ID], as well as the massive, two-volume *Nietzsche* [N], assembled from various lecture-courses and lectures, and *Kant and the Problem of Metaphysics* [KP]. There are also several important collections of essays, including *Pathmarks* [P], *Woodpaths* [W], *Underway to Language* [UL], *Elucidations of Hölderlin's Poetry* [EHP], *Early Writings*, and *Lectures and Essays*. (All but the last two have been translated into English. Besides *Being and Time*, I most recommend to first readers *What Is Called Thinking?*, *Pathmarks*, and *Woodpaths*.)

Next are the 44 volumes of lecture-courses in the *Gesamtausgabe*'s second part. These tend to be more thoroughly historical than some of the published works, and less forthcoming as to Heidegger's own views, though there are many exceptions to this. They span the period from 1919 to 1944, and so reflect Heidegger's great shifts in viewpoint. Of particular interest are (1) *Towards the Definition of Philosophy* [DP], from Heidegger's earliest lecture-courses, (2) two volumes from the period of *Being and Time* that fill out its ideas, *Prolegomena to the History of the Concept of Time* [PH] and *The Basic Problems of Phenomenology* [BP], and (3) *Introduction to Metaphysics* [IM], from 1935 and reflecting the start of Heidegger's "turning."

Third are the 39 volumes in Part 3 ("unpublished treatises—talks—thoughts") and Part 4 ("indications and notes") of the *Gesamtausgabe*.

These include Heidegger's "secret writings"—books that he
worked on apart from his lecture-courses but never finished for
publication, above all *Contributions to Philosophy* [CP] and *Mindfulness*
[M]—and other miscellaneous productions, very few of
them translated into English; of special value for Heidegger's late
quasi-mysticism is *Fieldpath Conversations* [FC].

Summary

The question whether Heidegger's life is relevant to his thinking is
much disputed, and mustn't be ignored. The issue obtrudes in a
way it doesn't with most philosophers, due to the large fact of
Heidegger's Nazism. How his political ideas and activities in the
decisive period 1933–34 are related to his philosophical thought in
Being and Time [1927] will affect appraisal of that work. In later years
Heidegger stubbornly refused to issue the apologies many critics
have thought requisite, but he did make fundamental changes in
his thinking that plausibly reflect lessons he thought he learned
from these events. We must look at the main facts about his Nazism
in order to weigh these philosophical connections. Beyond this,
there are many less dramatic ways in which his biography may
either affect or reflect his thinking. This chapter compresses as
much relevant information as it can.

Further reading

R. Safranski: *Martin Heidegger: Between Good and Evil*. Tr. E. Osers. Cambridge, MA:
    Harvard University Press, 1998. [A sympathetic biography that tries to introduce
    his ideas as it goes.]
H. Ott: *Martin Heidegger; A Political Life*. Tr. A. Blunden. New York: Basic Books, 1993.
    [A more critical biography centered on Heidegger's involvement in Nazism.]
R. Wolin (ed.): *The Heidegger Controversy: A Critical Reader*. Cambridge, MA: MIT Press,
    1993. [A useful collection of texts by Heidegger and others bearing on his
    Nazism.]

Two

Early development

For a long time Heidegger's early thinking lay fully in the shadow of *Being and Time*: if it was considered at all, it was only as the path to that book, and not for any merit it might have on its own. This view was abetted by Heidegger's own later tendency to dismiss this early thought and even to discourage attention to it. Moreover, apart from his two dissertations (in 1913 and 1915), he published very little in this period, and almost nothing in his first dozen years of teaching, before the publication of *Being and Time* in 1927. Most of the material from these years is his lecture-courses.[1]

Yet this early thinking is important in its own right—and indeed was so viewed at the time. Despite his very sparse publications, Heidegger was already gathering fame and influence, principally through his lecture-courses; transcripts from these were passed along, and carried the impression of a major new voice in philosophy. Hannah Arendt, who was already his student in these years, famously referred to this underground reputation as "the rumor of the hidden king" [1978 294].

So this early thinking deserves more attention than I will give it. It deserves to be treated for itself, and not just in relation to the later writing, as I will mainly do. In fact I'll be selective even in this. I don't want to anticipate the philosophical substance of *Being and Time*, so I'll largely defer treating Heidegger's path to his phenomenology; I'll mention it retrospectively in my chapters on that book (Chapters 3–6). Instead I'll focus here on three broad points.

First is Heidegger's insistence on the need for a different kind of understanding than we get in science, or the usual philosophy; we met this theme in the Introduction. It belongs to the "radicalism" I also touched on there: by attacking not just "what" other philosophers claim but the very kind of truth these claims mean to capture and convey, he tries to strike at the root of all other philosophy. We find this ambition already strongly evident long before *Being and Time*. We even find there his will to push this critique constantly further, turning it against deeper and deeper features of our usual thinking.

Second is Heidegger's relation to religion. This is the period in which he passed out of Catholicism, first into other forms of Christianity and then—apparently—out of and away from religion altogether. I summarized this transition biographically in Chapter 1, and now look at its philosophical substance. The transition is important first because it shows the trajectory within which he writes *Being and Time*—how that book expresses a secular stance that he will later think of as Nietzschean. But these early religious views are also important because, by his later "turning" from that book's stance, he will come back to some of them. So we find in these early writings the roots not just of *Being and Time*, but of the quite different later thinking as well.

These two themes, his radicalness about truth and his religious passage, are related. We can see the idea that we need a new kind of truth as a lesson he carried away from several points on this religious path. I noted on pp. 7–8 Kierkegaard's familiar claim that "truth is subjectivity," but a more decisive influence on Heidegger in these early years were the Christian mystics. He takes from them the demand for a special truth-experience transcending all our ordinary kinds; he gets a sense of such experience, in these years, that he never loses. It is expressed in a subdued and controlled form in *Being and Time*, despite that book's secularism. And it is given more rein after the turning; the turn is indeed in large part a rising of this element into authority.

These early years are characterized, I suggest, by the conflict between this religion-inflected critique of the traditional truth-project, and Heidegger's competing desire—this is my third theme—for a new philosophy that is yet more rigorous, more "scientific," than ever before. This (intellectually) conservative ambition for a more rigorous philosophy looks surprising in the light of Heidegger's late poetic thinking, but it was dominant in his student years. And it competes thereafter with that radical critique.

Heidegger starts, we might say, with a basic sense and conviction that *something* is deeply wrong with philosophy as generally done, but is tugged in two directions as to what this is: either philosophy has failed to be sufficiently rigorous, or the very effort at rigor is just what's wrong. The tension between these diagnoses is still not resolved by *Being and Time*, where rigorous theoretical inquiry is intended to aid and accompany an authentic relation to being.

I will use terms like "rigor" to gesture at this "conservative" ambition in Heidegger, which models philosophy on science and mathematics. It shows biographically in his consideration of a career in mathematics. And it shows in his thinking in the way it considers (proper) philosophy a kind of meta-science: scientific method applied in a second-order domain. Philosophy uses that method to understand not things—that's what science itself does—but our first-order understanding of things. It discovers the "logic" underlying that first-order knowing, and underlying especially the sciences themselves.

This ambition for a more rigorous philosophy shows most strongly in his student years, as he works to assimilate, and to find his own position within the profession—and in particular within two related strands of the then-current technical philosophy, neo-Kantianism and (Husserl's) phenomenology. These appeal to him because they promise to be that meta-science. I'll try very briefly to give a sense of how Heidegger adopted and merged these, before returning to those "radical" inclinations that will partly subvert them.

The 1913 doctoral dissertation—"The Doctrine of Judgment in Psychologism"—attacks various contemporary theories of judgment as psychologistic. It insists on the distinction between the "psychic acts" of judging, and the "logical contents" they are directed upon. Our path to a "logic of judgment" lies only through the latter, and not through any empirical or scientific study of those psychic acts. Instead we are to study those logical contents in acts of "categorial intuition"; the categories we thus arrive at are the very categories of being.

Much of this is continuous with Husserl in *Logical Investigations*, which Heidegger had read already in 1909. And the position is also neo-Kantian,[2] since it understands those categories not as real, as in Aristotle, but as transcendentally ideal: they are the *a priori* posits that are indispensable for us to have any experience. So while this logic disavows empirical psychology, it understands itself as based in a transcendental psychology; it is a theory of the preconditions for intentionality or meaning.[3]

The 1915 qualifying dissertation—"The Doctrine of Categories and Meaning of Duns Scotus" [DC]—interprets this Husserlian and neo-Kantian context back into (the text imputed to) Scotus. Once again the opponent is psychologism, together with historicism and similar relativizing threats to pure logic, understood as a special meta-science. So DC (*GA* 1 273): "the rod is broken over all physiological and psychological and economic-pragmatic theories of knowledge, and the absolute validity of truth, the genuine objectivity, is irreversibly established." But this objectivity lies in the necessity of a certain intentional structure.

Heidegger operates here with a telling conception of our intentionality—the first-order understanding that philosophy studies the logic of. He understands this intending (which lets entities be there for us) as the conscious positing of some content, in a judgment. And he analyzes this judgment to involve three moments: the intuitive showing or givenness of the object, a differentiation of this object into subject and predicate, and the assertion and communication of this predicative showing, to others. It is only by this full package of acts that we mean or intend entities; the way to the being of those entities is by an analysis of the logic of such judgments.

Heidegger's ultimate interest is already in "being," and the logic of our intending is studied as a means to it. Heidegger famously says (e.g. DL (UL 7)) that the source of this interest was his 1907 reading of Brentano's *On the Manifold Meaning of Being [Seienden] in Aristotle*. He takes hold of the problem of being from Aristotle, and interprets the neo-Kantian and Husserlian methods as good for it. So Aristotle serves him as his principal life-line out of the Scholasticism he was first trained in. He hopes to find being by those rigorous current methods.

But as soon as Heidegger leaves studenthood behind and starts teaching at Freiburg he begins to express and develop the radical critique of this effort at rigor and logic. Already in the supplement he wrote in 1916 for his dissertation on Scotus, we see him pushing off this way: "[T]he theoretical attitude [*Geisteshaltung*] is only *one* [form of direction], for which reason it must be a principal and fateful error of philosophy as 'worldview' if it contents itself with a spelling out of actuality and does not, as is its authentic calling, ... aim at a *breakthrough* to true actuality and actual truth" [CPC (S 66)].

This critique becomes most overt and emphatic from 1919 on, beginning with the famous lectures in the "war-emergency semester" [*Kriegsnotsemester*] early in that year. Some interpreters have suggested that it was here that Heidegger "becomes himself."[4] This is the period, we'll see, in which his religious passage brought him to the Christian mystics, and he had from them his strongest sense of a positive alternative to that rigorous philosophy.

The target of this radical critique is "the theoretical attitude" itself, as already suggested in 1916. By 1919 Heidegger says that it is "the general dominance of the *theoretical*, which deforms the genuine problematic" [DP 68]. What it is most important to understand is unavailable to this attitude; we can only "see" it by some other kind of attention. And tied to this critique of the theoretical is a dissatisfaction with epistemology. Although the latter is "born of a legitimate, energetic awareness of the necessity and value of critique," it "does not allow the goal- and end-questions of philosophy to come to their immanent meaning" [CTS (S 49)]. Much of modern philosophy has gone off the tracks due to its strong epistemological orientation.

What is this theoretical attitude inadequate for? For much of our everyday experience we'll see. And this makes it also inadequate for being, which must be found in or through the ordinary, engaged stance in which we mostly live. The theoretical attitude draws me out of my usual involvement in living my own life, within the context of a world I implicitly take—not just believe—to be there around me. Theory involves "a faded I-relatedness reduced to the minimum of lived-experience" [DP 59]. This inadequacy in theory itself poses a major dilemma for phenomenology, which needs to study that ordinary intentional stance.

We can see Heidegger borrowing, in this period, vocabularies from various contemporaries to describe the aspect of ordinary experience that resists the theoretical view. In particular he often uses "life," taken from various "life philosophers," though he will immediately insist on his differences from them.[5] It is "life-experience" [Lebenserfahrung] or "lived-experience" [Erlebnis] that is at issue, and theory's inadequacy is in being a "de-lifing" [Entlebnis] of it. DP 84: "the ur-bearing of lived-experience and life as such ... first becomes absolute when we live in it—and that is not achieved by any constructed system of concepts, but only through phenomenological life in its growing intensification [wachsenden Steigerung]." PIE 18: "the question arises whether a consideration of lived-experience is possible, that does not at once and necessarily theoretically disfigure it."

Another term Heidegger takes over for this purpose is "world": that lived-experience is characterized by the way an environment [Umwelt] "is there" for us as a sense-giving context. But he rejects the idea—in Jaspers and others—that it is there in the form of a "world-view": this depicts it as a kind of theory; it "freezes" it [DP 165]. The special presence of our world in this ordinary life disappears when the theoretical gaze is directed upon it: "When I attempt to explain the environment theoretically, it collapses upon itself" [DP 68].

Still another term he employs here he invents himself. In seeing something—Heidegger's classroom example is the lectern—"I am fully present in my 'I'," in such a way that I "appropriate" [er-eigne] the experience to myself; so the experience is not a process but an "appropriating event" [Ereignis]. DP 60: "Lived-experiences are Er-eignisse insofar as they live out of the 'own' [Eigenen], and live life only this way." Here Heidegger already tries to activate resonances in a word in the way that will be characteristic later. He does so with a term that he soon abandons, but will revive with similar intent much later on: Ereignis ordinarily means "event," but by bearing eigen can be heard to mean "make one's own." My lived-experience makes world and things bend towards me in a way that disappears to theory.

There are many other sources of this dissatisfaction with theory, for example his reading of German and Greek poetry and literature, which was intensive from early on. He says that he discovered Hölderlin in 1908 (before he was 20). Indeed he wrote poems himself in this early period. Although he doesn't yet (as he much later will) model philosophy partly on poetry rather than science, he begins to feel that poetry gives truths inaccessible to science—truths the thinker needs too.

But perhaps it was especially his religious shifts around 1919 that most strengthened this radicalism. It was early in this year that he informed his friend Father Krebs that "[e]pistemological insights extending to a theory of historical knowledge have made the *system* of Catholicism problematic and unacceptable to me, but not Christianity and metaphysics—these, though, in a new sense" [S 69]. But he goes on to claim that he "has experienced—perhaps more than your colleagues who officially work in this field—what the Catholic Middle Ages bears within itself regarding values."

We've looked at biographical factors in Heidegger's passage from Catholicism to Protestantism to an apparent non-religiousness. Here we are concerned with the philosophical ideas that explain or express this shift. The main such reason, I suggest, is this: Heidegger puts ever more stress on the importance of a nonrational religious experience, while, however, abstracting the object of this experience away from a personalized god, to identify it as being, itself.

The 1915 thesis shows Heidegger already inclined to an extreme abstracting and depersonalizing of God; it uses Eckhart's mystical notion of God as an undifferentiated unity. He gradually realizes, I suggest, that he is not talking about an entity or thing at all, not even an ultimate entity, but about being. This is reinforced by the way the neo-Kantian and phenomenological views treat their ultimate as the object of a transcendental meaning, "for" us and our intentionality; enclosure within this context confirms that what's at issue is no longer really "God."

Simultaneously, however, Heidegger's visit with mysticism serves to strengthen the religious element in a different respect. For although such experience is amorphous, it has a unique intensity—which is, indeed, part of its justification for its special epistemic status. In these years Heidegger claims there can be such intense and clinching experience of being, in place of God. What's crucial is to have the special experience: "Eckhart's 'basic conception', 'you can only know what you are'" [PR 240]. He quotes Schleiermacher: "'Thus now everyone can understand each activity of the spirit only insofar as he can at the same time find and observe it within himself'" [242].

In thinking of this religious illumination as available by noticing (in the right way) our ordinary lived-experience, Heidegger gives it a certain democratic character: it is potentially available in *any* of our experiences or situations, and with respect to any entities. It is indeed most to be had by somehow penetrating beneath the most ordinary attitude in which we generally live. So although the moment of illumination is itself quite exceptional, it is reached by turning a new kind of attention on what's simply and always available.

This experience is not, of course, theoretical, and can't be grasped theoretically. Christianity's appropriation of Aristotle was thus a fateful mistake, so that "Scholasticism, within the totality of the medieval Christian world of experience, severely endangered precisely the immediacy of religious life, and forgot religion in favor of theology and dogma" [PR 238]. Heidegger sees mysticism as an "elementary counter-movement" against this; it recovers the kernel of early Christianity, before its co-opting by Greek philosophy. This is Luther's main struggle too. And Heidegger calls for "an originary Christian—Greek-free—theology" [PIE 72].

He soon has second thoughts about Aristotle, however, and devotes several of his lecture-courses in the early 1920s to partially rehabilitating him. He reinterprets Aristotle as providing, in his ethics and other "practical" works, an analysis of the structure of our ordinary experience; see, e.g., the 1924 BCA. Much of this analysis (which has been disputed) he will transmute into *Being and Time*'s phenomenology of our everyday being-in-the-world. So we find here a rehabilitation not only of Aristotle, but of the ability of a rigorous method to bring out the character of our lived-experience.

Thus Heidegger's early years are characterized by the contest between his opposing ideas how philosophy must change, to help us towards being. He begins with confidence that a more rigorous and scientific theory will bring us the truth about being. But he also carries over from his religious roots an *extra ambition* with respect to

truth, an ambition that is reinforced by his sense of mystery in the
"worlding" of our ordinary life. This extra ambition invests the
idea of being with a religious potency, and demands radical changes in philosophy's method. As we'll now see, these opposing
ambitions are still alive in Being and Time, and their juxtaposition is
central to that book's appeal and influence.

Summary

Heidegger was 37 when Being and Time was published; he had
already crossed much philosophical ground. One major transition
was from his initial identity as a Catholic philosopher, through
Protestantism, and into the apparent a-religiousness of that book.
This passage brings him through religious and mysticist enthusiasms
that will reemerge in his later thinking.

We also find in these early years a strong allegiance to a more
rigorous and scientific philosophy, such as both neo-Kantianism
and Husserl's phenomenology seemed to promise. But this conservative aim competes with a radical ambition that gradually mas-
ters it; this radicalism finds those rigorous methods inadequate to
understand our concrete life-experience, which slips from view as
we try to understand it in theory and concepts. This sense of an
ineffable in our everyday lives draws both on that mysticism, and
on his devotion to Greek and German poetry. It will soon prompt
the changes in the method of phenomenology that he will detail in
Being and Time.

Further reading

T. Kisiel: The Genesis of Heidegger's Being and Time. Berkeley: University of California
    Press, 1993. [A detailed account of Heidegger's early philosophical development.]
J. van Buren: The Young Heidegger; Rumor of the Hidden King. Bloomington: Indiana
    University Press, 1994. [Stresses the radical elements in Heidegger's pre-BT
    thinking as anticipations of his late views.]
See note 1 for a selective list of Heidegger's early writings.

Three

Being and Time

Phenomenology

So we arrive at *Being and Time*. This is the book that made him famous, and for which he's most famous today. It is, like no other of his works, philosophy on a grand scale, with grand ambitions. It sets out to make a comprehensive statement, taking up and organizing all of his earlier ideas, and even all of earlier philosophy. It has unique status in Heidegger's corpus as a best, official statement—though of course only to this date (in spring 1927 he was 37 years old). For the book's authority is shadowed by the way (and the extent) that he himself later renounces its core ideas and even aims. *Being and Time* has a curiously divided status, as Heidegger's major work, but also as superseded, in his own view at least, by the smaller-scale books and essays of his later years.[1]

One of the great appeals of *Being and Time* is that grand ambition, by which it sets out to tell us everything that is most important. It sets out to uncover "the meaning of being," which is what philosophy, and all of us, have so egregiously lost sight of.[2] This grand ambition is reflected in its meticulous organization, and close attention to its own procedure and method. It has a fairly intricate structure, but tries painstakingly to make this structure fully clear. The Introduction—which will mostly concern us in this chapter—above all shows this intense methodicalness. To help display this important feature of the book, I'll spend more time here than later presenting the section-by-section path of Heidegger's discussion.

As a part of this procedural exactness, the Introduction (which has two chapters, and the book's first eight sections) develops at some length (in its §7) the *method* the book will employ, in its effort to clarify the meaning of being. This method is of course *phenomenology*—my main topic here. But phenomenology is just the announced part of a fuller method that Heidegger uses and displays from the very start. This fuller method is also germane to the "kind of understanding" he wants for himself and us.

The overt method of the book is strikingly traditional. Despite the critique of Descartes it later makes, *Being and Time*, like the *Meditations*, claims to "begin at the beginning." It doesn't, to be sure, lay down any first certainties, but it does claim to pose a most basic question—about the "meaning of being"—and then to reason out the best way to address this question. It tries to set aside all prevailing doctrines, to build a way to truth that anyone can follow.

Moreover, the book presents the insights it claims as a system, and insists on the importance of grasping them in this form. *Being and Time* seems in this regard very much in the German (and ultimately Aristotelian) tradition. The system offers us a synoptic view, which reaches down, through a hierarchy of levels, into detailed accounts. We then control each individual thing by seeing its precise place in the system. So it is with the book's elaborate analysis of Dasein (or human being).

In these respects the book's epistemic aims seem quite the usual ones. As we'll see, this appearance is somewhat misleading, and Heidegger will draw epistemic lessons that run against these points. Against the possibility of any best beginning for thinking, he will promote the "hermeneutic circle." And against the need for system he will promote an ultimate truth that is simple and direct. Indeed, it will turn out that this really important truth is not, in a sense, theoretical at all. So the careful path to an elaborate system turns out eventually to be a device to shift us into a rather different notion and method for truth. Nevertheless, it is by this path that Heidegger believes the more novel insights are best achieved.

The book opens with this strong display of method. A pre-liminary page announces an overall question—about "the meaning of being"—and the Introduction (its first chapter) proceeds meth-odically to: (§1) defend the question as unjustly neglected today, (§2) analyze the question's "formal structure," and then further promote it as an indispensable question both (§3) ontologically (i.e. regarding being), because it is a precondition for the "regional ontologies" that underlie all the sciences, and (§4) ontically (i.e. regarding entities), because the inquiry into being is definitive for the entity—Dasein—each of us is, and so is presupposed not just for us as scientists (knowers), but for our practical or life decisions.

This is the official structure, but more important is an argument Heidegger weaves across these formal steps. We are asking about being, but must proceed by "interrogating"—studying, examin-ing—entities. And since entities are rife, we need to ask whether any have priority, i.e. whether our search after being should focus on any kind of entity in particular. One naturalist answer might be to focus on whatever physics counts most basic—so perhaps on the simplest particles (or waves). But Heidegger proceeds differently. The question is of course something that a Dasein (a human being) asks, so this kind of entity is already singled out [BT g7–8]. And it's eventually established [g13–14] as the entity to be studied, by a murky argument purporting to show "that the ontological analytic of Dasein in general is what makes up fundamental ontology."

We must notice what's at stake here: nothing less than a choice (if only a tentative one) between realism and idealism—although Heidegger refuses to put the point in these terms, for reasons we'll see. (BT g14: "this priority [of Dasein over all other entities] has obviously nothing in common with a vicious subjectivizing of the totality of entities.") In order to investigate being we can and must study Dasein first and above all, because "there is" [*es gibt*] being only in or by Dasein's understanding of being.[3] We investigate being by studying that understanding. It is this basic idealist orientation that turns the book's attention to Dasein—which is where it remains, since the part of the book that was to return, after studying this special entity, to draw conclusions about being itself was never written. This idealism is with respect to *being*, we should bear in mind, and we must see to what extent it involves an idealism about *entities* as well.

Now I have been using the term "Dasein" for this special entity which each of us is. I will follow the general practice of leaving this term untranslated. (Indeed since it is now so usual in this role I will not italicize it, as I will the few other cases of Heidegger's German that I keep.) With Dasein Heidegger co-opts a term that German philosophers had used for being or existence generally. He applies it to us—to the entities we would otherwise label "humans" or "persons" or "subjects" or "agents." It refers to each individual one of us—each is a Dasein. It refers to us in our essential aspect, in which each of us is also typical.

It gradually emerges why this term Dasein is appropriate for this reference to us: its root or etymological sense of "being-there" should be heard to say how our intentionality gives us a "there" [Da], as a world or space of experience. This world is a field of possibilities that is the indispensable context for all our experiences. It's only by this opening up of a world—by our being in this there—that entities can then appear (be uncovered or encountered). Although this world is not itself the "being" we are seeking, the latter will be found through it. So the examination of Dasein will focus on this world-founding role.

The Introduction's second chapter proceeds with the same methodical care—yet again somewhat masking its arguments for important choices. Its first two sections offer orienting summaries of the overall course of (§5) Part I and (§6) Part II (not done). It then (§7) develops at length the phenomenological method Heidegger intends to use in studying Dasein, en route to the question of being. Finally (§8) it quickly outlines the book as a whole—including the large parts that were never published or even written.

I want to focus now on Heidegger's announced method, his phenomenology, which he introduces so methodically in §7.[4] Since he there offers this as only a "preliminary concept" [*Vorbegriff*] of the method [BT g28], we will need to fill out our account of it by looking ahead at later developments in the book. By this method, he proposes to understand first of all Dasein, i.e. oneself or the kind of entity one is, in its way of being, and then eventually being itself.

Famously, Heidegger learns the method from Husserl, but then adapts and alters it. Heidegger had read Husserl's *Logical Investigations* back in 1909–10, but it was not until 1917–18, when he was turning from Catholicism-Scholasticism, that he became a convert. Husserl had arrived in Freiburg in 1916, and Heidegger began to pursue him. The relation between their respective versions of phenomenology is a very vexed issue on which there have been extremes of disagreement.[5]

I'll try to show that Heidegger's main change to Husserl's method lies in precisely the dimension we're interested in: he revises it to provide a different *kind* of understanding, a different way of knowing or having the truth. Husserl has still too Cartesian a notion of knowing. Heidegger's new method is not a more effective way to get the understanding we've wanted; it carries a lesson to change what we want.

1. Studying intentionality

In studying Dasein we are studying the way it "is there," i.e. there in a world it takes to be around about it. We are studying the way Dasein "means" or "intends" its world. To be sure, Heidegger rarely speaks of "intentionality" in *Being and Time*: this is part of the break he wants to make with Husserl. He gives over the term to Husserl's sense for it, which he then has two reasons for abandoning: Husserlian intentionality is (1) a cognitive relation and (2) a relation to entities—and Heidegger wants to talk about more than these. But what he does want to treat—a non-cognitive relation, extending beyond entities to being—is still a kind of intentionality, I'll argue: it's another way to mean or intend. So I will keep this vocabulary in presenting Heidegger, and try to show how it can and should survive the criticisms he makes of Husserl.[6]

"Phenomena" are, if we use the term generically (rather than in the narrower and stricter sense I'll come back to), *what's meant*, i.e. intentional contents or meanings. A phenomenon is an *intentum* (intended or meant), the object of an *intentio* (intending or meaning). And phenomenology, in the Husserlian view Heidegger largely takes over, will begin by studying and describing these contents, as well as—inseparably—the way we mean or intend them.[7]

There are two important features of Heidegger's conception of this intentionality which we should notice from the start. They are, in fact, the first two things—he numbers them—that he says about Dasein in Chapter 1 of *Being and Time* (§9). (They have the status of working assumptions for the analysis of Dasein, which are to be confirmed, hermeneutically, by the success of the analysis to come.)

First, he hears a strong *telic* point in this "intending" or "meaning." The chief part of the way we're *"directed upon"* a content, is by being *"directed toward"* an end. What we intend or mean first and foremost is (in each case) an end or goal—what Heidegger will call a "for which." Thus the ordinary sense of "intend" suits it to pick out our way of meaning—though once again we must expel the implication of something cognitive or conscious. Other things have their meanings ultimately in relation to these goals. This point is at the root of Heidegger's "pragmatism," which I'll present in Chapter 4.

Heidegger builds this directedness into Dasein from the start: "The 'essence' of this entity lies in its being-towards [Zu-sein]" [BT g42]. This term Zu-sein is mistranslated by Macquarrie and Robinson as "to-be," which conceals its relation to the "towards-which" [*das Wozu*], i.e. what Dasein is being-towards. The principal towards-which is the for-which [*das Worumwillen*], a way for Dasein itself to be [g84]. And Heidegger mainly uses "existence" [*Existenz*] for this way in which Dasein is always directed towards "possible ways for it to be" [g42]. We always "stand out"—the root sense he hears in "existence"—towards these goals and roles; he will later call this our "projection."

The second important way Heidegger conceives of this intentionality is as reflexive or self-relating. An intentionality, in being directed upon an object, is always also directed upon itself. So, principally, the end that Dasein is directed towards is intended as its own; not only is that ultimate for-which a state of itself, but Dasein aims at it *as* a state of itself. I aim at my ends as "mine," and this self-relation extends to all of my other intendings as well: I mean them ultimately in relation to me. Intentionality, then, is ultimately first-personal.

This is the second thing Heidegger says about Dasein at the start of Chapter 1. "The being *about which* this entity is concerned in its being, is in each case mine [*je meines*]. ... Speaking of Dasein must, due to this entity's character of *in each case mineness* [*Jemeinigkeit*], always use a *personal* pronoun: 'I am', 'you are'" [BT g42].[8] This notion will also play a decisive role in *Being and Time*, for it lies at the root of the "existentialist" ideas I'll present in Chapter 5, in particular the ideal of authenticity.

So phenomenology studies this intentionality—but how? It might be doubted, at first, that any special techniques are necessary. Why isn't our own intentionality perfectly obvious or transparent to us, since we're the ones doing the meaning? Why is any new method necessary? It seems we already possess the understanding phenomenology seeks, by being already aware of how and what we're thinking about ourselves and things.

There's something importantly right here: we *are* trying to understand something we already *do* understand. The crux will lie, as I've said, in *how* we understand it, and there are serious problems here. But the fact that we're studying something already meant is vital to phenomenology. It entails that no novelties are to be expected. The point is to remind us of things so commonly understood that we fail to notice them adequately. BT g139: "Like any ontological interpretation whatsoever, this analytic can only, so to speak, listen in to some previously disclosed entity as regards its being." So our learning comes with a sense that we're recalling or remembering (Heidegger's version of Plato's point).

I want to stress both the *paradox* and the *presumption* of Heidegger's claim here: that he is merely reminding us of things we all already understand—yet that his reminder goes (almost uniquely) against the grain of all our philosophical and commonsense self-reflections. What he wants to show us above all is, on the one hand, "the most obvious thing in the world"—yet it is also something we constantly misunderstand when we try to describe it. The challenge, in developing his picture, is to present it such that it can merit these two claims—so that it can indeed be something both obvious and rare (esoteric). His accounts of us will, and must, oscillate between seeming tritely obvious, and seeming outrageously strange.

But what, more particularly, are the obstacles—why do we so easily go wrong? The main problem can be simply put: it's hard for us to pay attention to our own role in meaning what we do. We notice *what* we intend, our meant, but overlook (or look right through) the way we mean it.

Despite the reflexive character of Dasein's intending—the way its goals are *jemeinig*—it usually lacks an adequate view of itself. In intending, a Dasein takes *itself* to be intending, takes its aims as *its own*, but it does so without—as it were—looking at itself, and noticing itself as intending. We absorb ourselves in objects, and little notice our act of meaning them. So the *intentio* pays attention to the *intentum*, and not to itself, even though it is constantly saying "I," "me," and "mine."

This way we fail to notice our intending also spoils, in a way, our conception of intending's objects. We take them as real, i.e. presume that they are as and what they are "in themselves" or in their own right, and not (at least partly) in or by our intending. We don't regard the *intentum* as an *intentum*. This is particularly true, I think Heidegger holds, in our scientific view of things: we overlook how here too it is a certain way we *mean* these things that lets them appear, lets them indeed *be*, as we mean them.

Here we come back to the issue of Heidegger's idealism. We've seen how the basic project of *Being and Time*—to get at being by studying Dasein—already expresses an idealism regarding being.[9] But does Heidegger think that not just being but *entities* depend on Dasein's understanding of being? Carman has made a powerful case that he does not—but is instead an "ontic realist" holding that objects "exist and have a determinate spatiotemporal structure independently of us and our understanding of them" [2003 157], and that (in science especially) we can and do have knowledge of these real things. And there are passages in which Heidegger seems to say just this.[10]

However, I think all of these passages can be read as expressing a merely "internal" realism, which is spoken within an understanding of being and leaves out the way entities depend on that understanding.[11] It belongs indeed to the being of objects—which Heidegger will call "the at-hand"—that they are independent of all our experiences of them; within the framework of that understanding, they *are* real and independent.[12] And yet, I think Heidegger insists, they can only *be* thus real by virtue of that background understanding. Entities are, only by virtue of being, which lies in Dasein's understanding. Carman's reading makes the relation between entities and being too loose or indirect: it makes being necessary not for entities to be, but only for them to be meant or interpreted (or to "appear"). "Being" is a badly misleading term if it refers to the condition for entities' interpretability, and not the condition for what entities are.

So we typically overlook that background understanding of being, and indeed our intending generally. And because we don't know how to attend to this intending, we tend furthermore to seize hold of ready-made theories when we do describe it—theories that usually get our intending wrong, because they reflect the same motive to ignore that background. We need to learn to look for ourselves. So Heidegger's main words for phenomenology's improvement on traditional philosophy are that it "lets [something] show itself from itself"; he also cites the famous slogan "to the things themselves!" [BT g27].

But how are we to pay proper attention to this intending—and overcome that constant bias away from it? The first part of a strategy comes from Husserl, who offers a technique for it, his famous epoché, which suspends our ordinary assumption that things are real. "Bracketing" this claim lets us uncover objects *as intended* (qua *intenta*), and turns us back to the act of meaning itself, showing how it supports that content or object.[13] In this general sense of the epoché I think Heidegger takes it over.[14]

It's important that once we thus turn back to the *intentio*, to the act of meaning, we suspend our natural realism there too. We must not treat this intending in the way that psychology or biology does, as occurring in the midst of the world, as one kind of thing among others. We are interested in its role allowing a world of things, as meant or intended, to be; we need to treat it, as it were, from the inside out, rather than from an outside context in. So (§10) Heidegger distinguishes his project from those in the human sciences: phenomenology won't understand intending or meaning in the way a naturalist or scientist would, by seeing how these meanings arise in an organism.

Once we have recognized the intentional realm, and are able to pay the right kind of attention to it, our task isn't just to describe the phenomena that show up within it. We need also, and especially, to show its *structure*, and in particular this structure's deepest or grounding parts. And here we meet another general point that Heidegger shares with Husserl: he takes over a Kantian conception of this structuring, as the operation of transcendental conditions. That is, there are *levels* of intentionality or meaning, the lower levels serving as "conditions of the possibility" of the higher ones, the latter therefore depending on the former. What the phenomenologist needs to uncover, above all, are the possibility-conditions of the (first-order) phenomena. So he/she will employ "transcendental arguments," i.e. inferences from the evident features of experience to what makes them possible.

These conditions lie on the side of the intending—are imposed by it (by us) upon things. These conditions are in this way *a priori*, not drawn from experience. Yet these *a priori* impositions aren't explicit, aren't noticed; we make them unawares. Or, if we do notice them, we mistake them as features of the *intentum* by itself—of the object we think about. All of these points are in Husserl, but they are ultimately Kantian ideas. So BT g31 says that within "the Kantian problematic" phenomenology's phenomena would be the forms of intuition (space and time), which already "show themselves," but "unthematically," in all phenomena in the ordinary sense.

Because it studies a level in intending that is hard to see, Heidegger says that in its strict sense phenomenology "lets show itself" "something that is *concealed*, in contrast with what firstly and mostly shows itself, but at the same time something that belongs so essentially to [the latter] as to make up its meaning and ground" [BT g35]. We are looking for a way we mean and intend that decisively shapes all our experience without our noticing it. And we uncover it partly by inferring what it must be, for our experience to be as it is.

This inference to what our experience presupposes introduces a certain apriorism into phenomenology—or into one stage of its work. It begins empirically, by studying "appearances," i.e. our human (acts of) meaning; this is its "phenomenal basis." But phenomenology then steps back to infer the *a priori*, structurally necessary elements in this meaning. BT g50 n. x:

> Through E. Husserl we have not only understood again the meaning of all genuine philosophical "empiricism", but also

learned to handle the necessary tools. *"A-priorism"* is the method of every scientific philosophy that understands itself. Since it has nothing to do with construction, *a priori* research requires proper preparation of the phenomenal basis.[15]

Phenomenology must beware constructing, i.e. imposing, its own structures, and so must begin by getting the appearances right.

It is the step to the *a priori*, in transcendental argument, that brings us to the level of being. It reaches the level at which intentionality projects and constitutes that world of possibilities, and thereby the being of entities. This is where intentionality "discloses" being, on the basis of which entities can then be "uncovered." This is also the step to the "existential," as opposed to merely "existentiell" or particular. These term-pairs mark the decisive distinction between being and entities, the ontological and the ontical.

Now it is especially here, regarding this *a priori* level at which being is disclosed, that Heidegger comes to deny that "intentionality" is involved. He prefers to limit the term to the particular comportments that are based on that deeper structure: "It will turn out that intentionality is grounded in Dasein's transcendence and is possible only upon this ground—that one cannot conversely explain transcendence out of intentionality" [BP 162; cf. MF 135, 168]. Being lies in that *a priori* structure, which is a condition of the possibility of all meanings—and of entities as well.[16]

But although Heidegger elects not to call this transcendental relation to being "intentional," he still goes on to treat it as a directedness upon meaning. Indeed, it is important to his conception of phenomenology that this *a priori* level, though reached by transcendental argument, can be made to appear, i.e. can be experienced. It can be "brought to show itself," and to show itself "from within," and not just as an object of study. In these privileged experiences of insight we will notice ourselves meaning in these very ways, and that we've been so meaning all along.

2. Adapting the method

To this point we have mainly been attending to Heidegger's agreements with Husserl. Now let's turn to some of the ways he adapts and alters this Husserlian method. An important precedent for these changes was his earlier effort to adapt phenomenology to handle religious experience. The inadequacy of Husserl's method for this anticipates its inadequacy for the pragmatic and existential aspects of Dasein. Heidegger's dissatisfaction expresses that radical critique of the prevailing notion of truth, which we saw (in Chapter 2) took root in 1919.

Biographically, we should notice as background the way Heidegger and Husserl took one another "personally," so that doctrinal differences carried psychic weight. Although they both profit hugely from their interaction, they do so grudgingly and with a dose of ill will—which we find on both sides. Husserl felt betrayed by a most promising (and glamorous) student who failed to follow, or even to get the point of, the method he thought so vital. And Heidegger is strivingly eager to press his own originality, and indeed his greater stature. These interpersonalia give reasons to distrust their own accounts of their relationship.

Another difficulty in specifying *Being and Time*'s disagreements with Husserl is that the latter is a moving target: his views changed during the years of interaction with Heidegger, in part adapting to his criticisms.[17] The differences I will eventually detail are more apt regarding Husserl's earlier work, and less so for works contemporary with *Being and Time* or later.

My interest, however, is in Heidegger's conception of the differences regardless of its accuracy. I want to describe how he tries to "push off" from Husserl into positions he feels are his own; he may well (as other philosophers have too) overstate his own novelty.[18] He thinks that Husserl's changes in view come too late in the logic of his position; his phenomenology is doomed at its root by its subjectivism. Husserl's efforts to adapt it to handle pragmatic and existential phenomena don't go nearly deep enough—are artificial accretions to an unsatisfactory core.

So the central disagreement Heidegger thinks he has with Husserl is over his still-too-Cartesian conception of the intending phenomenology uncovers. *Being and Time* doesn't elaborate its differences from Husserl, but expresses them indirectly in its critique of Descartes.[19] For Husserl still thinks of human meaning (intending) as carried out by a kind of thinking thing, and shapes his method accordingly. The attack on Descartes' picture of us is thus an implicit critique of Husserl. And Heidegger's chief reason for giving up the term "intentionality" is his belief it is infused with this Cartesian, cognitive picture. I retain it because I disagree: I think we can annul this connotation by emphasis and reminders.[20]

Heidegger argues (first in §13) that the thinking that Descartes makes definitive of us, as minds, is instead just a "founded mode" of a prior, more encompassing way we mean and intend. Things matter to us much more widely and deeply than this. He calls this primary level of meaning, whereby "entities are" for us, our "concern." Husserl, he thinks, neither notices nor studies this level of meaning.

Hand in hand with this different conception of how humans mean, there goes a different method of phenomenology to study it. These two sides—the thing to be studied and the method of study—shape one another. The new idea of intentionality designs the method that will study it, but Heidegger is only confident that intentionality is this way because he has already begun to use (an ancestor of) that method. So we should think of the ontological and methodological points as evolving in tandem. But I'll consider them in that order.

i. Phenomenology's new phenomena

I'll treat Heidegger's reconception of intending (the object phenomenology studies) under three headings. He objects to three main elements in Husserl's view of the intender as essentially a thinking thing: that it is basically theorizing, conscious, and a substance. Human intending—or rather the deep level of it we're trying to lay bare—is none of these.

So first, Husserl makes primary our *theoretical* relation to the world.[21] He conceives of intentionality as deeply or principally aimed to know, and its content, its world, as what it posits (as true). Intending occurs principally in our beliefs and theories about ourselves and our surroundings—it is these that lay out the structure of the world, our *intentum*. So Heidegger in MF 134: "Thus every directing-oneself-upon receives the character of knowing, e.g. for Husserl, who describes the basic structure of all intentional comportment as *noêsis*; thus all intentionality is first a cognitive intending [*Meinen*], upon which other modes of comportment towards entities are then built." Values, for example, are treated as superimposed on a picture of reality already held in our beliefs: we value things only after we have located and identified them. Or indeed, values are treated as themselves beliefs—beliefs that certain things have value.

But here Husserl (like Descartes, and so many others) has begun—Heidegger claims—with what is really a *special* stance or condition, which we occupy only exceptionally. Proper phenomenological method requires that we begin with the way we are "firstly and mostly" [*zunächst und zumeist*] (Macquarrie and Robinson translate this extremely common expression "proximally and for the most part"). "At the outset of the analysis Dasein should not be interpreted in the differentiation of a determinate existing, but rather be uncovered in its undifferentiated firstly and mostly" [BT g43]. So we need to examine our "average everydayness" [*durchschnittliche Alltäglichkeit*].

As we'll gradually see, Heidegger thinks there is a fundamentally different attitude or stance "at the bottom" of our intentionality—not the stance we occupy when we think objectively or theoretically. We might call it the stance of trying.[22] Our primary *intentio* is willful and directed. It is an effortful directedness, which operates in the first person, towards ends "in each case mine." It is this "care" or "concern"—an industrious and ever-working *pragmatic* orientation—that basically gives us the world, and ourselves. This is the way we mean things in our everydayness, where we live most of our lives. Phenomenology must do justice to this basic pragmatic way we mean.

Since our intentionality is principally end-directed, phenomenology must mainly map not things but ends: the network of ends and means (that are themselves ends for prior means) that gives the ultimate orientation of our intending. We interpret every thing around us in relation to this elaborate network; it determines how things matter to us, and which features are salient in them. This network gives the principal structure to our "world." Of course the phenomenologist is interested not in the details of particular such networks, but in their broad and common structure.

A second way Husserl is still Cartesian is in holding that intentionality occurs only or principally in *consciousness*. Pragmatic concern or care is not mainly a conscious aiming. Of course Heidegger does not deny that we can mean things consciously, but he thinks this is only the tip of our intending, most of which runs along without the explicit awareness we usually refer to as "conscious." Indeed there is a spectrum of cases here, and reminding ourselves of some of these will show what uncertain borders the term "consciousness" has.[23]

Much of our meaning occurs, to begin with, in a kind of "background" awareness, such as that we have of our feet on the floor—before we think about our feet on the floor.[24] We sense our feet in their contact-points with the floor, and in their posture and kinetic potential beneath us, but we sense it (as it were) "behind" the conversation at the table, and the food, which absorb our attention. Our pragmatic intending has a figure-on-ground structure, so that what's explicit always rests on a background left in shadows and implicitness. We attend to a few concerns by pushing many others out of our conscious attention; they run, as it were, on autopilot, subliminally.

Now, is it right to say that we *are* aware here of our feet *at all*, even "in the background"? Perhaps sometimes we're not in the least aware, and what's really going on is just that we *would* immediately be aware of our feet's feel and posture if the feel "rose" to painfulness, or we had other reason to change their position. Consciousness is prepared, under various conditions, to pay attention *here*, and this is perhaps an indirect kind of awareness. We are, perhaps, "on the alert" to notice and respond to impingements on the various parts of our bodies, whose various postures and dispositions we keep track of implicitly, holding them available for immediate conscious notice and control.

So we constantly mean things "behind" our focal awareness, a penumbra that stretches even "beneath" awareness altogether. As we focus attention and make something fully *present* before us, we situate it against a background that is partly conscious and partly not, and which gives the context that supports the meaning we assign to that present thing.[25] So I understand myself, all the while I eat and converse, as doing these *with* this body I am bearing through this day, and disposing in postures in which I converse and eat. We can't adequately understand even how we consciously intend, Heidegger claims, without grasping this penumbral understanding.

We must combine this point with the previous one. This background that gives context and meaning to the figure is not, as it were, a picture of the surroundings of the figure. For the thing is principally intended pragmatically, and the background is too. It gives meaning to the thing by how it makes it matter. The background is the context of my projects, that gives practical meaning to the thing now present (to me). So I understand the posture of my legs not in an image of them, nor in any proposition, but in a practical preparedness to deploy them for various ends.

Another point here will be important later: we sometimes hold things in one of these backgrounds, and *resist* pressures that would otherwise bring them into focus or awareness. We know what it's like to be avoiding thinking about something. We do this intentionally—but mean to be as little as possible aware that we do. So the act of keeping in the background itself gets carried out in the background. Heidegger's existential story will place great weight on such cases of avoidance—cases we often call "self-deception." In them the background is, in one way, there for us, yet we are working to ignore it.

Heidegger claims that in these ways the most important parts of our intentionality are either implicit, or actively suppressed. In his pragmatic analysis (Chapter 4 below) our world of equipment and purposes is understood by a competence or preparedness that is very largely implicit. And in his existential analysis (Chapter 5) our competence for existence itself, or for being a self, is actively suppressed.[26]

There's a third way Heidegger finds Husserl too Cartesian, which reaches even deeper than the others. This is in treating the intending as carried out by a substance or thing, an ego or subject that is prior to the intending and directs it. So Descartes "substantizes" the self (as I'll put it), inasmuch as he "takes the being of 'Dasein' ... in the same way as the being of *res extensa*, as substance" [BT g98].[27] And this is adopted by Husserl in his account of intentionality.

How does Heidegger "de-substantize" Dasein? Not, I think, in the way argued by some interpreters,[28] who have read Dasein as not principally "in the individual," but in the social practice, or in "talk" [Rede], as Heidegger will define this. It's this overall practice that basically means or intends, on this reading, and not each or any single individual. Intentionality is carried out at the level of societies.

I will argue against this "social" reading of Dasein. In the sense in which the term applies to entities (we've seen that it can also refer to the being of those entities), I think it picks out entities that correspond to individual persons as we commonly sort them. It's for a different reason that Heidegger denies these entities are substances, as we standardly take persons to be.

If Dasein is not something social, and comes in the same units as persons do, it seems almost unavoidable to view "a Dasein" as some kind of thing, whether a subject, a person, or an organism. How could it not be a thing or substance at all? But if we hold fast to the idea that intentionality is something first-personal—and has structure precisely and only as such—we begin to see how this might not be so.

Above all—and I think this is Heidegger's ultimate complaint against substance—we find that intentionality has a very different temporality than substances do. We need to understand the temporal logic of intending "from within," and not impose a logic learned in relation to (third-personally observed) persisting physical things. Intentionality, as (in each case) mine, is "*present*" in a way that substances are not; it also "*persists*" quite differently.

A substance occurs fully and discretely in each present moment that it exists. But Dasein necessarily "means" by virtue of being stretched ahead towards a future and from back in a past. What it "is" lies in these relations, and not just in what is now. Nor are these relations analyzable into memories and goals—i.e. as present representations of past and future. This is not "what it's like" to mean, as we principally mean. It's not the real character of that first-personal intending itself.

A substance exists fully in each moment, but of course it can also persist through a series of moments or nows—indeed it's as persisting through change in qualities that substance is often defined. However, this kind of persistence is again very different from Dasein's. Dasein persists by virtue of a certain self-constancy, which is achieved only in the "steadiness and standfastness" of authenticity [BT g322]. For the most part Dasein fails to persist, because it fails to stand fast towards itself, in the way we'll eventually see. For now it suffices to have this further hint how Dasein's temporal structure differs from a substance's.

Finally, let's try to make more vivid to ourselves the upshot of these three Husserl-critiques, and Heidegger's positive conception of intentionality. As I dwell on some one thing—let's say an apple—and make it present to my focused awareness, still at the same time all the rest of my world "is there" for me, behind and beneath this awareness. This includes the position and posture of my bodily parts, and also the geography of my vicinity, but most importantly "where I am" in the various projects in which I hold myself involved, projects that reach out through my day, and through variously larger units of my life.

My principal relation to the thing is not theoretical. I attend to the apple not to study it but to wash it or store it or eat it, and each of these dealings has its meaning only within the context of those broader projects and ends. I am situated in relation to a past and a future, towards which I stand in quite different, but not opposite, relationships. Finally, I've spoken throughout in the first person here, and this is appropriate to the character of this intending, as "in each case mine." However, we must not suppose that this "I" is a substance or subject extrinsic to the intending. It is rather, we'll see, a certain project itself, which can be either better or worse pursued.

ii. Changing phenomenology's *logos*

If this is what intentionality is—if it has these features Heidegger claims—then we will need to go about studying it a different way. The changes Heidegger makes in intentionality affect what phenomenology's methods or strategies must be, and even the very kind of grasp or truth it should expect. So here we turn to the *logos* of phenomenology. If intending is not principally theoretical, nor conscious, nor by a subject, how should we examine and clarify it? How can we "make show itself" this intending which is mostly willful, "in the background," and nonsubstantial?

We should distinguish here between two ways of "showing." There is first of all the event of insight or understanding— the condition of being in a maximal truth towards the topic (the meaning). However, the *logos* is not this event itself, but rather the medium (or capacity) of *sharing* this insight. It puts the insight into words that are able, when rightly read, to stimulate or occasion that event of truth. So these words—the *logos*—"show" it by producing the event. Thus phenomenology is essentially related not just to its topic—trying to figure it out—but to an audience it aims to bring into the truth about this topic. (This audience can include oneself at later times.)

Husserl's misconception of intentionality distorts the method he adapts to it, preventing it from "showing" being in either of those ways. As we now expect, he makes the event of insight "too theoretical"; he still follows Descartes too far. BT g95: "The only genuine access to [entities of a world] lies [for Descartes] in knowing, *intellectio*, and indeed in the sense of mathematical physics' knowing." But this knowing stance can't adequately understand even sensation—a relatively simple kind of intentionality—nor the being of what is sensed, e.g. hardness or resistance. Descartes' mathematical formulations of these "extinguish" "the kind of being that belongs to sensory perception" [g97]. And he is still further from understanding how that sensory and intellective awareness are founded in being-in-the-world [g98].

Now of course Heidegger's phenomenology is also (in large part) theoretical; it employs that third-personal stance of "study." But it sees that this study's target is itself *not* (chiefly) a theorizing, but an attitude deeply unlike it, so that this study must adjust in ways Husserl didn't suspect. Meaning is crucially telic, i.e. an effort at ends that matter to it. To comprehend this mattering, phenomenology needs to occupy the intentional attitudes it studies, to understand them "from within."[29]

Phenomenology must include, to supplement its study of its objects, a participation in them—taking their point of view by intending that way oneself. One occupies the stance-to-be-under-stood, but in a particular way: such that the stance occurs in its own kind of explicitness, quite different from one's becoming "conscious of" it. One studies the stance in this perspicuous form, and gives a theoretical account of it. But that account is only a satisfactory "truth" about the stance, in conjunction with the special form of the stance itself.[30] So BCM 61:

> To awaken a mood means, after all, to let it *become awake* and as such precisely to let it *be*. If, however, we make a mood conscious, come to know about it and make the mood itself into an object of knowing, we achieve the contrary of an awakening. The mood is indeed thereby destroyed, or at least not strengthened, but weakened and altered.

This point affects also the kind of *logos* that can *share* this insight. Phenomenology can reveal intentionality only by breathing affective life back into words we have come to hear merely as theoretical concepts. It must reverse a tendency by which words lose their power to evoke the concern they are about: "in the end the business of philosophy is to preserve the *force of the most elementary words* in which Dasein expresses itself, so that they are not leveled off into incomprehensibility by the common understanding" [BT g220].

Surprisingly perhaps, what we mainly care about is not at all evident to us. At the root of all our meaning are ends that lie hidden from us. There is on the one hand an inertial drift of these ends into the background, where they are "taken for granted." But there are also motives that actively suppress notice of these ends, so that phenomenology must work against a positive interest in concealment. Phenomenology needs to wrest these ends out of this hiddenness, by foregrounding them within our projective effort.

For this purpose, and against all those obstacles to illuminating care, Heidegger employs one characteristic device: he pays special attention to experiences of "*breakdown*"—to cases in which our ordinary interpretive practice breaks down or fails, in such as way as to thrust us "off the rails" of the practice; so we see it in a condition of disruption yet "from within."[31] In Chapters 4 and 5 we'll see that the study of breakdowns is key for both the pragmatic and existential applications of the method. Here I'll just sketch the general reasons for this use.

When we experience a breakdown, and this prompts us to study it, this theoretical attention occurs in the wake of the ordinary experience and care—as we are falling out of it. So, in the first place, there is the advantage of proximity. We are "near" the experience, it is still fresh and vivid as we regard it.

Indeed, I think we should think especially of the case and time when there's an overlap and blending of these two attitudes—the ordinary one that is our target, and the knowing stance that regards it. While we are regarding the practice that has broken down, there are, as it were, still filaments of that telic, first-personal stance that can be "pointed to" and tasted by the third-personal theory. (This much we can do or have without breakdowns, simply by turning our attention to our attitude while we're in it.)

But much more important than mere proximity is what the breakdown does to that experience itself, before and apart from that view of it. It jostles the intentional practice out of its ruts, and makes us feel how it is at risk. It makes the structure of the aiming explicit *in its own way*, in the way that belongs to care itself: we notice it by our concern. We thereby "awaken" this aiming, as we might put it. So the deeper structure of our care is highlighted, in that very attitude itself, for the theoretical stance then to observe.[32]

Breakdowns illuminate, then, the background aims and ends that have underlain all my more overt and obvious meanings. They make me actively concerned about ends I have been taking for granted, all the while I was straightforwardly in the attitude that has now broken down. The deep-set goals that are ordinarily missed or suppressed are "lit up" by being thus disrupted and endangered.

I notice what has been important by feeling and handling it as under threat.

The theoretical stance then "pays attention" to this lit-up background. Or rather, as we've seen, there is a kind of intertwining of this study with remnants of the stressed concern. It is perhaps this mixed case, in which both stances participate, that is the privileged condition of truth or understanding, at which phenomenology aims. I think this fusion is what Heidegger calls "intuitive thinking." PH 41: "We only seldom engage in this mode of intuitive [*anschaulichen*] thinking, which instructs about the matter, but mostly rather in foreshortened and blind thinking"—i.e. thinking that has lost that linkage with concern. I will try to clarify this hybrid, intuitive thinking in the chapters to come.

All of this concerns the privileged state of understanding and truth at which phenomenology aims. But, as we've seen, the discipline has a second part: the task of "sharing" this insight by way of a *logos* or discourse. It finds words to "make manifest" the topic, so that it shows itself to that privileged view (that knows it best). The special character of this view affects how words are picked—what they're picked to do.

Since genuine phenomenological insight requires not just third-but first-personal grasp of the meaning to be understood, it needs words to induce or invite the "awakened" condition of the project or aiming it is trying to understand. (Ultimately this will mean that phenomenology must find words to help make us authentic.) The traditional aim at conceptual precision needs to be not replaced but supplemented by another, which is to induce, or enable us to find, the breakdown experiences by which our deepest aims are lit up.[33]

This is another main reason Heidegger rejects much of the existing philosophical vocabulary. It's not just that its concepts carve up things wrong, but that they are only concepts (as it were). They are useless at awakening the attitudes they are trying to clarify; this is perhaps what it mainly means to say that these terms are "theoretical." The challenge in understanding concepts is grasping their analysis (into other concepts). But our challenge with Heidegger's words is to be affected by a certain kind of breakdown in our ordinary stance. This is harder and less certain to achieve. It poses a different risk than the usual concepts: these words can always be understood "in an empty way" [BT g36], by one's lacking not their conceptual analysis, but the right first-hand grasp of the topic.

This is what Heidegger means when he calls his terms "formal indications" [*formale Anzeige*], inasmuch as "the meaning-content of these concepts does not directly mean or say what they refer to, but only gives an indication, a pointer to the fact that the understander is called upon by this conceptual context to carry out a transformation of himself in his Dasein" [BCM 297].[34]

It might be asked whether phenomenology doesn't have a further task, to *justify* its accounts of its topics. If it is a science of phenomena, it seems it should also give proofs or arguments to substantiate its claims—should give us reasons to believe them. However, I think Heidegger believes the justification also lies in those "awakened" engagements in our first-order projects. In those breakdown moments in which the structure of our aiming is lit up, we will find (Heidegger claims) the justification for the descriptions he offers of that structure. So by showing us the way to these experiences, phenomenology shows us where and how to assess its own accounts of intentionality.

Now it might seem that Heidegger's use of "transcendental arguments" involves a different kind of proving. Doesn't he begin with descriptions of our experience, but then argue from them to conclusions about what our deep structure *must* be, to make these experiences possible? However, we've seen that he thinks these founding structures must also be available in experiences—and it is the latter that justify the extrapolations we make from our ordinary intending. PH 87: "There can be no disclosure or deduction of essence from essence, *a priori* from *a priori*, one from the other, but each and every one must come to demonstrative sight [*ausweisenden Sicht*]."

3. A method for being and truth

Now the aim of *Being and Time* is "to work out the question of the meaning of *being* and to do so concretely" [BT g1], but I have not spoken much in this chapter about being. It might seem that this is because phenomenology is a method only for the book's preliminary project of analyzing Dasein, and not for the ultimate goal of revealing being. But in fact Heidegger insists that phenomenology is, most vitally, precisely the method for revealing being. "The phenomenological concept of phenomenon means, as what shows itself, the being of entities, its meaning, its modifications and derivatives" [g35].[35]

Here we meet again the decisive neo-Kantian idealism: it's by getting at the structure or logic of our meaning and intending that we find being, itself. The latter is, so to speak, fully settled by what (and how) we mean; it is, as it is for us. Hence the outward, objective view has no use in identifying being—neither physical science nor psychology can find it, and we need a science of phenomena instead. Being lies in the very logic of our intentionality, hence at a different level, indeed at a transcendental remove from all our usual meanings. It's a condition, a structural requirement, for every one of these meanings—something they all involve or rely on.

Heidegger puts huge stress on this difference in levels, and condemns the common tendency to overlook or understate this "ontological difference." It is a difference, it seems, with no intermediate stages: there's no approaching by degrees from entities to being. This shows that being isn't reached by *generalization* from entities; it's not, Heidegger often stresses, the most general genus or kind. As entities' transcendental condition, being lies at an absolute distance from them.[36]

Being is the background manner of intending that allows us to mean everything else. It is a deep expectation and aspiration we bring to bear in encountering any thing, an expectation less about the thing than about the stance or attitude in which we would ideally grasp it. As we'll see, the difference between at-handness and to-handness, the two kinds of being a physical thing can have, lies in the kind of grasp we aspire to. So, roughly, a rock, e.g., is to-hand if we mean it for use (in a wall), at-hand if we mean it for theory (in geology); its being is a function of which basic stance we bring to it.

When we see this difference in level between being and entities, and the former's transcendental role as condition for the latter, we see why Heidegger felt the need to mark it with a break in terminology, and to deny that our relation to being is a matter of intentionality at all. And yet I think his account of it makes clear that he continues to think of it so. Being resides in our understanding of being, which is surely a relation to meaning, i.e. intentional. Phenomenology's challenge is to illuminate this existing understanding, in which we "mean being."

We saw how phenomenology "shows" phenomena by inducing breakdowns that make explicit what we implicitly intended all along. This applies to the showing of being, as well. Being is given in an understanding that needs not just to be described, but itself "awakened" in each reader to an explicit state. This means awakening it as a first-personal attitude—taking it seriously and personally.

Heidegger develops the special character of his method's aim in his treatment of "truth" (see especially BT §44).[37] He presents this as principally a matter of "uncovering" or "unconcealing" (he uses a large set of related terms). This uncovering occurs at both ontical and ontological levels, both of entities and of being—and Heidegger will reserve different terms for each.

He attacks the standard interpretation of truth as correspondence or agreement.[38] This correspondence is taken to run between an intentional content—a "representation," perhaps—and the object of the claim; the first matches or mirrors the second. The intentional attitude towards this content is simply that of believing or positing or asserting it. What really matters is getting the right content for that theoretical stance.[39] Heidegger's core dissatisfaction with this prevailing view is that it locates truth principally in the content (and its relation to things), rather than in the attitude towards a content. Really truth is not a content we grasp, but a way of grasping, and especially in the most important case, of the truth about being. The change we need to make is in our stance.

Consider first the most obvious kind of case—ontical truths about things. Heidegger gives a rare example: "someone with his back turned to the wall makes the true assertion: 'The picture on the wall is hanging askew.' This assertion demonstrates itself when the man who makes it, turns round and perceives the picture hanging askew on the wall" [BT g217]. The assertion does, at one remove, the same thing as the experience of turning to see the picture's skew: it's an *"uncovering"* [*Entdeckung*] of the picture *as* askew. It brings explicit attention to an entity, in a way that "determines" it under a particular aspect. (The assertion, we should notice, shares or communicates this uncovering, as the original experience does not.) So, importantly, these cases involve a transition, from not-noticing to noticing; they presuppose a condition in which the entity in this aspect was quite unsuspected, or (more usually) forgotten.

This uncovering, not correspondence, is the gist of truth, Heidegger thinks.[40] Truth is thus not a steady state or possession but a transition or change, an event of coming-to-notice. It is well expressed in the Greek word *alêtheia*, un-forgetting, which means not "never forgetting," but that passage out of forgetting. The condition in which we do *not* notice or attend is primary and default. The assertion's truth—if it *is* true—lies in its enabling us to notice an entity in an aspect. This uncovering is not an event in Dasein alone (not a mental event), but in Dasein's relation to the entity,

Heidegger stresses. Truth "lies—taken almost literally—in the middle 'between' things and the Dasein" [BP 214].

All of this so far is ontical: both assertion and experience uncover entities. But they are dependent on a truth about being that Heidegger calls "*disclosure*" [*Erschlossenheit*], which is therefore more basically true.[41] What's disclosed is a world, as a network of possibilities a Dasein knows its way with. It's only because this is given implicitly that particular paths can then be "lit up" by an assertion, or by a direct uncovering. And the overall way this world is disclosed is being. Here we come to the ontological level: disclosure is a truth about being; it is being showing itself.

To be sure, for the most part—firstly and mostly—the world is disclosed to us only implicitly, only "in the background" in the way we've seen. But again there is a privileged experience in which being "shows itself" more adequately—in which our deep-set intending of being is awakened, becomes explicit. This happens in authenticity: "This *authentic* disclosure shows the phenomenon of the most originary truth in the mode of authenticity" [BT g221]. This is ultimate truth, the experience of insight that Heidegger (in *Being and Time*) most valued, pursued, and tried to convey. This way authenticity is bound up with phenomenology begins to show how the latter's aim is not just descriptive but valuative. In uncovering the truth about being, phenomenology also shows us how to live. How Heidegger can coherently think this will be an issue for us especially in Chapter 5.

Looking ahead, this phenomenological method will be applied in three movements: pragmatic, existential, temporal. In each case the task is to illuminate a different level of our being, and this requires a somewhat different mode of understanding in each case. But the general points we've seen will apply in all three movements. Truth about each level of Dasein lies not in an objective view about (of) it, but in an improved view within it. Such truth is occasioned by breakdowns in smooth functioning, in the transition into second-order assessing and coping. Truth lies in attending to those breakdowns a special way.

Summary

Being and Time is meticulously methodical. Its Introduction sets out its guiding aim—to treat "the meaning of Being"—and reasons out the one best way to pursue it. That the route to being runs through an analysis of Dasein (i.e. humans) indicates the book's deep "idealism": being occurs in Dasein's understanding of it. Phenomenology, as the method to study this understanding, is therefore also the route to being. The Introduction devotes its §7 to elaborating this method, to be deployed in the rest of the book.

Heidegger learns this method from Husserl, but then adapts it; we map it by seeing what he takes over, and what he changes. Above all he keeps phenomenology's subject-matter: intentionality, i.e. the way we "mean" things, "intend" them. We are in a way always already familiar with this, but tend also to overlook it, as we notice the things but not our meaning them. Phenomenology looks for deep structures of this intentionality, working in all our particular experiences. It uses transcendental argument—reasoning from our observed experience to what it presupposes—to identify these structures. When they're made explicit in the right way, we recognize them as what we've meant all along.

Heidegger revises Husserl's method to suit his different conception how intentionality works. Husserl had understood it as theoretical, conscious, and carried out by a substance, but Heidegger disputes each part of this. Our primary intending is willful and directed, and the theoretical attitude is a variant still dependent on it. This willful intending works mainly "in the background," the better to focus attention on particularly pressing concerns; indeed there are motives that actively suppress awareness of it. And finally, this intending is not carried out by an ego or self that persists as a substance through objective time; rather this intending has an intrinsic temporality very different from that of substances—and its own kind of persistence as well.

These revisions Heidegger makes to Husserl's notion of intentionality dictate changes in the method for studying it. Its willful character—its "concern"—can't be understood by a third-personal view upon it; phenomenology needs to occupy the intentional stances it studies. It needs to occupy them in a way that makes them explicit intrinsically, and not just to an external view. Heidegger puts great weight on "breakdowns" as giving this awareness "from within." When some tool breaks down while we're relying on it, we notice, by feeling, how it (and what hangs on it) has been mattering to us all along.

Along with this new method we need a new idea of truth. The prevailing conception of truth as correspondence doesn't look deeply enough. An assertion can "correspond to the facts" only because we can experience an "uncovering" of those facts, in which we come to notice something hidden before. And such uncovering itself depends on the "disclosure" of a world, as a network of possibilities within which we can frame the facts we uncover. Uncovering has better claim to be called truth than does correspondence, but disclosure is the most basic truth of all, and the kind phenomenology pursues.

Further reading

T. Carman: *Heidegger's Analytic; Interpretation, Discourse, and Authenticity in* Being and Time. Cambridge, UK: Cambridge University Press, 2003. [Treats BT with impressive rigor, and particular attention to the issues of this chapter.]

S. Crowell: *Husserl, Heidegger, and the Space of Meaning: Paths toward Transcendental Phenomenology.* Evanston: Northwestern University Press, 2001. [Linked essays arguing that Heidegger's early method is largely continuous with Husserl's.]

See note 1 for other works by Heidegger in the period of BT.

Four

Being and Time
Pragmatism

Heidegger fights three main campaigns in *Being and Time*, each opening up a different level of our human being. The first of these campaigns is what I'm calling his "pragmatism," which occupies most of Division I of the book, and especially its Chapters 2, 3, and 5.[1] We've already seen the point in a general way. He redescribes us, correcting the usual model, linked especially with Descartes, which treats us as principally theoretical or cognitive. Heidegger pragmatizes intentionality, i.e. the way we mean and intend. We most basically mean things by way of our "concern" or "care," and our positing or knowing is secondary and dependent on that more basic intending.

My purpose in this chapter is to elaborate this pragmatism. One obvious challenge is to show just how Heidegger conceives of the difference between (what one might call) practice and theory; the difference is more subtle than we might expect. For practice involves a kind of knowing—just (to lean on a familiar phrase) a knowing-how rather than a knowing-that. And on the other side theory is itself practical—as perhaps it must be, if practice is really basic. In section 1 I'll introduce this distinction, and in section 2 I'll discuss the problems this poses for our effort to understand practice.

This chapter's other main task is to introduce some of the elaborate *structural analysis* Heidegger offers for our practical intending.

This has been one of the most influential parts of the book. He analyzes Dasein under three main aspects, which are, roughly, how it understands, feels, and talks; together, these three allow us to "mean" or intend in that basic pragmatic way. I'll treat these three aspects in turn in sections 3–5.

Now I adopt the term "pragmatism" with some reservations. I don't claim that Heidegger is "a pragmatist," but only point out a pragmatist theme in his account of our intending.[2] He himself doesn't use the term for his point, although he does introduce the Greek *pragmata* in clarifying equipment [BT g68]. I think the ideas I'll bring out below are best named by it, although as always we will need to adjust its sense to fit his position.

Heidegger's presentation of this pragmatism is one of the great virtues of *Being and Time*. He shows a love for "menial" craft or handwork—his father was a craftsman—that is comparable to what Plato shows in his Socratic dialogues: both use it to model life generally. This theme in the book has special force or persuasiveness for many readers, despite the very thick new terminology he introduces in presenting it. I will try to convey what I think is the phenomenological aptness of his account.[3]

As usual for Heidegger, this aptness must strike us *despite* the initial newness or strangeness of his analysis. He claims to need his elaborate new vocabulary precisely because his account runs so contrary not just to Descartes, not just to the whole philosophical tradition, but to the universal commonsense viewpoint reflected and reinforced in our very language and sociality. It often seems that *everyone* before has gone wrong.

Despite such intimations of his near uniqueness, Heidegger of course knows where pragmatic points were pressed before. Aristotle's teleological account of humans (and all substances) is a clear ancestor, and indeed many of Heidegger's new pragmatic terms are modeled after Aristotle's (as *Worumwillen* echoes *hou heneka*). More immediately, Heidegger's pragmatism is a kind of offshoot of the long-standing German philosophical view that we (and the world) are essentially "will." But there are special features of this pragmatism by which it surpasses those predecessors.

I anticipated this pragmatism when I said in Chapter 3.1 that Dasein's intentionality is directed upon a content by being directed upon ends. That is, the first and necessary content is some set of ends one aims or projects towards. As we'll see, it is from these ends that meaning flows out into (to make) a world.

So the root point of the pragmatism is that intending is ultimately a *directedness*—an ability and disposition towards ends. Dasein is most deeply end-directed, or "telic." Heidegger's innovation lies in his analysis of the logic of the attitude in which we reach towards our ends. His general terms for this attitude are "care" and "concern." He has, I hope to convince, a fresh analysis which rings true to—and illuminates—our own experience.

Heidegger insists that we have our values *as ends*, by our practical set towards them. We value not principally by predicating "good" of a thing, but by holding it out ahead of ourselves as a goal we know a *route* to, a route that stretches (through a telic space–time) out towards this goal. That ordinary sense of valuing as a present act of predicating or "seeing as valuable" misses the temporal dynamism in the valuing which is really undermost, operating all along in us.

Since this pragmatism is Heidegger's reconception of our intentionality, it affects both aspects of it: both the content, and the way we intend it. His commonest term for this intentionality, "being-in-the-world" [In-der-Welt-sein], expresses this duality. "The world" is just that content (or the structure of that content), and our "being-in" [In-Sein] is the way we mean that content. Heidegger treats world in Chapter 3 of Division I, and being-in in Chapter 5.

Along with this different account of us (our intentionality), Heidegger also redescribes the method we need to use in order to understand ourselves. Since we're this different way than we suspected, self-understanding must occur in a different kind of state than we thought, and must be reached by a different method. We've already seen generally how Heidegger revises Husserl's phenomenology, and will now see in more detail one way this works: how we need a new kind of knowing-that, to grasp our own knowing-how.

1. Concern vs. theory

Heidegger offers his pragmatism as an analysis and mapping of the intentional stance we (i.e. humans) take in our "average everydayness"—which is the way we firstly and mostly live. It is this everyday stance that he determines as "being-in-the-world," and eventually also calls "care" [*Sorge*]. Chapters 2–5 of Division I give his analysis of this attitude or comportment in which we live the main and usual part of our lives.

He describes it especially by contrasting it with a *special* stance which, however, is more conspicuous to us, and so is usually taken for primary. This is the "theoretical" or "knowing" attitude in which we consciously reflect. Much of Heidegger's effort in the early part of the book is to drag his reader away from a bias (supposed) towards the view that we are principally believers, thinkers, rational beings. Instead this attitude is a "founded mode," dependent on the pragmatic stance, and indeed just a modified version of it.

Heidegger shows the importance of this contrast by devoting Chapter 2 to it.[4] The first of its sections [§12] gives "a preliminary sketch of being-in-the-world," by clarifying how we are "being-in": not by spatial containment, but by being *concerned* with the world—or indeed by being this very concern. So we are in the world in the way we are "in" a game—involved in it, devising and chasing success, feeling its ups and downs. And the next section [§13] presents, for contrast, "a founded mode" of being-in, "knowing the world." This arises by a certain stilling or restraining of concern; it depends upon "a *deficiency* in our having-to-do with the world concernfully" [BT g61].

Yet this secondary stance, arrived at by a *curtailing* of our primary attitude, gets misinterpreted as basic. Heidegger thinks that philosophers and psychologists nearly all treat theory as basic, and concern as a mode or development of it. They do so firstly for a very simple reason: when they set out to study themselves, they enter that theoretical stance, and so inevitably discover themselves as they are *in* that stance. So, if we set out to know ourselves, "the *knowing* explicit in such a task takes *itself*—as knowing the world, as the exemplary relation of the 'soul' to the world" [BT g58–59]. Trying to describe their own intentionality, theorists notice only this theoretical way of intending, and use it to model the way they are generally. So they treat practical concern as a valuing added on to some (theoretical) conception of the world. But they thereby miss the very different *structure* of the way they are for most of their days and lives. And everyday intending "becomes *invisible* if one interprets it in a way that is ontologically inappropriate" [g59].

An example of this mistake is the usual conception of perception. Perception seems to initiate my relation to the world by acquiring information about it. It seems to give a kind of prototheory about my surroundings: how they are independently of my aims or desires—though the latter of course then immediately use that perceptual "data." But really this is not, Heidegger thinks, the way we usually perceive; so PH 29–30:

> Let us envisage an exemplary and readily available case of "psychic comportment": a concrete natural perception—the perception of a chair which I find upon entering a room and, since it stands in my way, push aside. ... Natural perception as I live in it when I move in my world is mostly not a detached observing and studying of things, but is rather absorbed in concrete practical dealing with matters.

Our everyday perception meets things as they bear on our end-directedness, not as they are (or might be) in their own right apart from us. Nor is there a simpler "given"—such as sense-data—that precedes this interpretation (see BT g163 on hearing).

On the usual model, our aiming or intending is localized in our "desires" or "appetites" or "will," construed as merely one component of the psyche, and secondary not just to our perception, but to our "beliefs" and "intellect." One way to put Heidegger's point is that our aiming reaches out pervasively into these other components, infusing and controlling them. So perception, for example, is an instrument of our aiming, sensitive and receptive to meanings laid out by those aims.

But then how can there even be a theoretical attitude to contrast with concern at all? It seems that the latter exhausts the field—that everything is "pragmatic." And so in a sense it is: theory itself is a mode of concern for Heidegger—but a "deficient" mode. (He uses this notion of a deficient mode elsewhere as well, we'll see; it's his common device to explain cases that appear to be exceptions to his claimed essences.) Theory is a mode in which some of the most characteristic attitudes of concern are reduced and restrained, but it is still concern: it's just that we now strive and care for a project that requires us to restrain certain other concerns.

Heidegger tells a story in §13 [g61–62] about the transition into theory: it involves a certain stilling or diminishing not just of our particular concerns, but of the very stance in which we pursue them. In this stance, to put it roughly at first, our attention lies ahead of us in our ends—we lean forward in our aiming, and encounter things about us only by coming back to them from those aims. So we find and mean them in relation to those aims, in how they help, hinder, or otherwise bear on those aims.

The theoretical attitude begins when we put a pause in this aiming, when we loosen and take a rest from this stretched effort towards purposes, and look about at present things in their sheer presence, in themselves: "When concern holds back from any kind of producing, manipulating, and the like, it puts itself into what is now the sole remaining mode of being-in, the mode of just tarrying beside," and so can encounter entities "in their pure *appearance* [*Aussehen*]" [BT g61; also g172].

However, this "just looking" is not really all that's going on. The transition from concern to theory requires not just a suspension of everyday concern, but also its replacement by a new framework for encountering things, once the network of ends is disengaged. Heidegger develops this point much later in the book, in §69b. The theoretical view depends on an *a priori* projection of a particular way that objects can occur; he calls this "*thematizing*." This projection "free[s] the entities we encounter within-the-world so that they can 'throw themselves against' a pure uncovering" [BT g363].

Heidegger thinks this is the beginning of the attitude that enlarges into all our science and philosophy. Its essential direction is already set: it is the will to encounter or uncover things not as they are usable to my ends, but as they are in themselves. It is, even in the simplest case, still a care or concern: a concern to put out of play our other concerns. But as it advances to become science—and is entered as a discipline and career—the concerns that frame theory become ever more elaborate. The scientist's objectivity is a move within such aims as being a good scientist, earning a living, succeeding with peers, living up to professional standards, and indefinitely more.

Although this knowing attitude is still a mode of concern, it is different enough from the usual (or everyday) modes that it uncovers or encounters entities of a different kind, entities with a different "mode of being." This brings us to a major division in Heidegger's ontology. The stance of concern uncovers entities "*to-hand*" (as I'll render *zuhanden*, usually translated "ready-to-hand"), whereas the theoretical attitude uncovers them "*at-hand*" (as I'll translate *vorhanden*, usually translated "present-at-hand").[5] These are two of the three kinds or classes of entities that *Being and Time* posits—the third is Dasein.

Entities to-hand are "equipment" [*Zeug*]; they are "to-hand" in the sense that the hand is prepared for them, ready to reach out to

[zu] them, in order to use them, order them, or put them out of the way. In the best case the thing is so handy that it is (experienced as) also reaching to the hand, in its aptness for use—all the while the hand is shaping itself to grasp it. So we should hear the "to" in both directions: the tool is to the hand, and the hand to the tool.

Entities at-hand are "objects" [Objekte];[6] they are "at-hand" in the sense that they sit inertly before [vor] our idle hands as we consider them apart from our purposes. So the "at" or "before" is once again mutual: both thing and hand "just lie there." Yet it's still the hand the thing lies before, inasmuch as we have always the ability to revoke our restraint and "handle" it; the hand is still there for us, but as holding back. Thus Heidegger's term "at-hand" for theoretical objects implies his point that theory rests on concern.

I hope these images can be attached to these two key terms— "to-hand" (equipment) and "at-hand" (objects)—in what follows. Now what we would ordinarily call "the same thing"—some chair, for example—can obviously be encountered from either stance. We shift posture in a chair, tilt and slide and adjust it, and then the chair is to-hand. In an idle moment we notice the grain of its wood, and then it is at-hand. In these two cases we encounter what are, strictly speaking, different entities, because we encounter things with different "modes of being." As equipment the chair has the being of *Zuhandenheit* (to-handness). As object the chair has the being of *Vorhandenheit* (at-handness). We'll come back in Chapter 6 to this claim of an ontological difference.

Another way to think of the shift between these stances is as a shift from a first-personal to a third-personal attitude. We noticed briefly in Chapter 3 how Dasein's usual intending involves "mineness": in pursuing my goals I identify myself with them and pursue them as my own. An "I" is attached to our ends, and since things are encountered in relation to those ends (as to-hand for it), we engage them from a first-personal stance. The chair I handle is there for my purposes. By contrast, when I view the chair as at-hand I put these aimings "out of play"; I try to see it out of any relation to myself, i.e. third-personally.

Still another way to consider the contrast is by noticing the different kinds of "attention" these two stances involve. Theory attends to the object in its own right or as itself; it resists distraction by "personal" concerns or values. This involves "looking explicitly [*ausdrucklich*] at what is so encountered" [BT g61]. By contrast, coping's attention runs back and forth across the arc of means and ends in the project underway. Within the current situation it focuses especially on whatever cannot be done effortlessly—on what is recalcitrant or needs to be fine-tuned. Otherwise it is diffused ahead towards what's-to-be-accomplished. Coping strives more and more to make "painstaking" attention unnecessary, as it is when one is "in the flow."

Now attention, we might say, is a matter of bringing something "into the foreground," against a "background" which is intended, but to which attention is not now being paid. (Heidegger doesn't speak in these terms, but Merleau-Ponty shows their use for phenomenology.) Concern, as its attention passes to and fro along the intended route to the goal, gauging the steps and preparing for them, foregrounds the steps that need deliberate work. Entering the theoretical attitude pushes all such practical issues to a deeper background, where, however, they continue to operate, and from where they are always ready to be activated if conditions warrant. The philosopher wrapped up in a problem still has available a background sense where he stands in his day.

Heidegger claims not just that concerns are always orienting us "from the background" in this way, but that this orienting is a "condition of the possibility" for our theoretical meaning. This strong claim is at work in the reply to the "problem of the external world" that Heidegger makes in §13 and later. He argues that this problem is misguided, since it presupposes that we find ourselves in an "inner" (mental) realm and need to break out of it to be able to know external things.[7] Instead, he never tires of insisting, we are "always already" out there beside and involved with these things, and "know" them with a deep force that makes the epistemologist's doubt look quite superficial. That doubt is in fact a mode of concern, i.e. a way of dealing with the things and people one is steadily sure are there around one.

2. Studying concern

But now given our strong tendency to misinterpret concern on the model of knowing, how are we to go about studying and understanding it? If in studying we enter a theoretical stance that is quite different from our everyday manner of concern, how is it even possible to grasp the latter from the former? It seems that Heidegger may have painted himself into a corner, and doomed his project of analyzing concern or being-in.

Concern can't be studied in the usual fashion, so that phenomenology needs special techniques. These must side-step the special problems of access to this underlying practical stance: how it recedes under scrutiny, how attention to it disrupts it. Theoretic notice disrupts that practical flow of the projective attention described above, the way it runs implicitly and rapidly back and forth along lines of contriving effort, tending and improving them. So our challenge then is to make that projective concern explicit, to "light it up," in some other way than by scrutinizing it as object.

This points the way to Heidegger's strategy to "know concern": there is a different, non-theoretical attitude in which concern can be "lit up" for us, and theory can at least identify and point us towards this attitude. Thus the epistemic weight falls not on the theory but on that special attitude of illumination. Theory can describe this, but the attitude is different in kind from that in which we hear and understand the description.

Why do we need to "light up" this projective concern, if it's the way we live most of our lives? We've noted how it tends to implicitness, and even hides or conceals itself. There's an effort at work in our concern to push as much of what we mean as possible "beneath" attention or awareness—into the background. Smooth functioning depends on not being aware of an enormous number of details, which, however, still orient us. This lets us sustain more and more complex projects, which couldn't be handled with explicit attention to every detail. So of course there are ingrained devices to protect this implicit functioning and to discourage interruptions in it. All of this has the consequence that the to-hand, equipment, tends to "withdraw" [BT g69], to "hold itself in" [g75].

Heidegger asks near the beginning of §16: "Has Dasein itself, in the range of its concernful absorption in equipment to-hand, a possibility of being in which, with those entities it is concerned with within-the-world, their worldhood is also in a certain way lit up for it?" [BT g72] He goes on to identify our experiences of various kinds of *equipmental breakdowns* as special opportunities to "light up" our concernful relation to equipment.[8]

Heidegger distinguishes three species of breakdowns, and gives subtle phenomenologies for them [BT g73–74]. We notice equipment in somewhat different ways when it is (1) unusable, (2) missing, and (3) in the way. All these kinds of equipment failure make a break [Bruch] in our straightforward effort at ends—a break that functions differently from the one when we enter the theoretical stance. There we partly suspended our concerns; here we are frustrated in a particular concern, in such a way that we are thrown off the tracks, and notice it in a way we didn't while on them. We notice something that was there all along, but implicit.

This lighting up occurs in the transitional moment of the breakdown, when we are still fresh from the absorbed effort, yet no longer in it, and before we have absorbed ourselves in the new project to fix the breakdown. In breakdowns to-handness or concern "does not simply vanish, but takes its farewell, as it were, in the conspicuousness of the unusable" [BT g74]. We are off the tracks of our usual effort, though not in the artificial quiet of knowing. Once we set about fixing the broken equipment, we are back in the track of a new or adjusted project, and the epistemic moment is over. So our interest is in cases in which the transition is slow, and we're stymied and distressed.

A breakdown occurs in some item or sector of equipment, i.e. in some local part of our world (the world of our concern). This world is a web or network of kinds of equipment, connected along the lines of our end-directed projects. When one item in this web breaks down, we notice not just it, but its role in that web. Its inutility sends ripples forward through those projects: since we can't use this, we can't do the next and further things that depend on it. Just what ends we care about, and how much we do, are both illuminated this way.

The shoelace breaks, and we notice it in the uselessness (let's say) of the whole shoe, which in turn prevents the walk on an errand, which in turn means I fail to satisfy an obligation. I feel the broken thing not just where it is, but at all these further points in my projects. This lights up concerns I was implicitly intending all along. "The context of equipment is lit up, not as something never seen before, but as a totality constantly seen beforehand in circumspection" [BT g75].

Now these connections themselves are trivial; most would be easy to uncover in knowing study. What's important is how, in these experiences of breakdown, these connections are felt: I notice them in the very mode of my practical concern. I notice them with the kind of attention proper to that concern, a fluid attention that shifts along those telic routes, coping and devising. Concern's attention turns where there are problems, and a breakdown makes problems ramify. So this attention runs fretfully along the lines of my projects and efforts, feeling all the goals that are stymied.

Although Heidegger's talk of "lighting up" implies that the noticing is quasi-visual, it is indeed more a matter of feeling: I notice the broken thing by feeling these problems that radiate from its inutility. "This dwelling on such a conspicuous thing [as broken equipment] is however not a staring and observing but has and keeps the mode of being of concern" [PH 188]. Feeling has, we should notice again, a *telic* context and point: we feel in relation to our projects—in how we stand towards what we're trying to be.

It's in breakdowns, and by other experiences that show concern in its own manner, that phenomenology will read off the character of our practical intending. (It will *not* study social practices "from the outside," in the manner of anthropology or sociology.) We'll see in Chapter 5 that there are also more radical, global break-downs—anxiety, in particular—that will play a still more crucial role for phenomenology.[9]

Here in Division I breakdowns serve to "light up" our everyday concern, so that the phenomenologist can study it, and determine its structure. Let's turn now to the structure Heidegger claims to find by this study. Most broadly, remember, our structure is "being-in-the-world," and Heidegger splits this into the intentional atti-tude, being-in, and what it's "of," world. He treats the world in Chapter 3, and being-in in Chapter 5—where he divides it into three aspects: understanding, self-finding, and talk. I will often refer to these as *grasping—feeling—wording*.

3. Understanding and its world

The first aspect of being-in is the key part to Heidegger's pragma-tism.[10] Here we find his teleology, which lays out the main struc-ture of the world. His principal terms for this aspect are projection [Entwurf] and understanding [*Verstehen*]; another is existence [*Exis-tenz*]. I will often use, for reasons I'll give, the term *grasp* for this main way we "are in" a world. (Another useful term is "dexterity"— again emphasizing the primary role of the hand. Notice too that the "throw" [*Wurf*] in projection is to be heard as "from a hand.") All these terms refer to the way we are competently end-directed.

So we "project" towards ends, and "understand" our world in its use for those ends; our grasp or dexterity is of the world as a setting for our efforts at ends.

Thus projecting is a kind of aiming, and understanding a kind of knowing. But we must not conceive them in the usual way. The aiming is not a matter of representing goals, and the knowing is not a matter of having true beliefs how to achieve them. The aiming and knowing are built together into an able disposition to act with meanings and for reasons.

Neither the aiming nor the knowing is conscious, though they can be "brought to consciousness"—can be made to show themselves. They are carried out "in the background," in the way that— without attending to it—we both aim to and know how to tie our shoes. I project and maneuver towards goals "firstly and mostly" in this implicit way—without rehearsing any of my ends, or calling up beliefs about how to reach them. Consciousness and attention come in when there is a break in smooth functioning, or else when a task, unusually, requires close watch. But these episodes of explicit awareness take place against an immense and enveloping background which is meant or intended implicitly. It is only by my grasp of all this background that my overt particular acts of intending have their meaning.

I'll return soon to treat projection and understanding further. But first let's consider their intentional object—*what* we project and understand—which Heidegger calls "world." The world is not, very importantly, the sum of the things—equipment—around me. My projective abilities are of course exercised on particular equipment to-hand, such as these laces as I tie this shoe. But these abilities are themselves general—are capacities to use *kinds* of equipment. My world consists of the kinds of things for which I am prepared by my competent directedness. It is the vast network of these kinds, linked and organized in certain ways. The "closest" part of my world, over which my abilities are used most surely and often, is my "*environment*" [Umwelt] [BT g66].

A world must be distinguished from the entities that can occur "within-the-world," i.e. the particular items of equipment that we uncover to-hand. A world belongs to Dasein, as "that 'wherein' a factical Dasein as such 'lives'" [BT g65].[11] The world is the web of routes we know our way along; it is the system of ways we know how to handle things. Dasein must already "*disclose*" [*erschliessen*] a world, by its projective understanding of equipmental kinds, in order for it to be possible to "*uncover*" [*entdecken*] any particular equipment within that world. As Heidegger also puts it, our disclosure of a world "frees" entities to occur within it [g86].

Because a world, as the system of equipmental kinds, is still something particular, Heidegger says that it is "ontical." By contrast "*worldhood*" [*Weltlichkeit*], i.e. having a world, is a part of Dasein's being, and so is something "ontologico-existential" [BT g65]. Phenomenology's interest is in exposing worldhood itself, rather than the details of any particular world; it is ontological not ontical. Heidegger aims to find structures any world must have.

A world is analyzable into what Heidegger calls "*references*" [*Verweisungen*]. It is in fact a "referential totality" [BT g68, 70]. Heidegger gives a rough account of these references in §15, then a more decided one in §18, where he introduces the further term "*involvement*" [*Bewandtnis*] [g84]. I think the difference between "reference" and "involvement" is too subtle to concern us. Both name a teleological or practical role, which an entity or entities can be given; the generic term is "in-order-to" [Um-zu] [g68]. My world is the system of these roles I am prepared to assign to the entities I chance to meet—the ways, very broadly, I am prepared to put them to use. As my preparedness, this world lies in the background for me, ready to be applied to entities, thereby "freeing" them to be.

Heidegger introduces a rash of new terms to name the main kinds of references; as mentioned, this terminology resembles Aristotle's. First named is the "*towards-which*" [*Wozu*], which is the "work to be produced," or more generally the thing's "usability" [BT g70] or "serviceability" [g84]. It is, in other words, the end or purpose to which the item of equipment is assigned, and in particular the most proximate such end—what it does most immediately. But from this first use there runs forward a series of further involvements, as Heidegger says with his famous example of the hammer: "With the towards-which of serviceability there can again be an involvement; for example with this to-hand [entity], which we therefore call hammer, there is an involvement in hammering, with this there is an involvement in making-fast, with this in protection against bad weather" [g84]. Each end, in other words, is in turn "towards" (a means to) a further end.

So references or involvements make telic chains forward through sequences of means and ends. But they also radiate laterally to the other equipment this one needs to be used with; for the hammer: the nails, the clamps, the workbench. In knowing how to use the hammer, we know how to use it with these other things, i.e. as part of an equipmental ensemble, and indeed this ensemble is primary, reflected in the collective term *Zeug*: strictly, there never is *an* equipment [BT g68; cf. BP 163].

Moreover, there are also references "back": "In the work there is also a reference to 'materials'. It is referred to leather, thread, needles, and the like. Leather moreover is produced from hides. These are taken from animals, which were raised by others" [BT g70]. So this equipment also has references to other Dasein—the ones that made it, the ones it was made for. "Any work with which one concerns oneself is to-hand not only in the domestic world or the workshop but also in the *public world*" [g71]. Important will be the reference here to a *generic* other—the shoe was made not just for me but for *anyone* of a kind or class to which I happen to belong. All of these other references also belong to the "role" within which I interpret a shoe as a shoe. When I intend or mean it so, all of this lies in the background, is implicitly understood. (In the primary case it is the shoe-maker who understands this about the craft. But as we've seen we have an indirect understanding of all of it too, by our know-how as acquirers and users of shoes.)

But we haven't yet mentioned the most important reference of all, the one that lies at the terminus of the chain of towards-whiches we began to follow above. That protection against bad weather which the hammer serves, is itself "for [um-willen] sheltering of Dasein, which means, for a possibility of Dasein's being" [BT g84]. As we've anticipated (in Chapter 3.1), Heidegger calls this final end the "for-which" [Worumwillen].[12] Each chain of means and ends culminates in a (relatively) highest or ultimate end, which is a way the Dasein itself can be. I aim, that is, at possibilities of myself, and intend or mean things to-hand in relation to what I might be. "The primary 'towards-which' is a for-which. But the 'for [Um-willen]' always pertains to the being of *Dasein*, which, in its being, goes essentially about that very being [wesenhaft um ... geht]" [g84].[13] What ultimately concerns me is my own being.

In fact this for-which is really the primary member of that chain of towards-whiches, not the last. This is because it is at this point that Dasein principally commits or assigns itself—it's where the world "first" concerns it. I commit myself towards a certain possibility of myself, and other things have meaning in relation to this. "Dasein always already refers itself from a for-which to the with-which of an involvement, i.e. it always already lets, insofar as it is, entities be encountered as to-hand" [BT g86].

In assigning itself to ends, as ways it can be, Dasein shows the deep "mineness" we met above. I pursue my ends as mine, as better states of me. I assign myself to these ends, and implicitly identify myself both as assigner, and with the condition at which I aim. And the whole world, as a system of involvements, gets its meanings in relation to these ends, so that in a strong sense it too is "my" world. And, as I've put it, my stance towards this world is "first-personal." (Perhaps we can imagine an attitude that is end-directed but does not "mine" its ends.)

Heidegger reflects the priority of the for-which by retelling the hammer's telic chain in reverse order: "The for-which [protecting Dasein] signifies an in-order-to [making-fast], this a towards-this [hammering], this a beside-which [workshop] of letting be involved, this a with-which [hammer] of involvement" [BT g87]. It's in this direction—from ends through means—that meaning or significance flows through the world.

What are examples of these for-whiches? Heidegger's lone example in these passages is "shelter," as the ultimate end of the hammering. We aren't told what other kinds of things might count as such ends. Shifting to my example of a shoe, how should I identify its for-which? Is there one, or could there be a great many? There are certainly many candidates. Analogously to "shelter" we might think of "clothing myself," or "protecting my feet," but what about such other purposes as "suiting the occasion" or "showing status" or "gesturing sexually"? There might be a confused lot of such ways I use shoes to help me be. We should also wonder whether there might be still higher ends, for which even the highest of the shoes' ends are in turn pursued. Is there, as Aristotle argued, a highest end in which all of these chains culminate—happiness, or anything else?

Heidegger makes little effort to characterize the identity or structure of these for-whiches. But he thinks he has given us the tools to uncover this structure ourselves. My world, whose core is this network of for-whiches, lies largely in the background for me. But, unlike my visual background, it can't be made explicit at will. I can't simply choose to turn my attention to this or that sector of it. To identify my ends I must participate in breakdowns, since these make me *feel* what I'm aiming at and counting on, by feeling it at risk. When the shoe "breaks" in certain ways I may be more perturbed by failures in social appearance than by more obvious inconveniences: the breakdown can show me how the shoes have mainly mattered to me all along.

Now let's turn back from the world to the way we intend or mean it, which we began with above. (So we turn in *Being and Time* from Chapter 3, §§15 and 18, to Chapter 5, §31.) We "are in" the world chiefly by *projecting* towards those for-whiches, and *understanding* the chains of in-order-tos that reach towards them. We've seen that these are not really distinct, but sides of a single thing, our competent directedness, our *grasp*. We saw that neither projection's aiming nor understanding's knowing is a matter of representation or consciousness. As Heidegger puts it, possibilities are not intended "thematically" [BT g145], but in an implicit orientation and preparedness.[14]

In the primary case the ability (and inclination) is bodily, an habitual, "instinctive" readiness to handle kinds of things, and to move oneself through an environment. We begin learning the most rudimentary skills—how to grasp hand-sized things, how to pull closer some things and repel others—nearly from birth, and build countless elaborations upon them. What we acquire and develop are not just abilities (which might lie in us quite inert), but active dispositions or habits. And they are habits of performing not just isolated acts, but sequences and projects; they are "sets" to begin and carry out such projects. I am en-habited to projects pursuing goals through more and more complicated steps or means, and each means becomes a goal in turn. So as my abilities ramify, so do my orienting ends.

There is a constant tendency to push the exercise of these abilities into the background—below the level of conscious attention. We push them into the body, as it were, so that it carries them out "automatically" and unreflectively. The most basic abilities begin and remain here, and even skills learned in a conscious attention move there as proficiency improves. This lets them be carried out faster, and also frees that attention to supervise still further tasks. Still, we exercise these abilities with a different kind of attention, as we've seen, so that the body doesn't really act as a mere automaton.

Consider again shoes. Think first of the implicitness of our dealings with them, in putting on, wearing, taking off, storing them (they're still there for us in the closet). We don't steadily think what shoes we have on, but that information is not just at hand, but operating, as we walk on varied surfaces. They are also part of an ensemble of clothing we present to others, and we have an implicit sense of their degree and kind of stylishness. A great deal of our situation with these shoes works in the background all along. It gets lit up especially by breakdowns of various sorts. Notice how variously attention can fix: in the lacing if our fingers are cold or the laces tricky; where the shoes pinch or chafe; where the ground is icy or wet; where gum sticks; where they're inappropriate for the social situation. Think too of how finding ourselves barefoot in the city would vivify our reliance on shoes. (The dream of finding oneself naked in public gives experience of an ultimate breakdown in this sector.)

As an essential structure, understanding is a know-how for a whole system of projects; together, these constitute our "existing." "In ontical talk we sometimes use the expression 'understanding something' in the sense of 'being able to manage a matter', 'being a match for it', 'being able for something' ['*etwas können*']. In understanding as an *existentiale* that which we are able for [*das Gekonnte*] is not a what, but being as existing" [BT g143; cf. *BP* 276]. Heidegger hears "exist" in its root sense of "stand outside": we exist in being "out towards" our ends and the equipment we know how to use for them.

"Projecting" picks out especially our relation to a for-which: we principally throw ourselves forward towards (in each case) a possibility of ourselves. "Why does understanding ... always press into possibilities? Because understanding has in itself the existential structure which we call *projection*" [BT g145]. We are these possibilities, even though we are not yet them: "it *is* existentially that which, in its ability-to-be, it is *not yet*" [g145]. We are, also, who we're becoming.

So there is a division or ambiguity or contradiction in us, which Sartre will later state as our "being what we are not, and not being what we are." We are both the possibility we project towards, and the ability-to-be [*Seinkönnen*] that possibility. The possibility is intended as a fulfillment of that ability, and therefore as that ability "itself"—realized or come into its own. This is why, I think, Heidegger passes so freely between the ability-to-be and the possibility.

Possibility is basic to us. It is prior to actuality, inasmuch as our "actual" behavior, thoughts, etc. all get their meaning only on the basis (or against the background) of our projection upon possibilities: meaning "flows back" from these ends. What I'm doing depends on the person I'm trying to be in the doing. (This idea of possibility will be important in Division II's analysis of death.)

Again this aiming is not carried out deliberately: "Projecting has nothing to do with comporting oneself towards a thought-out plan, according to which Dasein arranges its being" [BT g145]. It is, in its wellsprings, implicit and unconscious. However, very importantly, it can be "brought to show itself": it is an intentionality that can be "lit up"—from within—and so experienced explicitly, as happens above all in those breakdowns. But it turns out that this isn't all these breakdowns light up.

4. Self-finding in feeling; thrownness

The second precondition for meaning or intending a world arrives as a surprise in §§29–30. Although projective understanding is not officially introduced until §31, it is already well clarified in §18's treatment of world: in explaining the latter as a system of equipmental references, Heidegger couldn't help but talk about understanding, which is an intentional grasp of precisely this structure.[15] The second precondition for intending is unexpected, because it seems not integral to that grasp of a world of equipment. It is also, I think, a subtler and less perspicuous idea.

Heidegger presents this second side to being-in as a kind of inverse to projective understanding. Ultimately the contrast will be temporal, as already suggested by the dual terms "projection" [*Entwurf*] and (now) "*thrownness*" [*Geworfenheit*]. Both involve a "throw" [*Wurf*], but the former is towards a future (goal), the latter from a past (source). Our intending, Heidegger claims, is always both. I'll come back to thrownness soon, but first we must meet its relative, the inverse to "understanding," which Heidegger calls *Befindlichkeit*. And here we strike one of the hardest problems of translation in *Sein und Zeit*.

Heidegger introduces the term so: "What we indicate *ontologically* by the title *Befindlichkeit* is *ontically* the most familiar and most everyday: mood [or tuning—*Stimmung*], being tuned [*Gestimmtsein*]" [BT g134]. He later clarifies *Befindlichkeit*:

> An entity of the character of Dasein is its there in such a way that, whether explicitly or not, it finds itself [*sich befindet*] in its thrownness. In *Befindlichkeit* Dasein is always brought before itself, it has always already found itself, not as a perceptual finding-itself-before [*Sich-vor-finden*], but as moody self-finding [*gestimmtes Sichbefinden*].
>
> [g135]

He wants his readers to hear such "finding" in his term.

For this reason I will translate *Befindlichkeit* as "*self-finding*"—and not with Macquarrie and Robinson's "state-of-mind," one of their poorest choices (though here all choices have faults). Self-finding is, as it were, a second direction in which our intentionality is always turned—or, better perhaps, direction *from* which this intentionality runs. It is a second way that we "give meaning" to things: we find them mattering to us "before"—independently of—our projects towards them. This finding is not a theoretical or cognitive discovery, but, in the primary case, something "felt." It comes most to the fore in our moods or "tunings," for we find/feel ourselves to be "delivered over" to these, in a way that can disturb our projective efforts.

This notion of self-finding is Heidegger's special way of handling what many before him have called our "affects"—both our feelings, and the way we're affected or "done-to."[16] Self-finding is the way we are affected or acted upon, in contrast with the way we reach out to act. But—crucially—it is this being-affected as an element (or structure) within our intentionality, and not as an objective property. It's not that I *am in fact* determined by the past, but that I have a sense of myself as affected, as subjected-to, which shadows or tempers my sense of myself as pressing ahead towards ends, as well as my sense of things as "there for" these ends. Hence it is a second way that meaning flows into things—another vector from which I intend them.

This second vector of meaning is clearest to me when I am "in the grip" of a strong mood. I feel myself "delivered over" or sub-jected to the mood: it's not something my projective effort is choosing en route to ends, but something received from a source separate from that effort, somewhere behind me. I experience things' meanings as set by such moods, and not just by my projects; indeed a strong mood can dominate and inhibit my projection—can interfere with my interpreting things with respect to my ends. And this is not, we should note, a *sophisticated* response to the mood, but something Heidegger thinks has been in moods themselves as long as there has been Dasein.

Moods are ontical versions of something ontological—something that is an essential structure of intentionality itself. Self-finding is most blatant or explicit when we feel ourselves in strong moods, but we are *always* turned back in this way, even during a frantic push towards a goal. Even as I cope with equipment to-hand, and dispose it to serve my ends, I have also the sense of myself as having arrived at this time and place from a past I am still subject to—and of the equipment as also having its meaning from this past. "Understanding is never free-floating, but always self-finding [*befindliches*]" [BT g339]. And we are never "free from moods [*stimmungsfrei*]" [g136]. Self-finding is going on "in the background" all along, where it sustains our meaning or intending.[17]

So things within-the-world also get meaning from this other direction, as it were. And just as was true of their projective meaning, so this affective meaning always involves our first meaning or intending ourselves. We've seen how I identify myself with the ends I pursue—they are me or mine—and how equipment is meant in relation to this projected self. And similarly as I feel equipment meant from the past, it is because I "find myself" as sent this meaning, and indeed as so "sent" and "meant" myself. This reflexiveness—expressed in the quotation on p. 107 from BT g135—is my reason for importing "self" into my translation of *Befindlichkeit*: Heidegger stresses how in finding things to be as I feel them, I am always first finding myself.

It's tempting to interpret this reflexiveness as involving a "look back" upon oneself, a self-observation. But this misrepresents it as a kind of understanding, hence within our projecting. Such self-observing can work either practically or theoretically, but neither shows us in *Befindlichkeit*'s way.

In everyday practicality, we can adopt the project of grasping some fact about ourselves, as it bears on how we'll pursue some end. Indeed we are constantly "looking back" at our given condition, the better to achieve our ends. We're pretty steadily (but implicitly) assessing, for example, our own capacities for various tasks. In this self-observing we can even grasp our moods, taking account of them as (sometimes) impediments to our projecting, which we need to master or at least compensate for [cf. BT g136].

This self-observing can also take a theoretical form: I try to still my interests and pay that special, present-focused attention to myself, which uncovers me as something at-hand. I take an objective view upon myself. And one important thing this view uncovers is that I am the effect of prior causes—determined, not a first cause. This discovery may be prompted by noticing how moods and emotions affect our actions.

But neither of these ways of observing our moods is what Heidegger means by self-finding. For "self-finding is far removed from anything like finding before [it] a psychical state. It has just as little the character of a grasping that first turns round and back on itself" [BT g136]. Self-finding occurs in those very moods themselves, and not in a reflective act which a mood may provoke. It lies in *feeling oneself affected*, as occurs in all the subtle feelings—self-feelings—that accompany our acts and attitudes. Such feelings are bound into all of our projects, in the very way our means and ends "matter" to us, for this mattering needs to be felt [g137]. Indeed even a purely theoretical self-scrutiny involves feeling and self-finding: "even the purest *theôria* has not left all moods behind it; the merely at-hand shows itself in its pure appearance to [theory's] inspection only when [the latter] can let it come to it in *calm* staying-beside" [g138].

Heidegger often insists on the authoritative way in which feeling discloses. In mood Dasein "is disclosed to itself *before* all knowing and willing, and *out above* their range of disclosure" [BT g136]. This disclosure by moods is "originary" [g134]. And in Chapter 5 we'll see how the special mood of anxiety and what it discloses are crucial to Heidegger's existential story.

Let's come back now to the other main term in Heidegger's account here, "thrownness." This translates *Geworfenheit*, which emphasizes the pastness, the "having been thrown." Heidegger uses this to name what, in self-finding, I most find out about myself: I find myself as thrown, i.e. as thrust into my present intentional situation ("the 'there'") by forces outside and behind me. So "mood brings Dasein before the That of its There, which, as such, stares at it as an inexorable enigma" [BT g136]. I find myself not just as acting but as being-affected, as made to be in some particular way. I find myself so, precisely because the finding occurs in feeling: the manner dictates the content.

Once again, we must not think of this thrownness "objectively," as the independent fact that I have been caused and determined to be as I am. This would be to interpret me as something at-hand, as an object. But I'm fundamentally a meaner (intender), and everything essential about me must be something within (a structure of) the way I mean. So my thrownness is not an external fact about me, but a way I invariably find or feel myself.

In feeling my thrownness I make no practical or theoretical posits about particular causes that have made me as I am. I do, however, experience myself as made, and, perhaps, as made by something different from myself. Thrownness involves subjection. So if I feel myself thrown from my own past choices, I experience a detachment or alienation from those choices, and myself as subjected to them.

Heidegger has a third main term for this second aspect of being-in, "facticity" [*Faktizität*]. This is the counterpart to "existence" or "existentiality." The latter refers to the sense in which I am my possibilities (as well as the ability-to-be them). "Facticity" refers to the sense in which I am as I feel myself to be—something thrown into a condition independent of and prior to my projecting. Heidegger sharply distinguishes this from "factuality" [*Tatsächlichkeit*]: "Facticity is not the factuality of the *factum brutum* of something at-hand, but a ... character of Dasein's being" [BT g135].

This second dimension to intentionality is also mostly implicit. It needs to be specially lit up for us to pay attention to it. And here too Heidegger thinks that it's *breakdowns* that are really revealing. Indeed, the same breakdowns we noticed in section 3 reveal not just our projects, but how they matter to us, how we feel in them and about them. They bring to explicit attention feelings that have been operating all along. When the project breaks down, we notice not just how we've grasped (at) these ends, but how we've felt them. All along we've felt them as affecting us, felt ourselves as "delivered over" to them. All along we've been finding ourselves in our feeling for ends, as well as in our projection.

5. Talk and *das Man*

Now it sometimes seems that the structure of being-in is bipartite—that understanding and feeling exhaust it. "We see in *understanding* and *self-finding* the two, equally originary, constitutive ways of being the there" [BT g133]. (See also the first sentence of §34.) But Heidegger has a strategic need to find a third element: he wants to give (in Division II) a temporal interpretation of being-in; this will read understanding as futural and feeling as retral, so that he needs a third aspect that he can tie to the present. However, his identification of this third is not very clear. In Division I it seems to be *Rede*, but when he returns in Division II it is identified as *Verfallen* or falling. I'll begin with the first, and then show why the latter is so connected with it as to take its place.

Rede, which I will translate "talk," is the main topic of §34, where it seems to be the third aspect of being-in, i.e. the third constituting condition of our intentionality. "*Rede is existentially equally originary with self-finding and understanding*" [BT g161; cf. also g295–96]. So understanding and feeling (self-finding) are not sufficient to enable us to intend a world of meaning. I will sometimes refer to this third condition as "wording," to be placed alongside "grasping" and "feeling." These are the three dimensions in which we are intentionally towards our world.

We've seen how grasping and feeling are contraries of a sort: they are a pressing-ahead and a feeling-thrown. The third aspect lies at an angle from this pair. Indeed, it initially looks so different from them that it seems a kind of category mistake for Heidegger to introduce it alongside them. It lies, very roughly, in the "linguistic" character of our intending, or in the way our meanings are "put into words."[18] And this seems not to be an attitude or stance at all, that should be set beside understanding and feeling. To see how it is we must work our way through some surprises and subtleties in Heidegger's account of talk and language.

The first point to notice is that talk (*Rede*) and language (*Sprache*) are sharply distinguished by Heidegger. Talk, as an aspect of Dasein's being-in, is more basic, and more obscure. Language or *Sprache* is much easier to identify: it is all the words Dasein uses in its talk. So language is not Dasein, but a special kind of equipment.

"The way talk gets expressed is language. This totality of words, as which talk has its own 'worldly' being, is discovered as something to-hand within-the-world" [BT g161].[19] This fits one ordinary sense of "language."

Rede—the "*existential-ontological foundation of language*" [BT g160]—is more difficult to translate. Macquarrie and Robinson render it as "discourse," but this connotes something too formal to me. We need a term that is at home in the most everyday occasions in which we exchange meanings with one another, so I have opted for "talk." But whatever term we adopt will need to be understood by special definition, since Heidegger's sense for *Rede* is so unusual. So just how must we specially hear "talk"?

We must start by pulling the term off of its ordinary referent, which is our vocal acts and conversations. These are events that occur "within-the-world," but "talk" needs to refer to a part of our structure as Dasein. It is the aspect of us that makes possible these vocal interactions; it is some crux in our capacity for them. So "wording"—like "grasping" and "feeling"—refers to a grounding ability, and not to the acts or events in which it gets exercised.

Now what goes on in these linguistic interactions—what's the crucial aspect that our capacity will explain? Heidegger's answer is that we "share meanings" with one another. This seems like a standard view, but Heidegger has a fresh analysis how this sharing works. It is not, principally, a matter of transmitting ideas or propositions from one mind to another. It is, rather, a matter of one Dasein inducing another to share its "concern"—its way of grasping and feeling about something. Communication [*Mitteilung*] "accomplishes the 'sharing' ['*Teilung*'] of self-finding-with [*Mitbefindlichkeit*] and of understanding of being-with" [BT g162].[20] If I say or show that "the shoelace is untied," this succeeds not by the other entertaining this proposition, but by his/her sharing this concern—caring about the thing, minor as it is, in parallel to me. "Sharing" is a process of aligning concernful meanings between Dasein—or indeed of one Dasein between different moments.

For this sharing we especially use "signs," which Heidegger treats in §17. Signs are equipment with the function of calling attention to an involvement that is either unnoticed, or noticed only "in the background"—bringing it to attention so that it can be shared. Words are signs, but many other things are as well: traffic lights and alarms, obviously, but also all of our gestures, including all the minute indications by which we convey our attitudes and concerns to those around us (as I'll put it, these are ways of "wording," too). As the alarm clock shows, some of these are signs by one Dasein to itself at a different time.

Heideggerian talk is the aspect of Dasein that makes this activity of sharing possible. And it seems this must simply be our linguistic (including gestural) abilities or skills. But this would miss the last crucial step we need to take. As our linguistic capacity, talk would be just a part or servant of our understanding (our grasp), which, as we've seen, is precisely our practical competence. Our ability to use language would be, by itself, no different from our ability to use any other equipment; it would be steered by that same projective stance, reaching ahead through means to ends. Of course we do have that ability. But talk or *Rede*, as an independent aspect on the same footing or level of generality as understanding, must be something different from this ability.[21] It must be some other condition on our vocal acts.

Moreover, this condition must itself be an intentional stance or attitude, as understanding and feeling both are. It must be a stance that is directed, analogously to projection's reach ahead and feeling's turn back. And it must be directed in a way that can plausibly support the temporal reading Heidegger will eventually give it too—directed somehow into or from the present.

My suggestion is this: talk or *Rede* is the stance in which we look, as it were, not ahead towards ends, nor back at our thrownness, but out towards an encompassing social practice—and to other Dasein as sharing in this practice. In this stance of *Rede* we view what we do and are with respect to (in relation to) "what one says and does"—i.e. to this shared practice. In this dimension, we intend meanings in relation to that practice: we mean what the practice means, or we mean in response to the practice. So *Rede* isn't the neutral capacity to use language, nor the capacity to deploy it for our projective ends. It's the capacity to mean in relation to what an encompassing social practice means, to mean out of one's engagement in that practice.[22]

Thus in "wording" things I mean them in a quite different way than by grasping or feeling them. I take their meaning to be given in the words that name them, and (in the main case) the meaning of these words to be settled in the practice around me. So just as in grasping (understanding) a thing I "press ahead" to my ends and come back from them to mean the thing, and just as in feeling the thing I "turn back" to my affects and mean the thing from them, so in wording the thing I step first out to the community of speakers around me, and mean the thing "from them," i.e. as they do.

This stance is at the root of all communicating, both in my speaking (by which I share my concern) and in my hearing (by which I share the concern of others). Indeed this underlies the non-verbal ways we communicate, by exchanges of bodily signals, by demonstrations meant to be copied. It is only because I can mean "what the practice means" that I can engage in any of these sharing activities. Still, the prime case is "talk" in the ordinary sense, which is why Heidegger calls the essential stance after it (*Rede*). We should think especially of conversation, in which both "let their words mean" something common that they both defer to.

In the everyday form of talk—the way we firstly and mostly "word"—we take that social practice simply as our model and standard. The meanings of things lie, in this stance, precisely in how the encompassing group understands and feels about them. We give them words meant to bear this common meaning. We make no response to the general practice, no effort to locate our own meanings in relation to it. And our grasping and feeling are subordinated to these social meanings, to this imitative talking: we want and feel according to the common meanings of the words we call our wantings and feelings by. Our concern is above all with "doing what one does"—and with so thinking and feeling too.

We'll consider alternatives to this everydayness later. One is authenticity, and we'll see how this modifies our meaning-in-relation-to-others. But for now let's focus on the everyday form of *Rede*. This is the way all of us live most of the time, I think Heidegger thinks, including even himself: measuring what we say and do by common standards, attempting to fit or align ourselves with the generality.

This subjection to others, this cleaving to their projects and values, is compatible with, and even involves, my distinguishing myself from others in many ways. I'm constantly measuring myself against others: "care rests constantly on a difference from others, ... whether one's own Dasein—lagging behind the others— wants to catch up in relation to them, or whether one's Dasein, with priority over others, is out to keep them down" [BT g126]. Heidegger calls this measuring Dasein's "distantiality" [*Abständigkeit*]. I'm trying to get ahead of others in these very projects we share— indeed the project often is precisely to get ahead this way.[23]

This everyday form of our social stance involves a peculiar relation to one's self. We've seen how both understanding and feeling involve relations to oneself, i.e. mineness, and the same is true of *Rede*. In understanding, I am who I'm trying to be; in self-finding, I am who's affected by feeling. And in reaching out to an encompassing community, I "find myself" there, too—I identify myself in relation to this community. Firstly and mostly, in my everydayness, I do so by identifying myself as an interchangeable or average member of the group.

This brings us to Heidegger's important notion *das Man*. I'll defer some of my discussion of this until Chapter 5, since it is one of the hinges on which he turns into the "existential" issues there. As Dreyfus noticed [1991 225ff.], falling (as well as *das Man*) plays two roles in the book: as something structural and essential, but also something psychological and motivated. Here we focus on the first role, reserving the second for Chapter 5. A crucial difference is that here, before we've seen the possibility of authenticity, this condition of falling or *das Man* is not yet *judged*: there's no standard it falls short of.

So *das Man* refers to an anonymous or average member of the social (and linguistic) group. Heidegger constructs the term out of the German analogue to our idiom "one says … " [*man sagt* …] or "one does … " [*man tut* …], used to describe the usual and prescribed practice:[24]

> We take pleasure and enjoy ourselves as *one* [*man*] takes pleasure; we read, see, and judge about literature and art as *one* sees and judges; but we also shrink back from the "great mass" as *one* shrinks back. … *Das Man*, which is nothing definite, and which all are, though not as the sum, prescribes the kind of being of everydayness.
>
> [BT g126–27]

We ordinarily speak of the group as consisting of "others," but we do so "to cover up the fact of one's belonging to them essentially oneself" [BT g126]. "The who is not this and not that one, not oneself and not some [people] and not the sum of all. The 'who' is the neuter, *das Man*" [g126]. This shows how Macquarrie and Robinson's translation of *das Man* as "the 'they'" is unapt: it implies "others than me." But since there are also problems with the alternatives (such as "the one," "the anyone") I will leave *das Man* untranslated.

Like understanding and self-finding, then, talk's way of "meaning" a thing involves a certain way of meaning myself. In it I identify myself with (I "mine") not my ends, and not my moods, but the community of talkers around me. In the everyday form of talk I identify and align myself with this social group. I defer to the meanings its words put on the things I encounter. I interpret myself as an average member of this group, as *das Man* myself. And insofar as I do so, my self is a *das Man* self: "The self of everyday Dasein is *das Man-selbst*" [BT g129].

Being immersed in *das Man* is one aspect of a more general condition which Heidegger calls "falling" [*Verfallen*]. For there are two ways we fall: into *das Man*, and into a certain kind of absorption in the world of involvements. Heidegger is not consistent, we'll see, on the relation between these—whether they are quite distinct, or one is the root of the other. It is only if falling into *das Man* is basic that Heidegger will be entitled to substitute falling for *Rede* as the third aspect of being-in. Early in Chapter 5 I'll try to resolve this issue, but here we should return to *Rede* itself, and notice two further points.

The first is what this analysis of talk or *Rede* tells us about our relation to "other Dasein," more generally. This aspect of being-in relates us especially to others, just as understanding relates us especially to equipment, and self-finding to ourselves (even though, as we've seen, each aspect of being-in is a way of meaning ourselves, things, *and* others). Because we intend or mean other Dasein in this fundamentally different stance than we do equipment, it's misguided to treat them as just another kind of entity "within-the-world." They are given to me by my essential turn outwards to co-intenders; they are a generality whose practices are the model and standard for my own.

The second further point about talk or *Rede* is its complex interaction with understanding (and with feeling, we'll soon see). For the most part these stances collaborate in our speaking, our language; but precisely because both are involved, there is room for conflict. Our language is aimed, as it were, in two directions: at the things that are its topics, and at the others we address. We choose our words to "fit" both topic and audience. Understanding aims words chiefly at the things—either to control them, or to know them, in either case to improve our relation to them. But talk aims words at the other people we speak or write for—tries to change our relation to them.

Heidegger is highly interested in the ways these different stances can either conflict or combine. They conflict, for example, in the phenomenon of "chat" [*Gerede*], a form of *Rede* in which a preoccupation with "sharing" dominates, and there is little interest in the topic itself. What matters to us is the conversational situation— saying the right thing, the thing that extends our alikeness and sharing. For we have, very roughly, two kinds of abilities, the ability to do *x* and the ability to speak about doing *x*. We speak with true authority where we have the ability to do, but we can learn to speak without acquiring that first-order ability at all. And this is what chat encourages us to do: to speak plausibly about a great many things, to be able to supply what's needed in all manner of conversations, on topics about which we have no real (first-order) understanding.

On the other hand Heidegger is also critical of an understanding that is so intent on correctness about its topic that it fails to speak *to others*, i.e. to address the concerns that bring them to the topic. Heidegger insists that philosophy address the deepest concerns of its audience, and not abandon them in favor of topics on which a stricter correctness is feasible. Philosophical truth must express both stances, and indeed the third stance of feeling as well. Heidegger writes *Being and Time* with this complex intent.

Now talk aims at sharing, and what it especially shares is understanding of involvements (practical concerns). For this purpose it uses, above all, language, as a kind of equipment that works in the manner of signs, which (we've seen) call attention to involvements, to facilitate sharing. To share them, talk needs to "articulate" involvements, i.e. to give them linguistic structure. It lays a grid of words over the world-structure we plotted in section 3: "The totality-of-meanings of understandability is *put into words*" [BT g161]. It thereby "articulates" that structure: "Talk is the articulation of understandability" [g161]. As we'll see, this linguistic structuring also changes the practice.

The same points apply to talk's relation to feeling. We of course share our feelings as well, and for this they too are linguistically structured.[25] We feel our moods under rubrics. Here too we can distinguish between our ability to feel *x*, and our ability to talk about feeling it. Chat involves a detachment from the source here too: we talk about things without their "mattering" or striking home to us. And we describe our feelings using social and average terms that are not really apt to their individuality.

Language is not only an instrument for sharing, it is also the sedimented product of a long history of such sharing. Each Dasein is brought up into a pre-existing language, and into practices and feelings that are articulated by it. Its principal relation to this language is its deep-running aim to assimilate itself to it, so that it speaks, feels, and acts "as one does" in the common practice.

This brings us to a much-debated question about the overall logic of Heidegger's account of intentionality. Does he think that meaning lies at the level of the individual, or of the social group or practice? Pointing to the weight Heidegger lays on *Rede* and language in constituting meaning and significance, some have argued that it is the language or the social practice that is the principal intender or meaner—and indeed that this is the principal referent of "Dasein."[26]

I can't address this problem head-on, but only point out how this book's overall approach to *Being and Time* takes the opposite view. I have taken Dasein, the intender, to be an individual human being, and the analysis of its being as the effort to identify structures essential to each such individual. More immediately, I have interpreted *Rede* or talk as an aspect of each individual's being-in, and indeed as a "stance" the individual takes, analogous to those taken in aiming and in feeling.

To be sure, this stance of talk makes me intend to align myself with the general practice. I intend my words to mean "what one means"—what they mean in the practice. And since our projects and even our feelings are structured linguistically, their meanings too are largely ceded to the social group. So PH 246: "This common world, which is there primarily and into which every maturing Dasein first grows, rules, as public, every interpretation of the world and of Dasein."

Nevertheless, for Heidegger the basic intentional event is the individual's meaning to cede authority, to defer to *das Man*. And the individual can, at least partly, win back this authority for him/herself, as we'll see is true in authenticity. This and the other "existential" ideas we'll meet next are very hard to apply plausibly to *Dasein* interpreted as a social unit.

Now as was true for both projection and self-finding, this way we mean things in relation to others works mostly implicitly, and needs to be "brought to show itself" by our attention to breakdowns. But once again the main interest here lies in the treatment of anxiety, as the breakdown that pulls us out of our falling absorption in *das Man*. And this belongs not to Heidegger's pragmatism, but to the existentialism to which we now turn.

Summary

Being and Time's analysis of Dasein (human intending) proceeds in three stages, purporting to go deeper and deeper into our structure. The first stage I call (though Heidegger doesn't) the book's pragmatism. It develops how our everyday intentionality is crucially end-directed: we disclose our world by reaching towards ends, and by understanding routes and means to pursue them. Heidegger gives elaborate analyses of both the structure of the "equipmental" world that is thereby there for us, and of the way we intend this world.

But first he tries to show why it is *not* our theories and beliefs that disclose our world; these are secondary to the practical "concern" that really does so. By pausing our willful efforts and "just looking" at things, we uncover them as objects that are "at-hand" before us. But this is a very special relation to things. More usually and basically we uncover them through our concern in our practical dealings, and for this they are equipment "to-hand," ready to be grasped and used. It is equipmental breakdowns that especially "light up" this concern, which works mainly implicitly.

Heidegger finds three necessary aspects in how we intend the world; they are quite different angles from which we mean things. The first he calls "understanding" or "projecting." It is the way we reach out towards ends, and "know how" to use what's around us to achieve them. By this practical ability we project a vast network of kinds of equipment, linked to one another and to our aims by "references," such as the hammer's relation to nails, to wood, to hammering, and to the chain of further purposes for which we hammer. The ultimate such references are to the ends of those chains, our final purposes, which are ways for ourselves to be. We project principally towards these "for-whiches," and understand both equipment and ourselves in terms of them.

The second way we intend things is in our *Befindlichkeit*, which I translate "self-finding": it is the way we find ourselves feeling about them, already and apart from the projects towards them we now pursue. In contrast with that projection I find myself "thrown" into moods that give a quite different kind of meaning to my world. Once again in thus meaning things I also mean myself: I identify myself not just with my ends, but with how I feel myself thrown into caring about things. So I'm not just who I'm trying to become, but who I find feels this way.

The third aspect of our intending seems quite different from the others: it is the way we defer to our linguistic community, and let meaning come to things from our shared language. Heidegger calls this way of meaning our *Rede*, which I translate "talk." It is not the concrete activity of speaking, nor the set of words we use in speaking, but the way we let these words, and our speaking, get meaning from the enveloping practice, and not just from our aiming and feeling. This deferral is indispensable for our having a world, but we also tend to exaggerate this aspect of meaning, at the expense of aiming and feeling. When that happens we identify ourselves too thoroughly with that practice, and our "self" is no longer our own; it has become what Heidegger calls *das Man*.

Further reading

H. Dreyfus: *Being-in-the-World; A Commentary on Heidegger's* Being and Time, *Division I.* Cambridge, MA: MIT Press, 1991. [This landmark work on BT gives a powerful account of its pragmatism (without calling it this).]

M. Okrent: *Heidegger's Pragmatism; Understanding, Being, and the Critique of Metaphysics.* Ithaca: Cornell University Press, 1988. [Analyzes BT's pragmatism as an argument about intentionality's transcendental conditions.]

Five

Being and Time

Existentialism

We come now to the second main theme or idea-set in *Being and Time*. Heidegger claims to find a deeper level to our intending and meaning, by broadening his analysis beyond its early focus, in most of Division I, on our everyday or usual condition. When we examine certain *exceptional* conditions we can be in, we discover a structure deeper than we noticed in the pragmatic account. (That there is this deeper level is another reason Heidegger is not a "pragmatist.") But in order to achieve this deeper truth about ourselves we need to change once again the *kind* of understanding we pursue/expect—and so change too our method (for reaching that truth). We must adapt phenomenology still further from Husserl, to study the "existential" structure of our intentionality.

This second theme or analysis is less to the foreground in Division I, although it is anticipated in a few places: in Chapter 4 on *das Man*, in Chapter 5 on falling, and in Chapter 6 on anxiety. More subtly, the groundwork is laid for this analysis right at the beginning of Division I, where Heidegger introduces *Jemeinigkeit* or "mineness." As we'll see, this is the central element in the existential theme, and he needs to build it in from the start. But these various pieces aren't put together into a coherent story until Division II; its first three chapters are the main statement of the second analysis.[1]

Now, as I did with "pragmatic," I will use "existential" in a non-Heideggerian way. For Heidegger, we've seen (in Chapter 4.3), "existential" picks out especially the projective aspect of our intending—the way we are towards possibilities. I will use it in a sense more common today, for a recognizable cluster of claims about "the human condition" that are distinctive of the so-called existentialists. Heidegger takes over many of these claims from Kierkegaard—as he may not sufficiently acknowledge.[2] But he brings these claims into a compelling, even canonical form, in which they were then taken over by the French existentialists and many others.

This second analysis in *Being and Time* introduces what is mostly lacking in the pragmatism: something like *values*.[3] The principal notion in this existentialism is authenticity, which stands out in the book as the ideal it most offers its readers—how, it suggests, a person should wish and try to be. Heidegger himself denies that his notion proposes a value, and we will need to take full account of his reasons. But I think we can and should still say that he "values" authenticity, if we build those reasons into how we hear that term. *Being and Time* surely offers us values, despite his demurrals: that he is "against" *das Man* and falling, and "for" authenticity and resoluteness (towards death) is inescapable despite his denials of any value-judgments in them.

I will try to give a sense of this principal value, and of its metaethical status for Heidegger. On what basis does he offer it to us? Does he claim it is discovered by phenomenological study of human intending? Phenomenology will, of course, discover any and all of our values as it studies our intending: our valuing is a way we intend. But how can phenomenology commend any of these values in preference to any others? Wouldn't that go illegitimately beyond the method's task to understand intending?

We should also ask some normative questions about the book's values. Isn't this ideal of authenticity too self-centered? Mightn't it be consistent with many or all kinds of mistreatment of others? It is remarkable how little attention Heidegger gives to the authentic individual's actions towards (or feelings about) others. And this seems reflected in the structure of the concept. Not only is authenticity a condition of me, but it's the condition in which I most achieve my mineness, and most am/have a self. We'll ask whether this self-accomplishment requires or encourages any particular relation towards other people. (Many worry that it is ethically neutral, or worse.)

Now in what sense are these existential findings "deeper" than the pragmatic? When Heidegger leads up to these findings, at the beginning of Division II, he describes the inquiry not as going deeper, but as getting wider: we're bringing "more" of Dasein's intentionality into our view, to grasp it more nearly "complete." Division I had focused on our average everydayness, and now we bring in various special conditions. The studies of both death (Chapter 1) and authenticity (Chapter 2) are explicitly undertaken for the sake of this completeness.

But it turns out that this wider view reveals not just further parts (or aspects or conditions) of Dasein that get added alongside everydayness, but an overall structure that the pragmatic findings must then be reinterpreted within. This overall structure is of course likewise intentional, and in Heidegger's strongly *telic* sense: it is still a matter of being directed, but in a different way and towards a different end. And this existential directedness is "deeper" than the pragmatic, because it motivates the latter. It is our stance towards our existential end that explains the manner in which we adopt and pursue our pragmatic ones.

Our everyday aims are bound up in capacities—and this is true for that structural, existential end as well. It is the object of a certain *Seinkönnen*, an ability-to-be, which encompasses a certain ability to do. This special *Seinkönnen* is a *meta*-capacity, since it's an ability to operate in a certain way *upon* our other, first-order capacities, including all of those discussed in Chapter 4. To put it quickly, authenticity is the exercise of a capacity to "choose" our other projects in a certain way. But we ordinarily fail to exercise it; we even avoid doing so, because it is our hardest work.

Heidegger thinks that this meta-capacity is essential to us, and in such a way that we have it as our most important task to be/do. How I most ought to be is authentic—understood as the adequate exercise of this capacity. Success within the terms of my particular (existentiell) projects is much less important than the way I exercise that essential (existential) capacity, which is a way of choosing and pursuing those projects. It's because this capacity is so basic that Heidegger sometimes says that authenticity is "more originary" [ursprünglicher] than everydayness. Authenticity enacts an aiming to which we're committed before all our particular ends.

Heidegger most distinctly conveys the decisive importance of authenticity by saying that it is what first gives us a *self*. The capacity, that is, is a capacity to become a self, to make oneself a self. Choosing in the right way just is to be/have a self. And doing so accomplishes our essential mineness, which he sets into Dasein from the book's beginning. This special notion of self is near the heart of Heidegger's existential ideal—and is what most makes it "existential." The notion is so important that we should spend some time on it now.

Heidegger has an unusual but not unprecedented idea of "self." I will try to carry us there by steps from a more familiar notion. Given that each of us is a Dasein, as analyzed so far, how should we speak of the "self" of this entity?

1. A first thing we might use "self" to refer to is simply this entity as entity—the entity "itself." In this sense every entity is a self, including everything in the great non-Dasein mass of things. When "self" occurs in compound personal pronouns such as "itself," we might say it carries this minimal sense.
2. A second thing "self" could refer to is not the entity but a part or aspect that is essential or definitive in it. So we might think

of a person's "true self" as some core or privileged part, perhaps a dominant part. So here "self" is used as a kind of honorific, for a part within the constitution of an entity. Again this might apply to any entity.

3. However, neither of these senses is in the right ballpark for Heidegger, since neither of them makes the self a matter of intentionality. Only something that means, that has a "there"—a Dasein—can be a self. And this is a third thing "self" might plausibly refer to: an intender or meaner, a Dasein. It's in this sense that I might refer to my different impulses or personae as selves within me—I'm thinking of them as micro-intenders.

4. But this is still missing something crucial: to be a self, the intentionality must also have that reflexive turn upon itself, which Heidegger calls mineness (see Chapter 3.1). What makes a self is not intending *per se*, but an intending that intends reflexively, i.e. intends itself. It is this reflex in intentionality that Heidegger calls *Jemeinigkeit*—the basis he lays at the start for selfhood and authenticity. This mineness, remember, gets cashed out later in the way all three aspects of being-in—my stances towards the world in projection, feeling, and talk—involve this reflexivity. In projection, I aim at the end as a better condition of myself the aimer; in self-finding I feel myself to be the feeler thrown; and in *Rede* I identify myself as a talker within the group or practice. So sense 4 is an important part of Heidegger's account of the self.

5. However even this mineness isn't enough to make me a self in Heidegger's full sense. Every Dasein has mineness, but not every Dasein is a self; to be a self I need to carry out or accomplish that mineness in a special way. For it turns out that this reflexive turn is usually corrupted or ruined in the everyday way we all live. This happens because there is something hard or painful about fully or straightforwardly intending oneself, and we embrace that everyday stance precisely to avoid this. So my everyday ways of grasping, feeling, and wording fail at

"mineness." To be a self I must overcome this drift towards concealing myself from myself. I must intend myself as I am, in truth. This achievement is of course authenticity—being one's own, being a self.

Our main challenge will be to describe this achievement, since it is *Being and Time's* principal ideal. The book arrives at this ideal following that methodological strategy of pursuing Dasein's "completeness" and "unity." I will introduce this route it takes to authenticity where it is relevant, but I think a different way of organizing the existential ideas will help.

For there is, behind that explicit argument, a story that we are all roughly familiar with, shared by existentialists generally. This is a story in a strong sense, a human drama, simple as the main elements of it are.[4] It is a drama of illness, diagnosis, and cure—a drama with a single role, into which the reader is invited to step, in imagination and aspiration. Heidegger sets this drama vividly before us, even though it's not reflected in the overt structure of his book. I will try to tell it in this chapter.

Now of course the illness here involved is not physical, but in our intending. The diagnosis will identify how this intending has gone wrong; it will attribute certain "motives" to Dasein for so going wrong. All of this will pose questions for us. How can phenomenology deliver such analyses and explanations? How does it discover what our motives really are—does it somehow introspect their operation? And how, above all, can phenomenology deliver the *values* this story involves: the negative value of the illness, the positive value of the cure?

A point to bear in mind in the following is that this web of ideas will be one of the main casualties of Heidegger's turning. He for the most part abandons these existential claims and ideals—though of course there are remnants. But the center drops out of this value when Heidegger diagnoses authenticity as expressive of technology, and turns against its fixation on the self.

1. *Das Man* and falling

In the simple drama of existentialism, the beginning is a picture of the egregiously unsatisfactory condition we're all alleged to be in. Heidegger's main term for this condition is "falling"; another, more negative, is "inauthenticity." With them he raises a complaint against how we all live, a complaint he means to be vivid and provoking enough to make us feel the need for his way out. "Dasein plunges out of itself into itself, into the groundlessness and nullity of inauthentic everydayness" [BT g178]; it thereby "*has lost itself*, and, in falling, 'lives' *away from itself*" [g179].

Here we meet Heidegger in the characteristic existentialist stance (or persona) of a *prophet* denouncing the outrageous *error* widespread or universal in society—error that involves a spiritual or moral failure. The term "falling" itself works this way, with its echo of the Biblical fall. This prophetic stance tends to annoy or thrill his readers, according to taste.

Of course it's a consequence of many or even most philosophers' views that most people fail to live as they should, that they're misguided and require the correction of a new and better theory—which the philosopher can provide. But existentialists express this with noticeably greater urgency and even alarm—stressing just how dire and misguided the usual way of life is.

Now it's natural for the prophetic stance to treat our problem as importantly *epistemic*: we're failing or refusing to know or recognize something. In religious authors this is God of course: spiritual depravity is a consequence of our turning our backs on God. For Heidegger, by contrast, we all flee and avoid facing something about ourselves, as Dasein. He puts great weight on this epistemic failure; it may be his main ground of complaint against falling and inauthenticity. Authenticity corrects this error, and gives truth, and indeed the very truth that phenomenology pursues.

There's a second stance or role that existentialists typically adopt in their critique of us all: that of psychological or social *physician*.

They depict the pervasive failing as not just spiritual or moral error, but a kind of illness, which is subject to diagnosis and cure. They base their negative assessment on a failure in the natural or proper functioning of the person or self—given some account of the structure of this self. So the problem is not (just) epistemic, but (as I'll put it) *functional*: it depends on diagnosing ways our intentionality is *mal*functioning.

Heidegger does not explicitly appeal to this medical model, and there's a way it may seem not apt for him: health, we feel, should be normal, and illness a breakdown and exception, yet he insists that falling is Dasein's usual condition. Nevertheless I think he leans on an abstract cousin of this functional argument. For he tries, with his "existential analysis," to map the essential structure of our intentionality, and to show that falling is a failure or breakdown in a key or deepest part of that structure—so that it's still a kind of malfunctioning, even if it's nearly universal.[5]

Values come into Heidegger's phenomenology by both these epistemic and functional routes, hence express those personae of prophet and physician. I'll show how his critical assessments of falling and *das Man*—his aspersions against the way we all live—are rooted in these two points. His ultimate complaints against falling are that it lacks truth, and that it's dysfunctional; he promotes authenticity on the ground that it corrects both faults.

But before we examine these complaints more closely, I must address a problem raised earlier: Heidegger says explicitly that these notions (falling, authenticity, *das Man*, etc.) are *not* valuative—so how can it be right to read him that way? Moreover, there's a reason to think those notions *can't* be valuative, given the structural status he gives them in Dasein's analysis. If we all *must* fall into *das Man*, how can it be wrong or bad to do so?

We face a quandary here. Heidegger depicts this condition in a manner that is clearly calculated to make it unattractive and unappealing, to make us indeed ashamed to discover ourselves so. But all the while he stoutly denies that he means anything negative, and insists on falling's structural role: "the interpretation has a purely ontological aim and is far removed from a moralizing critique of everyday Dasein" [BT g167; also g175–76, BP 160].

The problem, we've seen, is that he seems to have two conflicting roles for *das Man* and falling. On the one hand they are something essential to us, one of the three aspects of our being-in. They are allied, in this role, with talk or *Rede*, forming one of the three basic stances which together constitute our intentionality. We examined them in this role just now in Chapter 4.5.

But *das Man* and falling play a different role in the existential story we turn to now. They receive, above all, a value—a strongly negative value. And they receive it in a way that calls on us to try to escape or overcome this condition (of falling, of being *das Man*). *Being and Time* subtly but surely makes an appeal to its readers to change themselves in these respects—and thus strongly implies that they're able to change.

How can falling be both something structural-essential, and something we should strive to overcome? The pragmatic and existential themes intersect here, but falling's respective roles in them seem inconsistent. To serve as the "hinge" between these analyses it seems it might need to bear contradictory properties.[6]

The answer to this puzzle has, I think, a general character that others have suggested before: *das Man* and falling are structural and inevitable *as tendencies*, but these tendencies can take effect to varying degrees. There is, as it were, a steady momentum in us to fall, and this tendency ensures that we are constantly, in places or parts of our very complex intending, falling indeed. However, we can also oppose this tendency, steady as it is—can push (as it were) against it, thereby reducing, in places and parts, "how fast" (or "far") we fall. There are, besides, some places where it is especially important to overcome falling—and to do so there (yet not nearly everywhere) is to be authentic.

This general answer must be supplemented by a second point: there are two distinct sources of falling, on which Heidegger takes quite different views. The first source we've seen in Chapter 4: the basic stance of *Rede* or talk involves aligning with *das Man*. Every time we use language we defer to the authority of what one says (are the meanings of these words). This impetus towards falling is indeed something structural, and Heidegger raises no complaint against it. We can't imagine it away without stripping our world of its linguistic articulation (and all its other structuring by our sociality)—and without that there is no world.

What we meet gradually, with the existential theme, is a second source or impetus to falling. It turns out, as we look further into Dasein, that there are features of our deep structure that are difficult or painful for us to face. We recoil from these difficult truths, and this recoil adds to the steady slide involved in talk. It adds a motive, not present in the slide itself; it turns it into a "flight" or avoiding. It's this extra impetus that makes falling pernicious for Heidegger— makes it fully "inauthentic." It lets that stance of *Rede* or talk, in which we "mean things from" the community, swamp the other two aspects of our intentionality, in which we mean things from our ends, and in our feeling; it brings us into structural imbalance.

Let's remind ourselves of the first source of falling. We saw that what's essential to us is talk's stance outward towards others, and especially towards the generality of others with whom we identify and try to fit. We have an essential tendency to understand ourselves in relation to "what one says," "what one does"; this is one of the three "vectors" from which we mean (intend) things and ourselves: things mean what the general use of our language determines them to mean. So *das Man* is the who of the social group whose meanings I mainly lean back upon. And it is my who too, to the extent that I do so rely on it: I identify with it, in order to mean things so.

Without such entry into *das Man* there would be no language, since we can only speak and hear by aligning and subordinating ourselves to the common practice.[7] And without language there would be no world, since the network of practical involvements needs words, in order to have the articulation of a world. So this tendency is a "condition of the possibility" of our intentionality.

It's this impetus towards *das Man* that is to the fore in §27, where Heidegger introduces the notion. He stresses the structural role: "*Das Man* is an existential; and belongs as an originary phenomenon to Dasein's positive constitution" [BT g129]. In this role *das Man* gives me most of my world. Beginning at an early age I acquire by imitation and training—most centrally, by learning language—the great bulk of my abilities and projects. So "*das Man* prescribes that way of interpreting the world and being-in-the-world which lies closest. *Das Man* itself ... articulates the referential context of significance" [g129]. My self is *das Man* insofar as I have my projects *because* they are "what one does"; I engage in them *so that* I can comport with the general practice. I pursue them as "norms."

This is not to say, however, that our subjection to *das Man* is complete or uniform. "How compellingly and explicitly it dominates, can change historically" [BT g129]. And it can be resisted and overcome by individuals, in some manner and to some degree: "The self of everyday Dasein is *das Man-selbst*, which we distinguish from the *authentic*, which means ownly grasped *self*" [g129]. Although we must defer to *das Man* if we're to have an articulated world, still we can also individuate ourselves against this background deference. Since *das Man* is an essential existential, such authenticity must be just a form of it: "*Authentic being-one's-self* does not rest upon an exceptional condition of the subject, a condition that has been detached from *das Man*; *it is rather an existentiell modification of das Man—of das Man as an essential existential*" [g130].

Here in §27 Heidegger only hints at the second, non-structural ground of falling, which makes his clear dissatisfaction with the condition puzzling. But he gestures at this second source in a paragraph I quote in full:

Thus *das Man unburdens* the particular Dasein in its everydayness. Not only that; with this unburdening of being it accommodates

Dasein insofar as it has the tendency to take and make things easy. And because *das Man* constantly accommodates the particular Dasein with this unburdening of being, it keeps and hardens its stubborn dominion.

[g127–28]

Here he mentions a certain motive for falling: a tendency to "take things easy," which different Dasein have to different degrees. But in Chapter 4 we hear no more of this other source.

Heidegger returns to *das Man* in the second half of Chapter 5, and here too the first reason is uppermost, as we see in the account of *chat* [*Gerede*] in §35. This is the form talk or *Rede* takes for *das Man*. Although Heidegger's account of it is strongly deprecating, he still presents it as an aspect of the "generic drift" at work in talk as the third essential aspect of being-in.

A language is itself a communal property constantly reworked, and trained into each new member. As each acquires it, he/she acquires the "average" understanding "already deposited in what's spoken out [*Ausprochenheit*]" [BT g168]. This average understanding acquired in just learning the language requires no direct acquaintance with the matters the language is about: what we get is a capacity to talk about doing things with things, but only indirectly a capacity to do them. So: "In accordance with the average understandability that already lies in the language ... the communicated talk can be largely understood, without the hearer bringing himself into an originary understanding towards what the talk is about" [g168].

Most of my world is laid out for me only by my knowing how to talk about it, and most of my exchanges with others employ only this indirect know-how. Even where my understanding does come to ground in direct abilities—to do and not just to talk about doing—I lapse constantly back into an average understanding, and need over and again to win back a genuine grasp. "This everyday interpretedness, into which Dasein has firstly grown, never lets it detach itself. In it, out of it, and against it are accomplished all genuine understanding, interpreting, and communicating" [BT g169].

"Chat" is talk that has detached itself from an "originary understanding" of its topics, and contents itself with that "average understandability" deposited in the language. "Chat is the possibility of understanding everything without previously making the topic one's own" [BT g169]. Chat is content with this indirect relation to its content, because what it cares about is just the talking. It cares, that is, about the conversational situation, and about "saying the right thing" in it. So whereas talk can function to "hold the world open for us in an articulated understanding," in chat it serves instead to close it off, and to cover up the entities within-the-world; so it "perverts [*verkehrt*] the disclosing into a closing off" [g169].

The point, I think, is that here talk, one basic stance in our intentionality, too much rules the other two. Being with others swamps our competence at things, and even our feeling ourselves, so that we speak—and intend—too thoroughly with a view to "sharing" with others. Heidegger relies on an implicit contrast with the condition in which these three stances (grasping, feeling, wording) collaborate more equally. He relies, that is, on a version of the "functional" argument: chat is an imbalance and malfunction in Dasein's existential structure.

This functional argument is tied up with an epistemic one. When our basic existentials—projection, self-finding, and talk—collaborate properly, they "hold the world open" for us. Then talk doesn't distract from our direct concern with things, but plays its proper role of "articulating" our grasp of them. And similarly with our self-finding in moods: language can help us to know ourselves better in these, if our aim isn't principally at sharing in them. So the complaint against chat is epistemic too: it "closes off and covers up."

But why does talk tend thus to dominate? It's not talk itself that explains this, but another factor that enters on the side of talk, and unbalances Dasein towards it. Heidegger begins to suggest this other factor when he turns next (in §36), to "*curiosity*" [*Neugier*], another feature of everydayness. Curiosity is a distortion in "seeing" that expresses our need for "distraction" [*Zerstreuung*]: it "seeks unrest and excitement through constant novelty and changing encounters" [BT g172]. Our curiosity absorbs us in things, but in a way that stays at their surface. It craves the intensity of the first look and grasp; it avoids "dwelling" on things so as really to know them. Heidegger doesn't explain why Dasein so craves this distraction, but it clearly isn't due to that generic drift in *Rede*, towards *das Man*.

The presence of a second factor becomes still clearer when Heidegger introduces falling in §38. He presents it as having two sides, which correlate, I think, to chat and curiosity. Falling carries us into *das Man*, but it also absorbs us in the world. It is "completely dazed by the 'world' and by the Dasein-with of others in *das Man*" [BT g176]. This absorption in worldly concerns shows up not just in curiosity, but in our everyday "industry" [g177], the way we "lose ourselves" in our tasks. This absorption in things isn't well-explained by the impetus we've seen comes from *Rede*.

Falling is a broader phenomenon than *das Man*, since (I suggest) it can involve "losing oneself" in *any* of the three basic stances, projection, feeling, or talk. So it has three possible forms, each involving an excess in one of those stances. The excess in *Rede* is chat and immersion in *das Man*. The excess in projection is that absorption in things, that industry, which Heidegger often stresses instead. And the excess in feeling, which I do not think he mentions, would be self-distraction by intense sensation or emotion. Since falling has this generality, there must be another source for it besides the impetus towards likening in *Rede*.

Heidegger tries to make us see and feel that falling is not just attracted in its fall (into sharing, for example), but must also be avoiding—indeed recoiling from—something else. Only an aversion could explain the urgency with which we plunge into distractions of such various kinds. He in fact already identifies, here in

Chapter 5, what falling is away from, but only very schematically: Dasein has "fallen away [*abgefallen*] from itself as an authentic ability-to-be-self" [BT g175; also g176]. But he doesn't tell us what could be so painful or disturbing about itself to provoke this flight from it.

2. Anxiety

Unlike *Rede*'s tendency towards sharing, the second impetus into falling is not structural and indispensable, but in the nature of a contingent motive. As such it is also an impetus we can hope to overcome or eliminate—by contrast with the inevitable pull to share. So it's this second tendency that plays the main role in the existential drama Heidegger goes on to relate.

The main logic of the motive is that it is a *fleeing from* something. The idea that falling is a flight [*Flucht*] is absent from Chapter 4 and 5; it first appears in §40 of Chapter 6, in the course of introducing anxiety. "Dasein's absorption in *das Man* and its absorption in the "world" of its concern, manifest something like a *flight* of Dasein before [*vor*] itself as an authentic ability-to-be-self" [BT g184]. This new notion of flight gives a crucial turn to Heidegger's diagnosis of falling.

What this flight is *from*, above all, is "facing" something, i.e. facing a truth; so it has an epistemic character. Heidegger claims such flight is typical of everydayness, and draws several crucial conclusions from this. They flow from the simple point that we only flee something we already have some inkling of. And when we flee "facing" some truth, it must be because we already, in some manner, recognize it.

A first consequence is simply the priority in intentional logic here: more basic than the ignorance we flee into, is the recognition that motivates the flight. This changes the status of falling, insofar as it seeks such ignorance: it turns out that it is not as "originary" or ultimate as it had seemed. Since it is a flight, it presupposes a prior understanding—though of course this will have that implicit and background character we've been noticing. "[T]o be thus closed off [in falling] is merely the *privation* of a disclosure which manifests itself phenomenally in the fact that Dasein's flight is a flight *before itself*" [BT g184].

This is why Heidegger reverses his early claim that falling every-dayness is primary or basic. It is indeed far more usual than anxiety: "under the ascendancy of falling and publicness, 'authentic' anxiety is rare" [BT g190]. Nevertheless, because falling is a flight that presupposes recognition of the threat, anxiety is logically and intentionally prior to falling: "The tranquillized and familiar being-in-the-world is a mode of Dasein's uncanniness, not the reverse. *The not-at-home must be conceived existential-ontologically as the more originary phenomenon*" [g189].

A second implication is that we, as phenomenologists, can hope to identify what's fled by paying attention to the manner of the flight. What's fled is disclosed in the flight, though in the "privative mode" of avoidance. "[I]n turning away *from* it, it is disclosed 'there'. This existentiell-ontical turning away gives, phenomenally, on the ground of its character as a disclosure, the possibility of grasping the before-what of the flight" [BT g185]. Of course the phenomenologist will again need special methods to "wrest" this disclosure from experience aimed to hide it.

A third important point Heidegger draws from this flight is valuative: he encourages us to infer that it's *reprehensible* (I think this is not too strong an illocutionary force to hear in his depictions of falling and *das Man*). We should be ashamed of fleeing in this way. *Being and Time* tries to encourage us to stand fast and face what we thus usually avoid.

Now not all flight is reprehensible—what makes this so? Heidegger's first reason is its epistemic character: the flight is from a truth. And he can presume in his readers a prior value of self-understanding: it's what brings them to him. Beyond this, such epistemic flight has features that make it unappealing. Where an opposing force is too great, it makes perfect sense to avoid engaging it, and to try to stand out of its range. But it looks less sensible to ignore it or deny its existence. Moreover, this epistemic flight involves self-deception, and brings us into contradiction with ourselves: we superimpose an ignorance on a deeper recognition.

Heidegger's second reason why this flight is reprehensible is (as I put it on p. 131) *functional*: the flight subverts proper working. What we flee is precisely the battle that it most belongs to us, as Dasein, to fight. Here Heidegger relies on a claim to have uncovered a kind of ultimate essence, which involves an ultimate task. Dasein is the entity that "goes about" its own being, i.e. which takes the reflexive view upon itself; this is its mineness. Heidegger will present flight as a failure at this ultimate task—as giving up the effort to accomplish this mineness. As we follow his analysis of falling's flight, in this section and the next, we'll see how he implicitly relies on these two kinds of support for his evaluations and judgments against it.

Let's turn now to the question *what* Dasein flees. Heidegger has many answers, among them: itself, its being, the world, death, and guilt. But his immediate answer is *anxiety* [*Angst*], and its *uncanniness* [*Unheimlichkeit*]. "The falling flight *into* the at-home [*Zuhause*] of publicness is a flight *before* the not-at-home, which means the uncanniness" [BT g189].[8] Anxiety is the *proximate* "what" that falling flees, because it is the "facing"; the other whats falling flees are the things it is so difficult to face. So anxiety's crucial status is epistemic: it reveals deep truth, in the *kind* of uncovering adequate to it.

Anxiety is another of Heidegger's most characteristically "existential" notions. There's an analogous idea playing a similar structural role in most other existential systems. All give special importance to a feeling of discontent or malaise, directed not at any failures in our dealings or achievements, but at something deeper and more pervasive, a flaw or problem in our own structure. Anxiety is a self-finding [*Befindlichkeit*] or mood, but a very special one, in which we "find" something essential about ourselves—something that did not yet emerge in the pragmatic analysis that preceded.

Heidegger approaches anxiety by distinguishing it from fear, another mood which is structurally similar, but which "finds" us in mere contingencies.[9] Fear is of or about some entity within-the-world, something that threatens one of my projects or ends. But in anxiety the threat comes "from nothing and nowhere": there's no thing (or things) we're anxious over, and no goal we see some hindrance to. Anxiety is over something more sweeping and essential: it is "before" [vor] and "about" [um] being-in-the-world itself [BT g187].

Fear posits a threat to some project, so we feel it within that project—as a risk to its concern. In feeling fear we "find" ourselves at risk, due to our commitment to some project. Anxiety by contrast is of or about a threat to our very ability to have projects. It is the *feeling* of that threat, or indeed of that inability. So anxiety involves a loss of momentum and engagement in our projects—of ability to care about their ends. It is this detachment, but felt painfully as an *inability* to reattach myself: I wish I could sink back into caring about them, but have lost the knack.

So in anxiety the world looks pointless, "has the character of complete meaninglessness" [BT g186]. The things around me fail to solicit my interest by engaging my projects: there seems nothing worth doing with them. "The "world" can offer nothing more, and neither can the Dasein-with of others" [g187]. Even my leading ambitions, my life-goals, lose their appeal for me; I can't see how I managed to care about them. I *feel* how they are contingent, arbitrary, and inherently worthless—whether or not I entertain or believe any of these claims.

Anxiety, then, is a kind of breakdown, but not within any of our projects. It is a breakdown in our second-order ability to connect ourselves to our projects, to "be-in" our world. As such, this breakdown is important phenomenologically. Indeed, it's because it is "one of the most far-reaching and most originary possibilities of disclosure" [BT g182] that the discussion turns to anxiety in the first place.[10]

Those breakdowns in our first-order ability to accomplish our projects—when we're stymied by broken equipment, for instance—"light up" how those projects matter to us. These experiences have an epistemic authority, and to know the particular structure of my personal concerns, my world, I will need to appeal to them. Anxiety, as a breakdown in the second-order ability to have projects at all, lights up things more basic and universal.

So, first, anxiety shows me my world as a whole. In my alienation from my projects, I "see" them all stretched inertly before me, conspicuous precisely by my painful disengagement from them. So whereas a first-order breakdown lights up some local sector of my world—the part threatened by the broken tool—anxiety lights up my world as a world, *in toto*. "[O]n the ground of this *meaninglessness* of [what is] within-the-world only the world in its worldhood still obtrudes itself" [BT g187].

More importantly, anxiety also lights up my relation to this world, my being-in. I notice, by feeling its absence, how I am usually engaged with the world by projecting at ends and having things matter accordingly. I notice, as well, how these projects come to me especially from the authority of *das Man*, whose appeal is now lost. Anxiety shows, in fact, all three aspects of being-in, and their interconnection. For Heidegger immediately uses it, in the following §41, to tie these aspects together into a single structure. That is, anxiety is supposed to show us how our grasping, feeling, and wording constitute a unity, which he calls "care" [*Sorge*].

But anxiety shows me my world by disengaging me from it. It especially detaches me from projects that I have had in an everyday way, i.e. by falling into them, by taking them over from and as *das Man*. Anxiety deprives *das Man* of its tranquillizing effect: the assurance that in "doing what one does" I am doing what's really worth doing. It is a breakdown especially in my ability to let the general practice settle my ends. "Anxiety thus takes away from Dasein the possibility of understanding itself fallingly, from the world and the public interpretedness" [BT g187]. It is the feeling of pointlessness and dislocation that ensues once the support of customary values is lost, and I am left to my own devices, "individualized" [g188]. "This individualization brings Dasein back from its falling, and makes manifest to it authenticity and inauthenticity as possibilities of its being" [g191].

By this disengagement from my projects I thus discover, by feeling it, a deeper level to my intentionality. I experience how grasping, feeling, and wording have been making my meaning all along. But I experience this in alienation from it, and hence "before" having this meaning (this world, these ends) at all. My projects themselves become mere possibilities, and I find myself as the entity confronted with these options. So I find that "before" all those tasks I have within my projects, I'm confronted with the more fundamental task of deciding which of these projects will be *mine*. And, suited to this task, I discover in myself a deeper ability, a kind of meta-know-how.

Heidegger puts it this way: "Anxiety makes manifest in Dasein its *being towards* its ownmost ability-to-be, which means its *being-free* for the freedom of choosing and taking hold of itself" [BT g188]. My "ownmost" ability is my second-order capacity to choose among these projects; exercising this aright will be authenticity. Falling is, in fact, an effort to avoid exercising this capacity. It gives over the responsibility for the choice to *das Man*, and aims and values out of its sociality. So it is a kind of "choosing not to choose." Anxiety is a breakdown in my ability to ignore the choice.[11]

So anxiety feels not that meta-ability to choose, but precisely an inability for this task. This is why it is a distressing and uncomfortable stance or attitude. It is disengaged from projects and unable to reengage, either by falling back into its average concerns, or by a personal choice. So we might say that anxiety is a *seriousness* about oneself, but a seriousness that can make no progress. I can't lean back on the public understanding, I have lost that cushioning. But I'm unable to handle by myself the work that had been done by *das Man*.

Anxiety experiences how hard individual choice really is, since it needs to be "in the face of" deep structural problems in Dasein. Anxiety faces these problems too, having lost falling's way of avoiding them. We turn next to these structures, death and guilt. Since falling flees anxiety *as* a painful confrontation with them, they are deeper answers to the question "what falling flees."

3. Existential concerns

We turn now to specify what anxiety is anxious about—the truth that it so uncomfortably faces. We've seen that it is anxious about being-in-the-world—but which aspects or features of this is anxiety directed upon? Here we come, as it were, to the source: to the ultimate reason for the falling that infects everydayness. Heidegger's answer is "death" and "guilt."[12] But he has very special meanings for these, which require careful adjustments from the words' usual senses.

Death and guilt are the topics of Division II's first two chapters; here the existential issues are at center stage. Division II has the overall aim of deepening the analysis of Dasein offered in Division I; the latter was merely "provisional," because it focused on Dasein's average everydayness. Heidegger now aims at a more, or indeed at a most originary [*ursprünglichste*: BT g17] account, by widening the analysis beyond everydayness, so as to bring the "whole" [*Ganze*] of Dasein into view, and to reveal the "unity" [*Einheit*] of this full structure.

Division I's map of Dasein's essential structures was drawn with the eye on everydayness. That focus was appropriate, inasmuch as that is how we live "firstly and mostly"; no other starting-point is as appropriate. But we have begun to realize that there are aspects of our condition that won't readily emerge given that focus, since everydayness "flees" them, and suppresses its own awareness of them. We've noticed them by noticing how everydayness "turns away" from them, but now we should examine the special, non-average conditions in which Dasein "turns towards" these aspects that everydayness shuns. These special conditions will be more directly illuminating of our full structure.

We saw that falling flees anxiety. If anxiety is over death and guilt, then falling ultimately flees these, and this is where our existential challenge or difficulty finally lies. Our challenge will be, to "face" these and live properly with them. While largely deferring until section 4 that proper response (authenticity), we can address several questions about the problems (death and guilt) themselves. Why is it hard for us to face them—why do we flee them? Why do they provoke anxiety? And how does it help us avoid them, to lose ourselves in *das Man*?

i. Death

Division II's Chapter 1 is devoted to death.[13] Heidegger leads into the topic (in the introductory §46) in pursuit of Dasein's "wholeness." It seems that as long as Dasein is alive it is incomplete. For it is always "ahead-of-itself," i.e. defined by possibilities not yet realized. "In the essence of the basic constitution of Dasein lies a *constant unsettledness*. The lack of totality signifies something missing [*Ausstand*] in the ability-to-be" [BT g236]. So it might seem that Dasein is only complete in death. But although there is nothing "still outstanding" when Dasein ceases to project, there is also no Dasein. It therefore seems that Dasein can never be "whole."

It quickly emerges, however, that this very question about Dasein's wholeness is misguided, because it rests on a misinterpretation of Dasein as something at-hand (an "object"). And this makes Heidegger's route from wholeness to death seem a red herring—a misleading excuse for introducing death. He will try to vindicate the connection in the end, however. For it will turn out that (a proper) anticipation of death—not the event of it—makes one indeed "whole" in the sense appropriate to what we are.

Now our own route to the topic of death has been from anxiety: death is one of the things anxiety is anxious about. Death, Heidegger says, is a structural limit in or to us, which we prefer not to face, and which renders us anxious when we do.

So put, however, this seems a very trite point. That we're mortal, that the life of each of us will come to an end, that we are worried about this mortality, and often prefer not to think about it—all of this is obvious enough, and Heidegger would have little merit in resaying it. Yet he thinks he has strange and surprising things to tell us about death. His treatment of the topic is one of the most famous—and infamous—parts of the book, experienced by some as especially deep and inspiring, but by others as trivial, or non-sensical, or simply and plainly false.[14] We here face in acute form the general challenge stemming from Heidegger's claim to be reminding us of truths we already know, but somehow suppress or forget.

As I've mentioned, Heidegger means something different by "death" than we usually do, and some of those harsh judgments come from missing this change. But I think the difference or novelty in Heidegger's notion can also be exaggerated. Some interpreters have read his notion in a way that takes it out of any direct relation to the biographical event of death. They make it related to the latter only by analogy or resemblance—referring instead to something like our "loss of possibilities."[15]

But I don't think Heidegger means to detach death so thoroughly from our ordinary sense; he's not so drastically changing the topic. Instead, his main shift is to treat death *"as a possibility,"* i.e. within our projective intentionality, rather than as an at-hand, objective event. *"Death is,* as the end of *Dasein,* in the being of this entity *towards* its end"* [BT g259]. Death is a very special such possibility, and one that is not contingent but built into the structure of our intentionality. But this possibility stands, we'll see, in very tight relation to that objective event. It is, in a certain sense, "about" that event, and therefore competes with all the ways we usually think about it. The latter need to be reformed by the discovery of death as possibility.

What's hard for us is to see death as possibility. It's hard generally to notice possibilities as possibilities—they're transparent to the actualizations they intend. But it's especially hard to grasp death as possibility, because of the peculiar possibility it is. We avoid facing death as possibility by misinterpreting it as an objective event. This motivated misunderstanding of death is reinforced by a network of social practices designed to hide death's way of being possible; this is one of the most important functions of *das Man*.

Anxiety, however, is a *breakdown* in that everyday coping with death—a *felt* breakdown. And again the breakdown has an epistemic pay-off: anxiety faces death—has the truth about death—by virtue of so feeling it. It turns us back towards our own death, from our falling flight from it: "Being-towards-death is essentially anxiety" [BT g266]. So as the phenomenologist studies death, he/she will pay special attention to what anxiety reveals.

Let's look at the elements of this account more closely, following the chapter's order of discussion. After the introductory §46, Heidegger moves towards his positive account via a prolonged examination of the ways we ordinarily "get death wrong." I will summarize these critical sections, and then expand when we come to the concluding section (§53), where his focus finally turns to the positive notion.

§47 rebuts the idea that since we can't have experienced our own death, we must understand death by attending to the death of others. It offers an acute phenomenology for how we intend (think about) dead others, but insists that each must understand death from—and for the sake of—his/her own case. One Dasein can't substitute for another with regards to death, as we can in our public roles. "No one can take the other's dying away from him" [BT g240]. The insistence that our principal relation is to our own death, and that others, alive or dead, are of no real help in forming this relation, is a key point in Heidegger's treatment of death.[16] "Death is, insofar as it 'is', in each case mine [*je der meine*]" [g240]. So we must understand death as possibility, and as mine.

§48 examines the idea that death is an *Ausstand*, i.e. a completion that is missing or "in the offing" (Macquarrie and Robinson translate it "something still outstanding"). Heidegger reviews a subtle variety of ways this can be true of such things as debts (to be paid), fruit (ripening), and the moon (waxing to full). But the inevitable conclusion is that none of these is an apt model for death [BT g244]. Nor is death an "end" in some usual senses: it's not Dasein's fulfillment, nor its stopping, nor its being finished, nor its disappearing. What's wrong with all of these is that they are at-hand events that will accomplish an objective culmination or conclusion to a process. But death is *as* we are towards it, in our first-personal (reflexive) aiming.

§49 is again mainly negative, distinguishing our existential inquiry into death from the ways biology, psychology, and theology treat it. Biology studies the event of "perishing" [*Verenden*] in which an organism's life stops; in Dasein's case we can call this event "demise" [*Ableben*]. But we have already seen how irrelevant these events are. Heidegger also dismisses the most familiar kind of psychological study of death: "a psychology of 'dying [*Sterben*]' gives information about the 'living' of the 'one dying' rather than about dying itself" [BT g247]. Such studies treat the ways people cope in emergency or "death bed" situations, whereas we are looking for the way in which every Dasein is *always* being-towards-death. Nor is theology helpful. The question of an afterlife—whether I or part of me will survive my bodily death—is irrelevant to the analysis of our being-towards-death, since the latter is the primary or background attitude to which all questioning about an afterlife responds [g247–48].[17]

In §50 Heidegger gives a glimpse—though a quite schematic one—of his positive account. My relation to death, as "my possibility"—a relation that precedes and underlies all my efforts to ignore it—runs along all three of the dimensions of human meaning: my projection, thrownness, and falling (my grasping, feeling, and wording). First, I project towards death in my planning and devising: I take account of this possibility ("of no-longer-being-able-to-be-there" [BT g250]) in my purposiveness. Second, I am "thrown into" death, inasmuch as I also feel it a certain way: I feel it above all in the mood of anxiety—and not in that of fear, as might have been expected. But third, I am also related to my death in my social being, i.e. in the words, sayings, customs by which my community, *das Man*, deals with death. And here is where "firstly and mostly Dasein covers up its ownmost being-towards-death, fleeing *before* it" [g251].

§51 returns to the negative: Heidegger tries to show how this everyday way of being-towards-death, embedded in our common language and practices, expresses the effort to conceal or evade (facing) death. He details how our ordinary ways of talking about death, in our prevalent "chat," exhibit "concealing evasion before death" [BT g253]. In our everyday, "public" being-with one another it is of course recognized that people die, but this is taken as irrelevant to us now. Our talk "wants to say: one dies too, in the end, but immediately [*zunächst*] one stays unconcerned" [g253]. In this conversational stance we almost always adopt towards one another, we presume death relevant only where it is actual—concealing its true status as possibility. This evasion of death even extends to the death-bed: "the 'neighbors' often still talk into the 'dying one' that he will escape death and soon return to the tranquillized everydayness of the world of his concern" [g253]. Within this customary viewpoint anxiety over death gets interpreted as fear before an approaching event, and is stigmatized as a weakness. So chat guards against our taking death seriously.

But although we evade death in everydayness, this evasion is still a way of being-towards it. Thus a phenomenologist can still find out what death is, by examining what everydayness avoids. And this is what §52 proceeds to do, focusing especially on the "certainty" [*Gewissheit*] of death. Our public stance—our chat—does not deny death's certainty, but misinterprets it so as to remove its sting. So I conceive of my death as an event lying ahead of me on a time-line. I concede that this event is certain to happen, but I diminish this certainty as merely empirical: "So far as one knows, all humans 'die'" [BT g257]. And by placing it at some indefinite but sub-stantial distance from me (it's non-adjacent), I take away from death's certainty a most important aspect: "*das Man* covers up what is peculiar to death's certainty, *that it is possible at any moment*. With the certainty of death goes the *indefiniteness* of its when" [g258].

It is by its indefiniteness that this possibility bears in its dis-tinctive way on all my other possibilities. It is the possibility of being no longer able to project, and the indefiniteness of this puts all my projects at constant risk: I can lose at any moment my ability to be anything at all. So the indefiniteness of death makes it a constant threat to all the projects I identify myself by; this is why it's so unsettling, and why we try to ignore it. It also makes this ignoring especially unapt: if the possibility did lie at a fixed distance from us, it might be more excusable to defer attention to a later date. But by the kind of possibility it is, death is relevant in every moment.

For phenomenology, that very way I "chat" with myself about death reveals the more complete certainty I have of it: the latter motivates this chat. This certainty is not empirical, not in the "graded order of evidence about the at-hand" [BT g265], because it lies not in any beliefs or theories but in a deep-lying foreboding.[18] I push my death off to that distance and treat it as irrelevant "until I get close," as a way to hold off the anxiety before death that is always waiting "in the background" for me. I do know and feel that death can come at any moment, but I keep it in that background by repeating the commonsense account of death that I learn in *das Man*.

In the last and longest section on death, §53, Heidegger describes an "authentic being-towards-death," which turns back from this falling flight to face death. He presents this only as a theoretical construction, and will not claim to confirm its feasibility until he treats conscience in Chapter 2. I will defer until the next section talking about this authentic stance itself—it will be important to connect it with authenticity towards guilt as well. Here I'll skim off what §53 tells us about death itself—which authenticity grasps, since it chooses "in the light of" death. So what, finally, is it?

I've said that the most important point is that death "is possibility." Heidegger has stressed this all along, but just what it means comes out best as he finally describes what an adequate grasp of it "as possibility" requires. It's not enough, for example, to think about (or brood over) my future death. This treats death as possibility to the extent of viewing it as "something that is coming," but it "weakens" the possibility by "a calculating will to arrange about death" [BT g261]. Similarly, "expecting" [*erwarten*] death is to wait for its actualization, so that even here there is a "leaping away from the possible and finding foothold in the actual" [g262].

Indeed, death is a distinctive possibility inasmuch as it defies our effort to think of it as actual—to think it so from a first-person point of view, that is. (I can imagine my corpse, of course, but that treats me as at-hand, and grasps only my demise.) My other possibilities I can imagine myself achieving (or undergoing); I can anticipate how it would be to enact (or suffer) them. Death is distinctive in that it "offers no support for being intent upon something, 'picturing' to oneself the possible actuality, and thereby forgetting its possibility" [BT g262]. Death is "pure possibility," since it is not a way for me to be, but to become (or be towards). This unimaginableness of death can, if we pay attention, bring home to us how it is a possibility, and indeed what it is to be a possibility. And when we learn this lesson about death, we can learn to see our other possibilities as such as well.

As possibility, death is an *intentum*, something given in my projection, which is precisely and only *as* I am concerned about it. So we must consider it, as PH 312 puts it, "as a pure phenomenon." This shows us how Heideggerian death is still related to the event of demise. Death-as-possibility is "of" or "about" my cessation, the concluding of my life. But in our phenomenological study of Dasein this event—when and how it happens—is irrelevant. What matters is how I am towards the possibility: how I cope with it, and how I shape and mean it in my coping. The possibility is constituted by my ability or capacity in coping—once again by my knowing-how. "Being a possibility essentially means being capable of this being-possible" [PH 315].[19]

Of course it is not something I strive towards, as I do my for-whiches or goals. Nevertheless it is something that is what it is *as* I am towards it in a projective know-how, in a deep and pervasive striving. I am always in the midst of coping with this possibility, though of course "in the background." This know-how is partly, of course, my strategies for postponing the event (my demise). But, more importantly, it is my strategies for *living* with that indefinite possibility, which no amount of that prophylaxis can remove. It is the way I practice the pursuit of all of my other possibilities given this abiding constant threat to them.

It's not only in this special way it's a possibility, but in the special way it's "mine," that death is distinctive. Death is my "ownmost" and "non-relational" possibility. It is ownmost in that in this possibility Dasein's "very being is at issue" [BT g263]. It is non-relational in that I alone can deal with it, so that it "individualizes Dasein down to itself" [g263]. So death is "my" possibility in ways that none of my others is: the latter I copy from others, and I'm replaceable by others in them—in their usual or everyday forms, they're all social and socializing. Death is a possibility I have by my own essential structure, and this possibility cannot be grasped in the terms I get from my linguistic and social side.

As Heidegger puts it in *PH*, "I am this 'I can' in a superlative sense. For I am this 'I can die at any moment'" [313]. Death is superlatively mine because I have it as my possibility independently of any and all of the social meanings embedded in my language and practices. The roles, identities, and aims I pursue all have their meanings by the social-linguistic matrix I inherit and join: that determines what these roles mean and require, not I. And what matters for this matrix is merely that *someone* performs this role, not whether it's I. It's in this sense that I'm replaceable in it.

But I have death as a possibility "before" my entry into this contingent social domain—that is, at a deeper, more original level. I stand in a relation to it that has not been structured by language or by any of the prevailing social practices and outlooks on death. Its priority is shown by the way it (partly) motivates and explains my embrace of those structures. So I need to locate this original relation to death "beneath" all those structurings of it—to see how I "mean" it underneath all the ways I think about it. This is my relation to my death—to death as my possibility, not a possibility there for anyone else inhabiting that language and practices.

The lesson of death will work this way, then: seeing the special way in which death is a possibility, and is mine, I learn to stand towards my other possibilities *as* possibilities and *as* mine, as well. This shifts my deep relation to all of my ends (or for-whiches). But we'll wait for this until section 4 looks at authenticity.

ii. Guilt

Some of these points about death hold for guilt as well, and noting a few of the parallels will give us quick access to much of it. It stands at the same structural level in Dasein as death, but whereas the latter is a feature of our projection, guilt has to do with our thrownness or self-finding. Death is mainly given to us in projection's way, as a possibility, and guilt is mainly given in self-finding's way, by our feeling ourselves so thrown. But guilt, like death, is repellent to us, so that we usually avoid that recognition—except in authenticity, which embraces it.

Because guilt is a structural element in our intentionality, we must distinguish it from what we ordinarily call guilt. Just as death is not an event, so guilt is not any such fact about us as that we have sinned or done something wrong. Such facts could hold whether or not we notice them in any way. But guilt—as Heidegger means it—has its identity solely as an intentional object, uncovered by phenomenology, not by theology or morality.

I will try to substantiate these parallels between death and guilt. But I must acknowledge that there is a great asymmetry in Heidegger's handling of them. Death is the focus of all of Chapter 1, but Chapter 2 concerns authenticity, and guilt comes in only midway, as what conscience calls to us, in spurring us towards authenticity. I'll come back to this fuller project—as well as to "conscience"—in Chapter 2 when I treat authenticity in the next section. Here I'll focus on the treatment of guilt in §58, drawing from the surrounding sections where they add important points.

Guilt [*Schuld*] becomes a topic in Chapter 2 because it is what conscience calls to us: it calls "Guilty!" As an essential element in our intentionality, conscience has something important to say. The challenge is to grasp the genuine sense of this call. Once again Heidegger begins—and spends most of his time—telling us what this existential guilt is *not*, i.e. ruling out our ordinary senses for the term. Above all he rules out all accounts of guilt as a real or objective fact. It is not, for example, a matter of some "*lack*, as a failure of something that should and can be" [BT g283]. This treats guilt as something at-hand, a fact (or not) about me that others can know as well or better than I do. Instead, my guilt lies in a certain way I *take myself* to be guilty.

Heidegger then offers a "formal" definition of the term: "we determine the formally existential idea of the 'guilty' thus: being-the-ground for a being that is determined by a not [*Nicht*]—i.e. *being-the-ground of a nullity* [*Nichtigkeit*]" [BT g283]. He soon adds that this ground is also "null," so that guilt involves two nullities. Dasein's being-a-ground is its thrownness, and this grounds its projection. Hence one nullity lies in thrownness, another in projection, and together these are our guilt: "Care—the being of Dasein—thus means as thrown projection: The (null) being-the-ground of a nullity" [g285].

What, first, is the nullity in our projection? Heidegger presents it this way: "as able-to-be [Dasein] stands in each case in one or another possibility, it constantly is *not* others and has foregone these in its existentiell projection. ... Freedom, though, *is* only in the choice of one, i.e. in bearing not having chosen and not being able to choose others" [BT g285]. So my projection limits me at the same time that it identifies me: the choice of this possibility (whichever I aim at) involves renouncing indefinitely many others. Since I *am* my possibility, I deprive myself of those other identities.[20]

I take it to be implicit here that these foregone possibilities are no less valuable, intrinsically, than whatever one we choose. Indeed it may even be presumed that *no* possibilities have *any* intrinsic value. Here Heidegger concurs in the familiar existentialist idea that we're confronted with a "groundless choice." And since this nullity in projection is the one referred to in the initial "formal" definition of guilt—whereas the nullity in thrownness is added secondarily—it seems to be the main point of guilt. Surprisingly, however, Heidegger relies very little on this familiar idea; indeed this paragraph (on g285) is the only place he discusses this nullity, and he is brief about it here.

Instead his attention and weight are all on the other nullity, the one in our thrownness: it's this he treats as the crucial element in guilt. In his main use, guilt is really just that thrownness itself, and the limitation or threat this is for projection. It is the way we always find ourselves "thrown into" a particular set of ends and projects. This thrownness, moreover, is impervious to projection, and can't be taken up into it. "[Dasein] is never existent *before* its ground, but only *from* it and *as this*. Being-a-ground thus means *never* to have power over one's ownmost being from the ground up. This *not* belongs to the existential meaning of thrownness" [BT g284].

Whereas the first nullity, and also death, are limits on projection within its own domain—ways it can't make the future it wants for itself—this second nullity is projection's restriction to that domain, its inability to work back on the past. (So the others are internal limits on projection, but guilt is an external limit.) Guilt is the way we are subjected to the past, which our forward-reaching projection can't take control over. We are subjected not causally, but in the very structure of our meaning: we *must* mean our world "from behind," as it were—in the other vector we saw belongs to self-finding. Our moods display this way we've been thrown and subjected.

This problem is Heidegger's variation on an old family of problems. Classical forms include the body's intractability to mind, and determinism's threat to our freedom. A more recent ancestor is the problem Nietzsche devises will to power to solve: "the will's inability to will backwards" (in *Zarathustra* ii.2 "On Redemption"). Heidegger claims phenomenology shows that the ultimate root to all these problems is a conflict built into our structure as intenders or meaners. The root problem, he thinks, is that Dasein "never comes back behind its thrownness so as to be able to itself first release this 'that it is and has to be' from *its being*-a-self" [BT g284; also g383].

The deep problem lies in a duality in our way of meaning or intending: we're projective, but also mood-thrown, and both are essential to our intentionality. This division is the more disturbing to us because it makes a split between two ways we identify ourselves, two whos we are: I am my project-ends, but I am also my self-finding in moods. We will always find or feel ourselves as something different than we are making ourselves to be. We understand ourselves to be projecting *from* a self we also are, which is discrepant (of course) from the who we aspire to be.

We might put it: the conflict is between the two basic stances we take. On the one hand we are wrapped up in our striving and effecting, in what we're trying to do and be. But on the other hand we are also registering what we've come to be, and registering this especially in our feeling: we feel how we're doing, all the time we are doing. Often the latter stance serves the former: we keep track of how we're doing at what we're trying to do. But the more we pass over into this reflective view on ourselves, into "noticing how we are," the more discrepancy opens up between this and our projective aspiration. So moods are often experienced as hindrances to our effort.

Notice that Heidegger sees this problem from the side of projection: it is a problem for my being the who I'm trying to be that I am also already just so. In the conflict between these aspects of intentionality, it is thrownness that appears as a limit on projection, and not the other way around. So guilt lies in a deep structural feature of our intending—but in this feature *as* it is itself intended or meant.

Guilt is not over something we could and should be doing but are failing to do. Indeed the way one "reckons up infractions [in rules and norms] and seeks equivalents" is a strategy to avoid our original guilt [BT g288]. We try to restrict guilt to the performance or non-performance of specified dos and don'ts. We try to understand it, like death, as something at-hand that we can bring under control. Just as we temper death by interpreting it as an event lying at an indefinite distance ahead, so we temper guilt by restricting it to concrete infractions.

The deep problem is not that I've done particular things in the past that I need to atone for—and thereby control or wipe clean. The problem is the way my projective meanings for things always need to share with meanings coming from the past—meaning thrown into things from behind me. So the "call of conscience" is not really directed against our trespasses; it's a reminder of that insuperable limit. We can never overcome our guilt; our task is to be guilty authentically [BT g287].

Guilt is not just this structural problem as meant, but as felt. And not only is that structure constant, but we are constantly feeling it. In a typical move, Heidegger argues that even our feeling not guilty is a kind of evidence for this guilt, since we can see it as a self-concealing: "That this [originary being-guilty] remains firstly and mostly undisclosed, and is kept closed off by the falling being of Dasein, *reveals* just the mentioned nullity" [BT g286]. We fail to feel guilty by strategy, because implicitly we *do* feel it.

4. Authenticity

We come now to what might be called the answer to the various problems identified so far. As we've seen, these problems have three layers. First, we (phenomenologists) notice the falling in our everydayness, and the way we herd ourselves into *das Man*. Next we identify what that falling flees, the not-at-homeness of anxiety. And, third, we specify what this anxiety is before (over), death and guilt—the essential limits we grasp and feel ourselves to have. Authenticity then emerges as the adequate or appropriate stance towards death and guilt—and the answer to all three problems.

Our main sources on authenticity are §53 in Chapter 1 (of Division II), which describes an authentic being-towards-death, §60 in Chapter 2, which describes the authentic response to conscience's call to our guilt, and §62 of Chapter 3, which argues (roughly) that these are really two aspects of authenticity that entail one another. (I defer the temporal accounts of authenticity, later in the book, until Chapter 6.) Heidegger calls authenticity as facing death "anticipation," and authenticity as facing guilt "resoluteness."

Heidegger's two approaches to authenticity, via death and via guilt, have different epistemic status. He presents the authentic stance towards death hypothetically, as a way that Dasein *might* "become whole" by living with its death, but a way not yet substantiated; it emerges "only as an ontological possibility" [BT g266]. We need to show that it is concretely possible, and this is

what Heidegger thinks conscience does: conscience is a phenomenon we can all recognize in ourselves, which calls us to face our
guilt, and thus to become authentic. So it "attests" [*bezeugt*] to the
"existentiell possibility" of authenticity; it shows, as it were, that
we can live it.[21] (As we'll see on pp. 168–69, conscience may
"attest" in favor not just of authenticity's possibility, but of its
functional role—hence its value.)

Facing death and guilt pulls us out of our everyday concern. It
sets us into a second-order relation to all this concern by making
it problematic, "an issue." Death shows projection that all its
thrust forward is finite, moreover indefinitely finite. Guilt shows
thrownness that it will always fail to rise to what projection wills.
So they cast us out of our usual ways of thinking and feeling what
we're doing. They make these projective and affective stances
themselves problematic, and press us to view them as a whole. In
short, they step us back to the transcendental level in us.

How does authenticity handle the challenges posed by death and
guilt? It doesn't overcome or eliminate them: as authentic, I am
still towards my death, and still guilty. We've seen that these are
structural limits to projection, and authenticity can't change that.
But authenticity does two other things, and these, I think, are
Heidegger's own principal arguments in favor of it.

First, it faces these limits, is "in the truth" with respect to
them—in contrast with the avoidance and flight in which we live
firstly and mostly. BT g260 says that authentic being-towards-death
is towards it "without either fleeing it or covering it up."
And g265: "In anticipation Dasein can first make certain of
its ownmost being in its unattainable totality." So authenticity is
justified *epistemically*.

Second, it uses this facing of death and guilt to "make mine" its
projects—in the way we will see—which is their "structurally
appropriate" role, i.e. their function. So although authenticity
doesn't really "solve" either problem, it turns these limits into
advantages: I become myself by my relation to them. I also

become—in the way that is really appropriate to Dasein—"whole" and "complete." Thus authenticity is also justified *functionally*.

Consider first authentic being-towards death, which Heidegger calls "*anticipation*" [*Vorlaufen*]. The German says "running ahead," and what he wants us to hear is that our attention runs forward to death—not that we try to hasten it. (So it's not a matter of "actualizing" the possibility of death [BT g261].) Above all we face death *as possibility*: "[T]he possibility must, unweakened, be understood *as possibility*, it must be cultivated *as a possibility*, and *withstood as possibility* in comportment towards it" [g261].

This facing is of course not a merely theoretical attention: anticipation doesn't lie in a scientific knowledge or certainty that one will die. Instead, it is our projective attention that runs ahead to death—the attention with which we aim and orient ourselves in our projects. We aim these projects in relation to death, i.e. the possibility of being unable to project, of ceasing to be Dasein, a possibility that is indefinite in the sense that it "can come at any moment." (Hence "ahead" is potentially misleading, in suggesting that the possibility lies at some distance in the future.)

Because anticipation reaches "all the way" ahead to my death—recognizing that it may even be "now"—and sees it as the bound to all my possibilities, it gives me the "wholeness" that is really appropriate to Dasein. "Since anticipation of the unattainable [unüberholbare] possibility discloses with it all the possibilities that lie before it, there lies in it the possibility of an existentiell advance grasp of the *whole* Dasein, i.e. the possibility to exist as a *whole ability-to-be*" [BT g264]. In each moment that I thus stretch out to my death, I live as the kind of whole it behooves me to be.

However, this projective attention to death is also not a matter of *planning* over death's possibility—of taking practical regard of the various ways it might happen. As we've seen, this kind of calculating, preventative attention serves to "weaken" the possibility by its strategic management. It steps back from existing concerns to reason how to modify and pursue them in the light of death. It can then throw itself back into its concerns, and run them in the satisfaction that it has deftly handled death.

But in authentic being-towards-death we must *not* have it at our disposal, so as to feel that we have contained its threat and can proceed with our ordinary aims. Authenticity feels the threat precisely in those ordinary aims; this lack of insulation of death from existing concerns may be its most distinguishing feature. Authenticity faces death in these concerns, and this lets it judge these concerns from within, and not by strategic planning about death's bearing on them. In particular, death's indefiniteness changes the way I pursue these concerns.

Death—facing it—changes my relation to my other possibilities; it forces me to treat them too *as* possibilities, rather than awaiting their actualizations (taking these to be all that matters). As authentic, I aim at my projects in the practical understanding that they are each exposed to this standing threat.[22] I see, about my ends in each case, that I *am* these ends not as outcomes achieved, but as the for-whiches of my projective effort. I am these ends *as* I exist (stand out) towards them. So what counts is how I have them, and especially whether and how I've chosen them. Death shifts my attention onto my relation to my ends, and makes salient the question whether I have made them mine. So it turns me to face issues about all of my ends that I ordinarily shirk.

This relation to death takes away my everyday satisfaction with my projects as "what one does." Death is a possibility I have from my essential structure: the possibility of my ceasing to exist. And death is "between me and myself": all that matters is my own effort, and the only help anyone else can give is by inducing or spurring that effort (as phenomenology aims to do). Death brings me back to self-reliance, in relation to my other ends as well; it "individualizes me down to myself" [cf. BT g263].

But by this very act of pulling me back from my sociality, into the context of myself, authenticity equips me to choose ends for myself. By testing my ends, in my very effort at them, against the possibility of death, by choosing them and shaping them in the midst of this test, I make them "mine" genuinely. "Becoming free for its own death in anticipation, liberates [Dasein] from its lostness in contingently pressing possibilities, so that it can for the first time understand and choose among the factical possibilities that lie before the unattainable [possibility, death]" [BT g264]. So authenticity involves, as he says in the culminating paragraph, "an impassioned ... *freedom towards death*" [g266].

The other aspect of authenticity concerns our guilt; Heidegger calls it "*resoluteness*" [Entschlossenheit]. (The term is based in the verb *entschliessen*, (to) decide or resolve on.) Heidegger defines it at BT g296–97: "*the reticent, anxiety-ready self-projection* [Sichentwerfen] *upon the ownmost being-guilty.*" So resoluteness shares with anticipation the same mode of discourse, reticence, and the same basic mood or self-finding, readiness for anxiety. But these two aspects of authenticity project themselves upon different ends; they turn, as it were, in the two essential directions of Dasein, and identify themselves by these different essential poles. Just as anticipation reaches "all the way ahead" to death, so resoluteness reaches fully back to guilt.

Guilt—what conscience calls to us—is, we've seen, a second kind of limit on our projection: its dependence on a source it can't control, can't make by its aiming effort. Ultimately it is the way projection itself is only one side to our meaning: we intend things not just by coping with them, but by feeling them. So, in particular, our projective ends are only one side to who we are. We are, just as much, how we've been made. Authenticity can't overcome this limit—achieve control over this meaning we have in our affectedness. Instead it consists in facing this limit, living in the light of it.

But just how will it change projection to hold in view its own dependence on thrownness? "In resoluteness the issue for Dasein is its ownmost ability-to-be, which, as thrown, can project itself only upon determinate factical possibilities" [BT g299]. I take the main point to be, to confront these possibilities—our concrete projects and aims—with the felt-insight how we've been thrown into caring about them. We face, thus, "the problem," and do so in the very heart of our effort at ends. But the very step back to facing the problem puts us in position to answer it: by choosing, in this anxious recognition of their ungroundedness, certain of these possibilities, we make them our own, and indeed we begin to build our own identity out of them. Only the projects I can will while my thrownness in them strikes me this way are genuinely mine, and not *das Man*'s.

By choosing projects in this stance, and by being ready to choose them so again (by being ready for anxiety), I commit myself to them. I am resolute or decided, by embracing a certain identity *as* one I have been thrown into. I of course don't eliminate this thrownness, or subsume it into my projection. But I overcome the threat it had posed to my projection, by using it to make my projection what it should be, my own rather than *das Man*'s. In this achievement guilt-authenticity involves a kind of freedom of this projective stance, just as death-authenticity did.

This freedom lies in choosing, in the moments that really grasp my thrownness, which particular projects, among the many in the social matrix I inhabit, I will commit to and identify myself by. Whereas in anticipation I choose possibilities "all the way ahead to my death," in resoluteness I choose them "back to my guilt"— i.e. in a full sense of my thrownness into them, of how they are imposed on me, not of my making. And again this gives me a criterion for choice among these options: *can* I commit myself to a given project in this spirit? When I see-feel the ungroundedness it confronts me with, can I still will it? Some projects will be unsustainable when I attempt them in this spirit.

As with authentic being-towards-death, this authentic being-guilty lets us accomplish our "mineness." "In understanding the call [of conscience], Dasein is *heedful* [hörig] *to its ownmost possibility of existence. It has chosen itself*" [BT g287].[23] I turn towards something essential to me, something altogether independent of others and *das Man*, in noticing my guilt. Pursuing my projects in a way that takes account of this makes this projection mine, just as does projecting in the light of death. But, semi-paradoxically, in guilt I find my projects by resolving upon ones I have from *das Man*.

So put, there may seem an odd weakness to Heidegger's account of authentic guilt. The answer to the burden of thrownness seems to be too little more than just to embrace one's heritage—that is, some part of this heritage, and interpreted some way. By choosing it, I change it from *das Man*'s to mine. This seems too easy an answer, which leaves it puzzling why guilt (thrownness) would have been fled in the first place. And indeed it seems all-too-many people already "embrace their heritage"—throw themselves into projects and values they pick from their group's traditions.

Heidegger's answer to this charge of banality must be to stress the special way (or circumstance) in which the commitment must be made. What's hard is fully to feel the ungroundedness of a certain inherited value, yet to choose it in all seriousness. This relation to heritage will be something quite different from the usual following of tradition, which takes the embraced practices not at all as arbitrary but as singled out by virtue and reason.

Next Heidegger brings these two "kinds" of authenticity—anticipation and resoluteness—together in Chapter 3's §62. He tries to show that they are really two aspects of a single phenomenon. They require one another; neither is really itself without the other.

Guilt-authenticity requires/entails death-authenticity for two reasons. (1) Death is one thing Dasein has been thrown into; it's a part of our guilt. We are, as it were, guilty of being mortal. My being-towards-death is a very large "brute fact" about who I am, and I can only be authentically guilty if I face this way I've been thrown. (2) Really to face *any* part of my guilt, I must face it "unto death." "[O]nly *as anticipating* does resoluteness become an originary being towards the ownmost ability-to-be of Dasein. Only when resoluteness "qualifies" itself as being-towards-death does it understand the "can" of its ability-to-be-guilty" [BT g306]. We most acutely feel who and how we are when we feel ourselves thrown towards death.

And—although Heidegger does not address this reverse implication—death-authenticity entails/requires guilt-authenticity: really to face my death, I must fully feel how I am thrown towards it, subjected to it. I must also feel how I am thrown into a social web of ideas and practices towards death, and must resolutely take up some of these in how I live with it.

So far we've mainly been looking at the ways authenticity regarding death and guilt will change how we project. But the authentic stance towards them also involves or engages the other two aspects of being-in, self-finding (feeling) and talk or *Rede*.

The authentic feeling towards death and guilt is of course anxiety. "The *Befindlichkeit* ... that can hold open the constant and utter threat to itself arising from Dasein's ownmost individualized being, is anxiety" [BT g265–66]. (Here Heidegger is speaking about authentic being-towards-death; the same point about authentic being-guilty is at g295–96.)

This raises the question just how authenticity "solves" the problem of anxiety, as one of the difficulties falling flees. The answer, as with death and guilt, is that it doesn't eliminate what we flee, but shows us indeed how to live with it. Authenticity finds a way to project and strive in anxiety, overcoming its paralyzing or enervating effect.[24] Indeed it learns not just how to cope with anxiety, but how to turn it to use, and to the all-important use of making my projects (genuinely) mine.

Anxiety over death and guilt is the mood in which I need to choose my projects, the test I need to put them to. And I need to put them to this test not just once, drawing a general lesson, but recurringly. Choosing my projects in this way I make them mine, and I keep them mine only by an abiding deference to that manner of choosing, a readiness to test what I'm doing by anxiety again. It is in this sense that authenticity is ready or prepared for anxiety, *angstbereite* [BT g297].

Our relentless drift into habit and custom—into doing things by rote or by copying—erodes every resolution. We must commit ourselves again and again, by choosing what we do out of anxiety over death and guilt. In authenticity we learn to use anxiety as an acid test for our projects: *shall* I still do this when I'm anxious over these? Can I still will and value this end—carry on in this role—when I'm feeling death's constant possibility, and my humbling guilt? It's by choosing to do so precisely then that I make a *serious* choice of the activity, and make it mine.

The authentic mode of talk (*Rede*) about guilt is "reticence" [*Verschwiegenheit*]. When conscience calls us guilty, we don't "answer back"—don't defend ourselves. Conscience calls Dasein "as [something] to become still, back into the stillness of itself. ... [Reticence] takes words away from the common-sense chat of *das Man*" [BT g296]. And I think Heidegger would make a similar point about death (though he doesn't): here too our authentic response is made "prior" to any way it can be put into words or communicated. Death and guilt are meant by us more deeply than all our social and linguistic meanings, and we can and must address them at this level, without the intercession of those social meanings.[25]

We've seen that *Rede* is closely related to *das Man* and falling, which together were the third problem authenticity is meant to address. How does it do so? Again, not by eliminating it—our *das Man*hood is built into our language and our social being. Even the authentic Dasein still means most words in senses that defer to the common use. We are constantly subtly copying our micro-aims and -actions from those around us.

My world is a vast web of ends aimed at by all the very complex projects, dispositions, abilities I have been socialized and habituated into. How can I hope to make more than tiny parts of this my own? To an extent these ends are organized hierarchically, and authentic choice will obviously try to deal with the highest or most

ultimate ends. I try especially, in anxiety, to test and approve such
principal ends. But this will not suddenly realign all my particular
ends, since I generally have these not in the explicitness of attention and "from above," but "in the background" and by a gradual
accretion of imitative habits.

So inevitably the authentic Dasein will be only partially distinct
from *das Man*—will stand only in some places out of the average
understanding, through its individualizing choice. A tremendous
amount of work of "mining" what I do must be carried out
piecemeal, and there is always more of this to do—another reason
that this anxious choosing needs to go on and on.

Now in all of this I have been presenting authenticity as the way
of living Heidegger commends to us, offers to us to try to be. In
this sense at least, I think it's clear that *Being and Time* offers
authenticity as a "value," indeed as the highest or ultimate value.
And I think nearly all of his readers take the idea so—despite
Heidegger's own insistence that he is not making value judgments
in any part of his existential analysis.

He denies not just that authenticity is a value (or his value), but
also that being authentic is a way of valuing. For he wants to stress
its difference in kind from all the valuing we do within our projects.
Here too he prefers to mark the step to the transcendental level by
a change in term. We've already seen this with "intentionality": he
denies that our relation to being or world, the precondition for our
intending things, is itself intentional. Similarly, all the valuing we
do within our projects depends on a second-order commitment to
these projects—on our caring to push these projects ahead.
Authenticity is a privileged way of making (or sustaining) this
commitment to particular projects: it is choosing them in that
special circumstance and way.

Because Heidegger wants to change us at the "transcendental"
level, and not by specifying a different aim for our projects, he
denies that he is offering us a value. Authenticity is a different
relation to all our projects and values, and need not give us *different*

such projects. Nevertheless I think becoming authentic is still itself a meta-project, to which Heidegger wants us to attend more deeply or decisively than we do to our first-order projects: we're to judge and practice the latter by reference to it. And as the aim of this meta-project, authenticity is indeed a second-order value, which has indirect authority over other values, via that acid test of anxiety.

So I suggest that Heidegger *does* propose authenticity as a value. And he has two main ways of defending or justifying this value to us, as we've already started to see.

The first is epistemic: authenticity is the condition of facing the deep structure of my projection, which we ordinarily avoid and flee. Heidegger stresses that resoluteness brings us "into the truth." "In resoluteness we now come to the truth of Dasein which is most originary because it is *authentic*" [BT g297]. And "resoluteness is what first gives authentic transparency to Dasein" [g299]. Since we readers have taken on the project of phenomenology, we can be presumed to value the truth about ourselves. And we'll see that this transparency of authenticity, the truth we have in it about ourselves, will be crucial for the way Heidegger goes on in the book's third "wave," which we'll turn to in Chapter 6. I'll return to authenticity's epistemic role there.

Heidegger's second justification is functional: authenticity is the proper working of Dasein's essential structure.[26] In particular, it is the fulfillment or adequate achievement of the "mineness" that lies at my crux, in the way I "go about" my own being [BT g 42]. Instead of death and guilt scaring me into losing myself in *das Man*, they get turned into tools to "mine" (make mine) some of the possibilities I find myself after. In authenticity I become a self. "Selfhood is only read off existentially in the authentic ability-to-be-self, i.e. in the authenticity of Dasein's being *as care*" [g322].[27]

We achieve this mineness by exercising that second-order capacity we all have as Dasein: the capacity to choose our ends in the light of our death and guilt. I think this is what Heidegger means by his frequent expression "ownmost ability-to-be" [*eigenstes Seinkönnen*]. It is the ability to be authentic, though most often we fail to exercise this ability, and fall into *das Man* and inauthenticity.

Heidegger's reliance on such a functional justification for authenticity—his effort to establish it by analysis of our structure—is a large-scale feature of *Being and Time*. But he does not address questions we may have as to why Dasein has this basic structure. On a Christian view we are of course products of God's design, and if virtue lies in facing death and guilt, that is presumably why they are there in us. In Heidegger's detheologized analysis it's not clear whether death and guilt, as structural limits that yet enable us to become selves, are fortunate accidents, or somehow there in order to play this role.

The absence of an argument here is a threat to this way of justifying authenticity. For if this existential structure—projection, self-finding, talk, death, guilt, and the rest—is *not* a product of design, the implication that authenticity fulfills or accomplishes the *proper* working of this structure needs other explanation. Authenticity is not how the structure *most often* works, so Heidegger needs an explanation why it is how the structure *should* work. What sets the system that goal?

There's a second problem with this ideal of authenticity, concerning not its justification but its content. It may well seem too self-centered an ideal. In authenticity I accomplish mineness, I become a full-fledged self—the focus is on "me" in multiple ways. My fundamental project is the utterly private one of facing my own death and guilt and choosing myself through them. I individualize myself by separating off from the group-being of *das Man*, and this is the main way others come up in the story—as those with whom I "chat" and share in *das Man*. Heidegger pays little attention to more satisfying relations to others, not to love or friendship, for example.

Besides worrying that this ideal is too isolating, we might complain that it offers no ethics—no rules or guidance for how to treat others. Couldn't one be authentic, and yet any kind of terror to others, simply by choosing that terrible behavior in the light of one's death and guilt? Doesn't this follow from the second-order status of authenticity? Or does Heidegger think there is any way that authenticity will bring us to care about others?

Heidegger makes only infrequent mention of how authenticity will affect my relations to others.[28] The principal suggestion is that it enables me to care that others be authentic as well—this being their genuine good:

> Resoluteness to itself first brings Dasein into the possibility of letting the others with it "be" in their ownmost ability-to-be, and to co-disclose this [ability] in the solicitude that leaps forth and liberates. The resolute Dasein can become the "conscience" of others. From the authentic being-oneself of resoluteness there first arises the authentic with-one-another.
>
> [BT g298]

My authenticity reveals my essential task of achieving mineness by facing death and guilt. This self-understanding allows me to see that others likewise are defined by this task, and not by the concrete roles with which I mostly identify them. Understanding them as Dasein, my concern towards them shifts to this essential aspect.[29]

This argument's main thrust is towards caring about others' authenticity in preference to their contingent ends; when we see what's essential to them, we'll see that authenticity is what most matters. But there's the more basic question why we should care about others at all. Heidegger's general idea seems to be that I should care about others appropriately to the kind of entities they are: they are not to-hand equipment, but Dasein, and hence end-projectors themselves.[30] I should not just view but treat others as having ends, and this involves somehow—in a way and for reasons Heidegger doesn't say—caring about those ends myself.

But above all, as the above quotation shows, when I'm authentic I care especially about others' essential end, which is to become authentic themselves. So I become their "conscience," i.e. some kind of impetus or inducement to face the basic choice of themselves, in awareness of death and guilt. Heidegger's stress on this angle of concern towards others, and his inattention to any interest in their physical well-being, may not give us enough of what we think an ethics should.

Still, although Heidegger seldom mentions authenticity's aim to help others to authenticity, much less motivates or justifies it, I think the idea plays a hidden but framing role in *Being and Time*. The book itself is Heidegger's effort to "become the conscience" of his readers: to remind us of our death and guilt, and spur us to the personal effort over them that would make us authentic. His phenomenology, as a communication, has the purpose of bringing others to authenticity, since only here do they genuinely understand themselves as Dasein.

Authenticity is the end of the story told in Heidegger's "existentialism." It's the appropriate accomplishment of the "mineness" that lies at the root of us—the way our intentionality is crucially reflexive (we are an issue for ourselves). In authenticity we accomplish that reflexivity, by grasping, feeling, and wording in relation to our own, essential selves, the selves with the transcendental ability to choose projects not as *das Man*, but in the individuating experience of anxiety over death and guilt.

The comparison with Nietzsche may be helpful. He too puts great weight on a *choice* of one's projects (or values), but specifies very differently the circumstances in which this choice must be made to be validating. For Nietzsche I think it is *genealogy*, and the insight this gives into the drives that designed these values. Unless we understand what these values were designed for, we can't judge their suitability for us. By this genealogical truth about how our values were made, we get the kind of control over them that counts; we win a Nietzschean freedom. So Nietzsche's focus is on empirical insights about the psychological and historical roots of our moral values.[31]

Heidegger gives no such role to genealogy. The right way to choose is not with any such empirical insight, but out of an anxious engagement with death and guilt. We touch, as it were, the essential in us, and that gives our choice the power to render the projects we choose our own. We needn't, it seems, know anything in particular about those projects. To be sure, when we judge whether we can live a project "unto death and guilt" we will notice any laziness or banality in the project, as what can't be so lived. But this recognition comes in the intuitions we've seen Heidegger so stresses—not the naturalistic study I think Nietzsche favors.

This point of contact with Nietzsche—the idea that we need to choose a certain way if we're to become ourselves—is the crux to the "existential" strand I've been unfolding from *Being and Time*. We've seen that Heidegger himself has special uses for the term "existence," such that "existential" means something different in that book. And he will later deny that *Being and Time* intended an existentialism. As I will try to show, however, he well knew the book's affinities with the existential point in Nietzsche—and later turned deliberately against them. He recognized the affinity between authenticity and that Nietzschean freedom, and will give them the same diagnosis/critique: they express the controlling and "framing" will that Heidegger associates with technology. But this is work for a later chapter.

Summary

The second level of structure emerges as we pay attention to what our intentionality shows itself trying to hide. We find here *Being and Time*'s existential story: an abstract human drama that is in its main lines Kierkegaardian, though Heidegger gives it canonical statement. Beneath our pragmatic directedness we pursue a more essential project, for each of us the same. We are tasked with the need to realize and achieve our particular "mineness," to become our own self, no longer submerged in the collective *das Man*.

The drama arises because this task is so difficult that we avoid it—and this is the beginning of that existential story. Study shows that our everydayness is characterized by "falling," in particular into *das Man*. Heidegger introduces these ideas with clear valuative force, yet while insisting he's not making any moral judgments, only analyzing our structure. What's essential to us is the need to mean things from the practice, "as one means" the words we use. We go wrong in letting this aspect overwhelm the ways we mean in our aiming and feeling. We have a motive to go wrong this way: it's a tactic for fleeing or avoiding a distressing condition we're prone to.

Phenomenology next diagnoses this condition that falling flees: anxiety. Unlike fear, which concerns threats internal to our particular projects, anxiety is a disengagement from all such projects, an alienation that wishes it could care about them. It is a "global breakdown" in which these projects are "lit up," as well as their contingency: we are not compelled to them, but either choose them or fall into them. And this is what anxiety is anxious about: facing this need to choose its projects, and to choose them in the way that makes them our own and not *das Man*'s. And this is hard, because this choice must be "in the face of" certain deep problems in our structure.

This brings us to the root of the problem: we achieve mineness only by choosing our projects "in the light of" these structural limits. There are no aims that are settled already as ours, nor picked out by reason for us. Instead it all hangs on how we engage in our projects: whether we pursue them "unto death," and in the guilt of our thrownness. These existential limits are touchstones that test our aims. Can I will it while feelingly aware of death as certain but indefinite? Can I will it while also aware how I've been thrown into it?

Authenticity, the happy ending of the existential drama, is available to any of us. It lies in anticipation (properly facing death) plus resoluteness (properly facing guilt)—though really these are not independent but require one another. In anticipating death I recognize it as possibility, and this changes my relation to my aims or goals—I pursue them as possibilities too, rather than awaiting them as future actualities. And in resoluteness over guilt I choose my heritage while recognizing its contingency—the impossibility of making or justifying myself "from the ground up." Heidegger promotes authenticity to us on both epistemic and functional grounds: we best understand ourselves in it, and we also realize our essence by achieving the mineness at our crux.

Further reading

The existential ideas of BT can be profitably explored back to Kierkegaard (e.g. in *The Sickness unto Death*) and ahead to Sartre (especially in *Being and Nothingness*).

Six

Being and Time
Time and being

There is a third main wave of argument in *Being and Time*, which the disclosure of and by authenticity is supposed to make possible. The transition from the existential to this new theme happens in the middle of Division II's Chapter 3. Authenticity shows Dasein in its wholeness (§62), and this enables us to see (§65) the *temporal* structure of Dasein. This temporality is a deeper structure of our intentionality, Heidegger claims; indeed it may even be our deepest. He goes on, in the remaining chapters of Division II, to restate the preceding pragmatic and existential analyses in the temporal terms that are supposed to unify and justify them.

The first task of this chapter is to present this temporality, and Heidegger's effort to show all the intentional structures analyzed before as "modes" of our temporality. Once again the move to this deeper level of our intending requires a change in the way we understand it. It reorients us in our epistemic aim or why, and hence also in our method or how. Given that and how our deep structure is temporal, we need to expect and pursue still a different kind of truth about it.

The book ends with this account of temporality, but it wasn't supposed to end there. Heidegger previews in the Introduction where Division III, as well as an entire Part II, were meant to go. I will talk about these phantom parts of *Being and Time* in this chapter too. They continue the arc of the account of temporality: once we see Dasein's temporality, we see the way in which time is "the horizon for all understanding of being" [BT g17], and this will let us "answer" [g19] the book's opening question of the meaning of being. So Dasein's temporality gives the finally adequate jumping-off point for the book's goal, being. It lets us pass from our treatment of this entity (Dasein), to treating being itself.

Although we can't be at all sure how Heidegger meant this missing argument—from temporality to time to being—to run, I think speculations are worthwhile. We must remember that it is the question about being, and not the existential analysis of persons, that is really most important to him. And it will always remain most important, even though he will eventually doubt whether "being" is the best word for what he means. He never again gives such an analysis of our "Dasein." So to think about how *Being and Time* is related to the later works we will need to ask what it meant to say about being.

But it's not just that the upshot of *Being and Time* is that from which Heidegger turns, it is also a start on that turning. He later says that Division III was already going to "reverse" the book's beginning, and so begin the turning [see LH (P 249–50)]. Inevitably it was going to open up some difference between Dasein and being, some way the foregoing analysis of Dasein still left out something crucial. Heidegger always meant to make a large and surprising step from Dasein to being; this step simply came to seem more and more important and difficult. So we can begin to see elements of his later viewpoint, in the indications we have about the conclusion *Being and Time* was headed towards.

Indeed Heidegger was irritated, later, by the association of the book with existentialism: putting the focus on Dasein leaves the view too self-obsessed. Deeper than the relation to self is (or was going to be) the relation to being. So more vital than authenticity is getting that latter relation right—and so being in the truth of disclosure. We saw that both the pragmatic and existential movements of the book had their respective values. Revealing that temporal structure beneath them both shows deeper values, and finally the ultimate value of an adequate opening onto being.

The missing treatment of being was to come in Division III and was to be followed by a Part II which would amount—surprisingly because seemingly anticlimactically—to an historical second half to the book, with a matching three Divisions treating in turn Kant's schematism, Descartes' cogito, and Aristotle on time. The rationale for this historical turn comes from our temporality, inasmuch as this includes our "historicality." The latter is (roughly) our dependence on a shared tradition, which tends to "master" us by concealing its own role from us. But we, who are now studying being, time, and Dasein, are ourselves historical, and this study comes out of such a tradition. So to confirm (and study and transmit) the grasp of being we have reached, we need to clarify and disarm this tradition: "this hardened tradition must be loosened up, and the concealments it has brought about must be dissolved" [BT g22]. We thereby come back to the ur-experiences that preceded all these traditional accretions (see again g22). So Part II will carry out a "destruction" (which many read to mean "deconstruction") of the history of ontology, by analyses of Kant, Descartes, and Aristotle. Heidegger's later stress on historical philosophy stems from this last part of *Being and Time*'s plan.

1. Temporality

Once the existential movement has given us "the whole" of Dasein, in the peculiar sense we've seen, we can recognize (Heidegger claims) a deeper temporal structure that shows or explains this unity, and pulls together all the separate aspects of Dasein analyzed so far. So, as we did in noticing the existential beneath the pragmatic, here again we "step down" to a new level of our intentionality. Indeed Heidegger says that with temporality we arrive at the bottom level of all.[1] His development of this idea is another of the most appealing and influential parts of the book.[2]

In what sense is temporality supposed to be "deeper" than the structures uncovered before? Chiefly by being a "condition of the possibility" of those structures. Temporality "makes possible [ermöglicht] the totality of the articulated structural whole of care" [BT g324]. But, very importantly, Heidegger understands this condition as itself "there for" our intentionality—already given to it, though in the implicit and "background" way we've been stressing. When we see it we will recognize it as something we have meant—or as the way we have meant—all along. And this experience of insight will also confirm temporality's depth: how it underlies and unifies the pragmatic and existential meanings.

Temporality is, therefore, an attribute of intentionality (Dasein), and not of an objective or independent time. We might say that it is "the way we are in time"—though this too can be misheard, as making temporality a relation between us and an independent time. Temporality isn't an objective or external (even relational) fact about that intentionality, for example that it takes place in time, or the way it takes place in time. Instead temporality is something internal to intentionality, something that is, *as* it is given in intentionality—even though it is usually not explicitly or adequately so given.[3] (The same point will hold about "historicality": this isn't an external or objective fact about us, either, but rather something "inner" to intentionality.)

Temporality underlies and explains the pragmatic and existential structures, and their relation. It shows how the pragmatic analysis of our intentionality into projection, self-finding, and talk can be clarified by being restated in temporal terms. But it also gives a temporal sense for the existential drama that we've seen Heidegger writes across that analysis. Falling as flight from death and guilt, and authenticity as facing them, have temporal meanings as well, which show us better what these basic stances are.

There is also—we'll gradually see—a very special relation between authenticity, in particular, and temporality. *Being and Time* arrives at temporality only by way of authenticity: it's only by understanding authenticity that we phenomenologists can then see temporality. And authenticity needs to be understood, we've noted, "from within," i.e. in the stance of authenticity itself. So our temporal structure is revealed *when we're authentic*, because it's only then that we "stand out" into the temporal ecstases explicitly. Authenticity brings us into the special kind of understanding our temporality requires.

So Heidegger retells the pragmatic and the existential stories in temporal terms. Let me put it first very schematically (and crudely). The three parts of the pragmatic analysis are correlated with future, past, and present, respectively; and the existential drama of everyday falling is explained as a flight into the present away from our future and past. This temporal retelling thus unifies those earlier themes: the structure of pragmatic concern, and the root of our existential task. Our intentionality has this internal temporal structure, stretching out into these three temporal "ecstases." Yet it is hard for us to bear this temporal division, so that we tend to narrow in, in various ways, on the present. Authenticity turns out to be a way of holding our temporal stretch open to our (full) selves.

Temporality, then, occurs in two modes, authentic and falling. Heidegger stresses that the former has priority, and his first presentation of temporality, in §65, begins with it and presents falling temporality as a variation from it. This order reverses Division I's procedure of beginning with everydayness and treating authenticity as a special "modification" of it [BT g130]. But since then we have seen that authenticity is primary, in two respects—the two ways Heidegger implicitly supports the value of authenticity.

First is an epistemic priority: authenticity is the stance in which our intentionality is transparent—in which it "turns to face" the deep structures it ordinarily avoids. It faces especially our temporal structure. The phenomenologist must become authentic, and describe temporality from this personal stance. And so too for his readers: only as authentic is the "how" of our temporality evident to us; only so do we "see" ourselves stretched out in time's dimensions.

Authenticity also has a functional priority, and this holds for authentic temporality too: temporality is "most fully itself" when it occurs in its authentic mode. It is, in general, the ways we are "towards" future, past, and present—the ways we mean things along these three vectors. Yet it's only in the authentic mode of temporality that we are adequately "out" in these three ways. Falling temporality, though its commonest form, needs to be understood as a failure at this authentic mode, and as merely partial by contrast with authenticity's whole.

So it's when I'm authentic that I best notice my temporality, and also then that my temporality is most itself. Obviously these points are connected: I best notice it because it is now most itself, and vice versa. In authenticity I stretch explicitly to lengths I have tried before, but shied back from—hence the sense of recognition, as of something already there, but submerged. So authentic temporality is "originary" [*ursprünglich*], in that it is what I understand first how to do, but pull back from. By contrast Heidegger argues that "the 'time' which is accessible to Dasein's common understanding is not originary, but arises rather from authentic temporality" [BT g329].[4]

Let's begin now to add some detail to this temporal analysis. We've seen that it reinterprets understanding, self-finding, and talking (or falling) as rooted in our temporal directedness into future, past, and present, respectively. Heidegger has obviously been angling towards this alignment from early on. He prepares for it in Division I when he links understanding with projection and self-finding with thrownness—terms with obvious forward and backward references. And now he takes these temporal roots to show at last the unity of the care-structure. "Temporality makes possible the unity of existence, facticity, and falling, and in this way constitutes originarily the totality of the structure of care" [BT g328].[5]

What's at issue here are not future, past, and present "themselves," we've seen, but our intentional stances towards them. Heidegger calls these three stances the temporal "*ecstases*" [*Ekstasen*]. He means "ecstasis" in the original sense of "standing out": we stand outward into future, past, and present [cf. BT g329]. We stand out towards them intentionally, and they are *as* they are "objects" of this intending.

So the future, past, and present are not sectors on a time-line along which I move. "'Future' here does not mean a now which, *not yet* become 'actual', sometime *will be* for the first time" [BT g325]. And later: "The future is *not later* than having been, and [having been] is *not earlier* than the present" [g350]. Rather than segments of a single time-line, we should think of the three ecstases as three separate dimensions of our experience, three quite different axes along which we "reach out" in time, each in a distinctive way. The ecstases are, as it were, movements in these different dimensions, movements that accomplish meaning. They are much more diverse than the model of the time-line implies.

These ecstases are also not separate intentional acts such as planning, remembering, and conversing. Rather, each is an aspect or element in every intentional act, but often "in the background." Temporality "in each case temporalizes itself in [the ecstases] as equally originary" [BT g329]. We are always stretched out in all three dimensions, and can mean and intend things only so. Even in planning, for example, which might seem thoroughly future-oriented, we are also necessarily feeling this planning some particular way, and are planning in the midst of some immediate situation; so what I mean, as I plan, draws in past and present too.

Thus these ecstases are the grounding ways in which we intend or mean entities. And of course along with this intending of entities, we always also, as *jemeinig*, are towards (mean) ourselves. So each of the ecstases involves a relation by myself to myself. When I "stand out" from myself in an ecstasis, I also stand out *towards* myself: I discover or identify myself "out there," along each of these temporal axes.

We've seen that the authentic mode of temporality is primary. And for authentic temporality it's in turn the future ecstasis that comes first: "the future has a priority in the ecstatical unity of originary and authentic temporality" [BT g329]. It's primary inasmuch as a certain projection towards the future directs the other two ecstases: they are steered and motivated by it. Authenticity involves "the unity of a future as having-been making present" [g326].[6] (By contrast falling, we've noted and will see, gives priority to the present.) So let's begin with the "authentic future."

Heidegger's introduction of the authentic future may sound opaque: "This letting-come-towards [Zukommen-lassen] in itself of itself, which sustains that distinctive possibility [of death], is the originary phenomenon of the *future* [Zu-kunft]" [BT g325]. He takes the German word for the future in its root sense of coming-towards, and hears it as the way we "come towards" ourselves in projecting, inasmuch as we identify ourselves with the ends towards which we stretch: they are the who we're becoming.

Quite in general, I come towards myself in my ever-ongoing effort to "become who I am." So this ecstasis is towards "the future" in a teleological rather than a chronological sense.[7] The future is myself-in-aspiration, the who I'm trying to be. Some of this being I aspire to may be (by the clock) concurrent with my aspiring: I can do x with the aim of being the person who does it. And it's only by virtue of this projective identification with my ends that I can then have a chronological future to be plotted and planned.

But the originary future is an *authentic* coming-towards myself, in which I intend myself in my ownmost possibility—my death—and hence as I am really and "as a whole." I "intend" this possibility not of course by trying to die, but by choosing my projects in the face of death, thus making them mine. Thus this authentic future is "the coming [Kunft] in which Dasein, in its ownmost ability-to-be, comes towards itself [*auf sich zukommt*]" [g325]. It is the movement in which I really do come to myself in this futural, projective way: I am "ahead towards" this mortal self I essentially am.

As authentic I stretch "all the way out" to my death, which is the utmost limit of my futural temporality (despite my ability to imagine things happening after I die). But since this death "can come at any moment," including now, it doesn't lie at any chronological distance ahead. Indeed I am "furthest out" into my future when I take this possibility of death to lie (in another sense) "closest" to me—to bear on my most immediate projects. As thus indefinitely bounded by death, the authentic and originary future is *finite*, and the infinite time within our everyday or scientific view is derivative from it [BT g330–31].

As we began to see in Chapter 5 of this book, this authentic relation to the possibility of death transforms my relation to all of my other possibilities as well—it changes my whole arc to the future. I now choose and pursue my other possibilities in the light of death. I test all my particular projects by my ability to will them in the anxious regard for death. And as I live them in this spirit, I cease to await my projects' ends as actualities. I live them in my effort, made in the light of death.

Turning now to the past ecstasis, we see that this too is not a relation to a sector on a time-line, but another dimension in which we are "towards" ourselves—and from which we give meaning to things. Again it is not itself what we would ordinarily call temporal (or chronological). It is the way we identify ourselves not with our project-goals, but in our feelings—we are *as* we're feeling. That is, we are as we "find" ourselves already to be, thrown into being. I experience this other identity as settled outside and before my projection: in it I'm a who I can't help but be.

So the past—the originary past—is this way I find myself already being, or being in/as having been. Emotions make explicit this other vector in which I mean myself, and from which I give meaning to things. In them I notice myself thrown from a past in the principal sense that it "precedes" my projection in being independent of it. And my guilt is precisely that way an aspect of myself is immune to projection; it is my "inability to get behind my thrownness," to ground this aspect in my projective stance. I experience guilt as this limit on projection—a limit due to this other aspect of myself, in which I'm not my aspirations but a thing I find myself made to be.

Again we must focus on the authentic mode of this ecstasis, in which it both knows and achieves itself. Here I "take over" my guilt, my thrownness. "But taking over thrownness signifies authentically *being* Dasein *as it already was*" [BT g325]. As the authentic future faces and copes with death, so the authentic past does with guilt. It stretches "all the way back" to guilt, faces it by feeling it, and learns the way to live with it. It does so by choosing its projects *as* ones it has been thrown into.

When I anxiously feel myself thrown into one of my projects, I see it as *not* the product of my will. I'm turned back from my projective immersion in it, back from identifying with it in my easy and ordinary way. Authenticity embraces this alienated stance, as that from which I can make that project more genuinely and fully my own, by choosing it out of this felt thrownness. I make it indeed my own, in the only way it can really be my own, by my anxious, resolute choice. Pursuing it so, I mean it *from* my full stretch back to my guilt.

So I test my projects: which can I embrace from that anxious distance? Which projects *can* be done authentically will often be those that *have* been done authentically. So I will look for the ways I've been "thrown from" authentic choices already made by myself or others. This explains, I suggest, Heidegger's own use of history: he tries to find the points of authentic vision in his predecessors—to reawaken insights embedded in their basic concepts. Authentic Dasein tries to "repeat" authentic doings. This may involve choosing a "hero," and taking on "the struggle of loyally following in what can be repeated" [BT g385]. By reviving words and practices issuing from authentic sources, I can face my thrownness and find my authentic self in it.

We turn finally to the present ecstasis. Once again this principally names a dimension which is not itself what we would usually call temporal. Heidegger identifies it with the third dimension of our being-in, which is now most definitely falling rather than talk or *Rede*: "the third constitutive item in the structure of care—namely *falling*—has its existential meaning in the *present* [*Gegenwart*]" [BT g346]. By now Heidegger's notion of falling stresses a certain relation to things (entities within-the-world) rather than to *das Man* and language, a transition we noted began in the "existential part" of the book.

I think the dimension of the present is simply our *immediate* relation to things "beside" us—a relation that goes directly out to them, and not by way of either projection or feeling. So it is, perhaps, defined by contrast with the other two ecstases. In meaning things, we understand them in our projective projects, and are thrown into feeling them by our moods. But we also, distinctly from both of these, "are there" directly beside them. One of Heidegger's terms for this proximacy is *Sein-bei*, being-beside; he uses this "beside" [*bei*][8] to denote the present ecstasis, as complement to the "towards" [*zu*] of the projective future, and the "upon" [*auf*] of the thrown past [BT g328–29]. The idea, developed, will play a crucial role in his later thinking, in the notion of "presence" [*Anwesenheit*]; there the development of this relation to things is singled out as the hidden "destiny" and point of Western history.

Like the other two ecstases this "making present" [*Gegenwärtigen*] involves mineness: in standing out towards immediate things I find myself through them—I identify myself by and in these direct relations. Apart from what I'm trying to do/be, and how I find myself feeling, I am also "in" my immediate perceptions and activities. I am this very seeing and handling.

But what makes this temporal ecstasis the basis of falling? Heidegger claims we have a natural or usual tendency to absorb ourselves in this ecstasis in attempted exclusion of the others. We try to "lose ourselves" in immediate experiences—to lose precisely those other selves that lie in our aiming and feeling. So we "fall" into a kind of isolation within this immediacy, cut off—at least in intent—from projection and thrownness. And we have this deep tendency to shrink or collapse those other ecstases, because they reach out towards death and guilt.[9]

Heidegger develops this falling ecstasis towards the present by returning (at BT g346–48) to the phenomenon of curiosity. Curiosity is a "making present that gets entangled in itself" [g346]. It "craves the new" in order to make it immediate, but once it has done so it craves something else. It pursues a succession of absorbing immediacies, fresh experiences of novelties. So it degrades the futural relation to possibilities: "Curiosity is ... inauthentically futural and ... is not awaiting a *possibility*, but desires this as something already actual"; it also contracts the reach from the past in the way it "forgets" [g347].

The present ecstasis is the root of falling, but it can also be meant (or experienced) authentically. We do so by integrating it with the other ecstases, resisting that momentum towards pure immediacy. "In resoluteness, the present is not only brought back from distraction in the nearest concerns, but it gets held in the future and in having been" [BT g338]. It experiences entities "in the situation," i.e. in a context not isolated from future and past, but set by them—and especially with respect to the ultimate termini of those dimensions, death and guilt. The situation is fixed by those self-constituting choices I make in my anxious relation to my death and guilt. I "dwell" in the situation of these choices, by contrast with falling's distracted "never-dwelling-anywhere" [g347].

In experiencing entities "in situation," one experiences the "moment" [*Augenblick*], the authentic present.[10] "When resolute, Dasein has brought itself back out of falling, so as to be more authentically 'there' in the 'moment' of the disclosed situation"

[BT g328]. In this moment I am "here now" in the fullest and most explicit way possible, by seeing and doing in the light of my essential situation, projecting at possibilities chosen in the face of death and guilt.

Authenticity not only involves modes of each of the ecstases, but an overall way they are related and organized. It puts these ecstases in a certain directive or motivational order: "Coming back to itself futurally, resoluteness brings itself into the situation by making present. The having-been arises from the future, such that the future, having been … , releases out of itself the present" [BT g326]. So direction runs from future to past to present: I choose myself in my projects, unto death, which lets me choose also some of the practices I've been thrown into, and so brings me into my situation.

The temporal analysis gives an opposite account of inauthenticity. This gives priority to the present: it tries to dwell in the present, to absorb itself there, so contracting its temporal stretch. This unifies the different aspects and routes of falling; it explains their common logic. The aim to "make present" shows up both in our practical aim to place everything in maximal order, and in our theoretical aim to explain it as at-hand, to locate it in our objective scientific system. In both cases we bring the thing maximally near, make it maximally present or available to us. We'll see in the following chapters how this analysis survives, in altered (historicized) form, into Heidegger's later writings.

Besides that temporal analysis of falling, Heidegger gives one of everydayness. In everydayness Dasein "lives unto the day" [in den Tag hineinlebt], in the sense of letting the customary circle of the day's activities absorb it [BT g370]. It expects that the future will repeat that past: "Tomorrow, which everyday concern keeps awaiting, is the 'eternal yesterday'" [g371]. "The usual [Einerlei], the accustomed, the 'as yesterday, so today and tomorrow', the 'mostly' are not to be grasped without recourse to the 'temporal' stretch of Dasein" [g371]. What we see here, then, is another strategy for contracting our temporal stretch: by narrowing in on each day in its usualness, we look away from our thrownness and death.

The falling mode of the past ecstasis is a contraction of it in favor of the present. It pulls back from guilt, and towards immediacy, so that it's essentially a "*forgetting*": "The ecstasis (rapture) of forgetting has the character of backing away *before* one's ownmost having-been" [BT g339]. This of course is not a matter of failing to remember particular acts or events "in the past," but of disowning the meaning that comes from the past, how it helps constitute the meaning of things, and especially the meaning of me, who I am. "What we are, in which lies always what we have been, lies in some way behind us, *forgotten*. ... This forgetting is not the failure and absence of a recollection ... absence and failure to appear of a recollection. ... Understanding oneself by way of feasible and closely encountered things involves a *self*-forgetting" [BP 290]. This is a "deficient mode" of self-finding, in its temporal character.

This falling contraction of the past ecstasis does not eliminate moods, but gives them a certain skew. Heidegger takes *fear* as an example; he treats it as a falling analogue to anxiety. Of course fear involves an expectation about the future (some threat), but what makes it a mood or affect is the way this expected ill "comes back" to me by my feeling it. However, in fear I feel the threat in a way that doesn't bring it back to my authentic me that faces death and guilt. Instead, in fear I'm effectively stunned by the danger, losing hold of the situation as shaped from the standpoint that faces those limits—just as "the inhabitants of a burning house will often 'save' the most indifferent things that are nearest to-hand" [BT g342]. I "forget myself" in fear by failing to feel the danger in relation to the me making resolute choices.

Similarly, in the inauthentic mode of the future I direct and orient myself towards ends without choosing or willing them "in the face of" my death; I don't commit to them in that ultimate way. Indeed I even pursue them as a tactic to *avoid* "going out" as far as death. I stop short and content myself with goals belonging to "what one does," whose great appeal is that they let me avoid that anxious choice. So again there's a temporal contraction. Falling looks just as far ahead by the calendar, but not in the essential teleological dimension, the deep aiming of its projective effort. As I fall my projection is purposefully incomplete: it reaches ahead only partway, and not to the standpoint where I—my genuine I—would choose. This contraction shows up especially in the effort, so common in falling, to "live in the present." It also shows up in the conviction noticed before, that our ends are only real once they're present and actual.

Heidegger thinks it is this everyday and falling mode of temporality that underlies our "ordinary [*vulgäre*] conception of time," in which we view it as a series of "nows." "The ordinary characterization of time as an endless, passing, irreversible sequence of nows arises from the temporality of falling Dasein" [BT g426]. Heidegger spends the book's last (finished) chapter developing how this "now-time" arises by a "levelling off" and "covering up" of our originary temporality.[11] It converts that temporality into something merely at-hand, as we see in the way its nows have been stripped of the meanings that care gives them. The chief motive, again, is flight before death: "The inauthentic temporality of falling-everyday Dasein must, as such a looking-away from finitude, fail to recognize authentic futurity and therewith temporality in general" [g424].

The account of the authentic ecstases as giving (or being in) the truth about temporality revises yet again our conception of how we "grasp the truth." Once again this consists not in "looking at" the truth about this structure, but in "awakening" our experience in it—in this case within our temporal ecstases. I only really understand my temporal stretch by being explicitly so stretched out myself. And Heidegger thinks the ecstases are explicit only when I stretch "all the way out" in them. So I only understand how I'm futural when I reach ahead to death as my ultimate possibility. And I only understand how I'm retral when I reach similarly back to my guilt in my limiting thrownness. Even the present's true meaning requires that I reach fully out into what's immediate, by being fully "here now" in the situation set by my authentic choice.

Although these three ecstases run along different axes, still Heidegger claims that once we see them in their authentic modes, we also see their complementarity, in a way that pulls together the complex structure of Dasein (as falling thrown projection) into a strong unity. This distinctive temporal *way* of understanding suggests how this temporal point is more than just a unifying restatement of the pragmatic and existential ideas—is indeed a kind of level of its own.

This authentic temporality plays another crucial role in *Being and Time*. Not only do the authentic forms of the ecstases give us our best grasp of our own structure as Dasein, they also bring us in reach of the "meaning of being" that is the book's overall objective. But to get there we must pass through historicality.

2. Historicality

Temporality leads Heidegger to historicality, and Chapter 5 of Division II is dedicated to this important idea. Although the topic arises naturally this way, it comes to intrude into the existential analysis with a disruptive force. It underwrites the historical analyses that were to occupy *Being and Time*'s planned Part II. But it also suggests defects in the non-historical analysis that the existing part of the book carries out. Heidegger will draw this lesson fully in his later writings, which will promote history much nearer the front of his thought.

As usual Heidegger justifies his new topic (near the start of Chapter 5) as filling a lacuna in the analysis so far, a way it has still not brought the "whole" of Dasein into view. For although we have looked "all the way ahead" to Dasein's death, we have not treated its relation to its beginning, its "birth" [*Geburt*]. "Not only has being towards the beginning remained unnoticed, but also, above

all, the *stretch* of Dasein *between* birth and death" [BT g373]. The
account of historicality is supposed to clarify the "connectedness"
of Dasein from its birth to its death.

As with earlier such pleas to "wholeness," it may seem that this
effort to get at "birth" is a red herring. Heidegger doesn't return
to explain what he means by the term—as he should since he
clearly does *not* mean the event of biological birth. Nor does
he explain how historicality bears on it. Moreover, he has already
paid significant attention to this "view back," despite his bizarre
claim to have ignored it ("Dasein has been the theme only as
it exists 'facing forward', as it were, and leaves all that has been
'behind it'" [BT g373]). For the analysis of thrownness has played a
major role in the book, as has the associated idea of guilt; we've
seen how the past ecstasis is explained by these. But of course
there's more to say on these topics, and in particular on the way
we are thrown "from history." And we'll see that this at least gives
hints how we might indeed, by our historicality, stretch "between
birth and death."

The discussion of historicality extends Heidegger's account of
Dasein's sociality, and its aspect as *das Man*. My historicality is
especially the way I find myself thrown into a general social practice, a "tradition" that has come down to me as my "heritage."
Heidegger stresses this in the Introduction's preview of historicality: "Dasein ... has grown up into and within a traditional
interpretation of Dasein. In terms of this it understands itself firstly
and, within a certain range, constantly" [BT g20].

Since historicality is *Being and Time*'s last word on this social
dimension of Dasein, it invites a last look at the issue raised before
(Chapter 4.5), whether Dasein is ultimately something social, not
individual. "Historicality" sounds as if it refers to a feature or
property of a society, and some of what Heidegger says about it
may seem strong evidence for the holist view. So is it "a" Dasein
that has a history, or is it the society or people? We should notice
how the lead-in topic of "birth" seems already to situate

historicality within the analysis of an individual Dasein, as also does the claim that it "has grown up" into a tradition.

Some points about translation are relevant. "Historicality" translates *Geschichtlichkeit*, a word derived from the very common verb *geschehen*, to happen (or be done), and the intermediate noun *Geschichte*, a history or story. Heidegger plays on these connections. "The specific movement of *stretched stretching itself* we call the '*happening* [*Geschehen*]' of Dasein"; to analyze this we need "an *ontological* understanding of *historicality*" [BT g375]. So this term picks out a kind of "happening" which, I will claim, characterizes each individual Dasein. Each of us happens in the form of a story or history— which is not to be confused with the discipline of *Historie*, and is not to be grasped by the latter.

To be sure Heidegger does ascend to the social level when he talks about "*destiny*" [*Geschick*], which is "the happening of the community, of a people" [BT g384]. And Heidegger is a kind of holist here. "Destiny is not something that puts itself together out of individual fates, any more than being-with-one-another can be conceived as the occurring together of several subjects" [g384]. So, we'll see, there is an overall logic and direction to the society's (or culture's) evolution, which can't be explained by the choices of individuals.

Nevertheless the weight and focus of Heidegger's discussion remain with the individual. His interest in that "destiny" is in how it gets regarded or taken over by the individual, in his/her own mode of historicality. His term for the way destiny bears on the individual is "*fate*" [*Schicksal*]; this is "Dasein's originary happening, which lies in authentic resoluteness and in which Dasein *hands* itself *down* to itself, free for death, in a possibility that it has inherited and yet has chosen" [BT g384]. (Note the relation between *Geschick* and *Schicksal*, and the way both are related to *Geschichte*.) So our focus will be on an individual's authentic historicality, and the way this appropriates the social tradition.

As the term "fate" suggests, Heidegger also means to address issues descended from the old debate over freedom and fate. Like

Nietzsche (and others) he insists not just on the compatibility of these, but that freedom depends on a recognition of fate and vice versa. Of course, as we must always bear in mind, these notions are transformed by being moved within phenomenology—and treated in the analysis of intentionality. So fate is not an external power a Dasein is subject to, but a way of "making one's own" tradition and destiny: I only "have" a fate when I do this [BT g384]. And freedom is not a matter of being an "uncaused cause," but of making choices that are "mine" by my making them in the light of my death and guilt.

This is why Heidegger even identifies fate with freedom. "If Dasein, by anticipating, lets death become powerful in itself, then, as free for death, Dasein understands itself in its own *superior power*, the power of its finite freedom" [BT g384]. "Fate is that powerless superior power ... of projecting oneself, reticently and ready for anxiety, upon one's own being-guilty" [g385]. Fate is the way destiny looks, to a freedom that grasps its own power over it; it is a destiny that has been "made mine" in authenticity.

But this has brought us ahead of the story. Let's go back to get a better sense of the basic phenomenon here, historicality. This is, as mentioned, the way we have been thrown into a tradition that has come down to us "historically," as a heritage. Once again we best discover and show this phenomenon in its authentic mode, where it is most perspicuous and most itself. In §74, which begins the positive account of historicality, Heidegger tells how authentic Dasein will get its existentiell possibilities—its specific, individual projects—from "what has come down to us," i.e. from "*the heritage* which [resoluteness], as thrown, *takes over*" [BT g383]. But of course it doesn't take over all of it equally. It must cull, and it chooses among possibilities by seeing which can be lived out authentically, in the face of its death and guilt.

This selection among the available passed-down options works in two ways. On the one hand I test projects myself in that way, by seeing if I can live them "unto death." But on the other hand I also seek out projects that come to me from authentic sources, back within the tradition, at those moments they arose. Indeed, by working to revive authentic choice already embedded in projects or practices, we can get a better sense how to choose authentically ourselves.

This search for authentic sources is our best reason for attending to history. These sources are "heroes," in having founded practices that could be lived authentically, i.e. with the serious sense of our limits. I find what's pure or viable in the practice by seeing it as it was, in these cases, originally meant. Indeed only this really "comes down" to me, is really bequeathed to me as an individual self. Really I "inherit" only this authentic core—only this is that "heritage."

This point is planted in *Being and Time* very early on. The Introduction, previewing the never-written Part II, says that we need to get back to a "source" from which our traditional concepts "have been in part quite genuinely drawn" [BT g21]. The aim of historical inquiry is to recover the "originary experiences in which we achieved our first, and from then on guiding, determinations of being" [g22]. This route back through the tradition becomes all the more vital in Heidegger's later view.

It is in authentic moments facing death and guilt that new practices and ideas are made (Heidegger thinks). From these beginnings, practices and ideas decay, as they are solidified into a tradition, such that "what it 'transmits' is made so inaccessible, firstly and mostly, that it rather becomes concealed" [BT g21]— concealed by becoming habitual and self-evident.[12] Indeed this idea is hinted at at the very beginning of *Being and Time*, which argues for reviving a question about being that has been forgotten.

To be sure, resoluteness doesn't require that "one should *explicitly* know the origin of the possibilities" [BT g385]. But where the possibility is "gleaned explicitly," resoluteness becomes "repetition" [*Wiederholung*]: "The authentic repetition of a possibility of existence that has been—that Dasein chooses its hero—is grounded existentially in anticipatory resoluteness," where one "first chooses the choice that makes one free for the struggle of loyally following in what can be repeated" [g385]. So it's those uncovered originary meanings that I (seek to) repeat.

If we understand my "birth"—unclarified by Heidegger, we've seen—as this authentic source, we see how these points can provide the "connectedness" of birth and death he promises. I feel my choices "unto death" preceded and abetted by authentic choices at the very source of my thrownness. My thrownness reaches back past my biological birth to the heroic sources of the tradition I choose to repeat. So my thrownness can be *from* an authenticity congruent with the authenticity I am towards; in a way I am thrown from myself.[13] This reconciles, in a further way, my past and future ecstases. (In favor of this reading, see the use of "birth certificate" on BT g22, in context.)

This reveals the strategy behind that "destruction of the history of philosophy" that Part II was to carry out. This "destruction" does not really demolish, but turns philosophical positions so that they show the truth that lies behind them, i.e. their authentic sources. It shakes off the inauthentic accretions as the original ideas were converted into standard views. (So Heidegger says later that in *Being and Time* "destruction" [*Destruktion*] meant "dismantling" [*Abbau*] to uncover the originary; see Chapter 7, notes 9 and 10.)

All of these points are pulled together in the climactic paragraph of Chapter 5:

> Only an entity that is essentially *futural* in its being, so that it can let itself, free for death and smashing against it, be thrown back upon its factical there, i.e. only an entity that is, as futural, equally originarily *having been*, can by passing down to itself the inherited possibility, take over its own thrownness and be *in the moment* for "its time". Only authentic temporality,

which is likewise finite, makes possible something like fate, i.e. authentic historicality.

[BT g385]

My historicality lies, then, not in the cultural past that preceded me, but in the way my own life "happens" in the passage back and forth between my individuating death and those points in my heritage where I find my individuating projects born. I happen historically by meaning my world out of this authentic relation to that heritage. And inauthentic historicality is of course just a deficient mode of this: I shy back from going explicitly out to my death, and so the "heroes" I find aren't authentic sources, but serve to confirm my avoidance.

This analysis of historicality, and the claim that authentic Dasein must go back to test—and find its heroes within—the tradition that gives it its possibilities, motivate *Being and Time*'s planned Part II. Its three Divisions were intended to work back through three decisive moments in the development of our notion of time: first Kant's schematism, then Descartes on the givenness of the thinking thing, and finally Aristotle on time.[14] The main aim of this inquiry was to be, I suggest, the exposure of the question of being as the deep truth that these decisive philosophers each had inklings of—it gave power to their words—yet still could not quite say. But I'll need to suggest what this meaning of being was to be, in my next section.

The implications of this historical turn outgrow the framework of *Being and Time*; following it further compels Heidegger to rethink points that book is oriented by. The book couldn't be finished, with that framework. This is true, I think, even though Heidegger clearly planned the whole book in the light of the important historical turn. For Dasein's historicality emerges as an element within a rich a-historical analysis of being-in-the-world, which it doesn't then modify. Dasein "*is not 'temporal' because it 'stands in history', but on the contrary, it exists and only can exist historically because it is temporal in the ground of its being*" [BT g376].[15]

But Heidegger eventually comes to see important parts of that analysis as "historically local," i.e. as descriptions how Dasein now (in this age) shows itself. Moreover, he solidifies a certain story about what our local historical situation is, which throws those descriptions into a particular, unflattering light. That universal human momentum to fall gets translated into our historical limits (under technology).[16] Much of the transition into the later writings will be in drawing this historical lesson.

So, roughly put, the account of historicality is the intrusion of a Hegelian view within the Kantian questions at the book's beginning. Having looked for "conditions of the possibility" of any Dasein (intentionality) at all, Heidegger finds that one such condition is that this intending be historical. But as he reflects on our own historicality, he comes to see his phenomenology of Dasein as an episode in this history, as bound by it in ways it doesn't recognize.

3. From temporality to time and being

Division II concludes, anticlimactically, with a chapter treating "the ordinary conception of time," and developing especially how it is rooted in Dasein's temporality. We have already taken account of this above, and should reflect now on "where the book was headed" in the never-executed next parts of its plan.[17] This plan, outlined in §§5, 6, and 8 of the Introduction, was for the discovery of our temporality to prepare for a Division III in which the book would reach its original goal-topic, being; this would then be followed, we've seen, by a Part II, with its own three Divisions, treating these same topics historically, in Kant, Descartes, and Aristotle.

The final sentences of Division II anticipate what was to come: "How is this mode of temporality's temporalizing to be interpreted? Is there a way which leads from originary time to the meaning of being? Does time itself manifest itself as the horizon of being?" [BT g437]. But Heidegger's previews and plans do little to explain how this argumentative path—from temporality to time, and from time to being—was to run. We must largely reach out with speculation and extrapolation—based of course in what evidence we can find in both explicit pre-statements about being, and the overall direction or momentum of the discussion (i.e. what, given Dasein's temporality, it seems being will be).[18]

It is possible that Heidegger did not know himself quite what, in very much detail, he would say, but he clearly has at least an overall strategic idea about being. And we should not imagine that he didn't get past the book's analysis of Dasein because he lost interest in being. The latter is the ever-present aim of *Being and Time*, and it remains the crucial topic through all of his later writings as well. It's at this point—in the position on being—that the "turning" into his later ideas must occur. So to address this we must have some idea what *Being and Time*'s view of being was to be.

Indeed, as we've just noticed regarding historicality, it's likely that some of the things Heidegger initially expected to say, he found as he wrote the book he no longer wanted to say. His emerging ideas couldn't, he saw, be put within the framework the book had established. So we can suppose that "turning" away from these ideas to have begun even as he was writing *Being and Time*. And thus we should look not just for his initial plan, but for ways he was already shifting beyond it.

Let me come straight to what I take the overall idea to be; it can be put very simply. The main step is from the analysis of Dasein's temporality to an account of "the meaning of being." However, due to Heidegger's idealist framework this step does not have far to go. Being is not the highest genus of entities, arrived at by abstraction from them. Rather, it is the precondition for entities, the "making possible" of them, and this is accomplished by Dasein. Being lies in the opening-up of a world by Dasein; it is simply an aspect of that opening. Now the progressive analyses of *Being and Time* penetrate to the ultimate level at which this opening-up occurs, our temporality; in seeing the structure of this temporality we discover the ultimate "logic" of the letting-be of a world. And this means that we thereby already have being, which must be just an aspect of this temporality itself.[19]

This is by no means a "surprise ending" to the book. It is not only foretold in the Introduction, but also woven into the texture of Divisions I and II themselves. The guiding idea throughout is that being occurs in—and only in—something Dasein does, and that this in turn lets entities be. Of course it's not by Dasein's "ideas" that this happens; the label "idealism" is potentially misleading. Dasein is also not a subject or mind. It is, as I am putting it, an "intender," for whom there are meanings. Being is to be found at the root of this meaning or intending, which turns out to be temporality. Drawing direct lessons from this about being will fulfill the opening plan to find being by examining this entity, Dasein. So "being itself ... is thus made visible in its 'temporal' character" [BT g18].

Now if being is really as close to temporality as this, it may seem there's no step at all to make to it, so that Heidegger could have little to do in that third Division. But in fact there's a lot he still needs to say. Even though being is just temporality itself, "in a different aspect," it remains to say just what this other aspect is. How do we look at this ecstatic temporality, in order to see being in (or as) it?

The most obvious way to think of their relation is to treat being as what this temporality is "of"—its (very abstract) *intentum* or "meant." I think this is indeed the gist of Heidegger's point, despite his qualms about treating being as an intentional content or object (and also despite the difficulty in seeing what ecstatic temporality is "of"). Being is what our temporality, in particular our authentic temporality, "means" (or "sees"). It is something like a world, but more abstract and basic (permitting many other such worlds). And that temporality means this, is an ultimate "condition of the possibility" for there being entities.

Let me come to this point a different way. We have seen how Heidegger, from early in Being and Time, speaks about "the being" of Dasein, of to-hand equipment, and of at-hand objects. He treats these as three "modes of being"—the only three the book notices. We have taken these locutions as pledges he needs to redeem by eventually clarifying (the term) "being." But they also serve as indications of the work he needs this clarified notion to do: it must show, as varieties within itself, the different ways that Dasein, equipment, and objects can be. What grounds the possibility of these different basic kinds of entities?

Heidegger expected Division III to show how it is time that does so. As such, time would serve as an intermediary between Dasein's temporality, and being.[20] So the Introduction anticipates an "*originary explication of time as horizon for the understanding of being, from temporality as the being of Dasein as understanding being*" [BT g17]. Heidegger doesn't always keep a sharp distinction between time [Zeit] and temporality [Zeitlichkeit], but I think he usually treats time as "meant" by temporality. Time is projected by temporality, in a way that allows entities to be uncovered "in" this time. Temporality projects different varieties of time, and these make possible the different kinds of entities.

We get a foretaste of this argument near the end of Division II, in the account how our ordinary conception of time arises from ecstatic temporality [BT g420–21]. We get another sample in BP [302–13], which tries to show that experience of to-hand equipment is grounded in presence [Anwesenheit], as the horizon of a particular kind of ecstatic temporality. Things are to-hand to the extent they are "presences"; what lets them be is our own temporal stance, which projects this way of being in time. And I think Heidegger expected to give a further argument how at-hand objects are likewise made possible through our projecting another variety of time, by a modification of this ecstasis towards presence.

That the kinds of entities are determined in relation to time is dimly recognized by the many philosophers who divide things into those that are and those that are not "in time"—but they have an inadequate notion of time [BP 303, MF 144]. They fail to see how these times are projected by Dasein's own temporality—by the way it means in and from its three ecstases. They therefore also miss a third kind of time, which Dasein's temporality projects for Dasein itself: the kind of time it means *itself* as within. For Dasein lets itself be too, as an entity of its own kind, different from equipment and objects. It lets itself be, by projecting, in its ecstatic temporality, a most basic *intentum* and horizon: the kind of time that makes it Dasein.

And it's here, I suggest, that Heidegger thought he would find being itself. Being is the time that is meant by our very deepest intending, our ecstatic temporality, before it has been modified to make the times of worldly things. This deepest intending is that in which we understand *ourselves* in relation to time, as allowed to be by being in (or as) a kind of time. This time is, perhaps, simply that ecstatic temporality itself, but *as* understood by itself as the ultimate condition for being Dasein. For ecstatic temporality too always "knows what it's doing," is always reflexive. Dasein's most basic *intentum* is itself as ecstatic temporality, as temporality reflexively "means itself." This ultimate *intentum* must be being itself.

Of course usually we mean this *intentum* only dimly and implicitly: we *are* stretched out temporally, and mean ourselves as such, but this self-understanding is buried and unavailable. It becomes explicit only really in authenticity—in the authentic modes of the temporal ecstases. Only there do we adequately see (experience) our temporal stretch: how we are "out there" towards mortal ends, from a heritage, and beside the immediate. So it is only in this authentic temporality that we adequately see being itself—really witness the ultimate condition by virtue of which there are entities at all. And here again, at this ultimate point, phenomenology and authenticity converge: we get the ultimate insight into being only when we're authentic.

What do we then see and witness? I confess myself at a disadvantage here. But I believe Heidegger has or anticipates the revelation of an original intentional "clearing," beneath and before every other form intending can take. This clearing is that stretch from "birth" to "death," which is revealed as the ultimate ground of all the other ways I (or any Dasein) do and can intend. The revelation of this ultimate condition is perhaps to have some of the character of the mystical experiences we've seen Heidegger was earlier drawn to.

This account—speculative and allusive as it is—still gives us a point of departure and comparison as we now move to Heidegger's later writing, and try to see how it carries out a "turning" away from *Being and Time*.

Summary

Our third and lowest structural level is our temporality: the way we "stretch out" into the three temporal ecstases. It is only in authenticity that these ecstases are evident to us, because only then do we reach "all the way ahead" to our death, and fully back to our guilt. In doing so these temporal dimensions are explicit "from within," along with our third ecstatic relation to a present situation.

This temporal structure underlies the pragmatic and existential structures, which can therefore be restated in temporal terms. So the pragmatic analysis of Dasein into understanding, self-finding, and talk—grasping, feeling, and wording—is unified when we see the temporal basis of these three. And the existential analysis is integrated with this when we see how falling's flight from death and guilt is an effort to shrink the futural and past ecstases and to preoccupy oneself in the present. Authenticity by contrast achieves the full temporal stretch that belongs to us; it gives us even our most adequate relation to the present moment and situation.

Our analysis of the past ecstasis needs supplementing: we must see how it makes us "historical," in our relation to a tradition, our heritage. Authenticity picks out from this heritage the aims it can will unto death, and for this it favors aims that were created authentically, back in the culture's past. So it seeks "heroes" who founded practices that can be lived authentically—sustained even in the face of death and guilt. It's in this spirit that *Being and Time* meant (in the unwritten Part II) to go back to the history of philosophy, to deconstruct it by showing the authentic sources beneath later accretions and subversions.

Heidegger also failed to write Division III of Part I, which was planned to bring the analysis of Dasein to bear on the question of being. The argument was to run from temporality to time to being, but we have to speculate just how. I suggest: temporality is the way our intentionality means (and lets there be) time, such that entities can then be uncovered "in" such time. And since temporality is the deepest level of us, time is the basic way in which "there is" being for us. This is confirmed by seeing how the three modes of being the book has distinguished—of human Dasein, to-hand equipment, and at-hand objects—are each a way of "being in time" laid out by our temporality. Thereby the book was to arrive, I think, at the meaning of being asked for at its very beginning.

Further reading

W. Blattner: *Heidegger's Temporal Idealism*. Cambridge, UK: Cambridge University Press, 1999. [An illuminating treatment of the temporal theme in BT.]

Seven

Heidegger's turning

Famously, Heidegger undergoes a "turning" [Kehre] in the decade after *Being and Time*, a change in the basic direction or orientation of his thinking. The term is Heidegger's own; he applies it to a significant shift he retrospectively sees in himself. And indeed many changes are obvious from even superficial comparisons of that book with the later essays. We enter a distinctly different world in the latter, and must adjust ourselves to meet it.

I should say at the outset that the crux of the turning—what it was from and to—is open to debate; there have been rather different accounts of it. Heidegger himself offers, during this turning itself, no direct statement of what it amounts to, and only a few later accounts.[1] So I'll be giving a reading of it, not stating an obvious fact.

It is also debatable just when the turning occurs. I will take it to be during the latter half of the 1930s. *Contributions to Philosophy* [1936–38] is the most thorough statement of the emerging new view. But there are anticipations of it in the early 1930s, and I will also use these texts in treating his "later" view. Moreover, we will see that the turn doesn't arrive at a stable position. Heidegger pivots, and continues to pivot: all the rest of his career can be seen as a progressive turning. He steadily radicalizes his critique of the position he turns away from, so that his initial accounts of the turn come to be seen as incomplete and misleading.

The main philosophical influences on this turn are Nietzsche and Hölderlin; they clarified the direction he already wanted to go. Very broadly—and of course there are many exceptions to this—the turn is towards Hölderlin and against Nietzsche.

Heidegger turns from Nietzsche, seen as giving key statement to the modern stance, and looming behind the aspects of *Being and Time* he now wants to renounce. That book's pragmatic and existential themes are still Nietzschean: they express the spirit Nietzsche framed in his ontology of will to power, and in his lesson that man should take the place of the dead God as master of all. And this Nietzschean spirit is also linked with Heidegger's—and Germany's—political and moral error in embracing Hitler.

So the turn also has this biographical side: it is Heidegger's philosophical response to his unhappy experience with National Socialism. He never explicitly says this. Indeed I think he actively suppresses it, in his stubborn defense of his behavior in the Nazi years. (This also leads him, at times, to understate the turning by reading later views back into *Being and Time*.) But to an extent—that we will need to determine—this turning amounts to an acknowledgment of error, in the place that counts most to him, his core thinking about being.

The turn towards Hölderlin expresses, by contrast, a religious revival in Heidegger. He takes over Hölderlin's idea that the secular philosophy of human will expresses an age in which gods are absent—an absence we must properly regret. We need to look and prepare towards their return, in some new religiousness whose vocabulary he begins to construct. That this return to religion need not be to Christianity, however, we can gather from his adoption of Hölderlin's polytheism. It is this new positive aim that explains his changed discursive method and style. His later writing is often more "poetic" or "literary," and tends to renounce the quasi-Cartesian method of *Being and Time*, as well as its Kantian system.

I'll discuss Heidegger's "late" views in this and the following two chapters. In this one I'll try to clarify the turning itself: to identify the fundamental changes that occur after *Being and Time*. This will involve presenting an outline of his late position—which of course chiefly concerns being, and how it is concealed and unconcealed. His views about "language and art" (Chapter 8) and "technology and gods" (Chapter 9) will then be grounded in these central claims.

Since Heidegger's "later" writings extend over several decades, and since (as said) he continues to turn or pivot all through them, a really thorough account would need to be chronological. I will have to compress much of this development in order to present his position in its large-scale argumentative structure—though I will point out some of the stages as we go.

As I'll try to show, the main lesson of this overall shift is, once again, in the *kind of understanding* Heidegger thinks philosophers—and all of us—need. He radicalizes the critique he had already made against the usual epistemic aim of a theoretical-conceptual grasp of the at-hand. He broadens his target so that it now includes the pragmatic-existential understanding that *Being and Time* itself had pursued. His later writings push this lesson ever further, so that the kind of understanding we need is more and more different from all that is usual to us.

For Heidegger's later view there is no single dominant work—no book in which he gives detailed statement to the full range of his new ideas, as he had done in *Being and Time*. His interpreters' regret at this absence showed in the long anticipation and then reception of a "secret work" written 1936–39, just after his turning: *Contributions to Philosophy: From Ereignis* (often referred to as "the *Beiträge*"). This was long rumored his second magnum opus, and was so greeted by many when it was finally published in 1989. It is of great interest, and I will use it often in this chapter. But it (1) is mostly in very rough order, and (2) lacks the density, the thought-through detail, that characterizes *Being and Time*. There is no second "great work," and no comprehensive statement of Heidegger's view "after the turn." We will for the most part be looking at essays with narrower ambitions—though insofar as all of them try to speak of being (and *Ereignis*), they have (Heidegger thinks) the very highest ambition.

1. Character of the turn

I start with an overview of the new position, to show how the detailed accounts to follow will hang together. Here my aim is to show the position only schematically; many of these ideas will need to be both motivated, and understood rather differently than it might in this first telling seem (since some of the terms will need special senses). These ideas will also need to be "brought to life" out of this preliminary and flattening sketch, which little tries to give the very kind of understanding Heidegger will insist on. Still I think it will be helpful to start with a large-scale map.

Let's start with what doesn't change. Heidegger still holds that being [*Sein*] is the important topic: it is what we should all be paying most attention to, but that we're sadly, predictably neglecting. His main ambition as a philosopher is to bring himself and his readers into a proper relation to it, into the "truth of being." This gist is already in *Being and Time*, and Heidegger stresses it all the more emphatically as he goes. He adopts more and more the prophet's role: calling us back to this proper attention to being, from our misguided preoccupation with things and one another.

But as Heidegger goes on he treats this problem of being as harder and harder; this is the gist of the turning. Over and over he will suggest a way to state the difference of being from entities, which then a few years later turns out still to fall short of it, requiring yet another new formulation. This progressive radicalizing eventually impinges on the very word "being," and Heidegger adopts a series of other locutions for what he means, such as the antique *Seyn*, and writing *Sein* with a cross-out superimposed.

What is it in *Being and Time* that gets left behind? As we've seen, one key way that book went wrong was in arriving at historicality too late, as it were—or in failing to absorb that eventual lesson back into the book's guiding project. The main framework of *Being and Time* is Kantian: it tries to get at the ultimate "conditions of our experience," the essential—and ahistorical—structures of our intentionality. Historicality, along with temporality, emerges within that framework, as part of this ahistorical essence.

So the purpose of Part II's planned "destruction" of the history of philosophy was to clear away the concealing tradition that has kept us from recognizing both our own essence, and being. Its purpose was the negative one of removing a (relatively) superficial concealment, due to our history. After the turning, by contrast, being comes to be identified with (is treated as constituted by) its history, so that historical study is the direct and positive way to being.

One of the main elements of the turning, then, is the ascendancy of this historical lesson.[2] To understand ourselves, and being, we need to look not for an essential structure but an evolving or developing one. We need to look at the history of our (Western) understanding of being, to find out the logic in this history. So Heidegger shifts, more consistently than he could do in *Being and Time* itself, from a Kantian to a Hegelian project.

Now he could still have kept those pragmatic-existential lessons, within a new historical story: he could have made them the culmination of that story—as Hegel does for his own positions. But instead Heidegger uses history to diagnose and deflate those lessons. *Being and Time* turns out to describe not intentionality (Dasein) *per se*, but only *our current* kind of intentionality, whose historical context shows its limits—which that book, missing that context, therefore also missed. History shows how our way of intending has emerged by a "destiny," and as such has the task to transcend this current way.

The framing idea here—I'll try to put it as plainly as I can—is that there is, today, one fundamental and pervasive way in which *es gibt* (there obtains) being, and a world is disclosed for us. Here "world" refers to the presupposed network of aims and possibilities, within or as which entities can then appear to us. And "us" refers to "the West," i.e. to all the societies and cultures rooted in Europe, and ultimately in ancient Greece. (Heidegger is reluctant to speak about other cases.)

So there is a single overall way in which we "let entities be"— are set and prepared to mean and discover things: a general character or style to the network we presume. This basic level of world-constitution is temporal: we "have" the network of aims and possibilities above (beneath) all in the way we are *oriented in time*—as *Being and Time* already thought. But now this pervasive way we experience things in time is not an essential structure of any Dasein, but an historical phenomenon, a certain "epoch" in a very long-term historical event. That event or happening had a beginning, in ancient Greece, that both established its basic point and aim, and set up a logic of development that has swept on to our present epoch.[3]

Thus Heidegger thinks of this history as simple and linear: each epoch opens onto a single mode of being, which arises by a certain logic from that of the epoch before. And these successive understandings have all had a common core: *"presence"* [*Anwesenheit*]. The logic or "destiny" in those successive epochs is a kind of unfolding or unwinding of that "presence" (we'll have to see what this means), so that it all follows in a way from the original impetus given by the Greeks. Our own age represents a kind of culmination or fulfillment of that long destiny, inasmuch as being is now most fully presence.

It is Nietzsche who above all articulates our modern understanding—and gets at that unifying core—in his notion of will to power. And although Heidegger never says so, I think he saw it as also articulated in *Being and Time*, with its pragmatic-existential picture of Dasein: as defined by its projects with things, and its capacity to achieve an individualizing control over those projects, in authenticity. This personal control is so valued because it achieves "presence" in a maximal way.

These metaphysical positions articulate the current way humans stand related to things, to which Heidegger gives the title "*technology*" [*Technik*], and whose essence he calls *Gestell* or "*enframing.*" In it the "metaphysics of presence," the whole Western history of being, reaches a kind of culmination or completion. History shows, then, that we live at a critical moment, at which it is emerging just what this completion will inaugurate.

However—and this is Heidegger's inversion of Hegel—this culmination has a largely *negative* character. For what counts most is our "openness to being," and this has deteriorated all through that long process. Heidegger depicts the (Western) history of being as involving an initial "opening" or "lighting" of being, followed by a successive closing-off, so that this history has been, in this central regard, a deterioration or degeneration—a devolution. The completion of presence has closed off being. So instead of transcending limitations as in Hegel, history erodes an advantage it began with—though it devolves so far from it that it has, paradoxically, now a better chance to regain it.

In this story the modern condition or stance plays a role like that played by "nihilism" in Nietzsche—and not coincidentally. Heidegger thinks that Nietzsche not only speaks the metaphysics behind technology, but also begins to see the overall danger or threat to which this stance leads. Nietzsche thinks that his metaphysics gives him the way out of nihilism, but Heidegger thinks his way really epitomizes the stance at fault. Heidegger intends a more radical diagnosis of the problem, and response to it.

This diagnosis of our modern condition is coupled, of course, with a prescription: Heidegger points the "way out," or at least a direction that promises better for us. We need to initiate a "turning" ourselves, and a "second beginning," analogous to the first one by the early Greeks. This will eventually lead to a new specific understanding of being—but one less concealing of it than our own. This turning needs to occur at a cultural level, in our practices of acting, speaking, feeling, and thinking.

Heidegger plainly intends not just to point out the need for a new beginning, but to contribute to making it. His later works importantly aim to begin to construct the *new vocabulary* needed for the new understanding. This is how we must take, I think, the distinctive poetic-philosophical neologisms in many of his later writings. He gives examples of, first efforts at, the kind of reconstruction of our linguistic practices that we need in order to make a turn in our world.

It's important, however, that this "way out" does *not* involve trying to turn one's back on technology—not just because its viewpoint is all-pervading, but because, as the opening onto being that we have, it is only here that we can find "the saving power," as Heidegger puts it in words from Hölderlin. What we most need is to press down to the essence of technology, in a genuine "unconcealment" of this basic way being is there for us. We need to recognize the dimension or level of this opening of being, before we can grasp how to make a new start from it.

The special event in which being, which is normally hidden from us, becomes unconcealed is called by Heidegger "the truth of being," or *Ereignis*. Of course in a way being "is there" for us all along. But its unconcealment is itself concealed from us, and we must struggle to reveal it. It is in this moment of illumination, which will show us being as presence, that there is the possibility of renaming being. So the overall change in our practices depends on some individuals—thinkers and poets—achieving this special insight of *Ereignis*, and out of it creating new words for being.

The new understanding, to be embedded in the new language, will differ from technology in that it will somehow "hold open" the experience of being itself, as a part of the general social practice. By this those dwelling in the practice can be "preservers" and "shepherds" of being, thereby performing our (humans') essential role—as we are unable to do in our age of technology.

This account of humans as (properly) "shepherds" of being reflects a subtle but important shift in Heidegger's view on the overall relation between humans and being. To put it roughly or simply: he turns from a more fully idealist picture which has us the makers or projectors of being, to a more qualified view which gives being a certain independence from us. He adopts, that is, a greater "realism" with respect to being; along with his historical turn, this is a second main aspect of the turning. Those thinkers and poets are able to make their new words for being only because they are responding to something already "there" in being itself.

This implies, we should note, a shift from the basic strategy of *Being and Time*, which tried to get at being by analyzing structures of Dasein. That approach counted humans as determining being, which is therefore isomorphic to its temporal structure—what this structure "projects." After the turn being has an independence that precludes its being "read off" from us. FS 47:

> Meaning in *Being and Time* is defined in terms of a project region, and projection is the accomplishment of Dasein. ... The thinking that goes after *Being and Time*, in that it gives up the word "meaning of being" in favor of "truth of being", henceforth emphasizes the openness of being itself, rather than the openness of Dasein in regard to this openness of being. / This signifies "the turn", in which thinking always more decisively turns to being as being.[4]

So this new independence of being has consequences for the way we must go about understanding it. Heidegger now stresses the need for a more "receptive" stance towards being: we need to open ourselves up, or release ourselves into an attitude in which being can show itself. To be sure, this last phrase, recalling phenomenology's old motto to "let entities show themselves from themselves," hints how Heidegger retains some aspects of his old method. The key difference here is that we're no longer studying phenomena ultimately due to us.

In this treatment of being as more independent of us, and in his insistence on a receptive stance, Heidegger shows a religious turn in his later thinking—or of course a return, in particular back towards the mysticism he was drawn to in his twenties. The inadequacy of human willing, including the kind *Being and Time* meant by authenticity, teaches a receptiveness towards being. Being is not a god, but in our proper relation to being we welcome gods—new gods, befitting our new relation to being.

This first overview of Heidegger's later position gives, I hope, an overall orientation. But it requires now (a lot of) both clarification and justification. With this flat and blunt summary we don't understand it in the special way we must.

2. The history of being

Let's start by looking more closely at Heidegger's history of being. This begins, we saw in a general way, with the early Greeks, who experienced an initial unconcealment of being as "presence." This opening set in motion a development with a logic that has led through a series of reinterpretations of being as presence, culminating in our own. This evolution, however, was in one crucial respect a devolution, and we should be discontented to find ourselves here at its fulfillment. This large story is so far very abstract; let's make more concrete just where and how the claimed history runs.

Heidegger does not tell the story by describing the general social practices of the successive "epochs" in his history—although I think he does claim to clarify these. He focuses instead on the series of metaphysical systems, projected by a fairly traditional pantheon of great names in the history of philosophy. Each epoch's understanding of being is articulated in the words and ideas of one of these metaphysicians. (It is also articulated in poets' words, as we'll see in Chapter 8 of this book.)

So by studying the series of these metaphysical vocabularies and systems, we get at the single main stream of our history. And since all of these systems treat being as presence, there is further unity to this history. Heidegger stresses often how the great philosophers all "say the same." "This history [of Western European thinking] is at bottom a sequence of variations on this one theme, even where Parmenides' saying [of the sameness of thinking and being] is not itself named." [WCT 242] The grasp of being as presence ramifies, from this metaphysical source, into the concrete social practices: they too manifest a will to treat entities as being insofar as they're presences.

The contrast with Nietzsche is stark. Nietzsche also thinks we need to study the past to uncover the real meaning of our current outlook and values: he uses "genealogy" to reveal both the social forces that built our morality, and the interests thereby installed in it. But Heidegger's historical interest is quite indifferent to psychological or social forces or motives. The destiny of being runs straight over—and renders irrelevant—any such individualities and interests. What matters about great philosophers is what they have in common: the ability to "hear" this destiny of being as presence.[5]

We may wonder at this elevation of metaphysics. Is it plausible that these abstruse theories express attitudes basic to the general practice? Heidegger thinks that they express them not just retrospectively—by describing existing practice—but prospectively: they initiate these attitudes by putting them into words. This initiation is not, however, an act of personal creativity, but is due to the individual's responsiveness to a general momentum. Metaphysicians intuit the basic problems of the age, and "what's coming next." So they articulate—put into basic words—the next or coming understanding of being. These words are then readily adopted through the culture, as what seems naturally next—and with the words the practice gets new meaning.

Here is one of Heidegger's summaries of the history of being, naming the sequence of metaphysical concepts:

> [P]resencing shows itself as the Hen, the unifying unique One, as the Logos, the gathering that preserves the all, as idea, ousia,

energeia, substantia, actualitas, perceptio, monad, as objectivity, as the positedness of self-positing in the sense of the will of reason, of love, of the spirit, of power, as the will to will in the eternal return of the same.

[TB (OTB 7)]

Heidegger wrote separate books (or book-length course notes) on most of the philosophers behind these many concepts.

I will focus on the very first stage of this history, the pre-Socratics, then just sketch its later route. Is the theory more or less plausible when we look at its details? Heidegger's account of the pre-Socratics seems to many especially willful and bizarre, imposing odd Heideggerian senses on terms and phrases that just won't bear them. Is it good history (of philosophy)?

But before we so evaluate his history we should remind ourselves why he himself thinks we should care about history—what we should want from it. These are the criteria by which *he* thinks we should evaluate his histories, what *he's* trying to do in them.[6] These ambitions are rooted in a kind of meta-history Heidegger tells, of something going on behind or beneath what's usually studied. We should weigh whether those ambitions can justify his seeming abuses.

Heidegger thinks our main interest in thinking about philosophy's history ought to lie not in the past *per se*, but in better seeing the essential character of our own current opening or clearing: how being holds for us now.[7] The character of this opening is usually concealed from us by our immersion within it. The main challenge is to somehow "step back" from this overall view: to find an angle upon it that nullifies its usual obviousness. History can give us this angled view that lets us see being fresh. It helps to this in several connected ways.

First, to think our way genuinely into one of these past metaphysical stances we must step partly out of our own—must at least tug against it. If we take these other words seriously their difference illuminates our own, by a kind of friction against them.[8] Or, those other words open a dialogue with our own, that lets ours speak more explicitly than before. This idea that "difference illuminates" is of course a familiar justification for the study of history, but Heidegger has new ideas about how this works. His interpretations are pitched to bring us into this certain kind of dialogue.

Second, this study of past systems is also valuable because in earlier phases of our history its deep meaning of presence was less concealed. The general movement of our culture's history has been to cover over the original "openness" to being that occurred with the pre-Socratics. Our own age is the culmination of that tendency, in which being-as-presence is especially hard to notice. By looking back, to the beginning especially, it is easier to locate the transcendental dimension, where being resides, as it were, because it is thought more naively and undisguisedly—which is not to say fully adequately.

Third, these systems help reveal being because they are original speakings of it. Metaphysicians genuinely see being as presence—within limits we'll examine on p. 232ff—and so give it words. These words alter the general practice, but then gradually become such common coin that they lose connection with that original vision. By going back to the original speakings we have better prospects for that vision than from the refracted and banalized versions of it expressed in the general practice. If we study these metaphysical systems in the right way, we can cut away this sedimented custom and share in the uncovering of presence and being.[9]

Fourth, this recovery of these original thinkings enables us eventually to see the general logic of their series.[10] And this illuminates our own epoch's view still further. By stepping down to the transcendental level, we see the arc of development that has produced our view, and gives it its meaning. We can only see its dominant meaning by gaining this larger historical perspective of how it has come to be. So it's not enough to know that sequence of epochs, crystallized in those concepts; we need to see the logic by which they evolve from one to another, and into our own.

Fifth, this image of an arc or throw leaves out something important about this history: its different stages are not "left behind" as this image suggests. Instead they are embedded and preserved within later ones. Indeed they are even directive of later ones: they set the aims that still lie ahead of later ones, or are realized by them. WCT 76: "One still supposes that the handed-down is something we have really [*eigentlich*] behind us, whereas it rather comes towards [*zukommt*—futures] us, since we are delivered over and destined to it."[11] So history uncovers attitudes deeply embedded in us, working beneath our distinctively modern views. And in this way the study of history is quite directly informative about our current state.

Hence the ambition of Heidegger's history is to reveal our current world as the upshot of a long telic movement—of what he still (as in *Being and Time*) calls a "destiny." This long movement gives the real meaning of our own stance. It's only by coming to grips with its "first beginning" (the pre-Socratics) that we become heirs of this heritage [CP 138]. And by grasping the arc of this history leading to us, we also see the way to throw it forward, in a new direction. These should be our ambitions in studying the history of philosophy, and these are the criteria for evaluating historical studies—or so Heidegger insists to us. How does this work in practice?

i. The pre-Socratics

Western history—at least its "history of being"—began, Heidegger thinks, with the pre-Socratics. They made a "first beginning" by having—and putting into words—an original experience of being as presence. This gave deepest content to all of the understandings of being that have followed; it set them all a deep goal and project.[12] These Greeks' experience was also epistemically superior to our own, in one crucial respect (although in others they knew very little what they were up to): being was more unconcealed for them.[13] Our own task is to recover such unconcealment, in order to make a second beginning.

Since they play this crucial role, it's worth examining Heidegger's account of these first thinkers.[14] We can use them to begin to clarify some crucial ideas that we have so far left quite obscure. They can also illustrate how he more generally handles the philosophers he discusses. His accounts of the pre-Socratics initially look extremely odd; I'll try to show that they have more sense and interest—in particular given the special historical aims just mentioned—than so at first seems.

One term we especially need clarity about is *presence* [*Anwesenheit*], which Heidegger claims is the fundamental character of the whole destiny begun by the pre-Socratics. Can his story about the first philosophers help us with this? Let's note, to begin with, that the term does *not* refer, directly, to the temporal *present*, for which there is a quite separate German term, *Gegenwart*. We must bear in mind the important difference between these, which is obscured by the need to translate both by variants on "present."

Gegenwart refers to the present time, but *Anwesen* to the way in which something is present in the sense of showing up (as when a student answers "Present."). In most translations the difference can't be seen. I will try to preserve it by using "present" for the former but some form of "presence" for the latter. So "present things" are things existing now, but "presences" or "what presences" [*Anwesendes*] are the things that show up or occur "close by," now or at other times. Their showing up, their being, is "presencing" [*Anwesen*]. In our Western destiny, the being of entities is the presencing of presences [*Anwesen des Anwesenden*].

The principal idea is *proximity to*: presencing is a nearness or closeness or immediacy *to* some locus or thing.[15] (The student "presences" where the roll is called.) An entity is, as or what it is in this proximity. Moreover, this nearness is crucially to *a viewpoint*, for

Heidegger—a viewpoint which, by that entity's proximity, best sees or understands it. The projection of being as presencing thus involves this standard of immediacy to a witnessing view. And along with this immediacy comes an adjunct: when something is brought near, it comes into lasting possession. So presence involves not just immediacy but durability. Both points can be carried in the idea of "grip" (as by a hand). Entities are what they are when in close firm grip.

Heidegger claims that the pre-Socratics first articulate the West's understanding of being as such presence. But they do so with a certain indirectness. They don't say that entities are by virtue of being presences; nor do they even say what presence is. Instead they analyze the logic of the event in which "there is" being as presence for us. They describe what it is that happens for us, that opens a world or clearing of presences. In what may seem a great anachronism, Heidegger thinks that the great pre-Socratics—Anaximander, Heraclitus, and Parmenides—all focus on this trans-cendental event; each analyzes a different aspect of it, and these aspects cohere in a single view.

I've just spoken of the clearing as "happening for us," and this way it is something we undergo, or receive, is important in the pre-Socratic vision. Being is not something we accomplish our-selves; it doesn't issue from an act of projection in the strong sense of *Being and Time*. And this is the element of realism in the original Greek viewpoint: the clearing happens by our receiving being, not creating it. The subsequent development of metaphysics is towards idealism—in the specific sense that it progresses towards claiming full authority and credit for the opening of being. Although I won't forgo active verbs for describing our relation to being, these need to be heard with this qualification.

Now Homer already talks about entities—recognizes all the things he names *as* entities. So there is a world there already in Homer, and in the everyday practice. Moreover, Homer already treats entities as "presences," and understands this in distinction from the temporal present. Heidegger brings out this difference [AS (W 260ff.)] from a passage near the beginning of the Iliad in which the seer Kalchas is said to know "what is and what will be and what was." Here what is (now) presences in a privileged sense, in which the future and past are absences [Abwesende]. But in a broader sense the latter are presences too: they are inasmuch as they did or will presence. So there is already this ambiguity pre-philosophically: "On the one hand ta eonta [entities] means what presently presences [das gegenwärtig Anwesende], but on the other everything that presences: the present and the non-present essences [Wesende]" [AS (W 261)]. The seer is distinguished by a privileged insight into this wider presence.

But Homer, and his seer, notice only the entities that are within that wider or narrower presencing. They don't notice the background step by which presence is raised up as the criterion for entities to be. It was the achievement of the first philosophers to notice and name this constitutive event—to distinguish from entities this being that gets demanded in advance. They name this being—this insistence on presence; they determine and specify it. They do so because they see being in a fresh vividness. "The representing of what is … is always already beyond what is—meta. To have seen this meta, i.e. to have thought it, is the simple and thus inexhaustible meaning of all Greek thought" [WCT 98].[16]

Among the pre-Socratics Heidegger most often treats Heraclitus and Parmenides, but he also has an important essay on Anaximander. He says that these three are the only "inceptive thinkers" among the pre-Socratics [Par 2]. He treats them not as reacting to or building upon one another in turn, but as each presenting a part of the same view. Even Heraclitus and Parmenides, who seem polar opposites, say the same, merely describing different aspects of it.[17]

These thinkers all "say the same" inasmuch as they're all describing the basic projection of being as presence.[18] Working backwards:

The *energeia* which Aristotle thinks as the basic trait of presencing, of *eon*, the *idea* which Plato thinks ..., the *Logos* which
Heraclitus thinks ..., the *Moira* which Parmenides thinks ...,
the *Chreôn* which Anaximander thinks as the essencing in presencing, name the same [*das Selbe*]. In the concealed richness of
the same the unity of the unifying One, the *Hen*, is thought by
each thinker in his own way.

[AS (*W* 280)]

These thinkers grasp the One, i.e. the single condition for all entities, the requirement that they "presence" in some way. This
underlying posit is implicit in Homer, but inarticulate, and fleeting
in a way to preclude development. The first philosophers set
themselves the task to articulate this One, and each gives it a principal name. In this they aspire to a kind of understanding deeper
than Homer's and his seer's—of a One that's prior to all the latter's
many truths about entities, even divine and future ones.

Heidegger's claim that each of these philosophers has a theory of
being is perhaps plausible. But his insistence that all of these theories interpret being as presence, and so all say the same, is not,
initially. How does he find common reference to presence in those
theories? The pre-Socratics seldom or nowhere speak, it seems, of
presence, and those principal names they introduce seem quite
unconnected with it. Heidegger needs to interpret them quite for-
cibly to find this in them, we'll see. He will explain and justify this
force by arguing that these philosophers don't adequately understand what they themselves are about. Despite their epistemic
advance they suffer from a special blindspot, which makes them
leave out what's most important—but which he, Heidegger will
supply.

Take first his reading of Anaximander, "the first inceptive thinker" [*Par* 2], whose famous fragment is "considered the oldest
saying of Western thinking" [AS (*W* 242)]. Heidegger starts with
Nietzsche's conventional translation:

> Whence things have their arising, there they must also pass
> away *according to necessity* [*to chreôn*]; *for they must pay penalty and be
> judged for their injustice*, according to the ordinance of time.

He accepts only the italicized part of this as direct quotation, but
takes the rest, as Theophrastus' paraphrase, to be good evidence of
Anaximander's view.

Heidegger reads the first clause of the direct quotation as referring to being, and the second as a statement about entities in general. So he takes *chreôn*, usually translated "necessity," as the first
recorded word for being [AS (*W* 274)]. But he argues, partly on
etymological grounds, that we should hear it to mean not necessity
but "usage" [*Brauch*—also translatable as "custom"], which he glosses
as "to hand over [*aushändigen*] something to its own essence [*Wesen*]
and to keep it in secure hand [*in der wahrenden Hand*] as so presencing
[*Anwesendes*]" [AS (*W* 277)]. He eventually offers this very idiosyncratic
translation of the quotation:

> along usage; for they let jointing [*Fug*] and thereby also regard
> [*Ruch*] belong to one another (in the surmounting) of dis-jointing
> [*Un-fugs*].
>
> [AS (*W* 280)]

What can be his point in this risibly willful and obscure rendering?

The usual reading of the fragment has it refer to the generation
and destruction of things, and explain these by a cosmic force or
principle of equity. Heidegger brings out the condescension hard to
avoid when we read it so: Anaximander sadly lacks an adequate science
to explain things' changes, and imports a cause or reason from the
human sphere; so "[m]oral and juridical notions get mixed into
the picture of nature" [AS (*W* 249)]. He makes predictable mistakes
in an early and still primitive or childish kind of thinking.

Heidegger rates Anaximander much higher,[19] by taking the point
as not causal but transcendental—hence within an ontological

framework that is in a broad sense idealist, though with the realist qualification I mentioned. What's at issue is not a causal agent or power operating to create and destroy particulars, but a logic in the constitution of meaning—the opening of an intentional space, a world or clearing, within which particulars can then "be," i.e. can "presence" (the realist qualification is that we don't open this space on our own). Anaximander has had a glimpse of this underlying event, the opening up of a world of possibilities, by the founding insistence on presence. His basic word for being, to chreôn, names this event, and not a cosmic force operating on things.

Heidegger connects chreôn with cheir, hand, and stresses this in his gloss above. He connects them through the verb chrao, which he presents to mean to handle something, to take it in hand.[20] So it is the hand at work that projects being as chreôn. What unconceals the world of kinds is our manual capacity, the system of ways we know how to handle our surroundings and ourselves. This echoes the role of the hand in Being and Time's account of equipment as "to-hand"— as getting its identity or whatness from our competences over things (see Chapter 4.1 and note 5 in that chapter). Anaximander's chreôn, Heidegger claims, names this practical, physical control, embedded in the customs of a people. It is this that gives us things, and abiding things, stabilizing them out of the buzzing confusion of our surroundings.[21] Entities show up as immediately available for use, and this is the sense in which they are "presences."

Very importantly, however, in naming being Anaximander does something more than describe a transcendental event (the clearing): he prescribes a certain end. The event of clearing, by chreôn or usage, is a precondition for all experience, but it is also something that occurs in degrees—and that we have as a task, to perform more fully or adequately. Our practice unconceals a world of entities, but this unconcealment is incomplete; it calls for improvement. Unconcealment lets entities be, and also assigns us a certain task or standard for letting them be. This valuative or imperative element is a crucial part of the "ontology" Heidegger attributes to

Anaximander—and to all later thinkers. They all not only describe the world-forming of being, but tilt it towards the privileged act or stance that best lets entities be.

The term "usage" already has a valuative element: the constitutive event reveals things as there to be used—for the ends of the practice that lets them be. But besides these many ends embedded in the practice, which we handle things for, there is a single essential end Anaximander claims we have at the transcendental level. This is to perfect or "realize" unconcealment itself, such that entities can most fully "show up" or "presence"—and indeed most fully "be." And it's here—to name this principal value built into Anaximander's (and every subsequent) theory of being— that Heidegger's term "presence" [*Anwesenheit*] does its main work. Handling or usage aims to unconceal things most fully, by making them abide "in hand," and this is Anaximander's inaugural thought of presence. But just how do we handle them so that they so presence?

Back within the pragmatic framework of *Being and Time*, a maximal presence would lie in a full control, the full subjection of a thing to our competences. We've seen that Heidegger attributes some of that framework back to Anaximander, but he also revises it according to his turning. He redescribes the kind of "handling" that—in the original pre-Socratic vision—constitutes a world. For he proceeds (in both AS and the parallel *WCT*) to interpret it in the less aggressive, more receptive terms we've seen he turns to. "'Usage [*Brauchen*]' does not mean the mere utilizing [*Benützen*], using up and using out [*Ab- und Ausnützen*]. ... When we e.g. handle a thing, our hand must measure itself to the thing. Usage implies measuring [*anmessende*] response" [*WCT* 187]. And so: "Usage is: letting into essence, is securing in essence [*Wahrung in Wesen*]."

Anaximander's *chreôn* discloses entities as to-be-used *only* in a certain manner, or under a certain constraint. There is a crucial limit on the aim at presence, as abiding control. This is spelled out in the second clause of the fragment, which tells how usage aims to let entities be. The clause is commonly translated: "for they give justice [dikên] and recompense [tisin] to one another for their injustice [adikias] according to the arrangement of time." But Heidegger thinks this easy rendering into our own familiar concepts hides Anaximander's point.

He translates dikê not by justice but by jointing [Fuge], which he claims Anaximander contrasts with the adikia or disjointing that lies in entities' tendency to cling to their presence. Entities presence (are presences) by "whiling" [Weilen] or lingering each for its time; presences are "each-whilings" [Je-Weiligen]. But they presence not in isolation from one another, but rather in their joints and connections to one another—in a web of dependences. And this sets a kind of limit on their self-assertive whiling. Usage shows entities as giving over their whiles to others within the jointed whole. By contrast, "[t]he dis-jointing occurs when the each-whiling seeks to stiffen itself in a while in the sense of mere constancy [Beständigen]" [AS (W 268)].

Heidegger likewise retranslates tisis, commonly rendered "recompense" or "penalty." Instead he offers the archaic (German) term Ruch, related to our "reck," and like it now used only in a negative form (our "reckless"). I'll translate it "regard," though we must hear it as broader than the "human trait" of consideration or esteem [AS (W 270–72)]. Usage reveals entities as showing a regard for one another, by allowing their whiles to give over to those of others. That is, the practice that opens a world sees the essence of entities as being so to give way to one another. Again this works not as a cosmic force, but as an aim in the constitutive act by which custom lets a world be.

So Anaximander thinks of the overall clearing as releasing things to a handling that fits itself to their essence, and expects them not to cling to their whiles. This is how entities most fully presence, not by persisting, and not by a handling that secures them permanently for its purpose. As mentioned, this amounts to a qualification or limit on the aim at abiding control, involved in our modern (and in *Being and Time*'s) idea of presence; it is the loss of this qualification that sets off the fateful momentum towards modern technology.

Notice the general character of Heidegger's reading: he reinterprets Anaximander as concerned with the human event of "having a world," within which entities can appear. But this event is something that happens to humans, rather than being devised by them. And it imposes on humans a requirement to accomplish most fully things' presencing, by letting them give way to one another in their whiles. This tempers the pragmatic character of the "usage" that constitutes the world.

Heidegger has a strategy here, and with the other pre-Socratics as well. He shapes his readings of their respective ideas of being-as-presence in two directions. On the one hand he points it forward as ultimate root of our own technological stance. So Anaximander's usage will eventually become our way of handling everything in a system of scientific and practical control. But on the other hand he insists that we are wrong when we (as typically) read our own stance back into theirs, since we miss and lose the advantage that distinguishes them. So Anaximander has a healthier idea how custom (usage) can aim to handle things, which Heidegger tries to retrieve.

He has the same strategy with Heraclitus, whose chief word for being he takes to be *Logos*. Again he gives this term a surprising, seemingly willful reading. Here the fragment is Diels-Kranz 50; in a standard translation:

> Listening not to me but to the word [*logou*], it is wise to agree [*homologein*] one is all [*hen panta*].

The usual interpretations of this point out that *logos* has the primary meaning "word," but that from this extend the meanings "account" and "measure"; so Heraclitus' *logos* is something like the overall formula or proportion in the world, capturable in a verbal account.

Heidegger, by contrast, interprets *logos* as "laying [*Legen*] that gathers [*leset*]." He justifies this as retrieving a more original meaning of the Greek verb *legein* (cognate of *logos*) than speaking or saying; it means "the laying-down and laying-before which gathers itself and others" [Lo (EGT 60)].[22] And laying, he goes on to say, is a "bringing-together-into-lying-before" [61]. This indeed seems, as he suggests it will, "an arbitrary interpretation and an all-too-alien translation" [66]. This impression is strengthened when we later hear his translation of the whole fragment:

> Attending not to me but to the laying that gathers: letting the same lie: the fateful essences [*west*] (the laying that gathers): one unifying all.
>
> [75]

Again this seems not just willful but bizarre.

What's going on here, I think, is once more an account of what (Heidegger says Heraclitus thinks) we do, in having a world. Heraclitus names, as decisive, a different aspect of this event than Anaximander: entities can appear because we lay down a persisting structure, that gathers our experience together within a single web. Indeed it also gathers us with one another in relation to the same web, brings us to share the same world. Entities appear only against the background of such a common (shared) structure. So the key term *logos* describes not a worldly thing or force, but this structural operation of establishing ("laying") and unifying ("gathering") that gives us a world.

The "laying that gathers" is the act of imposing this structure in having experience. It interprets and configures its intentional objects in the light of that background network of ends and abilities—that very network that Anaximander names *chreôn* or usage. It gathers that network together; it focuses this accumulated structure in its handling of entities now. (And it then builds each new experience into the background too, laying it down in an efficient memory.) By so focusing these manifold considerations upon each entity it experiences—by concentrating the many into one—it makes each entity most fully a *presence* to it.

This gathering is also expressed in the last two words of Heraclitus' saying: *hen panta*, one many. Heidegger says that this is not the *content* of the *logos* (what it says), but its very manner or way [Lo (EGT 70)]. "The *hen panta* lets lie together before us in one presencing things that usually absence [*abwest*] from and so against one another, such as day and night, winter and summer, peace and war, waking and sleeping" [71]. By having a world, and bringing this many to bear on each entity, we expose them (and us) to contrary descriptions and evaluations. Given this world, the overall framework we bring into each experience, seawater shows up both as pure and as poisonous; the one world we lay down, as background for every entity, is the condition for opposites.

This laying-gathering is not just a transcendental condition for entities to be, it also states an essential, most proper aim. For *legein* occurs in degrees, and our task is to carry it out more properly or adequately. There is a standard for laying and gathering, to which we need to hold ourselves. And once again it is here that Heidegger thinks Heraclitus means "presence"—without knowing that he means it. The point of establishing and unifying a background structure against which to let entities appear is to make them maximally immediate to us. It's in the fullest presence that they are best unconcealed. To this end we try to lay down and gather more and more into the structure we bring to our experience of things. This will culminate in modern science-technology.

Again as with Anaximander, however, there's another, tempering side to this deep aim embedded in Heraclitus' idea of being. Besides this functional or pragmatic aim at things' presence, *logos* has the interest to "keep safe" these things. So again the proper stance involves a certain care towards entities: "Because *legein*, as letting things lie together before us, lies solely in the safety of what lies before in unconcealment, the gathering that belongs to such a laying is determined in advance by safekeeping [*Verwahren*]" [Lo (EGT 63)].

So *logos*, like *chreôn*, has negative and positive aspects. On the one hand it points ahead to technology: the Greeks' idea that entities most are insofar as they "presence" on the ground of the fullest structure will carry us, as a fate, towards technology. But on the other hand Heidegger claims to find something healthier, more positive in Heraclitus' relation to being—and to entities, in the idea that they most fully presence when we regard and secure them.

But what about that usual interpretation of *logos* as word or account? Heidegger denies that Heraclitus is talking about language when he names being as *logos*. Heraclitus fails to see that the transcendental act, constituting a world, happens only through language. So Heidegger posits a strange situation: he imputes his own idea of being-as-presence to Heraclitus, and claims for himself the point about *logos* as language.[23] When Heraclitus does talk about language, it's only about its ontical role in revealing individual entities, not its ontological role of making a clearing for all of them.

What, finally, does Parmenides contribute to this pre-Socratic insight about being that Heidegger assembles from them? It is Parmenides who speaks most directly about being, and the thinking that understands it. He connects them in a brief, enigmatic fragment, Diels-Kranz 3: *to gar auto noein estin te kai einai*. This is often translated:

> For thinking and being are the same.

Heidegger pays repeated attention to this saying, which he calls "the guiding principle of Western philosophy" [IM 154], though by virtue of being misunderstood. Once again he gradually constructs an obtrusively odd replacement for the usual translation:

> For the Same is taking-heed-of and so too presencing (of presence).
>
> [Mo (EGT 92)]

We face another challenge to interpret his interpretation.

Heidegger notes how the fragment, in identifying being and thinking, has often been taken to state an idealism, of either a Berkeleian or Hegelian kind. This takes Parmenides' claim to be that being is settled by thinking, such that to be is to be the object of a subject's representing. But this misses his sense of both *einai* and *noein*. It also misses how Parmenides relates them: he's not clarifying being by so restricting it to (the objects of) thinking, but restricting (genuine) thinking by telling us what it is about [Mo (EGT 84)]. And when he says it is about *einai*, he means, Heidegger claims, not really being, nor yet merely entities, but precisely the "duality" of them both, a duality encapsulated in another of Parmenides' key terms, *eon*, which suggests both entities in their being, and the being of entities [86].[24]

So Parmenides' point is that *noein* is the "taking heed" of the duality between being and entities—it doesn't *constitute* that duality, as the idealists suppose. The latter is instead accomplished by the *legein*, by the "letting-lie-before" that Heraclitus had in view, and which Heidegger thinks Parmenides also refers to (so that his Parmenides is a kind of idealist after all). "Only as so lying-before can presence as such concern the *noein*, the taking-heed-of" [Mo (EGT 89)]. It is only through establishing this background framework that a clearing is opened up for entities, which thinking can then treat. Moreover, Parmenides believes this framework is laid out by the same "usage" that Anaximander names.[25] Thinking is then the condition in which we "take heed of" this duality.

It's with this notion of a privileged thinking that value is embedded in Parmenides' "theory of being" as well. The world is laid out prior to thinking, but it is laid out with an essential task: to realize it by thinking it. This thinking is, on the one hand, a matter of "presencing" the duality of being and entities [Mo (EGT 88)]. But on the other hand Heidegger insists, as we by now expect, that this presencing is tempered or limited a certain way. It is not the representing and objectifying that thinking became, when that limit was lost. So he stresses that *noein* is not a "grasping" [*Greifen*], hence does not work by concepts (*Begriffe*); it is rather a "taking-heed-of," i.e. into "the gathering in which what lies before is, as such, kept safe" [*WCT* 211].

Returning to Diels-Kranz 3, its key word is *auto*, the same, which Heidegger says is the real subject. "What keeps silent in the puzzle-word *to auto*, the same, is the revealing bestowal of the belonging-together of the duality with the thinking that comes to appearance within it" [Mo (*EGT* 95); cf. *ID* 27ff.]. But he stresses that this key idea—of the sameness of *legein* and *noein*—needs further thought, and indeed we will see it is an ongoing issue in his later writing: the relation between the background act by which a world "is there" for us all, and the special state—the "truth of being"—in which this unconcealment is "realized."

Heidegger draws one more important element of the pre-Socratic view from Parmenides, claiming it is named by his word *moira*, commonly translated "fate," but which Heidegger calls *Zuteilung*, apportionment. This is "the sending [*Schickung*], gathered in itself and thus unfolding, of presencing as presencing of presence. *Moira* is the destiny of 'being' in the sense of *eon*" [Mo (*EGT* 97)]. That is, *moira* is the "sentness" of being as the presencing of entities; it expresses the sense that we have been *given* this kind of opening—being as presence—not chosen it ourselves. We have indeed been "sent" *ourselves*, by this gift of an opening, with a momentum, along a path, not at all subject to our choice. It is this sentness of being—and of ourselves with it—that will unfold in the history of philosophy, and in the cultural history it articulates.

In sum, Heidegger interprets these three pre-Socratics as having a privileged glimpse of being, and of being as presence in particular. (Or, more strictly, they had a glimpse only of "the being of entities," or of "entities in their being," or of the "duality" of being and entities—and not of being itself.)[26] They give names to this being, and when heard properly these names articulate different parts of a unified view, a view that strongly mirrors Heidegger's own. This seeing and naming of being was a pivotal cultural event, setting in motion our real history, as the implications of this original opening to being were very slowly unfolded—but in a way that progressively "closed off" that opening. Let's look more quickly at the arc of this further history.

ii. Being's history

Heidegger tells an extremely detailed "history of being." This history is punctuated, broken into epochs, each with its own decisive words for being. It is philosophers (and poets, we'll later see) who make these words, and institute these epochs, as he tries to show by close attention to a number of major philosophers. He taught courses or wrote books on many of these, including Plato, Aristotle, Kant, Schelling, Hegel, and Nietzsche; he gives more local attention to many more. I'll try to convey the overall direction he imputes to this history by encapsulating his accounts of the most major figures.[27]

The pre-Socratics initiate this history both by what they see and say, and by what they fail to see and say. They experience being as presence and put it into their basic words, but they see it not in itself but only in its relation to entities (the duality). They already have the tendency that will mislead all their successors, the tendency to interpret being as a special entity. Moreover, they fail to name presence *as* presence. We can see that they all take it so, but they can't, so that each gives his own articulation of presence, without noticing that common character.

This failure to recognize presence itself contributes to the fatedness of this opening to develop as it has. Not seeing the secret to the series to which they belong, philosophers have been subject to its logic. Heidegger calls this logic of development in the history of being *destiny* [*Geschick*]. "*Es gibt*" being, but this giving "holds itself back and withdraws," so that it is a sending [*Schicken*]. Being is sent/destined [*geschickt*] [TB (OTB 8)]. Heidegger's image is of an initial impetus—that original opening—that throws, and so of course releases the process to work as it must.

The logic or working of this destiny is telic. Embedded in the pre-Socratics' idea of being is a certain goal: the ideal of a maximal presence in which entities show themselves most unconcealedly. This goal gets taken over as presupposed task by each later thinker, who strives to improve and perfect this presence. So what the pre-Socratics say lies not merely behind us but also ahead of us, as this goal we are still working towards.

We've seen that presence involves immediacy of relation, but also a relation that secures, i.e. abides or lasts; it is, as it were, an *effective* immediacy, that is able to maintain itself. Presencing takes both epistemic and pragmatic forms. In both cases it involves what I have called "grasp," either by understanding or by having-to-hand. The thing presences before us by being maximally available, whether for inspection or for use. So Heidegger says that both at-hand and to-hand (in *Being and Time*'s terms) are perceived under presence [TB (OTB 7)].

Hence the overall tendency of being's history is to convert this presencing into the most thorough *control*: things are, as they are when they are subject to this fullest control. This control can take the form of a theory, that places the thing precisely in a complete picture of the whole, or in a practice, that makes complete use of the thing within a system of aims. This tendency towards a maximal control culminates in our own current opening to being, technology.

It's important to see how this drive towards control works crucially at the ontological level. In metaphysics, there is a glimpse of the projective act by which a background "world" is presupposed—the web of possibilities that Heraclitus calls *logos*. This "laying that gathers," i.e. the laid-down network that unifies our experience of things, comes to a kind of self-awareness. Hence it becomes visible as an act or project that can itself be worked on, improved, and perfected. How can we craft this background framework we bring to experience, so that it will let us experience things in maximal presence? Metaphysics is the effort to control the background event so as to improve control of particulars. Its destiny is its progress in this regard.

The long process by which the transcendental event—the opening of being—is recognized and improved is a transition into a fuller, more explicit idealism, where that event is increasingly interpreted as humans' own *act*, and designed and improved as such. This movement has its start in Plato, in his interpretation of *on* (being) as *idea*, is pushed further in Descartes' account of the *ego*'s certainty in (some) representations, and still further in Hegel's idea of absolute knowing as *self*-knowing [CP 141]. Not just entities, but the very condition for entities, is brought into ever fuller presence and control.

However, this progress towards the goal of presence has involved a regressive "closing off" of being down through this history. For as we become more and more what we must be to exercise the most perfect control of things' presence, we slide ever further away from the transcendental stance towards being. We lose sight more and more of the fact that it is indeed presence that is being for us. And this is true in spite of that momentum towards idealism. (I'll return to this "oblivion of being" in section 4.)

Among the Greeks this aim towards perfect control is held in check by the "saving" features we noticed in the pre-Socratics, in particular their stance of reception and reverence towards both entities and being. The fullest presence is not one in which we control them, but one in which they show themselves, and we receive their showing as a gift. Heidegger supposes that the Greek thinkers take this view because they are closer to—still fresh from—the experience of being itself.

There is already a falling-off in Plato, however—and here we can begin to review this further history. Plato slides further from being towards entities.[28] He misinterprets the transcendental as relating to a special domain of entities. His key word *idea* is a new way to specify presence: we stand in the most immediate and lasting relation to the *idea*, which thus "is" to the highest degree. Only in relation to these *ideai* are there other, sensible and transitory things at all, which are given to us only indirectly despite our illusion of their immediacy. These *ideai*, however, are clearly entities, so that Plato has lost even the "duality" (between being and entities) seen by Parmenides: the deepest he can think to go is to a domain of special entities, not to the world-constituting event of being, which lets any entities be.

By interpreting being as an entity Plato inaugurates metaphysics. By interpreting being as the highest entity, he makes his metaphysics an "ontotheology." "This highest and first cause is named by Plato and correspondingly by Aristotle *to theion*, the divine. Ever since the interpretation of being as *idea*, thinking about the being of entities is metaphysical, and metaphysics is theological" [PD (P 180–81)]. Meaning comes onto the scene through ideas, and we and things around us have meaning in relation to ideas as ends.

The perfect presence—in which entities most "are"—is the nearness of an idea to the knowing mind. Knowing is now first conceived as the grasp of ideas, and with this Plato effects a decisive change in the notion of truth (here I touch on a topic we'll examine in section 5). Truth ceases to be what Homer and the pre-Socratics thought it to be, unconcealment—evident in the structure of the word *alêtheia*. Plato (according to Heidegger in PD) makes truth the "correctness" of a gaze to the *idea*, and so initiates the correspondence notion of truth. Heidegger counts this a large step in the wrong direction.[29] (He later takes back this charge, however, allowing that the notion of truth as correspondence long preceded Plato; see TB (OTB 70)).

Heidegger is more sympathetic to Aristotle than to Plato. (He owes an old debt to him, having acquired his life-long question about being from Brentano's work on him.) He takes Aristotle to preserve more of the original pre-Socratic standpoint, in particular in his notion of *phusis* or nature. In an important paper on this notion, Heidegger uses it to elucidate unconcealment, the genuine kind of truth missed by Plato.[30] It's not, however, that Aristotle quite recognizes unconcealment himself. His treatment of *phusis* is "an *echo* of the great beginning of Greek philosophy," a "derivative [*Abkömmling*] of initial *phusis*" [EC (P 229)]. For the pre-Socratics were talking about being when they said *phusis*, whereas Aristotle takes it to be the essence of just one kind of entity, things "by nature," things with a nature.

Still his account of it is our best clue to excavate that original notion. *Phusis* is: unfolding from a source that remains indistinct or hidden. This is how Aristotle sees all living organisms—the plant sprouting out from the closed-in seed. But the pre-Socratics applied it (Heidegger claims) not just to entities, but to the basic or background event that "opens a world," an intentional space in which entities can then appear. *Phusis* describes how the clearing is opened not by our deliberate choice, but through a hidden source. This world is "unconcealed," and entities enabled to show up in it, by a source itself concealed. (Heidegger takes Heraclitus to express this in Diels-Kranz 123: *phusis kruptesthai philei*, nature loves to hide.) We can measure Aristotle's drift from the original experience of this unconcealment, by the way he applies it to a mere class of entities.

Let's survey rapidly the main stages since. The overall direction of movement is from a more realist position among the Greeks, in which being is thought as received by us, to the modern idealist position that claims authority over being for humans. This idealism perfects the aim at presence founded by the Greeks: metaphysics gradually designs the background projection of being, so as to maximize entities' presencing. Each of the great metaphysicians adds another element to the position that will eventually constitute modern technology.

Descartes takes a first decisive step: he founds the modern age by making man the *subiectum*. He does so by interpreting presence as the certainty a subject can achieve about objects it represents.[31] By contrast the Greeks did not yet think of subjects and objects, Heidegger claims. And although Plato treats being as *idea*, the latter is not a representation, but something independent of us. By locating truth in the certainty of a subject's representations, Descartes identifies a field of immediacy over which we can exercise a new kind of control. "To represent means here: of oneself, to set something before one and to make what has been set in place secure as thus set in place. ... Representing is no longer the self-revealing for ... , but rather the grasping and gripping of [*Ergreifen und Begreifen von*]" [AWP (*W* 82)].

Leibniz may be even more important in articulating the modern view.[32] In *The Principle of Ground* Heidegger interprets Leibniz's principle "nothing is without a ground" (i.e. a reason) as the demand that guides modernity by expressing our understanding of being: "a realm opens up for an expressly arranged determining of the ground of entities. This brings the possibility of what we call modern natural science and modern technology" [PG 55]. Since Leibniz we have challenged ourselves to perfect the background web of reasons and explanations, against which we can place and secure each thing we encounter.

Kant is obviously crucial for his transcendental move, by which humans' role in projecting a background—being—is first made explicit. But Kant attributes this projection to a representing subject that "posits" objects in order to unify its sensible given. In "Kant's Thesis about Being" (in P) Heidegger treats the well-known passage in the first Critique that denies "being" is a real predicate and says "it is merely the positing of a thing." This positing is carried out by a representing subject descended from Descartes'; it depends on that subject's transcendental apperception, which "makes possible the object as such" [KT (P 348)]. Hence for Kant being is "the objectivity of the object of experience" [350]. Things are full presences when we grasp them by a science fully grounded in transcendental understanding (as given in the first Critique).

Hegel carries further the subjectivization of being.[33] Now the full and ideal presence occurs in absolute subjectivity, which is achieved through the "experience of consciousness," i.e. through the historical process by which consciousness discovers, by skepticism over its knowledge of phenomena (entities), the absolute knowledge of its own projection (being). So Hegel is the first philosopher to make thinking historical.[34] But his ambition in this thinking is to appropriate history and thereby surpass it in a knowing which Hegel still conceives in the Cartesian way as correctness and certainty [CP 142]. Hegel hasn't seen the basic aim of that history—the grip of an ideal presence—and so still operates inside this framework. Paradoxically, what we need in order to recognize this framework is to give up the aspiration to transcend past stages, but instead to "step back" to their disclosive view [ID 49].

Nietzsche represents the culmination and completion of the metaphysics of presence. I will present Heidegger's reading of him in more detail in the next section, but notice here how Nietzsche carries forward the idealism in Kant and Hegel: it's not a matter of discovering the necessary conditions of human experience, nor of completing a necessary historical dialectic, but of our freely making a world by our will. So the human takes a final control over the transcendental act of constituting a world (being), and thereby control over entities.

So much for now on the history of being. We'll return and approach this history from further angles when we look at Heidegger's notion of "metaphysics" in Chapter 8, and at his account of Nietzsche in Chapter 9.

3. Being in itself

Besides strongly historicizing his idea of being, Heidegger makes another large change in it, which affects how we must hear the history. One way to put it is that he moves towards a realism about being; this is why he counts the overall trend from a Greek realism to a modern idealism as a devolution. That is, he now accords being a certain independence from us—humans, Dasein—which

Being and Time didn't allow. Though evident, the change proves very difficult to characterize, since Heidegger refuses the usual philosophical terms for it, including, especially, "realism" itself. And indeed, we must bear in mind that being is not "real" as a thing or entity. Immediately, this change seems to stand in tension with the first, since being's historicality seems to involve its dependence on us; in this way idealism persists in the later works. We must try to see how these views can fit together.[35]

Let's start by reviewing *Being and Time* on this question. We've seen (near the start of Chapter 3) that this book seems to settle early the question of realism-or-idealism—settle it on the side of idealism. *Es gibt* being, being obtains, only by virtue of Dasein's understanding being, i.e. only by its opening a world, its "clearing." Being is not—as usually supposed—the highest genus of entities, discovered in or about those entities. There are indeed "kinds" of entities—equipment to-hand and objects at-hand—but these are distinguished not by intrinsic features, but by Dasein's different ways of clearing a space in which to encounter them. To-handness and at-handness, the modes of being of equipment and objects, are the ways our pragmatic and theoretic stances project their background worlds. These modes of being occur, as it were, not in the things but in Dasein.

It might, however, seem that *Being and Time* does take a realist stance on the third mode of being it treats, Dasein's own. The book claims to be analyzing Dasein's being, and seems to treat this as independent of the way Dasein interprets itself. Indeed the book stresses how wrong we usually are about our being. To be sure this would be a very attenuated realism—in a sense in which Berkeley too would be a realist, when he agrees that not everything is ideas, since there are also the minds those ideas are in. For Berkeley these minds are real and independent of any ideas of them, and for Heidegger the same would be true of Dasein and its understanding. But such an attenuated realism has always been called idealism.

Moreover, I think *Being and Time* in fact denies even this attenuated realism. Dasein's being is not, in fact, independent of its self-understanding. At its deepest level Dasein *does* understand itself, Heidegger claims, and this understanding makes it what it is. Its own being is *constituted* by this essential self-grasp. We do indeed often "get it wrong," but this happens in the more superficial ways we think of ourselves. Our task is to face and live by that deeper understanding. Even our own being, then, is "ideal"—made to be by our (underlying) intentionality. This is another reason for denying that Dasein is a substance.

To be sure, *Being and Time* intends a kind of realism—an internal realism—about *entities*: given that such-and-such a world has been cleared, it's not up to us what particular entities then show up within it. It is our world, our web of purposes and grasps, that lets such a thing as "clouds" appear, but just when and how they appear is settled outside us, as it were by clouds themselves. Yet still the latter only are, by virtue of our opening that world. Heidegger's (early) position mirrors Kant's of an empirical (or internal) realism contained within a transcendental idealism.

In his later writing Heidegger deliberately backs off from this idealism of being. This belongs to the general turn he made away from the pragmatic-existential schematization of Dasein, which now seems to him Nietzschean in a bad sense: it expresses a hubristic assumption by man of full authority over the world. And in this light idealism looks like another way for the human to claim ultimate authority: it alone lets entities be.

The metaphysics of presence, our destiny, bears this aim to assume control, over entities and all their conditions. Things are, in that experience in which they are most *presences* to us—i.e. are immediately before us, in a way that will last. The history of metaphysics progressively enhances the control taken over these presences, by improving the background framework of "grounds" against which these presences can be fixed. Hence our destiny's deep push is towards idealism: being is what we constitute it to be, by that projected framework.

Heidegger believes, provokingly, that modern science and technology are idealist in this sense. Of course they pride themselves as the most hard-headed realism. Yet ultimately they take things most fully to be as they are when fixed in precise place within a comprehensive system—the system of science, the system of technology. They bring these background systems strongly to bear on every thing they meet, allowing it no chance to "show itself from itself." Things can "really" be only *as* they are so fixed and controlled. They are in this way allowed no independence from us: they can keep no secrets or mysteries. But this deep idealist premise is not noticed within this scientific-technological stance. It can't see its own deep posit of being as presence.

But if being is presence in and by this posit, isn't Heidegger's position idealist too? Here we come to the countervailing thought: that although humans hold open a clearing by their understanding of being, still they depend on being to reveal itself to them. So they understand it not indeed by the imposition of a "posit," but in a receptivity and listening. "Thinking completes [vollbringt] the relation of being to the essence of man. It does not make or cause this relation. Thinking brings [this relation] towards being solely as given over to [thinking] itself from being" [LH (P 239)]. As we try to make sense of Heidegger's idea here we meet central puzzles or mysteries.

His ultimate idea has always been, we've seen, that there's an ontological difference between entities and being—that being is no kind of entity, and that we must guard against the constantly evolving temptations to think of it so. We've understood being's non-entitihood to follow from its transcendental status, as the condition for entities to be. And we've understood this condition to be realized in the background event by which an intentionality "has a world," within which entities can then appear—can presence. So being seems an achievement in and by intentionality, its opening up of an intentional space or world. How can this picture allow being that independence from us?

Now there's already a problem with this picture: why isn't that "intentionality" an entity, violating the rule against understanding being in terms of entities? If there can only be entities once there is a clearing (of being), then no entity can be a prior cause (or explainer) of the clearing. When we say that humans "have" or "open" a world, this cannot be by bringing it about it, since they *are* only by virtue of it. The answer, I think, is that this meaning or intending of being is not a cause, or even an entity, but rather an aspect or element of the clearing—a part of its very structure.

And the same point applies, I suggest, to being: this is another aspect of the clearing, and not an entity either, that could stand apart from us and affect us. To be sure, some of Heidegger's language encourages the idea of being as an independent cause. He sometimes even seems to treat it as an independent intentionality— as when he speaks of it as "granting," or when he says that it "desires" to be thought [WCT 6], or when he says that it "turns away" from us today [7]. He seems to put it in the role commonly credited to gods, so that many have read his late idea of being as a code way of speaking of God.[36]

But surely we must read this language as figurative, since it is Heidegger's ultimate and firmest conviction that being is not an entity; we've seen his hostility to any such "ontotheology." And he specifically attacks "the almost ineradicable habit of representing 'being' as an opposite standing on its own and then sometimes approaching man" [QB (P 310)]. No more than we can be before (prior to) the clearing, can being be before it. It can no more cause the clearing than we can.[37] So it too must be not a prior cause but a part of the initiating event of the clearing itself. We and being are structural elements in that transcendental event, which Heidegger eventually calls *Ereignis*.[38]

Does this return us to idealism, with being again "within" some kind of mental space? No, because that event has a different structure than that of a mind/subject with ideas/representations. In his account of the *Ereignis* Heidegger means to reconfigure the very structure of intentionality or meaning; at the deep level at which *es gibt* being for us, this does not occur in that proprietary fashion. The way our usual thinking "grips" its ideas belongs within the project of presence. When we step down to the level of *Ereignis*, we come back before that projection is made—back before we make ourselves a subject surveying a content.[39]

This, I think, is how we must understand the independence of being—the way Heidegger shifts towards a quasi-realism: it's not by positing being as an entity over against us, but by giving it a stronger role in the basic intentional event, the clearing or *Ereignis*. Intentionality takes a different form at this level: meaning and meant are related differently than usual. The usual is to subordinate the meant to the act of meaning it: an idea is after all something that occurs "in" a mind, it has a one-sided dependence on a mind. An intentional "content" has a similar dependence on an act of meaning. But the ultimate intending, the intending of being, happens with a different logic or structure. It happens with a more mutual dependence between us and being.[40]

Nor is it merely that we must *view* being so—must interpret it as separate, as given not made, in order to have the idea of it at all. This would license realist talk, but only within idealist quotation marks. Heidegger is indeed much interested in helping us to shape our attitudes to be receptive to being. But when being arrives it must come not as an idea, but in that different intentional relation in which it really is more and different.

The point, once again, is meant to have practical import. This event is accessible to us: we can experience this step back before the assumption of presence. We can set aside the intentional stance that ensues from that assumption, the stance of "presencing" the things we mean; we abandon the role of subjects wielding our ideas. We thereby reach the ground on which this meaning of being occurs, and in it being will meet us as something fresh and separate from us as our ideas never can be.

It's by redrawing the structure of the intentional relation in this way that Heidegger gives being its kind of independence. We now see how he can do so without either (1) turning being into a real entity apart from us, or (2) rendering that independence just "how we have to think of being" (which would subjectivize it once again). Being "is" this way it shows itself in the event of clearing a world. But it shows itself not as an idea we possess and control—it's not as an idea that we are towards it in this founding event.

4. The oblivion of being

Before turning to Heidegger's account of the truth about being, we should look at what this truth must be won *against*. Its achievement is rare and difficult, because strong tendencies hide or obscure being from us. Heidegger, as prophet, sounds the alarm about forces that pull us relentlessly away from the truth of being. Together he calls these the "*oblivion*" [*Vergessenheit*] of being—which is thus something dynamic. These forces operate at several levels.

Most broadly, we've seen that Heidegger's history of being plots an overall decline, in this all-important dimension of our access to being. Being is what it most behooves us to think, yet the history of Western ontologies shows an ever-worsening ability to think about being. Each epoch stands further from "the truth of being." More-over, each epoch within its course enacts a gradual falling off from an insight achieved at its own beginning. And this falling-off also happens within each individual: each of us tends likewise to slide away from any inklings of being we might get. The oblivion of being works on all of these levels.

Now Heidegger's term *Vergessenheit* means literally "forgotten-ness"—a deficiency in memory of something once already seen. We'll examine his conception of this memory. The term reveals the strong relation to Plato's famous thought that our souls, upon incarnation, forget the Forms and need help to remember their acquaintance with them. Heidegger partly models his point after Plato's, but with a crucial change in the account of the kind of truth we tend to forget.

These critical claims about a tendency to untruth are closely interwoven with Heidegger's more neutral claim that *concealment* [*Verborgenheit*] is pervasive and inevitable. One of being's defining aspects is that its clearing or unconcealment is always bound up with a concealment; this may indeed be Heidegger's principal point about being. It is in order to express it that he so favors the Greek word for truth, *alêtheia*, hearing it to mean an unconcealment that overcomes a prior concealment. PD (P 171): "Truth initially means what has been wrested from concealment." He will also employ the term "earth" for this inevitable hidden.

We must distinguish from this inevitable and essential conceal-ment that "oblivion" which he is clearly critical of, and exhorts us to overcome. (Notice how this problem repeats the one over *Being and Time*'s neutral and negative notions of "falling" treated in Chapters 4.5 and 5.1.) Often it seems that the latter is just a form of that concealment—perhaps a greater degree of it, or a special application of it. Oblivion includes a failure to see the essential role of concealment in being: "concealing appears as what is first of all concealed" [ET (P 148)]. By contrast the truth of being will include an unconcealing of being *as* (involving) a concealment. So is oblivion just the second-order form of concealment, or else some higher degree of it?

Heidegger does sometimes treat oblivion as homogeneous with the inevitable concealment in these ways. But I think he also means more to distinguish them. Concealment, as I will develop in section 5.ii of this chapter, is the way being, in our most adequate experience of it, must be shown as granting itself partly from a greater, hidden store. To experience being in this way we must therefore suspend our importunate demand to bring everything into presence before our knowing view. Oblivion, by contrast, is our momentum away from that experience, due to several factors (or forces), among them that very insistence on presence.

Oblivion has "forgotten" being not of course as per Plato—by not remembering the soul's pre-history before this incarnated life. The "forgetting" is principally synchronic: a human is constantly positing being as presence—this posit sets the underlying aim—but "forgets" or overlooks that he/she is doing so, even while doing it. There is no requirement that this human has earlier "seen" this explicitly. What makes it apt to call this oversight forgetting, however, is the way it generally worsens, Heidegger thinks, at those several levels mentioned before. The West has "forgotten" the more adequate sight of being by the early Greeks; each historical age gradually "forgets" the vivid idea of being it began with; and individual humans too "forget" whatever glimpses of being they may have had.

The claim that this dynamic oblivion is usual poses a puzzle: why should it be our essence to house and think being, if this deep momentum pulls away from it? Why are we so ill-constituted that we have to fight this deep tendency in order to stand in proper relation to being? I don't see that Heidegger ever recognizes such questions, and it's not clear whether he has the resources to deal with them—except of course by asserting that once one achieves insight into being, in the event of the truth of being, one sees (with conclusive clarity) why this event involves this risk and task.

The claim about a tendency to concealment obviously goes back to *Being and Time*, where our "falling" has epistemic import: it is crucially a tendency to misunderstand our own being. There Heidegger attributes this tendency to two sources, first an inertial drift into the implicit and generic, and second the effort to avoid being because death and guilt are bound up in it. These arise at the pragmatic and existential levels of the system, respectively. They are tendencies in the individual Dasein whose intentionality is structured in those pragmatic and existential ways. How does this earlier idea of falling get modified into the late notion of oblivion? We can plot this at each of the levels at which oblivion occurs.

(a) Take first individual oblivion: after the turn Heidegger continues to think individual persons have a tendency to forget being. There is a drift or momentum away from the truth of being in each of us, that pulls us relentlessly in the wrong direction, into an absorption in entities. But Heidegger now reconceives of that misdirection—our forgetting—in the light of his turn against the pragmatic and existential accounts.

The existential diagnosis of falling drops out almost altogether: we don't forget being out of anxiety over our death and guilt. Those existential worries—Heidegger comes to feel—express a self-obsessed subjectivism, which takes itself able to answer, all by itself, its essential task (which is to choose/make itself while in the individualizing relations to death and guilt). The ideal of authenticity owes no dependence on anything beyond Dasein's own nature—and no need to "listen" to anything beyond the "call of conscience" that comes from that nature. So this whole motivational system drops out of Heidegger's later thought.

But I think there are more survivals of the diagnosis in the pragmatism of *Being and Time*, which attributes falling to an unmotivated tendency towards the generic and implicit. There the drift to the generic is due to the nature of language—that words can be "passed along" and understood in an average way. And the drift to implicitness is due to the foreground/background structure of intentionality, which has to push most meanings into implicitness, in order to give effective, focused attention to one or a few. What's secure and doesn't need to be attended to is pushed into background—and being thus becomes the very deepest background.

Heidegger keeps these points in his later view: being falls into the deep background as we deal with particulars. "Prior to all else it stands before us, only we do not see it because we stand within it"

[*WCT* 98]. We fail to notice the deep formative event of opening a world, and are able to see only the things showing up within it. "The oblivion of being announces itself indirectly in that man always observes and handles only entities" [LH (P 258); cf. *WCT* 236–37]. Moreover, whenever we do try to think about this condition for entities, we tend over and again to interpret it as an entity itself. We must push constantly against this powerful bias to the ontical if we're to notice being.

But these points, which still seem accounts of the human situation in general, are pushed to the side by Heidegger's new historical analysis: it is our cultural insistence on presence that is most to blame for our forgetting of being. Under technology our thinking is shaped to give a prodigiously effective control of all its objects. But this kind of thinking is radically unsuited to witness being. Its very effectiveness is due to how thoroughly it has pushed being into the background, so that entities can appear as maximal presences. The insistence that entities *are* to the extent that they can be fixed in the systems of science and technology prevents being from showing up at all.

By this historical analysis forgetting becomes something we have been "destined" to. For it stems from the appearance of being as presence, which (as we saw in section 3) required an initial "granting" by being, of itself. M 193: "oblivion of being would never be a mere oversight of man, rather it would eventuate by being itself." Our Western history then unfolds the implications of that "first beginning," and our technological world is its fated culmination. This long story principally accomplishes the loss of being. This historical oblivion happens both within each epoch, and in the passage from each to the next.

(b) Take now the progressive oblivion within each epoch. An epoch is founded by a thinker's (or poet's) access to a new way of understanding being, which he/she states in new basic words. These words have their maximal freshness in the thinker's own mouth. In this potency they embed their new meanings in the language, so that entities appear to its speakers in new light, under a new regime of being. By this novelty speakers have some sense of being, itself, and its role in letting entities be. But as these words and meanings grow settled they merge into the implicit background that sets up a world. And so they eventually suffer the fate we've seen, of being "passed along" as tokens out of all relation to the original experience by the thinker. Hence each epoch deteriorates, drifting out of the vision that initiated its understanding.

(c) Take last the oblivion operating from epoch to epoch, over the long-term course of our history, as our fate. This is the progressive "closing off" of being that happens by the logic of our Western understanding of being as presencing. There is a devolution from epoch to epoch in this history: being is increasingly obscured as the understanding of being as presence advances, and each ensuing epoch's understanding enables a grasp of a fuller presencing.

To be sure, even that pre-Socratic beginning involved a forgetting: "In the beginning of Western thinking being is thought, but not the "Es gibt [It gives]" as such. This withdraws in favor of the gift that Es gibt, which gift is thought henceforth exclusively as being with regard to entities, and brought into a concept" [TB (OTB 8); also NW (W 196) and AS (W 275)].

But the working-out of the understanding of being as presence— the development of ever-more effective ways to bring entities into fullest presence—draws epochs ever further from the pre-Socratic experience, flawed as it already was. IWM (P 281): "What if the absence of this relation [of being to the human essence] and the oblivion of this absence determined the entire modern age from afar? What if the absence of being left man more and more exclusively over to entities, ... and this abandonment itself remained veiled?"

As this suggests, the worst feature of our contemporary forgetting of being is that this oblivion is itself forgotten. In our own age being "remains absent in a strange way. It conceals itself. It holds itself in a concealment that conceals itself" [QB (P 313)]. Heidegger appropriates Nietzsche's term "nihilism" for this extreme modern form of the oblivion of being [IM 217]. His prophet-like complaints are aimed against this meta-concealment. But we still need, most importantly, to hear his positive account how being can be thought adequately.

5. The truth of being

Despite the pervasiveness and inevitability of concealment, there is possible for us an event in which being is unconcealed. To accomplish this is the task of "thinking" [Denken]—which is of course not metaphysics, and even no longer philosophy. Thinking is indeed distinguished by this aim at the truth of being, not at any truths about entities. This deepest truth—or rather "unconcealment" [Unverborgenheit], as Heidegger eventually prefers to call it—is a special and rare event in which a person comes into proper relation to being. His name for the privileged experience in which we dwell in the truth of being is Ereignis. This term ordinarily means "event," but bears (to Heidegger's ear) the same root—eigen (own), as in Eigentlichkeit (authenticity). So it is the event in which we "come into our own," by coming into that proper relation to being.

These three topics—thinking, unconcealment, and Ereignis—are so crucial in late Heidegger that all of his other ideas really serve to promote and develop them. So we'll be pursuing them further in the following chapters, in particular by seeing the roles that art and religion play in these achievements. Here I want to focus first on points bearing on the general epistemic character and status of these three notions.

As we'll see, there are important ambiguities in these notions—or certain double applications Heidegger makes of them. Sometimes he applies them to individuals, but elsewhere he treats them as large-scale social occurrences. Sometimes they seem to be happening all along, as a condition for everything else, but elsewhere he presents them as rare and revolutionary events. And sometimes these notions seem purely epistemic, but elsewhere he gives them a creative and constitutive role. We will need to resolve these seeming conflicts by showing how these ideas fit together in a unified account.

Heidegger's terminology is especially fluid on these topics. Although his point looks (to me) fairly constant in its outlines, he steadily modifies his preferred terms to express it. About each new expression, he quickly sees how it can be misinterpreted back into our ordinary model of truth, and revises his terminology again to plug this new hole. (He no doubt frustrated many students each time they learned the new term-set.) To track these adjustments would give the fullest sense of his epistemic point. But I will have to elide most of the complexity here, and compress these shifts and adjustments into a single argument.

i. Thinking

"Thinking" is Heidegger's favorite term for our path towards the all-important truth of being. He abandons first "metaphysics" and then "philosophy" as rubrics for this.[41] Generically, thinking is the activity whose end is truth. But Heidegger reserves the term for its highest or fullest form. So, first, it is that activity carried out well, carried out as it should be, best for the sake of truth. And, second, it is for the sake not just of truth generally, but of the most important and ultimate sort of truth, which is the truth of being. Thinking alone brings us into relation to being itself, rather than entities. Science, since it never gets beyond entities, "does not think." Nor does common sense nor any other of our usual cognitive practices, since all of them reach only to entities. Indeed thinking is particularly difficult and rare in our modern age.

Heidegger's most important lesson to us is to think; it's the effect he above all wants to have. We his readers want honestly now to do so—what then are we to do?

Schematically put: we need to turn our attention to a different topic, and attend to it in a different way. We need to think about being instead of entities, and to think somehow not with concepts or representations. CP 326: "En-thinking [Er-denken] of be-ing [Seyn] does not think up a concept but rather achieves that freeing from mere entities, which makes apt for the determination of thinking out of be-ing."[42]

Consider first thinking's topic: how do we bring our attention to being? Being resides at the deepest level of constitution, by which es gibt a world or clearing in which entities can appear. Thinking must reach down to this most basic "giving" of our world. And Heidegger has a proposal—a further claim—about what it will find when it attends to this level: thinking sees that the clearing is most basically constituted as presence. His account how we understand being as presence can help us to locate the level of constitution he means.

It's important to bear in mind that being and presence are not the same: the latter is an interpretation or specification of the former. Thinking needs not only to notice presence, but to see it as an interpretation of being. Our danger today is that we see only presences, and not how we're interpreting being in this. So I dis-agree with Blattner's forthright assertion: "For later Heidegger, being means presence" [1999 289]. It means this within our his-torical horizon (our "Western destiny"), but Heidegger wants thinking to peek above that horizon, to see how there could be different openings on being than our own. The most important thing is to prise being apart from presence, so that we can see it as just a way for being to obtain. So WCT 235: "we would fall into a mistake if we supposed the being of entities meant only and for all time: the presencing of presences."[43]

How then do we interpret/constitute being as presencing? As we've seen, we do so by presupposing a certain project or aim: to bring things to presence. Ontology occurs as teleology: we open a world by the way we're directed at ends. Presencing gives the world not in pure factual neutrality, but as a field of concerns, in which we have one fundamental concern: to maximize entities' presence. Entities are, insofar as they are presences, and they are presences to different degrees. Our ("Western") interpretation of being aims to bring everything to fullest presence, either as a resource or in a theoretical system. Hence being as presencing is the transcendental "project" (in *Being and Time*'s term) that serves as ground for all our more particular ways of finding and using things. But almost always we overlook that general expectation, pervasive as it is, and care only about our tactics and achievements in emplacing things.

So, since thinking is about being, we can come to think by somehow carrying our attention down to this basic project of presencing that underlies our world. But probably it is not enough to be told this. The telling may *in a way* bring our attention to this project, but obviously not in the right way. We need some further advice as to how to pay attention to this aim at presencing.

As always the crucial question is *how* to think about being. Thinking considers it *not* by the route I've just now followed—by fixing the point in concepts and representations. A concept [*Begriff*] tries to "grasp" [*greifen*] its topic, which is too aggressive a relation. (Heidegger now "turns against the hand" in his core imagery, just as he turns against *Being and Time*'s pragmatism.) *WCT* 211: "Thinking ... is not a grasping, neither the seizing [*Zugriff*] of what lies before, nor the attack [*Angriff*] against [it]." Such relations to the topic involve a "third-personal," or an impersonal or external view upon (about) it. But genuine insight into that deep constituting act requires that we occupy or inhabit it. This is requisite especially, perhaps, because of the telic or end-directed character of that act.[44]

So the point is not just to discover being as presence, but to do so in the right place (in ourselves): there where we are all the time projecting it, there in our effort to bring things to presence. We must see how we do so, in the very doing of it. We hold open the clearing all the time, as we live every day and moment in our world. But we do so unawares. And we continue to do so unawares even if we can say, in intellectual engagement with Heidegger's propositions, that precisely this is what we are doing. We need to bring the propositions to touch the very intentional act they treat, if they're to "bear truth." BC 10: "We are thus concerned solely with attaining the ground and the relation to the ground, not with getting to know 'concepts' as mere casings of representations." We must somehow "awaken" that deep constituting act. We must make it (as we've seen Heidegger already thought in *Being and Time*) somehow explicit in itself. Rather than bringing it before our impersonal scrutiny, we bring that activity in us to its own awareness.

Just as some of Heidegger's strategies for thinking serve more to illuminate the what—being as presence—so others serve more to give us the content *in the right way*. I'll develop in the next chapters his uses of poetry and religion to adjust us in the needed dimension. Here I'll focus on a more general strategy he employs for this purpose, of illuminating our projection of being-as-presence "from within": he tries to *disrupt* this projection, to disturb and frustrate its smooth operation. He tries to make it an issue or problem how to continue to interpret entities as presences. The basic projection is thereby "put in question" not just intellectually, but for itself, in its very projecting.

This strategy has its roots in *Being and Time*, in its heavy reliance on *breakdowns* in our everyday understanding of our world—and especially on the "global" breakdown of anxiety. Heidegger continues in his later writings to call attention to such moods as boredom [e.g. WM (P 87)], which suspend all our purposes. These are moods or feelings with a transcendental status, in that they step us back from the "internal" problems of managing our projects, to the meta-problem whether to live that life as a whole.

But much more important in the late writing is another kind of disruption—one that Heidegger not only directs our attention towards, but tries himself to induce. He tries to throw off its tracks the activity we readers are immediately engaged in, the theoretical and intellectual project we bring to his writing. He tries to disrupt this project *as* it expresses the deep projection of being as presence. Our ultimate intellectual aim, so far unnoticed by us, is at an unmediated presentation of the object to our knowing. The precision of logic-partitioned argument with analyzed concepts expresses this aim at an ideal presence and immediacy. He tries to make us notice this deep aim by inducing an intellectual disruption reaching down to it.

Heidegger's late essays have, I suggest, a typical structure. The essay begins straightforwardly and reasonably, with Heidegger using familiar terms in recognized ways. This may continue a considerable while. But eventually, sometimes gradually and sometimes abruptly, we transit into an unsettling intellectual space. Heidegger begins to introduce a new vocabulary, explaining its terms by ostensions and definitions we can't quite make out. He makes sweeping claims, and seems to justify them by punning connections among the terms. Nothing familiar remains; we can't set our feet down, and can't grasp what's being said.

He thus gives up much of the method of *Being and Time*. Although that attacks Descartes vigorously, we saw how it employs a Cartesian regimen. It confidently pursues precise definitions and sound arguments. Its analysis of Dasein gives a systematic, partitioning account of it, cleaving it neatly into threes (and sometimes twos and fours). By contrast the *Beiträge* abandons this effort to place everything precisely in a system; it attacks "system" as falling within the domain of mathematical thinking [CP 45]. That epistemic ambition is dictated by the projection at presence, Heidegger now diagnoses. And his aim is now precisely to frustrate this ambition.[45]

Heidegger tries to make us feel the inadequacy of this method, so aimed at presence, for certain questions: the way the demand for full presence of the known prevents access to a certain truth. The point here is not to prove the proposition that science or analytic reason can't recognize this truth, but to "light up" the underlying posit of presence in this reasoning, while it operates trying for grasp. By our difficulty "presencing" what Heidegger is saying, we feel our insistence on presence as our guiding intellectual goal. So we come to notice the deep level of our constitutive act of letting being be.

We experience the grounding role of this project, in feeling how all our relations to things are unsettled by any disruption in it. By getting down to the bottom of the grip this project has on us, we see how we are "destined" to it. But we also have a glimpse past this bottom, feeling the contingency of this interpretation of being. We come back before the constitution of being as presence, to face the transcendental choice whether to let being be so. We thereby reach the level in ourselves at which thinking occurs. Heidegger hopes our path to thinking, then, will run through the very frustrations we feel with his writing.

Of course our allegiance to presence will only be disturbed if we feel that it is blocking our access to real insights—not if it is simply rejecting nonsense. So Heidegger must simultaneously give us— give even to our epistemic eye that insists on presence—a sense of some(thing) that can't be brought to presence. This is of course the work of his positive account of being as thinking's "what." But he tries to convey its "how" by giving this positive account in a way that frustrates effort to convert these felt insights into the definitions and arguments needed to "presence" them. We are thereby to feel our allegiance to presence as a project, and our choice of it as at issue—to feel this down at the level at which we really do choose that project.

Heidegger's strategy here, of chafing us into noticing our insistence on presence by frustrating it, is thus paired with a positive effort to give us a sense of a new truth, a sense we can only really get by beginning to operate under a different epistemic regime. We get our glimpses of being only by beginning to "look" in a different way, momentarily free of the insistence on presence. And the further challenge, beyond revealing the constraining insistence on presence, is to develop that new epistemic stance, and to let it step, at appropriate moments, into the place of the old. We must not conceive this as a matter of designing a new epistemic method, however. To think that we can engineer a path to the truth of being is one more expression of the scientific and technological stance expressing being as presence. The new "method" we need is, in an important way, a matter of foregoing method, or at least faith in the sufficiency of method. It requires that we give up, in the moment, the very perspective of design, in which we treat problems as to be handled by designing and then executing a solution to them.[46] So our earlier question "What then are we to do?" (in order to think) invites mistake if it is looking for an executable procedure.

It's because suspending our insistence on presence strikes so deeply at our overall stance and set that Heidegger's prescription acquires some of the paradoxical features we've seen. His prescriptions are designed to guide our effort—but an effort to suspend this very kind of effort, through a stance that has no designs. We can only really think (about) being by giving over the responsibility to accomplish this by our own design. We need, that is, to acknowledge—feelingly—that it's "not up to us" whether we succeed—that indeed the idea of "success" is as wrong here as those of "achieving" and "accomplishing."

Two points should be separated here. On the one hand there is this idea that we must "will not to will," and so enter a stance that lets happen or be. It's this that enables us to step down to the deepest level of our projection, to realize how we have ultimately insisted that being is presence, but that it needn't be. This first point concerns the stance we need, to see being. LH (P 241): "Thinking … is of being insofar as thinking, belonging to [*gehörend*] being, listens to [*hört auf*] being."

But Heidegger further holds that adopting this stance—though the most we can do—is still not enough. It's not enough to guarantee that being will appear, since that depends on a granting by being of itself. Being is not "there" sitting inertly for us to find; it must somehow "show itself" to us, and our receptive posture is merely hopeful. Thinking "listens" to being, but being is not all the time speaking; we must wait and hope that it will.[47] At the moment, unfortunately, being mostly turns away from us; it "withdraws" [WCT 9].

In all of this we need to remember what we saw in section 3: that "we" and "being" are not entities that jointly cause Ereignis, but elements in it. We are elements in a special intentional event, which is a condition of the possibility of entities. So rather than standing in causal relations, we and being are related as meaners and meant. Being's greater "reality" (than in Being and Time) is not a matter of its existing independently of our intending, but of the special logic of the intentionality it belongs to. Being must be meant not as an idea, held beneath our mental scrutiny, but as meaning that gives itself "from above." It's not a matter of having the idea of something higher, but of having (meaning) being itself in this special other way.

So, on the one hand, we need to revise our epistemic methods and to think in a different manner—more "receptively," somehow. But, second, we need to reduce our expectation from these methods: they're not sufficient, in themselves, to secure us the all-important truth. We depend on some kind of initiative "from outside." Our problem may be "that thinking has withdrawn from us, and not that we have withdrawn from thinking" [FC 18]. Together, these points often give a passive and even despairing tone to Heidegger's late writing. "We are to do nothing but wait," a waiting that must not even represent to itself what it awaits [FC 71, 75 (= DR (DT 62, 68)); also FC 140ff.].

This stress on "reception" comes only after the Beiträge, in the late 1930s, as Polt has shown [2005 384–85]. Biographically, it expresses Heidegger's disillusionment with Nazism, and with "engagement" towards revolutionary reform in general. Yet it also has roots in Being and Time, which gives phenomenology the task of "letting things show themselves from themselves." This stress on reception culminates in the term *Gelassenheit*, releasement (see Rel and DR (both in DT) as well as FC). Heidegger insists that the lesson is not passivity: the very distinction between activity and passivity arises within "the domain of the will," which releasement escapes [FC 70 (= DR (DT 61))]. Passivity, as we usually conceive and denigrate it, is the condition of a will that "weakly allows things to slide and drift along." But the releasement involved in true thinking involves a strenuous engagement—only not by a will, wielding ideas. This engagement allows thinking to "unconceal" being, as we next must see.

ii. Truth and unconcealment

Let's look at the epistemic good this thinking achieves. This brings us of course to "truth," or more aptly, as Heidegger thinks, it brings us to "unconcealment" [*Unverborgenheit*]. We took a first look at these topics, as they're treated in *Being and Time*, back in Chapter 3.3. The later view is continuous in the gist, but finds a richer development we must treat more closely. Indeed truth and unconcealment become leading topics.[48] Heidegger's views on them are among the most infamous parts of his later thinking. This is partly due to his dubious etymology (of the Greek term for truth, *alêtheia*) to support his idea. More importantly, doubts focus on his attack against "truth as correspondence," as well as on the obscurity of his positive idea.

I think it's clear, to begin with, that Heidegger does promote an epistemic good: a privileged condition of something like knowing or understanding, in which it achieves something like truth—even if these particular terms have implications he means to reject. (I'll use "epistemic" for this reference to something like an understanding of truth.) What he encourages us to hope for through him is a rare but all-important insight. This good is what thinking "achieves," though we've seen it can do so only by forgoing a set (or stance) towards achieving. Despite all these hedges or qualifications I think Heidegger's aim is still clearly descendent from (and keeps a deep affinity to) the truth-aim philosophers have traditionally had, for themselves and for their readers.

This link to the traditional aim is indicated by Heidegger's embrace of the image-system that associates truth with *light* and *vision*. Truth appears as if to the eye, in an illumination or "lighting-up" that allows it to see this truth. He favors this over the alternative trope treating truth as something *grasped*, since the latter encourages that aggressive and controlling stance he thinks cuts us off from being. Indeed the image of lighting must also be modified according to that point: illumination is now not a matter of exposing the object to a scrutinizing, categorizing view, and so bringing it to presence. The lighting-up is not of something "before our gaze," not even our mental gaze. It is by pursuing this point that we eventually see, I think, how Heidegger can believe that the special *seeing* of truth he means is not a matter of bringing it to presence.

Let's start with the attack on the understanding of truth as "correspondence"—i.e. as a match or fit between a representation and its object. This attack is disturbing because it seems to renounce what's important to us about truth. Why should we trust what he says if it's not meant to correspond to how things really are? We, at least, care about "getting it right," and if Heidegger doesn't we won't expect to learn from him.

But I'll try to show that Heidegger *does* think his statements "correspond" to his topics—he just denies that this correspondence is the kind of truth or illumination those topics themselves require. The purpose of his statements is to point the way to that other kind of insight: to suggest routes to it, and even to describe it as it is, so far as possible. But he wants constantly to remind us that these things he says, accurate though they are, are not even a part of the truth that matters—they're altogether different in kind from it. The point is not to believe them, but to step from them to an epistemic stance above belief—above even true justified belief.

The correspondence conception treats truth as an external relation between the representation (the intentional content) and the object. (So ET (P 138): "the traditional definition of the essence of truth: *veritas est adaequatio rei et intellectus.*") The *way* that content is intended is hardly mentioned, but is taken to be a simple and characterless believing or positing of it—together perhaps with its evidence. But as always Heidegger's vital aim is to persuade us that truth *about being* requires a very special intentional stance, different from belief—that everything hangs on this different relation to a content. Truth—as we saw was already maintained in *Being and Time*'s existentialism—is (Kierkegaardian) "subjectivity," i.e. a matter not of what but of how.

Heidegger explains correspondence-truth by situating it upon several deeper epistemic events—four kinds of unconcealing he claims it presupposes. Boring down through these levels reaches deeper and deeper kinds of truth. Let's quickly distinguish these levels, before returning to examine his claim that these amount to kinds of truth.[49]

1. We begin with what correspondence-truth most immediately presupposes. Such correspondence (to the facts) is attributed, we've seen, to an intentional object, as what is believed or posited; sometimes Heidegger treats this object as a proposition or statement. And his first point, made already in *Being and Time*, is that propositions can only "mean" things at all on the basis of a background disclosure of a *world* to which we comport ourselves. This disclosed world is the context only within which we can understand a statement, and evaluate its correctness. ET (P 142): "A statement is granted its correctness by the openness of comportment [*Verhaltens*]; for only through this can what is opened up generally become the standard for the presentative [*vor-stellende*] correspondence [*Angleichung*]."

2. But the opening of a world, as this context of entities, itself presupposes an understanding of the kinds of entities that can

show up there. The things in that background web can take their places there only because we know what it is to be (and how we can discover and verify) things of their sorts. So there is a deeper unconcealment of *essences*—or what Heidegger some-times calls "the being of entities." He thinks it is this level that metaphysics has principally addressed.

3. This disclosure of a field of essences depends in turn on a still deeper unconcealment, of the overall character and aim of this organization by essences. For the West, since the Greeks, this steering unconcealment has been of being as *presence*; it lies beneath all the various interpretations of the being of entities proposed by metaphysicians. We reach down to this unconceal-ing of presence by thinking back with the pre-Socratics, and by other strategies we'll see.

4. But Heidegger claims to find an unconcealment still more basic than presence. For we can come "back before" the posit of presence to engage more immediately with being, itself, before it is specified as presence. We then see that this engagement with being has been operating all along, beneath our insistence on presence—that the latter in effect answers a question posed at this bottom level. And here we have the possibility of determining being as something other than presence.

But what, we may ask, do these several levels of grounding have to do with truth?[50] Heidegger claims, in "On the Essence of Truth" (begun 1930): "But if the correctness (truth) of state-ments becomes possible only through this openness of comport-ment, then what first makes correctness possible must with more original legitimacy be taken as the essence of truth" [ET (P 142)].[51]

But why, from the point that correspondence-truth is only pos-sible by virtue of those underlying projections, should it follow that those preconditions are also (kinds of) "truth"? Projections of a world, essences, and presence are also presupposed by the *falseness* of (some) beliefs and statements, so wouldn't those preconditions be just as much kinds of "untruth"?[52]

Heidegger eventually pulls back from claiming they are kinds of "truth"—he concedes this term to the prevailing sense that it means correspondence.[53] Instead he claims they are kinds of "unconcealment" [*Unverborgenheit*], and that this, not truth, is the crucial epistemic good. He favors this term, we've seen (section 4), because of the way it entangles the epistemic good with its prior and enveloping opposite: it is an opening in the midst of concealment.[54] It is the bringing to an unobstructed vision—and the bringing to this out of, and within a larger context of, concealment.

Now I've called unconcealment Heidegger's epistemic good, yet it seems to be something that happens all the time. We're always, implicitly, projecting being as presence, classifying entities by essences, and presuming a background world; because of these unconcealments we can make and assess claims about particular things. But if these unconcealings, as preconditions, are always going on, they don't seem to be a "good" the way truth is meant to be: something not automatic, something that we need to work for, and indeed come to books of philosophy for.

Heidegger's idea is that these founding unconcealments, though automatic, bear the task to extend or improve their unconcealing. This makes, on the one hand, each rise to the next, more concrete level. Yet this ascent comes at the expense of the understanding "below": its unconcealing, though ongoing, is itself concealed, is held down in implicit assumption. Moreover, our deep disclosure of being as presence reinforces this suppression. The grounding aim at presence makes us press upward through these levels, out of our relations to being, and into correspondence-truths about entities.

So our epistemic challenge is to unconceal those deeper unconcealments. This means, however, to unconceal them in the very kind of unconcealing they are. It means to "see" world, essence, and presence in those founding acts themselves—to render those acts explicit. This happens not by casting light on them before our studying gaze—nor by capturing them in propositions—but by lighting up from within our own doing of those acts. Let's see how this epistemic logic works at the four levels of unconcealing we've distinguished.

(1) The first level beneath our correct (or not) beliefs is the world as a context of entities projected as there in the background. This world is there around us, for us all the time. When we ask whether a belief is correct we foreground some relevant part of this world; we raise it to doubt, while all the rest stands fast and determines the meaning of our inquiry. When I ask, "What is this?," whether everyday on the street or scientifically in a lab, all my other relations to things and people keep their places. That background motivates the question, and determines the kinds of evidence I'll let answer it.

So the implicit world-context underlies our explicit beliefs. This world is itself unconcealed: it is there for us in its distinctive, background way, as a kind of map we project around us—and most revealingly behind us where we are not seeing or attending. This map, set in our practical comportment—in our dispositional readiness to behave in the ways we can—not only is descriptive, but is cathected by our interests in these background things: they are things we "can do with."

Although we implicitly rely on this map, we don't count it final: we are also all the time working on it "in the background." Our deep sense of this map views it as incomplete, as well as partly—but in unknown parts—mistaken. This is the task set us by the clearing of being as presence: to unconceal more by our map, so that by it we can bring things to fullest presence. Our discoveries about things are integrated into the background holding, and become implicitly presumed from then on. So we are constantly, by explicit attentions, improving how well that implicit map unconceals a world we know how to live in.

These explicit attentions also improve on our background just in themselves, just by being explicit; they accomplish the grounding aim at presence. When we formulate a belief we bring a part of the background to the fore. This bringing to attention mustn't be supposed the primary case, such that every bit of my world begins in some explicit recognition of it, from which it recedes to become part of my background. Much of the background has never been made aware, much less begun in awareness. But we also have— again mostly implicitly—a sense of that background as improvable by that attention; we experience that explicit focus as improving unconcealment.

However—and this is his crucial thought—Heidegger insists on a countervailing point: our explicit attention to particular things at the same time conceals from us the world as unconcealed. It's when we're most focused on some particular that we most lose sight of the background world: we feel ourselves to stand in direct and solitary relation to that thing. Attention, by its focus, pushes the world into still deeper background—conceals it all the more. So in our very effort at explicitness we tend to lose further sight of the world-context.

This is true even when what we try to make explicit is the background itself. It disperses and disappears as we direct our attention upon it. And when we try to frame it in statements, these distort and degrade the understanding we have implicitly and practically. If we're to unconceal this practical coping, it must happen in the coping itself, and not by external attention to it. There is an unstudied way of handling things, Heidegger thinks, in which the structure of our coping is lit up "from within." ET (P 147): "where entities are not very familiar to man and are scarcely and only roughly known by science, the openedness of entities as a whole can prevail more essentially."

(2) At the next level down is the system of types or essences we are prepared for: every entity in the world we comport towards must belong to some type, which tells *what* (kind of thing) is

located at that position in our world. Our world can be populated with entities only because of this more basic projection of essences which entities can then instantiate. Here we take a first step down into being, though only to the most superficial level of it, which Heidegger comes to call "the being of entities."

Again this projection of essences has epistemic status. These essences are unconcealed for us: in them we see the structure of the world, but more than this we see *how to have a world*. We see how to organize experience into that of determinate (kinds of) things. We see a noematic structure—to use Husserl's term—which lets us then see, in part by discovering, a world of entities (of those kinds). Of course we "see" these things only implicitly, in our competence for them.

In this same implicitness we also see that these essences are unconcealed within an enveloping lack. We feel the incompleteness of our typology, and how many kinds remain hidden. Once again we make improvements by work at the higher, more concrete level—in this case the application of these essences to structure a world. Just as world is revised by scrutiny of beliefs, so essences are revised in the light of world—by the viability of the world they permit. Do these essences structure a world that works? Even more than our revisions of world, those of essences happen far in the background.

But having a world not only lets us unconceal essences better, it also amounts, itself, to a further way of unconcealing. It corrects a felt limit in our view of essences: it instantiates them in entities, and so makes them operable or liveable. We act upon entities, not their being, and in this respect the essences themselves are incomplete. They give us a system of possibilities, and the task "to let entities be," "to let entities be as the entities they are" [ET (P 144)]. Those types are disclosed as calling us to find out the truth about how particulars stand.

Again the deep aim at presence strengthens the push to make concrete and explicit. But again this explicitation comes at an epistemic loss. When most occupied with a world of entities, we "lose sight" of those essences that underpin the world. We rely on them, but they are transparent to us: we look unnoticingly through them at the entities they allow. It is only at exceptional ("revolutionary") moments that these essences become explicit. They particularly do so in metaphysics, which examines and revises this first level of being.

(3) But metaphysics fails to reach the next level down, which is the disclosure of being as presence. This is not a highest genus to which all those essences belong, but something like the point or aim in discovering them; it lies at an angle from the ascent in generality through essences. The deep disclosure of being as presence sets the ambition with which we project those essences, and the world that depends on them. We want our types to make a world of entities "presence" before us in such a way that we can grip and secure them.

This projection of being as presence is itself an unconcealing; the general point of the world shows up for us. Our guiding project is to bring to presence, and this prescribes how unconcealing works at the levels of essences, world, and statement-truths. Our effort to "see" unconcealingly is pursued as an effort to "grip" in the secure closeness of presence. This motivates the projects to capture essences in concepts, and the world in an array of propositions— pursued by metaphysics and science, respectively. The correspondence conception of truth is a further expression of the insistence on presence.

We've seen that each ascent in level brings epistemic loss as well as gain, and Heidegger mostly blames being as presence for this. Our drive to bring everything to firm control makes each unconcealing suppress or distort the levels beneath it. If unconcealing happens by presencing, then what can't be brought to immediacy and control—those founding levels—must drop from view. It's the insistence on presence that induces us, for example, to interpret the world as given in a system of propositional beliefs—whereas it really lies in our implicit comportment. And because presence develops and perfects itself historically, there is a progressive worsening of this concealing.

(4) The project of presence, as unconcealing, appears for us in the context of alternatives that remain hidden. Being shows itself as presence, but might have appeared in other basic ways, not visible to us. And this brings us to the last level, which is the givenness of being itself, before and without its specification as presence. We can come back even before that all-guiding decision, to what Heidegger sometimes calls "the truth of being," or *Ereignis*. And it is from here that we have the possibility of projecting being as something other than presence. But I'll defer treating *Ereignis* for a moment.

Let's return to sum up regarding Heidegger's epistemic good. Why, in the end, is this an unconcealing rather than a truth—if we take the latter to mean the correctness of beliefs or statements? It's because our great epistemic challenge is to move against that strong current pushing us upward to those beliefs—from background to foreground, from abstract to particular. If we're to understand ourselves down to the bottom, it must not be by looking "from above," and trying to describe and capture that bottom in propositions.

Rather, we need to find our way down to the places we unconceal world, and essences, and being as presence. We need to light up these unconcealings "from within," rather than directing an external scrutiny upon them. We need not the sight of an illuminated object, but "insight," an illumination within the stance itself. So we will notice "what it's like" to project a world, or essences, or being as presence. We will improve that unconcealing in itself by bringing it to its own explicitness.

Heidegger adopts "unconcealing" to name his epistemic good, because he thinks this way of becoming explicit is the true way to unconceal these grounding unconcealings. It brings them to the only kind of lighting or showing that does not distort and conceal them; it corrects the usual tendency to conceal them. It is a kind of intensification or perfection of the grounding unconcealment going on all the time.

Because it occurs at this level it engages and engears the whole machinery of the person's concern. The unconcealment of world, essences, and presence is not just factual but valuative (with due hedges about these terms). For example, the world that's unconcealed is crucially one in which "things are to be done." It is a world structured in relations to *aims*. So in "making explicit" my projection of a world I experience how I aim or will—and also feel—towards the things "there" for me in the background all along. The "seeing" that I do in this way must happen in that very aiming and feeling.

iii. Ereignis

This idea is of highest importance in Heidegger's late writings—their apex thought. It stands first ontologically.[55] It also names his ultimate good or end, what his writings (implicitly) most preach and call us towards. We need to locate *Ereignis* with respect to the other main epistemic notions, thinking and unconcealment. And we need to form as concrete a sense as possible of what it is—which will be hard, because it lies in the center of his mysteries. It's when Heidegger is discussing *Ereignis* that his prose gets most esoteric and elusive.

Heidegger understands *Ereignis* a bit differently through the period of his late writing.[56] Although I will be able to defend this only indirectly, I think these are shifts in emphasis within a fairly stable view. He has a single point, but with several parts, different ones of which he chooses to call *Ereignis* at different times. But the point stays the same, and keeps its primacy. This explains those dualities—and apparent contradictions—in his account of it, as both individual and social, both indispensable and rare, both epistemic and constitutive.

We began to develop this complex point above: *Ereignis* is the bottom level of unconcealment, "before" the interpretation of being as presence. But it is also the (second-order) unconcealing of this unconcealment—the epistemic good. So *Ereignis* is on the one hand something happening in all of us all the time—a deep structure of our intentionality. On the other hand this level is most deeply buried and concealed by those above it, so that it is the rarest achievement to unconceal this fundamental unconcealing—an achievement that is also *Ereignis*.

Another part of the point gives *Ereignis* a world-historical significance. To unconceal that undermost unconcealing of being is a precondition, he thinks, for hearing a new interpretation of being. So that rare achievement made the very beginning of Western history, among the archaic Greeks. They faced the question how to let being be, and answered: as presence. And Heidegger's hope is that this will happen again, now that that original projection of being as presence is reaching its culmination in technology. By coming once again back before that projection, we will reach the stance from which it is possible to initiate some different basic interpretation of being.

In this aspect *Ereignis* is an historical event for the society, in which it finds not just a new world, but a new way of having a world—of letting being be. It is constitutive and not merely epistemic—constitutive at the social level. It sets up for a culture an ultimate orientation that then destines it for a succession of worlds. The second-order unconcealing that makes this possible is an epistemic good for individuals. It's in this aspect that Heidegger dangles *Ereignis* before us as the personal end we're to take up.

But why call this *Ereignis*? The term has posed great challenges to translators, who have rendered it very differently; a few choices have been: "enowning," "Appropriation," "event of appropriation," "disclosing that brings into its own." The discrepancy among these renderings, and the difficulty even recognizing the term in some editions, is one of the obstacles in reading late

Heidegger in English. The main problem is to do justice to two central senses that can be heard in the German word itself.

First, the word ordinarily means an event or occurrence, and I think Heidegger retains this, properly adjusted: *Ereignis* is a "happening" of unconcealment, its coming-about. To be sure, Heidegger denies that the word means an "occurrence and happening [*Vorkommnis und Geschehnis*]" [TB (OTB 20); also ID 36]. Events happen to entities, but *Ereignis* happens to being, and to humans only in their defining relation to being. Still, with the qualification that *Ereignis* happens not within a world, but in the transcendental forming of world, its event-like character is crucial.

It shows this event-character in two of the aspects we've just distinguished. *Ereignis* is the historical event in which a way of having a world is constituted, and a destiny set in motion. This happens by the whole society acquiring that unconcealing as an implicit presumption that shapes the further ways it unconceals. But *Ereignis* is also the personal event of unconcealing the uncon- cealment of being—of lighting up that level in oneself. And this personal event is also transformative: it inaugurates a new epistemic regime.

In both of these senses, I think, it is an event in an honorific sense: not just a continuation or prolonging of an ongoing state, nor the repetition of something that has occurred before. It is an event in which unconcealment—whether first-order and implicit, or second-order and explicit—comes about *initially* or primarily. And this event *sets up* or inaugurates something that lasts. CP 41: "The *beginning* is *be-ing itself* as *Ereignis*, the concealed mastery [*Herrschaft*] of the origin of the truth of entities as such. And be-ing as *Ereignis* is the beginning."

Second, Heidegger hears *Ereignis* to be built on *eigen*, own—just as was *Eigentlichkeit*, authenticity, so crucial in *Being and Time*. It seems this is not the real etymology of *Ereignis*, but Heidegger takes it to connote that something "comes into its own," in this special event of truth.[57] Something comes into the condition that is distinctive of it, and proper to it. In particular (although we'll see he also puts it in other ways) the human—either an individual or a society—comes into its own by coming into proper relation to being. So there is the same broad idea we found in *Being and Time*, that the epistemic event of seeing/knowing being accomplishes ownness—what we were (in some sense) meant to be. The epistemic good is also a functional or essential good: in the truth of being, we realize or achieve ourselves.

Of course we've seen how the turning involves a critique of authenticity, which gets diagnosed as expressing a Nietzschean self-assertion. This critique makes Heidegger reconfigure the "own-ness" achieved in *Ereignis*. Now he stresses how coming into our own is also a matter of belonging to being (of being owned by being); this reflects the point developed in section 3 about the enhanced independence of being from us. So M 11 speaks of "the Er-eignis wherein entities are owned over [*übereignet*] again to the belongingness to be-ing." And CP 211: "Da-sein is owned [*ereignet*] by be-ing," and "[a]s *owned* [*er-eignetes*], Da-sein itself becomes *more its own* [*sich eigener*] and the self-opening ground of the self."

As to the way *Ereignis* unconceals, once again this works "from within." CP 3: "It is no longer a case of talking 'about' something and representing something objective, but rather of being owned over into Er-eignis. This amounts to an essential transformation of the human from 'rational animal' (*animal rationale*) to Da-sein." We need, by thinking, a personal "experience" [*Erfahrung*] of *Ereignis* [TB (OTB 26)]. This is a potent experience of illumination, which occurs as suddenly as lightning, to which Heidegger compares it; what flashes is "the truth of being" [Tu (QTE 44)]. So—yet again—our aim is not to think objectively about *Ereignis*, but to enter into it, to experience the event ourselves.

Not only is rationality not enough for understanding, it can even distract or divert us from the needed experience. Heidegger says that *Ereignis* is something that can't be conveyed by knowledge or even questions, but "must be experienced" [TB (OTB 26)]. And he warns his readers against relying on his propositions: "The saying of *Ereignis* in the form of a lecture remains itself a hindrance of this kind. It has spoken merely in propositional assertions [*Aussage-sätzen*]" [TB (OTB 24)]. Descriptions of *Ereignis*, framed in such assertions, can only lead us up to the place from which we must leap into an attitude different in kind.

To be sure, there's more to be said, but it needs to be said in a different way. We must look next at Heidegger's late views about language. There are more ways to speak, he insists, than with concepts and propositions. By turning to his account of language, and poetry in particular, we can throw light from a different angle onto the *Ereignis* he promotes to us.

Summary

After his 1933–34 Nazi engagement, and perhaps as a rethinking from it, Heidegger carries out a "turning" that makes basic changes from *Being and Time*. He recoils from what he now sees as a Nietz-schean element in it, expressed in its focus on authenticity as an individual's realizing its mineness. He draws by contrast towards a neo-religious stance he finds in the poetry of Hölderlin, in which our proper relation to being is not imposing but receptive. And being comes to us not up out of our essential human structure, but from history—the contingent history that lies behind us in the West, and that has an overall direction we can uncover. This history has issued in our current technological stance, whose orienting understanding is articulated by Nietzsche.

Heidegger thinks our history began with the pre-Socratics, and that we can discover in them its original orientation, which has steered it ever since. His readings of Anaximander, Heraclitus, and Parmenides are famously idiosyncratic, but we find in them Heidegger's idea of the original "openness to being" that is the ultimate reason for our predicament today. We find how they understood being as "presence," by describing the transcendental event in which a world is given within which entities can occur as presences. Each describes a different aspect of that event, so that their ideas are complementary. We find in them both the roots of our current lostness in technology, but also saving features, due to these thinkers' presence at the source.

The "history of being" the pre-Socratics began, shows the reworking and gradual perfecting of their project of presence. Metaphysics, beginning with Plato, takes increasing control of the transcendental event in which a world is projected; it crafts that event so that entities can be ever more securely presences for us within the world projected. So there is a deep momentum towards an "idealism" regarding being that understands it as made by us human subjects. Metaphysics culminates in the Nietzschean idea that man steps into the place of God and creates the world for his own sake by his choices.

Against this impetus into idealism Heidegger now shifts towards a realism about being. However, it's a peculiar realism, in that being still depends on us—depends on our "meaning" it. But this intentional relation has a different structure than that of a subject with ideas: it is less proprietary than that. Being is meant only in a stance that "receives" it as something independent. Moreover, this stance means being as not only revealing a world, but doing so on the ground of a primary concealment. Yet it is hard for us to see this basic way being is meant, due especially to our historical destiny of presence, which inculcates an aggressive stance incompatible with that insight. So being and its concealment are themselves concealed, a condition Heidegger calls the "oblivion" of being.

It is the task of thinking to unconceal being, and this is the new truth-goal Heidegger sets for us. It aims at the privileged experience of *Ereignis*, in which the most basic way a world is opened for us itself becomes explicit to us. So we witness the deep understanding of being as presence—how its aim operates in all we do. Again Heidegger insists on the special way this truth needs to be seen, which dictates an unusual "method" for the thinking that seeks it. His later essays work to jar and disrupt our ordinary thinking, which operates under the regime of technology and presence. By thinking back to the historical steps that formed this regime, we can learn to notice its operation in us now. And when we light up in this requisite way the deep clearing of presence, we become available for some different basic sense of being, a "new beginning."

Further reading

L. Braver: *A Thing of This World: A History of Continental Anti-Realism*. Evanston: North-western University Press, 2007. [This wide-ranging book hinges on its long chapter ascribing a new paradigm of anti-realism to later Heidegger.]

M. Wrathall: *Heidegger and Unconcealment: Truth, Language, and History*. Cambridge, UK: Cambridge University Press, 2011. [Although these essays treat topics all through Heidegger's thought, they handle "late" issues with special clarity.]

Eight

Language and art

Humans' essential task is not just to unconceal being, but to "house" it, and we do so above all by and in our language. Indeed this housing is really included in that unconcealing, and so vitally that without it our previous account was incomplete. Similarly, it was only by artificial delay that we were able to treat unconcealing without mentioning language's role in it. Heidegger thinks language is essential for unconcealing being, and that the main reason this unconcealment is usually concealed—the "oblivion" or forgetting of being noted in Chapter 7.4—is that we stand in a faulty relation to language. He stresses that our route to being lies through language, so we may well hope to improve our (murky) sense of being by turning to this.

Language was already important in *Being and Time*, but it comes right to the center of things in Heidegger's later thinking. This weight he puts on language, as the philosopher's topic, is comparable to that which Wittgenstein and much analytic philosophy give it. But of course Heidegger has a quite different account of what language is, and why it's important; he studies it with a very different angle of attention.

Heidegger's principal claim about language is easy to state: it has a "constitutive" ontological function, and not just a "representational" epistemic one. That is, language brings entities to being, instead of merely referring to entities already there. But this deeper role of language is very difficult for us to notice properly. We are strongly inclined to think of language as a tool at our own disposal. If it is instead constitutive in this way, it has been working quite beyond our supervision or control. It has, in fact, been making us, as it has made our world.

This constituting role of language poses an obstacle to our understanding it: we can't "get back before it" to an independent stance from which to reflect on it. EL (UL 75): "What we speak of, language, is always ahead of us. ... Thus we are continually lagging behind what we must first have caught up to ourselves, in order to speak about it. Accordingly, in speaking of language we remain entangled in a speaking that is persistently inadequate."

Now this is, heard one way, a familiar enough point. We are always embedded within a particular language, and unable to step out of its culturally local perspective. We speak English, or German, and so abide by that particular way of delineating things and values. To be sure, we can learn other languages, sometimes abetted by their kinship with our own. But this expands our horizons only modestly, compared with the great host of other linguistic perspectives we can see there are.

This is a "local" version of the problem—it concerns having this language (or these languages). But the problem also has a global form, and it's this that Heidegger mainly means. The very fact of having a world *by language*, of having being determined this way, sets constraints on how being "obtains" for us. It has the consequence, we'll see, that a certain kind of "concealment" accompanies every unconcealment of being. It also has the consequence that we are furthermore at risk of (liable to) a more egregious kind of concealment—a kind widespread and dominant today. It is not which language we speak, but our relation to it as language, that interferes with unconcealing.

We live in an age of "universal, rapidly spreading devastation [Verödung] of language," such that it "still refuses us its essence" [LH (P 243)]. We're used to using words in a way that conceals

their real role from us. Our ultimate task is not to change our
theory about language, but our relation to it, our way of "dwelling"
in it. Nor is it a matter of changing how we "use words," but rather of
entering a different kind of relation to them (and language) than
that of use.

We don't adequately understand the constituting role of language
by representing it in (other) language. "Much speaks for it, that
the essence of language refuses to come to language, namely to the
language in which we make assertions about language" [EL
(UL 81)]. Instead, we must understand it by changing our relation
to language, and in particular by participating in a special mode of
the constituting language itself. Developing this will re-cover
ground we looked at in Chapter 7, and I hope cast light back on it.

The solution is a new way to language—a way by now we can
anticipate. Instead of trying to speak "about [über]" language, we
must "from *out* of language, let it, in itself, say its essence" [EL
(UL 85)]. We need to "listen" for language itself to speak, to listen
"for the countering word" [75]. *Ereignis* is the "saying in which
language promises [*zusagt*] its essence to us" [90], i.e. grants us
being.

To follow Heidegger we need to distinguish several aspects or
forms of language, and his different handlings of them. The sections
of this chapter will treat these in turn.

First and most general is the role language plays of housing being,
i.e. of embodying an age's understanding of being. Those tiered
unconcealments of being, essences, and world (see Chapter 7.5.ii)
happen especially by language. And the way these unconcealments
are, as we've seen, usually concealed is also due to language—or rather
to our misrelation to it. Our prevailing interpretations of language,
and our deep sense of it as a tool or instrument, interfere with the
way it unconceals—serve to hide that unconcealment. Different kinds
of language do worse or better at addressing this generic problem.

This misrelation to language is epitomized in metaphysics—the
first more particular kind of language I'll treat. Heidegger tries to

analyze that misrelation by examining metaphysical language. We've seen that although he is highly critical of metaphysics, he also gives it a really remarkable importance and value: it makes (some of) the basic words that house an age's understanding of being. But it gives these words in a manner that hides that understanding from itself. We traced Heidegger's history of metaphysics in Chapter 7, and can add to it now metaphysics' way with language.

Along with metaphysics, being has always been housed in a second discourse, poetry; Heidegger is clearly far more favorable towards this. Poetic language opens a world in a way that displays its own role—as metaphysical concepts do not. We must see how this might be so. We must also explain how a society's understanding of being can be based both in metaphysics and in poetry—and whether these conflict not just in how but in what they say. And does poetry's history involve a "destiny" in the way we've seen metaphysics' history does?

Finally, there is the new "language for thinking" that Heidegger anticipates, on the basis of these accounts of metaphysics and poetry. It's the way philosophy will speak once it has broken loose from metaphysics, and learned a lesson from poetry. Heidegger has not just hopes but ambitions here: he is trying to begin to build this language in his own way of writing. So "thinking and poeming must return to where, in a certain way, they have always already been but have never yet built" [QB (P 319)]. We must consider whether Heidegger's distinctive late writerly "style" reads better in the light of this special aim.

1. Language as the house of being

Let's begin by looking at language's generic role, to "house being."[1] Heidegger develops this, as always, by first identifying and attacking the conception he thinks is usual and prevailing. We commonly think of language as our instrument. And we think that this instrument works a certain way, for a principal purpose: it works by naming or *representing* the things around us, for the purpose of *communicating* about them with others. Heidegger will dispute these obvious-seeming claims.

1. The instrumental view treats language as a dispensable means for conveying thoughts, that exist independently of language.[2] As an instrument language is at our disposal, subject to a project of design: we can better shape our words to what we want to say. So we see it as "a mere means of expression that can be taken off and exchanged like a garment, without that which has come to language being touched by it" [QB (P 298)].

2. We think that language principally serves us by representing things. This "representing" can be understood in many ways, for example as mirroring, or resembling, or indicating. But in any form of this representational view language plays a secondary role. Things around us, also things in us (our attitudes towards those things around us), are already there before language, for it then to match or denote. Language "comes along after" both us (its user) and things (its referents).

3. And we think that by this representing, language serves us in one main way: it lets us communicate, i.e. transmit to others, our individual ideas about those things. Again language comes in later, to convey to others a content already fully there in one's mind (or intentionality). Language subserves the wish of these individuals to come together into a group by sharing their views.

All three points seem clearly true, and Heidegger of course does not deny that language does these things. But these views all go wrong in thinking that any of this—serving us by representing and communicating—is the main or essential thing language does. They are true, but only about language in an ontical sense. They fail to see a deeper role it plays, its essence, of which these are merely results [HE (UL 55)]. And in this essential role it is very much *not* a tool, and neither represents nor communicates; it is not dependent or secondary in any of those three ways. To see this deeper role we have to change the expectations that belong to that usual picture.

Heidegger thinks the error is quite deeply rooted and extremely widespread. WCT 200: "Do we want with this reference to shake all science and philosophy of language in their foundations, and to expose them as a sham? By all means." The error is embedded in metaphysics, but reaches out into the everyday relation to words in the age it sets up (articulates). We treat language as this kind of tool by long habit through our lives, and this is the key to our "alienation."[3]

This standard conception of language rests on the supposition that there is a meaning or content "already there," for language then to represent (2). But language gets to work earlier than that. It makes or constitutes these meanings—they wouldn't be there without it. Language is world-disclosing. This is not, however, anything we can *use* it for (1), since it only adequately plays this role when we give up our effort to work it. Nor does language open a world within individuals who then come out towards one another (3); it runs essentially at the social level, so that shared meanings are primary.

OA (W 46): "language brings entities as entities into the open for the first time. Where there is no language, as in the being of stone, plant, and animal, there is also no openness of entities, and consequently no such [openness] of the absence of entities [Nicht-seienden] and of the empty." More succinctly a bit later: "language is the happening in which, each time, entities first disclose themselves as entities to man" [46].[4]

Let's try to make more concrete to ourselves what Heidegger means when he says that language discloses being, and constitutes our world—and why it does so in a way that runs against the drift of those three standard views.[5] This amounts, I think, to the claim that we would lack intentionality, be unable to "mean" anything, if we, like stones, plants, and animals, lacked language.

Now if world is a "background" framework of aims and understandings—the view of *Being and Time* that remains largely in place—why must it depend on language? We might suppose we could have plenty of aims and understandings without language: we'd still feel thirst and still see water as good for it; so we'd have a world, just a simpler, less finely divided one. It seems likely that language developed, spread, and is even now acquired, because of ways it improves pursuit of those original aims. It seems merely to modify an existing schema, sharpening and complicating and extending a structure of intentions that is already there.[6]

Heidegger is torn, I think, between two positions here. Sometimes he is willing to allow that there would be *another kind* of world or clearing of being in this case. So animals, as language-less, are not worldless but "world-poor." A (*EGT* 116–17): "Because the animal does not speak, self-revealing and self-concealing, together with their unity, have a wholly different life-essence among animals." On this line his point is that *our* intentionality is essentially structured by language.

Elsewhere he seems to hold that *any* intentionality requires language. And since it doesn't seem that this is definitional, he then needs a transcendental argument that language is a "condition of the possibility" of having a world. It's not clear just how this would go. But most likely (I think) it would run through the claim that only language gives the kind of persisting and authoritative framework needed for a background world—the point we've seen he stresses in his readings of the pre-Socratics (see Chapter 7.2.i).

Whether his claim is descriptive of *our* intending, or insistent about *any* intending, what matters is that language works by *instituting*— i.e. installing to last—a world. That language is a stable and lasting framework is, I think, the first and main thing Heidegger means when he calls it the *"house"* of being. Language houses being by serving as the enduring structure, only in or through which entities can show up as entities. EL (UL 63): "The being of anything that is dwells [*wohnt*] in the word." This image is *not* meant to imply that before language there already was being, but wandering around unhoused—though Heidegger does think that being can be better or worse housed.

Language gives this consistency and stability through time by virtue of being a body of meanings independent of me (each of us) and to which I defer. It houses being on the time-scale of history, not just of lives or days, and this makes the crucial difference between us and animals. I submit my spontaneous sense what words mean to the broad and lasting practice, so that my words' meanings aren't personal, but settled out around me in that practice. I own allegiance to it, am committed to its authority beneath all my pretense of control over my words.

Indeed my deference to language is still more radical. It's not really that "I defer" to language, since this suggests that there's an I there apart from language and related to it. It's rather that I come to be at the same time as language does for me: through language there's instituted something stable enough to be a self, over against a stable world. My own continuity is secured only by my being planted in language: I come to be as a speaking thing.

But what exactly is this "language" that has this authority? Language is not, as we might have expected, a "system of signs," together with their rules for use. HE (EHP 56): "What we usually mean by 'language', namely, a stock of words and rules for joining them, is only a foreground of language." Those words and rules are tools employed for language, not the thing itself. So language's authority does not lie in its semantic and syntactic rules—the ways these constrain my intending.

For the same reason we should not, I think, describe language as a "practice"—if we mean this in its third-personal aspect, as the fact that a community of speakers say such-and-such things in such-and-such circumstances. This is another exterior aspect, that could be studied by another science, a sociology.

Language itself, in its "interior," is a way of intending. It is crucially *point of view*: an overall point of view on the world as understandable by this language. So, most obviously, it views the world as divisible into the kinds named by its words: their "definitional" senses pick out the types of things, properties, events, etc. the world can show to this view. Less overtly, a language views the world by what its grammar specifies there can be types of—as our grammar of nouns, adjectives, verbs expects to find those things, properties, events. A language is a view of the world as divided up—"articulated"—in the very ways it speaks the world.

Heidegger's idea is not just that a language specifies what a point of view is of—the (kinds of) contents it has, the world it discovers. Language lets there be point of view at all. Not any kind of consciousness—any bare sensing or feeling—counts as "letting entities appear." The latter is the crucial event for Heidegger, his analogue to what Kant calls "experience." And like Kant he sets persistence conditions on this, that would deny that fleeting and fragmented sensations thus "let appear." Language gives the last-ingness needed for viewpoint; language is indeed the persisting viewpoint itself, in toto, which we participate in.

A language's viewpoint is not that of any one individual, but is pieced together out of many. Nor is it just a viewpoint that many individuals share, but something more inclusive, and divided; it includes the society's variety and disagreements in use of these words. So it is enormously complex, an intentional realm that individuals can explore their way through. By these internal differences, this comprehensive viewpoint takes the form of a "conversation." In learning a language I enter a part of this point of view, and my sayings become part of its conversation.[7]

Indeed the language's comprehensive viewpoint includes also its history: all the ways each word has expressed the world in the past. The latter remains present in the viewpoint, so that we are in conversation not just with our contemporaries but with the history—past and to come—of our co-speakers. Indeed this conversation also extends across to "other" languages, as German or English interprets Latin, which interprets Greek. What I mean by my words is dependent on all of this, which is also accessible for me to explore.

Heidegger denies, however, that the diversity encompassed by a language is all equal. Some meanings, as expressed in some crucial words, are "essential" in a way that makes them authoritative. It is in recognizing this authority that individuals *don't* disagree: "we are *one* conversation [*Gespräch*]. The unity of a conversation consists in the fact that in the essential word there is always manifest that one and the same on which we agree [*einigen*], on the ground of which we are united and so are authentically ourselves" [HE (EHP 57); also PG 90]. It is these meanings—the viewpoint embedded in them—that we must of course especially pursue; this is how we "listen to language."

By contrast I do *not* listen to the "common practice," to how and what things are said most of the time; WCT 119 decries such "floundering in commonness" [cf. 192]. This general usage does not have authority by its numbers, nor by its status as a default or standard position. Heidegger tells, early and late, a deflationary story against the common way of using language. Because of the iterability of words and statements—language's means—they can be "passed along" in absence of the view or experience they properly express, and this is precisely how they come to be common [cf. HE (EHP 55)]. Initially genuine statements get repeated non-genuinely as simply "what one says."

So it's not this common practice that has authority, but the genuine uses of language, in which they really do express the relevant experience. These are the standard to which our own saying is set: we refer ourselves to the privileged experiences in which words are spoken with full sense. And these genuine uses of language include above all those that unconceal being—when words are first invested with meanings, before they devolve to convention. These meanings are still there in the language, but we miss them, and miss them more and more as we become inured to our words. So WCT 191–92:

> [Language] allows both of these: first, that it be reduced to a mere system of signs, uniformly available to everybody, and thus carried through as binding; and the other, that language in

one great moment says for once a single thing, which remains inexhaustible, because it is always incipient and therefore unreachable by any kind of leveling.

Viewed most narrowly, this single thing is the original, archaic opening of being as presence. More widely it includes too the later epochal statements by metaphysicians and poets, each specifying the mode of presencing pursued by an age. Language is a house that has been (and is being) repeatedly rebuilt. These rebuildings are always only incremental, however, so that meanings do not replace one another, but accrete around the earliest, original choices, that stay active in all that follow.

Although thinkers and poets carry out these rebuildings, they don't create their own designs. The true source of the new meanings they build into our words is what Heidegger calls "destiny." This is a kind of logic of development in our social-cultural history, a very long-term movement, drawing out the ultimate consequences of the original posit of being as presence. Thinkers and poets are sensitive to this movement, able to hear "what must come next." For they have "stepped down" to the level of being, where the basic choices about our meanings become visible. They put what's next into words, fuse the new outlook into them.

Thinkers and poets change language only insofar as their new uses disseminate and become common coin. They "house" the coming viewpoint in words that are memorable—in different ways with thinkers than poets, as we'll see. So their meanings are built lastingly into the language, and get acquired as each individual learns it, remembers it, and defers to its authority. However, this very way meanings get "built in" exposes them to be misunderstood. The thinker or poet means them within the privileged experience of being, but when they're part of the general inheritance—of the background framework each grows up into—they're grasped in a much-attenuated manner.

To reach those grounding experiences we must break through this rote and routine with which we ordinarily use words. This is why Heidegger, once again, singles out experiences of breakdown as especially revealing:

> But where does language itself come to word as language? Strangely there, where we do not find the right word for something that strikes, distresses, or inspires us. Then we leave unspoken what we mean and ... undergo moments in which language itself has distantly and fleetingly touched us with its essence.
>
> [EL (UL 59)]

We step down to the stance from which an experience requires new words that may or may not come—words fully adequate to that experience. (This reverses our usual stance, in which routine words take the place of experiences: we talk without caring.)

I think these are the broad lines of Heidegger's later view of language. But there's a lot of detail to be added, which will give better point to parts of it. We'll take closer looks at three particular relations to language, one that Heidegger criticizes—metaphysics— and two that he praises—poetry and thinking.

2. Metaphysical language

After his turning, Heidegger mainly uses "metaphysics" for the way philosophy has been done so far, a way he means to turn from. So it is most often a term of opprobrium: it marks the way these predecessors—all the (other) great figures in the history of philo- sophy—fell short.[8] They fell short, above all, in their clarity regarding being. They gave names for being, but didn't see clearly enough what they were naming, nor what they were doing in so naming it. So their discourse "conceals" being in a way Heidegger tries to diagnose—and to rise above.

Our focus will be on this negative aspect of metaphysical language, seeing what goes wrong so that we can then see what goes right in poetry and thinking (sections 3 and 4). But it's important to bear in mind that metaphysics is also enormously esteemed by Heidegger—indeed given a cultural role that many might think wildly inflated. "Metaphysics grounds an age in that, through a definite interpretation of entities and through a definite conception of truth, it gives it the ground of its essential form" [AWP (*W* 57)]. "Our Western languages are in their different ways languages of metaphysical thinking" [ID 73]. It is the metaphysical systems of philosophers such as Plato, Aristotle, Descartes, Kant, and Nietzsche, that "gave language" to the "understanding of being" of the whole society (or culture) in their eras. Without their crucial words there would have been no "clearings" of being at all.

To play this role these great philosophers had to go far further than almost anyone else—far further down towards being. Although they are all metaphysicians, and misguided as such, they also do genuinely think. They just do so behind the scenes, as it were, in a way not at all explicit to themselves, a way even inconsistent with their own theories. IWM (P 278): "in its answers to its questions about entities as such, metaphysics speaks out of the unnoticed openness of being."

It is the language of metaphysics that opens up a world for a "people." But its way of giving words for being simultaneously closes off that world, prevents us (that people) from living as transparently in that world as we might. So by diagnosing the error in metaphysics we can get at what cuts us off from being. Thus LH (P 245) says that the question of the truth of being "only comes to light if in the midst of metaphysics' rule the question is posed: 'What is metaphysics?'"

A metaphysics is, in brief, an ontology; it gives an "account (logos) of being (on)." Its limitations lie both in the way it thinks being, and in the way it gives an account, i.e. the way it puts being into words. We made a start on the first limitation in our look at

Heidegger's history (in Chapter 7.2.ii). I'll first recall and amplify this, then turn to the second limitation, in its language, our focus here.

Metaphysics' chief "error" regarding being is its tendency to treat it as a kind of entity.[9] LH (P 252): "It thinks from entities back to them with a glance in passing toward being." Heidegger struggles how to state this criticism so that it is consistent with his view that what makes metaphysics so important is that (in some other sense) it *does* think and talk about being.[10] Sometimes he says that metaphysics treats only "entities as a whole": "It means entities as a whole and speaks of being" [IWM (P 281); also M 333]. Or it treats "entities as such" [IM 20]. Elsewhere he says that it treats only "the being of entities," and not being itself [LH (P 246)].[11]

This error is reflected in the way every metaphysics is not just ontology but ontotheology. For its theory of being always has the two aspects we saw on pp. 232–38: it understands being both as "being-what"—the most general genus to which all entities belong—and as "being-that"—the ultimate entity that explains all the others, the god.[12] Heidegger finds a theology even in Nietzsche—in his idea of the eternal return of the whole.

The understanding of being as ultimate entity obviously violates the "ontological difference" Heidegger insists on. To treat God—or any other cosmic force or principle—as the ultimate explainer of entities is to fail to step back from the domain of entities to the clearing or opening of a world-for-us, that is being itself. God is an entity within the clearing, but what we need is insight into the clearing itself, and the event in which it opens for us. This event is the precondition even for God or gods (and even for us).

But metaphysics also goes wrong when it posits being not as an ultimate entity but as the "what" of entities; this too stays on the side of entities, failing to bridge the gap.[13] Here metaphysics treats an entity's "being" as its genus, and treats "being itself" as the highest and all-encompassing genus. But it's misguided, Heidegger thinks, to try to push up to being from below in this way—by generalization from the characteristics of entities. To find being we need to notice in ourselves that basic stance or project that "lets entities be" as presence; this stance lies behind our conception of entities as sortable into genera in that way.

Why do Plato and all his followers make this mistake of interpreting being through entities? How had the pre-Socratics (partly) avoided it? I think Heidegger's guiding idea is that the pre-Socratics directly experienced being showing itself as presence, and the later thinkers do not. In that experience Anaximander and his cohort saw how presence is "granted" in the *Ereignis*; they articulated and transmitted this understanding, even without naming presence itself.

Later philosophers, beginning with Plato, take over that understanding, without themselves going "all the way down" to being's revelation. Since they don't experience its revealing as presence, presence becomes presupposed—a requirement whose source they can't notice. M 347: "Metaphysics must think being as entitihood [*Seiendheit*], it must take presencing and its constancy itself as the most constant." They operate implicitly with that understanding. Presence, as a project, takes a grip on them, and their failure to see this lets it compel and push them a certain way.[14]

Now let's turn back to language: how does metaphysics' flawed relation to being show up in its relation to language? Metaphysicians use it, of course, to state a flawed content—their misunderstandings of being in terms of entities. But less obvious is the *way* they use language, and what they expect of it in this use. This too is now shaped by the presupposition of presence: metaphysics wants language to "bring to presence," to set things in immediate and lasting grasp. Moreover, metaphysics treats language itself as such a presence.[15]

Metaphysicians do use language effectively, for they succeed in housing their viewpoints in memorable words, by which they can be securely fixed both in individual and group. But they make their words memorable by a different method than poets, or than the new thinkers Heidegger foretells. They make them memorable by a definitional clarity that captures in formulas precise senses of these words. By this these words come to a kind of presence, which then becomes a model for our relation to words generally.

Metaphysics, with its posit of presence, does more than change the language's words: it changes users' relation to their words, changes what they understand themselves to be doing with them, as they speak or think them. It transmits the general conception of language as an instrument, for the statement of facts about things, with the supposition that those facts and things are there quite apart from language. It works on its language to make (as it thinks) its words fit the facts. Hence this way of using language conceals its own work in opening a clearing and so "letting entities be"; it hides its ontological role.

Metaphysics tries to make its words exactly map being, by specifying technical senses for them all; its words become *concepts*. It thereby makes the word itself arbitrary, with all meaning hanging on the definition, which is crafted quite precisely to suit its idea of being. It breaks the word's link with all its prior history of senses; it wants meaning to come to the word solely through the definition. The word is to be (as it were) transparent to the definition, and the latter gives its meaning full presence: the word's meaning is locked up in the formula, and is lastingly immediately available in it. So nothing in the meanings of these words is hidden or concealed.

Metaphysics thus suppresses and denies what Heidegger will call (we'll see in section 3) "the earth." The earthy aspect of language is the concealment it always involves—inseparable from its uncon-cealing. This includes, for example, the mere sound of words, and in this their web of links to other words in the language (with all its history). These involve a brute contingency in the way a word means, which makes it uncontrollable by current definitional fiat. That web of links is too vast for survey, and can be meant, by any individual, only "in the background," and never brought to full presence.

Metaphysics transmits to the general practice its own ambition with language—its aim to bring words' meanings under control as concepts, eliding implicit resonances. The word's meaning is to be what we give it, by our definition now—is what we say it is. The word's meaning isn't at all a matter of its sound, nor of its history of uses. So it becomes a part of general practice to deny the relevance of language, understood as the whole "conversation" of sayings of the word that envelops our use. Heidegger of course wants to reverse this, and persuade us that meaning comes to words from language—from that enveloping conversation, which we must learn to hear.[16]

That metaphysical crafting of language takes its ultimate form in our own technological age. Metaphysics culminates in (what Heidegger calls) enframing [*Gestell*], the essence of technology; we'll examine this in Chapter 9. And this enframing dictates a certain relation to language:

> Enframed speaking turns into information. ... En-framing, the everywhere-ruling essence of modern technology, orders up formalized language, that kind of notification by virtue of which man is shaped, i.e. directed, into the technological-calculating essence, and gradually abandons "natural language".
>
> [PL (UL 132)]

Language is no longer allowed to be natural, but is brought to reason and control, the better to bring us under control.

This enframing relation to language is also reflected in a "meta-linguistic" philosophy, as Heidegger says in this rather startling passage:

> Recently the scientific and philosophical investigation of languages is aiming ever more decidedly at the production of what one calls "metalanguage". Scientific philosophy, which is out to produce this super-language, understands itself

consistently as metalinguistics. ... [M]etalinguistics is the metaphysics of the thoroughgoing technologizing of all languages into the sole operative instrument of interplanetary information. Metalanguage and sputnik, metalinguistics and rocketry are the same.

[EL (UL 58)]

They are the same in expressing that project of enframing and control. Our crucial struggle is against metaphysics: "What is to be decided is whether ... metaphysics, in turning away from its ground, continues to prevent the relation of being to man from coming to light ... in such a way as to bring man into belonging to being" [IWM (P 280)].[17] And this struggle must focus, we've seen, on the faulty relation to language metaphysics involves.

3. Poetic language

Our way out of this faulty relation to language lies through poetry, which bears language's positive, saving powers. Whereas metaphysical language, in opening being, does so in a way that simultaneously closes it off, poetry is more thoroughly "unconcealing"—and so more true. In fact all arts, and not just poetry, play this special role of revealing being. But poetry does it more basically, because it works in language. We must try to specify how poetry "speaks" differently from metaphysics: not just how it says different things, but how it says them a different way, better suited to open being for us.

Poetry is not the only such unconcealing language. It may be tempting to hear Heidegger as subordinating all philosophy to poetry, as the real site of truth. But we'll see in the next section that there is also a language of thinking—of the genuine thinking that should replace metaphysics. This thinking is descended from metaphysics, and bears its principal identity there; it is even something metaphysicians already carried out, only implicitly and incompletely. It is something independent of poetry—and with a value independent of it too. But to learn to think more adequately, philosophers should pay attention to poets.

Poetry, and art in general, are almost completely ignored in *Being and Time*. But notice this passing remark at g162: "In 'poetical' discourse, the communication of the existential possibilities of one's self-finding can become an aim in itself, and this amounts to a disclosing of existence." Since this disclosing, possible only in authenticity, is the ultimate good in that book, this suggests an importance for poetry that is puzzlingly not pursued.[18]

i. Art

Let's start with some orienting points on the broader topic of art—covering a few well-known ideas in "The Origin of the Artwork" [OA], one of Heidegger's most famous essays.[19] He attributes great things to art here; I think we can distinguish two main ideas. He defines or identifies art by two things (he claims) it does, or is able to do—one for society, the other for an individual. At the social level, art functions to set up or "found" the (current) world of a society or people. And for an individual already in such a world, it can do something more: specially "light up" this world, and being itself. These are, of course, both aspects of the "unconcealing" we've seen is Heidegger's epistemic good. We can add detail to that good by seeing how art promotes it.

Take the social point first. Heidegger gives extraordinary cultural-historical importance to art: it shapes (constitutes) the background world of meanings within which all of an age's experience runs. The age's artworks lay out how it is ready to see and value things. In "Origin" Heidegger gives one of his rare examples in a famous account of a Greek temple:

> The temple-work first fits together and at the same time gathers around itself the unity of those paths and relations in which birth and death, disaster and blessing, victory and

disgrace, endurance and decline win for the human essence the shape of his destiny. ... The temple, in its standing there, first gives to things their look and to humans their outlook on themselves.

[OA (*W* 20–21)][20]

We should note that it's debated whether Heidegger's point is really that art *constitutes* a world, rather than specially lighting and revealing a world a people already has.[21] I think he does mean the ontological point and not just the epistemic one, but that the difference between these is less due to the kind of thing a world is—due to the unity and clarity it requires, as noted in section 1 of this chapter. The world that comes to be from the artwork is a unity of the shared practices: it gives them a point—indeed a long-term historical point, a destiny. Moreover, the artwork pulls a world together by the way it *manifests* that point: it calls repeated attention to it by its conspicuous presence. So there might indeed be a rich set of shared practices that preceded the artwork, yet lacked that manifested unity, so that the group remained "worldless." Thus Heidegger converts "having a world" into an honorific (we've seen this is a frequent move), such that only properly unified societies have worlds. This somewhat runs the epistemic and ontological points into one another.

We've seen that Heidegger thinks our history is broken up into "epochs" distinguished by their respective understandings of being. It seemed that these epochs were instituted by metaphysicians—that their basic words project being. But here, in "Origin," he seems to give the crucial role to art: an epoch's understanding is embodied in essential artworks. The artist embeds a new "look and outlook" in a physical thing that then "stands there" as a public presence for the people—around which they live, and by which they orient their lives. This artwork gives a concrete presence, a visual (or auditory) emblem for the basic values and world-view of the group—and so lets them *have* those common values and world-view.

Let's defer the question how this is related to the founding by metaphysics. It is at least clear that (he thinks) art *can* found a world. Indeed it sometimes seems that it only counts as art if it *does* do so. "Always when art happens, i.e. when there is a beginning, a thrust enters history, history first begins or begins again" [OA (*W* 49)]. The artwork is in this sense itself an origin—of each successive world of outlook; this is the pun in the essay's title, which Heidegger reveals only near its end.

These claims about art's world-founding role may strike us as far-fetched. We think of art as isolated in galleries and museums, and how can that have any such sway? But Heidegger agrees, and sometimes draws the conclusion that there *is* no art in the modern age, since none of what we call art plays that world-founding role. Either we lack a world in that honorific sense, or our world gets its manifest unity from some other source.

The account in "Origin" of art's social role shows nostalgia for the Greek and medieval pasts, where art was principally religious. The temple and cathedral, including their associated sculpture and painting, give convincing embodiment to the qualities of the divine, and the human, that deeply orient their societies in their worlds. We can better see how "look and outlook" might be shaped this way. Heidegger holds out, in the background, hope that art might some day play this role again.

However, he now comes to see a different role for art than founding a world—it must do something else in our modern age. Art doesn't now found a world, but it can—it should—remind us of what we're lacking. Art shows what's missing when we fail to come together this way. It unconceals the concealment we're now subject to: how we lack a unifying point to what we do—our nihilism. It can even, more positively, begin to put in place pieces of a new world, with that manifest unity ours now lacks.

Unfortunately art mostly *doesn't* play this helpful role today, because—in Heidegger's pessimistic view—it has been largely subverted to service of technology and enframing. Art is a "resource," whose economic and cultural value is assessed and compared with that of other resources. We come to it in the wrong way. This misuse is reflected in our theory of art, our aesthetics: with the rise of aesthetics "great art comes to an end" [WPA (N v.1 84)]. Aesthetics is metaphysics applied to art, and so works to bring it under the dominion of presence. "Aesthetics is the ... modern metaphysical way of delimiting the essence of the beautiful and art" [HHI 88].

Art can only play that helpful role as an exception to this, hence not at the social level, but individually and privately. So it is no accident that Heidegger's example of a modern artwork is of a painting that works by specially and privately affecting individuals. He treats at some length Van Gogh's painting of "peasant shoes": "In the rugged heaviness of the shoes there is the accumulated tenacity of her slow trudge through the far-spreading and ever-uniform furrows of the field swept by a raw wind" [OA (W 14)]. Reflecting on how the painting shows these shoes, he comes quickly to a word for the "essential being" of this equipment (and all equipment): "reliability" [*Verlässlichkeit*]. I'll return to this notion, and its difference from *Being and Time*'s "to-handness," but for now the important point is that the painting reveals to us this being, as—usually—observing actual shoes and their use would not. "Van Gogh's painting is the opening of what the equipment, the pair of peasant shoes, in truth is. This entity steps out into the unconcealment of its being" [16].[22] Art's epistemic power makes it a vital topic and resource for thinkers pursuing the truth about being.

This second way the artwork unconceals seems quite separate from the first.[23] Van Gogh's painting doesn't found or institute the world of the peasant woman—nor presumably the world of its viewers. It gives, it seems, an isolated insight that need have no impact on the broad structure of one's world. It is an insight into a structure (reliability) the world (of equipment) *already* has—a structure it has for us as well as for the peasant woman. So here the artwork seems to play *only* an epistemic role.

Nevertheless I think Heidegger hopes that this epistemic effect will lead to a constitutive one: the artwork can light up the world in a way that *gives* it a manifest unity it had lacked. It does so by embodying a new overall point or aim. So that Van Gogh painting can show us a different overall stance towards things: it gives us the ideal of a subtly different relation to equipment than *Being and Time* had offered. It points the way out of enframing and technology, by beginning to construct, in responsive individuals, the new world we can hope will come. As they live in the world thus (partly) opened by the artwork, they become what Heidegger calls its "preservers."

So these two examples, of the temple and the painting, are less separate than initially seemed. The temple constitutes its people's world, but the painting has the power to begin to construct a new world for us. In both cases the artwork gives truth. OA (*W* 44): "*Art is, then, a becoming and happening of truth.*" Here Heidegger thinks he breaks sharply from Nietzsche, who claims that art and truth contradict one another [WPA (N v.1 148)].

ii. Poetry

But our interest is especially in language, and how it unconceals. So let's turn now to poetry, the linguistic art for Heidegger, to try to make more concrete how those ontological and epistemic functions might work. How do the poet's words found a society's world, and/or "light up" the essential character of the world for an individual? The other arts largely drop out of the picture in the writings after "Origin,"[24] and the focus is all on poetry.

What counts as "poetry" for Heidegger? In "Origin" he distinguishes wider and narrow senses. In the wider (and "essential") sense poetry [*Dichtung*] is the poeming [*Dichten*][25] of truth, which means the founding [*Stiftung*] of truth—i.e. it is setting a new outlook into a culture by embodying it in a work. In this sense, he says that all art—including sculpture, painting, architecture—is poetry, since art generally is "the setting-into-work of truth" (this, we've seen, is art's first function) [OA (W 44–47)].[26]

By contrast poetry in the narrower sense—poesy [*Poesie*]—is linguistic art, artistic language. And this is the primary art, because it is language above all that lays out a world. OA (W 46): "since language is the happening in which, each time, entities first disclose themselves as entities to man, poesy ... is the most original form of poetry in the essential sense. ... Building and shaping, on the other hand, always happen already and only in the open of saying and naming." So the other arts, as we might put it, lay out a world by changing the "look" (or "sound") of things. But there can only be a look to the world if there's already a language for it—and this is what poesy affects. Poesy changes that aggregate language, and so restructures a people's world—the system of ways they are prepared to discover or interpret things.

It's this narrower—and more usual—sense of "poetry" that Heidegger usually means (by *Dichtung*) in his later writings, and from here on I'll stick to it. As linguistic art, poetry plays the primary role of founding a world. HE (*EHP* 59): "in that the poet speaks the essential word, through this naming entities are first nominated [*ernannt*] as what they are. So they become known *as* entities. Poetry is the wordly founding of being."[27] And it also plays the secondary role of lighting up a world already there—or lighting up our lack of a world, in a way that promotes finding one.

But if poetry is linguistic art that founds or lights up a world, which things will count as poems? How many of the verses we ordinarily call poems will be such? And will any other things count? Street slang (or popular music) changes language, but not in the way, we'll see, Heidegger requires of poetry. He focuses conservatively on what we'd all call "poems," by a few German poets of the eighteenth to twentieth centuries: Hölderlin [1770–1843] first and foremost, but he also examines poems by Stefan George [1868–1933] (in EL, Wo), R.M. Rilke [1875–1926] (in WP), and Georg Trakl [1887–1914] (in LP). He also pays attention to some Greek poets: Homer (in AS)

and Sophocles (in IM, HHI). As we'll see, the traditional character
of such poetry plays an important role in Heidegger's argument.

These count because they are "great" poems—OA (*W* 19) says
that "only [great art] is under consideration here"—i.e. are able to
play either the founding or the epistemic role. They found or light
up basic or central aspects of the world—and don't just change
stray details of the linguistic practice, as we might suppose, for
example, slang does. Indeed they found or light up *the aim* of our
general comportment towards the world.

In the primary case the poem changes the language—gives words
new meanings in the general practice. HE (*EHP* 60): "Poetry is the
primal language [*Ursprache*] of a historical people." Heidegger quotes
Hölderlin: "But what endures [*bleibet*] is founded by poets" [EL
(*UL* 68)]. Poets make new basic words, and thereby disclose a new
truth, a new world. We see this in Greek poetry: Homer, Aeschylus,
Pindar voiced answers to the dilemmas of the people—and the
people came to voice these themselves as the language was inflected
by their poems.

But we've seen that Heidegger thinks modern art no longer plays
this role. The world is now set up in different ways than by art. Art
works less as social and constitutive, and more as individual and
epistemic: it can reveal, in private experiences, the deep character
of our prevailing world, made in those other ways. It can also give
us glimmers of a world we might have, that would set us better
towards being; if such poetry can play a social role, it is by beginning
the long work of designing such a world.

This is the main significance of Hölderlin, Heidegger's essential
poet, about whom he seems to have written more than about
anyone but Nietzsche.[28] Although Hölderlin's poems haven't made
our age's world, they do articulate its essential situation, to those
who can hear them. They voice an alienation from the age, and
the age's alienation from itself: we are "not at home." (Having
been a structural feature of Dasein in *Being and Time*, this *Unheimlichkeit*
is now historical.) They reveal our spiritual poverty, our distance

from the gods, the oblivion of being. So Hölderlin regards himself as a "poet in a destitute time," in the phrase of "Why Poets?" And indeed, "[h]is poetry dwells in this locality more intimately than any other poetry of his time" [WP (*W* 203)].

This diagnosis of our situation is the "content" Hölderlin expresses, and all great poets of the modern age must say this same thing. "Hölderlin is the forerunner of the poets in a desolate time. That is why no poet of this era can overtake him" [WP (*W* 240)]. But our interest is in the particularly poetic way he expresses this content—the different way his words "light up" this situation than discursive or argumentative prose can do (including my bland statement of the point just now). His poetic point must stir us more deeply in order to be understood.

The first way poetry works is by effecting—this is now a familiar idea—a certain kind of breakdown: a breakdown in our relation to language. The poet's unexpected words throw us off our usual path through language. They strip off our usual assumptions about the meanings of words, and this brings us back to original decisions. Again Heidegger thinks this breakdown has great epistemic value: it lights up our relation to both language and world.

Poetry steps us back from our customary discourse, our habitual—and therefore unnoticed—uses of words for things. It frustrates our effort to hear words in everyday ways. So it prevents us from sliding straight through the word to the thing, and missing the gap, as we usually do. To step back to notice words this way is to suffer (or effect) a breakdown in the prevailing meanings—or rather in the automatic and habitual way of assuming these meanings.

In reminding of the gap between word and thing, poetry (paradoxically?) brings things closer to us—lets us experience them more freshly and fully. Ordinarily our relation to the thing is mainly a relation to the word, which passes for the thing; we feel the thing as if instilled in the word. Our concern doesn't reach out vividly to the thing, instead hovering around the word. Poetry, with its unexpected words, calls attention not just to them but also to the things, which look new themselves when named by these new words. So we recognize at once both the independence of the thing, but also the word's crucial role in letting it appear.

To help us find the tone of this special breakdown, Heidegger refers us—in a passage quoted on p. 287—to times "where we do not find the right word for something that strikes, distresses, or inspires us"; in such cases we "undergo moments in which language itself has distantly and fleetingly touched us with its essence" [EL (UL 59)]. For we come back before language's framing of the world (its essential function), to the situation in which it is still open how to put being and entities into words.

However, the poet effects this breakdown while on the way to doing a second thing: giving words new meanings. In reading poetry we experience, with the poet, the latter's "discovery" of the new word (or meaning). Moreover, we experience this discovery as responding to the need to say things the available words aren't up to. The poet wants to "bring to language something that so far has never yet been spoken" [EL (UL 59)]. Moreover, the poet houses this new viewpoint in _memorable_ words (words memorable for reasons we'll see). The "right word" is the one that _memorializes_ the new experience; it makes it something lasting.

Heidegger delineates this breakdown experience in poetry quite specifically. On the one hand we feel that there was something there waiting to be said by the poet. But on the other hand we also feel that without language to say it that "something" could not really be. (If we feel in the right way the word's lack, we feel that things can't really be "that way" without it.) And thus we recognize, by feeling it, the constitutive role of language: how it "nominates" entities into being. Heidegger develops these points in a reading of Stefan George's poem "The Word," and especially its last couplet: "So I renounced and sadly see: / Where word breaks off no thing may be" [EL (UL 60), also Wo (UL 140)].

So by poetry we participate in an ontological event: in speaking fresh words that found meaning, we experience new things "coming to being" by these new words. This, I think, is what all (great) poetry does, for Heidegger: it lets us experience words forming world—and being. But—and he stresses this—we experience these new words not as invented by the poet, but as spoken through him by "language itself." There's an inevitability or necessity in these words, and the new outlook they give us; they are not just the personal fiat of the poet.

We hear the poet's words to come from a source behind him—and so indeed they do, Heidegger thinks. He attacks the Romantic cult of genius in which the artist creates the work in an heroic originality of will and self-assertion. Nietzsche gives powerful expression to this idea, but Heidegger reverses it: the poet succeeds by being receptive and attentive to the situation of the people in the age. The poet is somehow "open to" and "hears" what is destined, i.e. the words needed next as the current ones lose their force. The poet is responsive to "the withheld determination of historical Dasein itself" [OA (W 48)].

The poet receives the new words from language—understanding the latter to be, as we saw in section 1, the comprehensive point of view embodied in the sayings of the people, through its history. So the language is not just the "uses" of words as the linguist may study them, and not just the "practices" in which these words are embedded, as the sociologist may study them. Instead it is the "meant" or "felt" viewpoint which these uses and practices merely express. The poet enters this meant medium and finds his new words there, "sent," as a destiny, from the very sources in this language.

Language is the overall view of the world which is expressed in the great synthesis of the uses of its words, through a history. But this synthesis is not a mere sum of all the individual uses at specific times and places: some uses are essential and determinative, whereas others are parasitic and deficient. Language speaks principally in those essential uses, which express the deep structure of the overall viewpoint. They express, above all, the ultimate aim or purpose which all the other uses presume but neglect.

The poet "listens to language" by entering the viewpoint expressed in these seminal uses of words. So Heidegger depicts poets as strongly traditional—as hearkening back to the sayings of their major predecessors, and responding to them. Thus Hölderlin carries out a "poetic dialogue" with Sophocles [HHI 55]. These earlier poets articulate the "mission" [Sendung] the people has been sent upon, and thereby also the "mandate" [Auftrag] it is its task to achieve [LQ 106].

However, we still haven't come to the special character of poetic language. Most of the things we've so far said of the poet's methods— how he induces breakdowns and initiates meanings—are true of the metaphysical philosopher too; metaphysics also gives new words that jar us out of linguistic complacency, in a way that fixes them for us. What distinguishes poetry is its different way of making its words "memorable," and the different relation to language this sets us into.

Metaphysics makes its words memorable, we saw, by offering them as concepts. These are recommended by the special clarity with which they are defined, as well as by the metaphysician's adjoined arguments that they fit precisely along the real joints in things. These concepts are meant to be transparent onto things so that the latter lie exposed and available to us. Concepts aim at securing a "pure presence" of things to the subject or intellect that has them. This presence is meant to be not just immediate but lasting—to give a lasting control.

The poet offers new words in a very different spirit. What takes the place of definition, as the way to these words' meaning, are the stories and human situations the poet's verses install us in. We must gather their meaning in the experiences—sensuous, perceptual, emotional—they elicit, as they bring us to inhabit those situations. We inhabit them in an unaccustomed vividness, and it's this that makes the words memorable. They reinstall us in those moments. By the web of experiences the poet's words set us into, they give us a new stance—some part of a new way to live. And they give us not merely the conception or description of this stance, but the affective and willful taste of it.

In this different way poetry makes new meaning, it's very important that this meaning not be completely transparent, as the concept aspires to be by its accompanying definition. Wo (UL147): "The poet must renounce having words under his control as the portraying names for the posited entities."[29] Indeed poetry purposively and essentially gives its world in a way that is not transparent, and not susceptible to conceptual capture. It founds a different kind of world, by sustaining certain mysteries and indeterminables within it. Heidegger's term for this aspect of the way art founds world, is "*earth*" [*Erde*]. Poetry makes its words memorable by and in their "earth," and by this bars full openness.

Here we arrive at the large idea in "Origin of the Artwork" that I mentioned I was keeping aside. This is "earth," used in contrast and conjunction with "world'; this contrast-term is not present in *Being and Time*. The earth is (as it were) the penumbra of mystery that must surround the clearing or world—a mystery that penetrates into every entity that shows up in the world, as something to it that precedes every way it shows up, every way we can discover it. In the words we learned above, earth is that concealing which is the essential concomitant to the unconcealing of being. It is also what cannot be brought to presence. It is a principle of breakdown embedded in the clearing itself.

When the artwork "lights up" a world, it also reveals that world as from and upon a ground, an earth, that is not revealed. Our world is that system of paths we know our way along, all that we are prepared for. It is the "open" or "clearing" in which our concern and effort move. Artworks such as Van Gogh's painting can reveal this world—can let us see/feel what is normally in a deep background. But in doing so they show it *as* emerging from something independent, something inscrutable and uncontrollable by our most searching concern. So the artwork reminds us—in a way metaphysics' concepts do not—of the limits of our world. There is something all our skill and knowing can never control, something that comes before it. Art's reminder of earth gives us a particular modesty in our world.

One essential way the artwork does this—gives earth—lies in how it presents itself to us in its materials, its bricks or paint or bronze or words. It fuses its meaning in these materials, so that it can't be abstracted away in concepts and statements. So, for example, with the painting: no concepts can capture the contribution made to its meaning by the particular hues and textures of its paint. An artwork displays its materials as essential to what it says—by contrast with a tool, whose materials "disappear into usefulness" [OA (*W* 24)]. The tool works best when we don't notice what it's made of, but the artwork calls attention to itself this way: it "sets itself back into the massiveness and heaviness of the stone, … into the lightening and darkening of color, into the ringing of tone, and into the naming power of the word" [OA (*W* 24)].

Turning back to poetry, its words aren't concepts because their meaning depends on their "earth." The latter includes, for one thing, their sound—their rhythm, their rhyme, the particular way they're shaped in the mouth, how they feel in the mouth to say. And the poem's earth also includes, I think, the particularity of the images and situations it embeds its message within. So Sophocles projects ideals and attitudes not by defining virtues or goods, but by telling stories about individual men and women; his meanings are in these stories, and can't be extracted as concepts and precepts without interpretation and loss. All these factors in its meaning make the poem elude conceptual capture, as it does translation.

In science, in philosophy, in everyday talk these factors are counted irrelevant; attention passes through them to the sense or content, and it seems unapt and juvenile to weight them much. Those features seem merely cosmetic, and to work at them seems an effort to influence by underhanded means. Against this the poem insists, and makes the reader accept, that these factors are much of the point. And if we hear poetry right it persuades us that this is really true of language more generally: it works by something it cannot express outright.

EL (UL 98–99) develops the importance of language's "sensuous side": "That language sounds and rings and vibrates, hovers and trembles, is in equal measure characteristic of it, as that the spoken has a meaning." But this sensuous side has been misunderstood by being treated only "from the perspective of physiology and physics, that is, technologically-calculatingly in the widest sense." Instead, Heidegger insists, we should view this sensuous side as showing our roots in "earth." These roots run through the mouth, in speaking: "body and mouth belong to the flow and growth of the earth, in which we mortals flourish, and from which we receive the sound-ness of our roots." And so: "Language is the flower of the mouth. In language the earth blossoms against the bloom of the sky."

The poet's language calls attention to its own sound—but sound not as physics or physiology might study it, i.e. not as brute or meaningless wave-lengths or pitches. A word's sound is something different from its sense and reference (its content), but is itself another kind of meaning. It is a meaning that branches out into obscurity, as roots do in soil. So it includes, above all, that the content is said in a particular language, within which the words stand in massively complex relations of (mingled) sound and sense to other words. These relations, moreover, have a history, and each word links back to formative uses in the culture's deep past.

Poetry insists that we hear these echoes and reverberations (whereas metaphysics tries to wipe this slate clean and determine the meaning solely through definition). Heidegger's many sound-connections among words—the way he runs through series of terms built on the same root, for example—are meant to expose these elements in words' meanings, how these other terms resonate in them. This is true for poetic language, and also for natural language, apart from its regimentation in concepts with definitions. Words bear these overtones as their "earth": sense reaches out multifariously and indefinitely through language, as plants' roots reach down through ground.

So the poet gives his words' meaning over to the language to co-determine. His fresh words evoke vivid stances in us, and have a part of their meaning in our experience of those stances. But meaning also flows to that experience from the language—from the manifold viewpoints expressed by its words. The poet means to keep his words open on that side too—to let meaning accrue to them from the meanings they have elsewhere. In particular, he offers his words within the cultural practice and tradition of poetry, hence in a kind of dialogue with other poets. So his words have meaning in relation to theirs, and these relations inflect, as we notice them, the experiences the words evoke. (This is another reason slang may not count as poetry for Heidegger.)

More particularly, the poet speaks in a particular dialect, rooted in a particular region and locale. This makes his words express "earth" in a more literal sense: their meaning draws too on a particular region or landscape or "soil." Heidegger remarks in particular on Hölderlin's use of words from the Schwabian dialect. The geography of this region in southern Germany (Heidegger's own), and especially its rivers, figures prominently in Hölderlin's poems. This way a localizing "accent" contributes to the meaning of a poet's words reinforces that this meaning can't be defined or captured in concepts.

The poet's words are conspicuously multivalent. By the standard of the concept they are indeterminate, though this is not a matter of mere vagueness [HHI 121]. Indeed each poetic word's links run off in opposite directions, so that it always has contrary meanings. Heidegger develops this with respect to Trakl: "'Green' is decay and bloom, 'white' is pale and pure. ... Yet this meaning-more [*Mehrdeutige*] of poetic saying does not flutter apart into an indeterminate meaning-many [*Vieldeutige*]" [LP (UL 192)]. Yet these divisions are not chaotic or arbitrary; the ambiguity "resides in a play that, the richer it unfolds, remains all the more rigorously held in a concealed rule" [QB (P 320)].

In these several ways there is an ineliminable obscurity in poetry, a mystery that can never be cleared up. A poem gives us a world with that mystery embedded in it. We participate as it makes new meaning, but the meaning is "set back" in the sounds and situations so that we can't "capture" it in the familiar terms we have in control. We can't fix it as a propositional content. It can't be grasped by the representing subject, but needs to be understood "in the body," in our feeling and will.

This dichotomy of world and earth, so famous from "Origin," is superseded in later works by what Heidegger calls "the fourfold" of earth, sky, mortals, and divinities—all as something like regions or aspects of the world. I'll come back to this when I talk about Heidegger's treatment of gods in Chapter 9, but for now we should note that this schema preserves the stress on a mystery in things, but now allocates it into lower and higher sectors, "earth" and "gods."

Poetry, then, carries its responsive reader out of the stale habit of language, into a situation in which the usual words don't suffice. The reader then shares in the experience of language's founding role, by speaking with the poet his new words, giving a new world, but a world inflected by (concealing) earth. So the reader participates in the ultimate event of Ereignis, in which world comes to be. And when poetry plays its social role—as it did among the Greeks, does not do now, but may do in the future—the whole society learns to speak these words, and to live in this new world. But it learns to live in it *as* made by language of this earthy, impenetrable character.

So, in the optimum, the new basic words the poet injects into the language change the world of the people who speak it. But Heidegger conceives of this "thrust" as decaying and lapsing over time: as the poetic words become common coin they lose their freshness and surprise. They continue to hold users in this world they project, but their own role in making this world drops from notice. And as they grow usual, it's harder and rarer to notice their "earth," the indeterminable meaning in their mere sound. As they become the habitual language, the light dims, that had shown words' founding role.[30] The world itself takes on a different status: no longer experienced as made by these words, it comes to seem obvious and inevitable. So poetry is not a higher form of everyday language; the latter is a forgotten and misused poetry.

Poetic words thus become hard to understand even among the people whose world they make. Nevertheless, Heidegger thinks they retain their potency, if we approach them right. They keep their power to "light up" a particular world-and-earth, even for people from other ages or cultures. It is of course the aim of his explications of poems to show how this can happen.

One important tactic for reviving the original sense of a word is to expose its etymology. Heidegger is often ridiculed for this. But his main point is not to assign these root senses to the word, but to locate the formative moment in which the root meaning is poetically converted into a new sense not analyzable into its root. Those root senses of course inflect the word, but only in helping us to have the experience the poet frames with the word. Etymologies can help us to regain that experience, and so to hear a word's poetry again.

But in order for us to get this effect, our aim mustn't just be to understand some other age or people. Instead of touristing in poetry, we must bring to it all of our concern, and so use it, in the end, to make ourselves a better home. In the "oblivion of being" we now suffer in our technological age, we must use poetry to begin to build a new language, to house a new world—to house it poetically, i.e. so as to give us this world with its earth, and its gods, both of which technology precludes. Hölderlin above all, he thinks, gives us words for this task.

Our own role is to be "preservers" of that poetry, by learning to live openly in the world it unconceals. Preserving is needed because of the iterative nature of language: "[b]ecause the word, once it is spoken, slips out of the protection of the caring poet, he alone cannot easily hold fast the spoken knowing ... in its truth" [HK (EHP 49)]. Poetry is preserved by those who live in the world *as* opened by its words. "Preserving the work means: standing within in the openness of entities that happens in the work" [OA (*W* 41)]. "[F]or a work only actually is as a work when we transport ourselves out of the habitual and into what is opened up by the work" [47]. We preserve poetry when we sustain the power of its words to show themselves making our world.

I've deferred several times the question of poetry's relation to "thinking," which, we've seen, is what Heidegger promotes to replace metaphysics. I've described poetry largely in its contrast with metaphysics; we can improve this account by contrasting poetry next with thinking. The relation between these two, both favored by Heidegger, is much subtler than is either's relation to the rejected metaphysics.

4. Thinking's language

Having reviewed Heidegger's critique of metaphysics and his praise for poetry, we turn now to what seems the obvious consequence of these, his effort to write a poetic philosophy. We turn, that is, to Heidegger's own language—to the style that is so striking and controversial a feature of his later work. Why does he write like this? How does he mean us to read him? And does he want us—as aspiring thinkers or philosophers ourselves—to write (and even think) this way too?

His lesson is not to give up philosophy for poetry. He identifies himself as a thinker rather than a poet. He writes very often *about* poems, but only exceptionally does he write verse—though he much esteems two philosophers who do, Parmenides and Nietzsche.[31] Nor does he write in the dramatic-fictional style of *Thus Spoke Zarathustra*, in which ideas are embedded in a story about an individual life. And although he does use the favorite literary genre of philosophers, the dialogue, he uses it rarely.[32] His later writing is abstract and discursive; it proceeds as a kind of argument. It still belongs, more clearly than much of Nietzsche's, to the family-line of metaphysics. In his writerly genre, at least, he doesn't switch sides.

This affinity to metaphysics is of course much closer in *Being and Time*, where he coins his philosophical vocabulary in strong imitation of Aristotle.[33] He takes words from everyday discourse and converts them into technical terms. In particular he very often converts prepositions into abstract substantives; he does so especially in mapping *teleological* structure (e.g. *das Wozu* [the towards-which], *das Worumwillen* [the for-which]), which makes the resemblance to Aristotle still more striking (compare *to hou heneka* [the for-which]). On the other hand the architectonic effort of the book to build from basics reminds of other members of the metaphysical tradition: of Descartes (I suggested in Chapter 3) as well as of several German predecessors. Its language organizes its subject-matter with great care to set each point down in systematic place, where it is justified and also controlled by points before.

We've seen that Heidegger continues, in his later writings, to rate metaphysical language very high: it comes closer to expressing being than ordinary discourse, and so deserves the closest attention. The metaphysician's words come from "near the source," and carry a force that can be revived. Heidegger's writings about past philosophers are often extremely compelling for the way they breathe life and freshness back into terms now stale for us. And his own terms in *Being and Time* carry this freshness themselves, for many readers. In this respect even metaphysics—and Heidegger's own work before his turning—can constitute a form of "thinking."

Nevertheless, he learns a lesson from poetry that makes him pull away from metaphysicians' ways of writing, including his earlier own. This is not just a matter of his appropriating a number of poets' words. Nor is it just that he thinks and writes *about* poetry. He goes on to present his lessons in a style that seems sometimes—at crucial moments—to mimic it, without the verse form. For example EL (UL 101): "When the word is called the mouth's flower and blossom, we hear the sound of language rising like the earth. ... The sound rings out in the resounding assembly call which, open to the open, lets world appear in things."

At issue is far more than simply Heidegger's "style," taken as something cosmetic. Making thinking poetic is not done to "refresh and beautify the dull progress of thinking" [WCT 19]. His way of using words is his way of thinking, per se, and not an added ornament to it. He insists on the very special character of this thinking, lying above all in its special relation to its own words. So if thinking is to use words "poetically," this will reach deeply into its very method or procedure: it will affect, above all, the way thinking gives grounds. We must consider whether this poetic element in Heidegger's way of thinking makes it no longer the kind of "reasoning" we would want for truth.

Heidegger says that thinking and poetry lie very close: thinking "goes its ways in the neighborhood of poetry" [EL (UL 69)]. But often he seems to make them more intimate still: they include or involve one another. Sometimes it seems that poetry is a kind of thinking: "the lofty poetry of all great poetic work always vibrates within a thinking" [EL (UL 69)]. Other times it seems that thinking is a kind of poetry: "The thinking [Denken] of being is the original manner of poeming [Dichten]" [AS (W 247)]. Each seems to be a case of the other: "All reflective thinking is poeming, but all poetry a thinking" [PL (UL 136)]. These mutual involvements threaten to erase the distinction between poetry and thinking, and to merge or blend them with one another.[34]

But, I suggest, rather than merging thinking and poetry Heidegger sets them in a complex relation we can analyze.[35] They are, to begin with, two species in a genus, with a common project: unconcealing being by language. Because they share this project they are also in a way collaborators; they "say the same thing." But they do so best when they say this same thing in their respective, distinctive ways:

"What is said poetically and what is said thinkingly are never identical; but they are sometimes the same, namely when the cleft between poeming and thinking cleaves cleanly and decisively" [WCT 20].[36]

I think there are two main points to see. (1) We must look at what thinking and poetry have in common; it's important that Heidegger largely draws this generic character from the example of poetry. (2) We must identify the specific differentiae of thinking and poetry—how each does that same thing in its own way; here is where that "gulf" between them appears.

(1) Thinking and poetry are both: unconcealings of being, in and by language, such that language's role in the unconcealing is also unconcealed. The thinker's or poet's words make possible and available a viewpoint for which the very being of entities is clear or explicit—and clear *as* dependent on those words. Their words express and bear this viewpoint, which notices the basic project that controls, from the background, what kinds of entities can appear. Their words bear this viewpoint *conspicuously*, in a way that brings home how words "let be."

So both thinking and poetry are events in language, but this means something different than we usually suppose. We might have said that they are "uses" of language, but Heidegger denies that language is a tool put to work by the thinker or poet. Language is not a system of words and their uses, but—we've seen—a comprehensive stance or point of view, opening upon a world; it is this viewpoint *as* expressed by and embodied in words. Thinking and poetry are sectors in that overall viewpoint, likewise expressed in particular words. By being "housed" in the thinker's or poet's words, a new possibility arises in that viewpoint: in particular, these words "say" the viewpoint becoming clear or explicit to itself.[37]

Thus neither the thinker's thinking nor the poet's poeming is an event in the individual's head; they happen in the space or medium of the language, and are accessible to all speakers of it. These new sectors of the viewpoint are laid out, of course, by certain (sequences of) words, the "saying" of the thinker or poet. Those words—the treatise, the poem—embody that new view: they "house" it, in Heidegger's favorite expression. But although the thinker and poet make (or assemble) these words, they are not ultimately responsible for that new possibility. It arises by a "destiny" within that overall viewpoint—that way of having a world—so that really it is language itself that *says* (or speaks) in these words.

What's crucial to thinking and poetry is to house not just any new possibility in the language, but one that "lights up" being as founded in words. In the fullest case, they light being down to its ultimate level, its specification as presence; they not only say presencing, they *show* it *as* embodied in their words. And it's here that the contrast with metaphysics lies.

Metaphysics does not belong to this genus, even though it satisfies its first two conditions: it is an unconcealing of being, in and by language. Its words are indeed, like thinking's and poetry's, (transformative) "events in language," fundamental extensions in its overall viewpoint. But metaphysics fails the third condition: it doesn't unconceal the role of its own language in being's uncon cealment. Indeed it suppresses recognition of this role—and of being itself (as presence).

Metaphysics is in the grip of being as presence. It is driven by enframing, first and foremost in its relation to language: it picks its words as tools to set everything in a maximal order. Our habitual enframing not only wants words that express its control of the world, it also wants control over these words themselves, wants to fix them with definitions that render them maximally present and available. So we've seen how metaphysics treats its words as empty vessels getting all content from its definitions—and treats these definitions as inferred or read off from things: definitions report the discovered kinds of these things, and words are arbitrary names for these kinds. But this hides the way metaphysics' own words really work (i.e. mean).

Because metaphysics doesn't step back/down to the ultimate level of being's clearing, it can't notice its own particular relation to words—this enframing ambition with them. It also can't notice how these words in fact elude that ambition to control them, and carry out their work of opening a world in a quite different way than by its definitions. Metaphysics misses the earth or mystery in its words, which is the necessary complement and limit to its clarity. It uses words with the objective to eliminate all mystery, and so actively interferes with access to being. It misaligns us for the insight to being; being can't be known by concepts. PG 90: "what was in different ways named 'being' and 'reason' and, in such naming, was brought into a certain light, does not allow of a definition in the academic sense of traditional concept formation."

So a post-metaphysical thinking must change what it wants to do with its words. We need "a transformation of our saying and … a transformed relation to the essence of language" [QB (P 306)]. Thinking needs to think its words not under its control, but as gifts. Rather than imposing their senses by willful definitions, it must receive them somehow from being itself, which thinking can learn to do from poetry.

Heidegger's later writing deliberately models thinking's new relation to language on poetry. Thinking learns from poetry a certain modesty in its relation to its words: to abandon the effort at a rigorous control, and to let them take their meanings from the language, as it extends around and behind us. It learns to set its words afloat in the language, letting them draw sense from their history, as well as from such subliminal and "chance" aspects as their sound-relations to other words. Thus the sense of the words diffuses outward (and backward) through the language, and cannot be "presenced" or contained.

This semantic strategy is reflected of course in Heidegger's incessant play on words' resonances and echoes in other terms, as well as in his often-speculative etymologies. His reliance on such sound-relations provokes the complaint that his philosophizing depends on mere puns—or on a claim that words' "real meaning" is found by etymology. But he has grounds for this procedure.

First, this strategy lets words "bear earth," and so sustain us in that reverence for mystery that we need for the revelation of being. This is why they can't get their meanings by definition and fiat—can't have sharp-edged and controllable meanings at all. By making their sense lean conspicuously on their sound, and on the undertones and associations they carry, Heidegger lets his words "preserve earth"—in the way we've seen holds in poetry.

He also has a more positive aim in that strategy. The thinker, like the poet, has his words get meaning this way, because it lets them tap the illuminating power buried in these words' past. Thinker and poet thereby recover a potency in these words, which they had in their formative uses, but have lost to routine. "Words [*Worte*] are not terms [*Wörtern*], and thus are not like buckets and kegs from which we scoop an at-hand content. Words are springs that the saying digs up, springs that are to be found and dug anew again and again" [*WCT* 130]. The power in these old words is carried in such "chance" features as their sound.

But the thinker, like the poet, is only able to tap this buried potency by also saying something *new* with the words. The past senses are brought to life only by virtue of issuing in a fresh view or stance towards things; this fresh view brings life back to those old senses, and they further vivify it in turn. It's the meaning our own time needs that most lives for us. So thinker and poet let their words draw sense from their history, while also adding a new sense to that history; they must do both to do either.

The thinker further follows the poet in the way he sets this new sense forth: it is fixed in a vivid new experience, that the words express and evoke. The words bring to life, they insert us, their readers, within, a "felt outlook" that stands apart from routine. They give us the world in a fresh aspect, which we feel more genuine than the habitual view it interrupts. The old words get new sense by being tied to this experience; this opens a new region in the overall viewpoint which we've seen is the language. The key difference between thinker and poet comes at this point, I think: in the different kinds of experiences they evoke, and give their new meanings in. But let's approach this difference more methodically. (2) Heidegger stresses thinking's difference from poetry. He attributes to each its own role or function. HHI says that thinking has "its own proper origin, one equally essential, yet therefore basically distinct from that of poeming" [112]. The difference is not, we should see at once, the one Nietzsche insists on, that thinking wants truth but poetry is antithetical to truth. Because thinking and poetry both disclose being, they are both "true" in the most important sense, of *alêtheia*. Nor is the difference that poetry deals with values and thinking with (something like) facts. For thinking's words are valuative too, and poetry gives a look to things and says how they are.

Heidegger's clearest way of separating the two is by assigning them different topics: "The thinker says being. The poet names the holy" [AWM (P 237); cf. HHI 138]. This divides between thinking and poetry the aspects Aristotle attributes to metaphysics: ontology and theology.

We should notice right away how this undercuts the view that Heidegger makes thinking subordinate or subsidiary to poetry.[38] For being clearly "lies deeper" than the gods for him. M 217: "the thinking of be-ing is a deed deeper than any immediate veneration of god." Gods are, or are not (or are, as for us now, distant or away), by virtue of being—by virtue of how "there is" being for us. So although indeed the poet appears first in an epoch, and the thinker relies on this precedent, the thinker goes further and deeper.[39]

I'll examine Heidegger's account of "the gods" in Chapter 9, and will be brief here. Our interest is in how the poet's and thinker's different "topics" bear on their different "uses" of words. For they speak, he stresses, in different ways.[40] The point is not, I suggest, that the thinker has words for gods but not being, and the thinker words for being but not gods. It's rather the way that *all* the poet's words involve an implicit reference to gods, and all the thinker's words an implicit reference to being. In particular, all their words are (respectively) meant as *from* gods, or from being; this gives them quite different tones.

The idea that the poet gets his words from divinity is most explicit at the starts of Homer's poems, but Heidegger thinks that any "true" poet must feel this. He must feel, that is, that his words, and the new outlook on things they embody, come as a gift from a source that means or intends (and has other human-like properties) yet is discontinuously higher or better in a way that gives that new outlook decisive credit. These words open a world that "is there" due to this higher source, and that shares in the latter's glory. And this is why and how the poetic words disclose the world as *beautiful* [WCT 19]; their particular form of truth lies in this uncovering of beauty.

So the poet experiences this new vision as received, in moments of revelation that he undergoes rather than accomplishes. The poet can transmit this outlook through the words that frame it, but he can't show the reader a route to the poetic experience itself—one must wait to be "struck" as by lightning (which is Hölderlin's image for it). And this, I suggest, is the key procedural strength of thinking over poetry, as Heidegger now thinks it: the thinker finds "paths" that lead to the revelation of being, paths on which he makes his own way. Although finding these paths requires a receptiveness, a readiness-to-be-affected, they still give us an active ability to come towards *Ereignis* ourselves.

The thinker has a different kind of experience with being: not that of a momentary reception or gift, but of finding or following a "*path*" [*Weg*]—which is a crucial term in Heidegger's notion of thinking, and where (I claim) it differs from poetry.[41] His writing describes a path, which has a different temporal logic than telling a story. This is how he reframes the age-old philosophers' claim to surpass poets by the giving of *arguments*, of *reasons* in favor of seeing the world their new way. Thinking makes a path to being; it finds a way to come into being's vicinity. It dispenses with reliance on the authority of others (the gods), and finds a way to see being directly.

To be sure, this "path" is not at all a clear and fixed road. It is a "wood path," a *Holzweg*—as he explains in the prescript to *Holzwege*: "In the wood there are paths that are mostly overgrown and end abruptly in the untrodden." Heidegger elides in several ways the extent to which this path gives us *control*. It must be entered by a leap [PG 60], or else it makes possible a leap. And it is pursued not by aggressive exploration, but by a "waiting" or receptiveness that refrains from representing what it awaits [FC 75 (= DR (DT 68)).

However, this receptiveness is not towards gods—not a waiting for experiences of them. It waits to hear something in the human medium of *language*, understood as that overall viewpoint stretching back through history. It recognizes that whether gods are here or absent depends on that medium, which it can explore—make its paths within—by efforts of its own. So although this thinking can't make a road that lastingly controls the space it moves through, it can improve its ability to find its way through it, each time anew.[42]

In one aspect thinking's paths run back through history, but in another they run "down" to the foundations of our current world-view. These paths pursue that history because it shows how those foundations were laid—because it helps to bring those foundations to the special kind of explicitness they need. Those foundations were laid in words, and become explicit by our properly hearing words. And it is the experience of this special kind of insight (truth) that gives the crucial clues or signs along the path. Thinking finds its path by following a thread of illumination, in which this truth-experience is extended to more and more decisive levels of our meaning a world.

Heidegger's later talks and essays follow paths in just this way. They begin more locally, trying to establish a sense of the kind of insight at stake, by raising some familiar philosophical issue, and showing how it has become *too* familiar—showing this by breathing life back into its terms, whose prior roteness becomes evident. This sets the standard of vivacity in words that we are to try to sustain as we move from these more local—or ontical—questions towards the deep stance and aim that shapes those questions, and is also expressed in those words.

This way of finding a path is the thinker's "method," which Heidegger hears through the Greek: "'Path' in Greek is *hodos*; *meta* means 'after'; *methodos* is the path upon which we go after a matter: the method" [PG 63]. Thinking's method is to follow the clue of the new kind of truth, back into history towards the formative sayings—by thinkers and poets—that remade language and experience. In these primary sayings thinking finds the original and still-guiding senses of our words. It recovers the potency buried in these words, and by them takes the stance that reaches all the way down to being.

This path that distinguishes thinking from poetry amounts to a kind of reason or "ground." This is how Heidegger transmutes philosophy's claim to provide—as poetry cannot—an argument that justifies what it says. Arguments themselves can't really justify, he thinks, since justification happens only in the actual experience of the truth of being. WCT 233: "What has been seen can be demonstrated [*ausweisen*] only by being seen and seen again. What has been seen never lets itself be proved [*beweisen*] by adducing grounds and counter-grounds. Such a procedure forgets what is decisive, the looking." Thinking's method is all about this "looking"—it takes this experience itself as its clue.

It's this insistence on reasons, and on making a path, that brings thinkers past gods and down to the level of being. And it's by this that a people has a full-fledged history. It was the pre-Socratics' pursuit of reasons that brought them (but not Homer) to the level of being, and opened the great discussion of it that followed in later philosophy. This fateful discussion has brought us to our modern dilemma, in which we find ourselves in the grip of enframing and technology.

Summary

Humans understand being only by virtue of language: we "house" being in our words. So language plays a founding and constitutive role, letting a world be there for us at all. This really crucial role is concealed by our prevailing conception of language as a tool by which we communicate information about a world that is there independently of language. This instrumental conception reflects our own alienation from language, and in particular our effort to subject it to the same control by which technology "presences" all entities. Our misrelation to language is a key element in the "oblivion of being"; our way to the truth of being depends on our finding a new way of speaking and hearing our words.

A language is not a system of signs with their rules of use. It is an overall view of a world as understandable by its words. So it involves intentionality or point of view. It is a comprehensive intentional space that includes all of a society's diverging uses of words, and indeed the history of uses reaching back in the culture's past; all of this has been one "conversation." This vast space can be explored by individuals who already live in some sector of it. Those myriad uses are not all equal, however: some meanings housed in some simple words are decisive for opening the culture's world. These are not the commonest public meanings, but the "originary" meanings expressed by thinkers and poets.

Since Plato Western thinking has been metaphysics, which exhibits a flawed relation to language. Metaphysical thinkers have, to be sure, played the crucial role of articulating the culture's under-standing of being; each houses the current understanding in the new basic words he introduces. But these thinkers mistake the very being they articulate, by misconceiving it as either the highest genus of entities, or as an ultimate entity itself. And this error is tied to their misuse of words: they propagate that instrumental conception of language by presenting their words as "concepts" pulled quite out of the cultural space and assigned meaning entirely by the metaphysician's definition.

In strong contrast with this metaphysical relation to language is what we find in poetry. One large aspect of Heidegger's turning after *Being and Time* is the weight he now puts on art, and on poetry in particular. Our culture's understanding of being has been articulated not just by philosophers, but by poets. We find in their way with words lessons that can help our thinking too. By contrast with metaphysics, which makes words blank markers controlled by definitions, poetry relies on their sound, on their associative links with other words, and on the concrete stories and situations it embeds them in. So its meanings are not transparent and contained, but draw on such sources impervious to definition and control. Heidegger calls this aspect of poetic meaning "earth"; poetry reminds us of the crucial role of earth in meaning.

Heidegger's own later writerly style shows his effort to use lessons from poetry to find a non-metaphysical way to think. Thinking learns a kind of modesty in its use of words, allowing their meanings to accrue from the language; in this medium every word bears manifold senses, many due to its "mere" sound. Thinking relies on words to revive the originary meanings housed in the language by poets and thinkers. It differs from poetry first in speaking not from gods but from being, and second by following a "path" to being (whereas the poet depends on being struck by revelation). Thinking's path, which runs back through those formative thinkers and poets, is what remains of the argument philosophy has prided itself in; it involves a kind of method with grounds, which separates it from poetry.

Further reading

J. Young: *Heidegger's Philosophy of Art*. Cambridge, UK: Cambridge University Press, 2001. [A distinctive account of Heidegger's later views on art, and especially his readings of Hölderlin.]

Nine

Technology and god

Now we turn to two topics that form the gist of Heidegger's diagnosis of the present age. Technology is one of his names for our current understanding of being—for the distinctively modern way of having a world. It is the aspect under which he principally objects to the modern age. Our technological understanding or stance (not our technological stuff) is "the great danger" to humanity in its essential aspect. And a key part of his recommended response to this threat is that we learn to feel the absence of gods, and our need for them. We should hope and prepare for a new arrival of gods (or of a god), as most famously expressed in the title of his late *Der Spiegel* interview, "Only a God Can Save Us" [DS]. Gods will save us once we receive them back into our world, in a way that overcomes the technological stance that now stifles us. So although thinking is principally about being, and thereby goes deeper than poetry (as we've just seen), it still also thinks about gods, especially today.

The heightened religious element in Heidegger's later philosophy is one of its most important features. We've seen that he has always preached the need for a new kind of understanding, as far more vital than adding to the stock of what we understand. After *Being and Time* this new condition of insight—the event of illumination he sometimes calls *Ereignis*—acquires many affinities with mystical experience, reviving and building on this interest from his twenties.[1]

By embedding relation to divinity within his mature idea of *Ereignis* as the truth of being, he makes a quite distinctive theology.

Heidegger thinks out his stance on these topics in relation to Nietzsche, and in particular to Nietzsche's account of the "nihilism" Western society is entering, as advancing knowledge destroys faith in the religious and other myths that had supported our values. Nietzsche's "way out" of nihilism is, very roughly, to put man where god was—or rather to put the overman there. We must give ourselves the new ideal of advancing beyond what humans have been so far. Knowledge, in particular by genealogy, will clear the ground of values that have inhibited us, and let us achieve a new freedom and power.

Heidegger argues that Nietzsche's way out of nihilism shows that he hasn't diagnosed the problem deeply enough: his solution is really another symptom of it. It is precisely the dominance in us of a will to power and control, a will that attempts to set in place and "enframe," above all by the twin routes of technology and science, that is responsible for our nihilistic loss of values. The solution isn't more self-assertion, but rather a humbling to higher power. We must "take gods back" by ceding to them the ultimate say as to the meaning of things.

This is the simple gist of Heidegger's position, but the interest lies in how he tries to persuade us to it. Although he often derides argument, he still gives us reasons or grounds of a sort in favor of his diagnosis and prescription. He tries to lead us, in each of his essays, on a "path of thinking" all along which we have grounds, of the appropriate sort, to proceed as we do. We saw in Chapter 8 how such reasons distinguish thinking from poetry. His principal grounds will lie in special experiences he helps us to induce in ourselves; in them we inhabit technology "down to the bottom," which exposes its limits, and lifts us in a way out of it. As always our most difficult challenge will be to make clear this new kind of insight, since it goes so strongly against the grain, he insists, of our whole outlook. He thinks we will see his ultimate reason if we can find our way to this experience, which he tries to point us towards.

1. The critique of technology

We must be clear from the start that this is not a critique of particular items of technology, nor of the physical dangers these might present (for example from nuclear war or global warming). It's a critique of our current overall outlook and stance, our modern "mode of revealing." This is expressed most characteristically in our ever-advancing technology, but is also at work in our science, philosophy, and indeed in all our endeavors.[2]

The problem lies not in our employing a complex system of tools, but in the "spiritual" stance that compels us into this use. So Heidegger's critique has an extremely abstract and spiritual character. It remains an open question whether shifting that stance would change the specific technologies we employ in our lives. It is even an open question whether we couldn't have much the same array of equipment, yet not detrimentally, due to some different relation or stance towards it. So Tu (QTE 38): "If a change in being—i.e. now, in the essence of en-framing—eventuates [*sich ereignet*], then this in no way means that technology, whose essence lies in en-framing, will be eliminated."

Heidegger thinks he has noticed something pervasive and decisive about our current intentionality (how we have a world, how entities "are there" for us)—something that reaches out into all of our doing, thinking, and feeling, even when we're not using or devising anything technological. It is so pervasive that it is hard to notice: we struggle to get a sense of any alternatives to it, for our guesses at these are still inflected by this deep-rooted attitude. It is the general way being is given us, and so at once the very closest but the hardest to see.

Heidegger's principal term for this pervasive stance is "*enframing*" [*Gestell*]. Intuitively, first, this alludes to a "frame" or framework, both practical and theoretical, within which we place or set everything we encounter. As enframing, we think of entities as having each its proper and precise place within this frame, and feel ourselves challenged to set them there. In our epoch of being, entities show up for us as "to be enframed." They are what they really or most are *as* or *when* they're enframed, for it is then that they are most fully "presences" before us. Enframing is the upshot of our long historical understanding of being as presencing: it best accomplishes the destiny set in motion by the culture's beginning, in Plato, and ultimately in the pre-Socratics. Let's start with Heidegger's description of this enframing stance, before considering his objections to it. (It will be hard, predictably, to present this description without valuative overtones.)

Gestell or enframing is the stance that culminates the ancient effort to "presence" entities—to consider them entities *to the extent* and *as* they are brought to presence before us. Enframing is the most refined and perfected ability to presence things; it does so by settling them precisely within the scientific and technological schemata. We take for granted that everything is what it is just *as* it is determined by science's considered account of it, and by its functional role in our organization of things. Each of us defers to those larger, social schemata, and through them participates in their ultimate presencing of things.

There are two key ways we go about enframing entities. First, we *set them to work* within our framework of equipment—we discover the specific uses a thing can have, and bind it into a network of processes that extract this value from it. A famous passage in "The Question about Technology" describes how the Rhine is turned into a "water power supplier" by the power plant built on it, and how it also serves "as an orderable object for viewing by a travel group, which the vacation industry has ordered there" [QT (BW 321)]; these of course are only two of the myriad uses made of it. We set it more and more intricately and fully "in place" in the world organized around us in this technological spirit. Heidegger thinks this is something quite different from the kind of tool-use that has characterized humans all along.

The second way we enframe entities is by *explaining* them—setting them in place within the framework of science (which includes the scientifically practiced humanities). We demand that nature be "orderable as a system of information" [QT (BW 328)]. So we bind and control the thing not (now) by putting it to use, but in a way that prepares for that use, and which Heidegger thinks is the same in spirit. And he insists that modern science's enframing of what it studies makes it different in kind from the theories about their surroundings that humans formed in earlier ages. "When today we use the word science, it means something essentially different" from medieval or Greek science, for (he eventually says), today nature and history are "set in place [*angesetzt*] as that upon which man directs himself" [AWP (W 58, 66)].

We might wonder how this enframing is different from the imposition of a "world" or "referential totality," which *Being and Time* attributes to all Dasein, not just those in the modern age. Every Dasein (we saw in Chapter 4 on that book's pragmatism) encounters entities within some pre-established world as a system of ends (for-whiches) and equipmental roles, i.e. within a system of "references." How do enframing and technology go beyond this? How is a framework different from a (being-and-timely) world?

A first point to remark is that *Being and Time does* still stand too much within enframing, and draws its picture of how Dasein opens a world in enframing's terms.[3] So I think there are large parts of the book's existential analysis that Heidegger would later deny are essential—they describe only *modern* intentionality. In particular, its notion of world leaves out the aesthetic and religious aspects that are indeed deficient in our own, but can be found in the past, and hoped to come. And the book's ideal of authenticity does not correct this defect, since it only subordinates one's pragmatic will to control the world to a deeper project to choose—and control—oneself (who one is).

Nevertheless technology or *Gestell* is something more than just having a world in *Being and Time's* way. It is, we might say, that pragmatic stance intensified or perfected a certain way, a way that turns it nightmarish. The web of references has been enhanced so that it closes tight over things; everything we can notice has been taken account of, and fixed with great efficiency for theoretical and practical purposes. All blank spaces on our map of things have been filled. The accumulated results of methodical and disciplinary study have rendered enormously elaborate and precise the framework we bring to things' experience—into which we constantly force both things and experience. Heidegger's claim is that this is our ultimate commitment: we are settled on pursuing just such control. Each of us experiences this control as achieved not individually, but through the organized group; by participating in it, the individual shares in that control.

Let's look more closely at how modern science, even in its beginnings and before any practical application, already expresses enframing. We might have thought that technology is "applied natural science" [QT (BW 328); cf. FC 3], but this gets it backwards, Heidegger thinks. *Gestell*, the essence of technology, is not an outgrowth of science, but is already present in it. So *Gestell* "already holds sway in physics. But it doesn't yet itself come to appearance in it. Modern physics is the herald of *Ge-stell*, still unrecognized in its source" [QT (BW 327); cf. FC 116]. The distinctive effort to enframe already shows in early modern science, though only to an eye that looks back from technology, where enframing has completed itself. Indeed, because enframing is a kind of completion of presence, it is already implicit at the very beginning, among the Greeks.

In "The Age of the World Picture" Heidegger distinguishes three features of modern science by which it enframes. First, early modern physics takes the lead in making science "*mathematical*." This sounds like a familiar point, but Heidegger uses the term in a very special sense (drawn from the Greek): it refers not to the use of numbers, but to the way physics sets up its researches by first projecting a rigorous ground-plan [*Grundriss*] that circumscribes the entities it treats.[4] This framework of definitions and laws is what's "known in advance" (*ta mathêmata*, in Heidegger's etymology) before research begins. Sciences have one by one become rigorous by following physics' lead in projecting such a ground-plan.

This prior plan is a precondition for the distinctive *method* of modern science, its second key feature. By this method, some candidate to join the framework as a "law" is laid down as hypothesis, and then examined by experiments set up to confirm or disconfirm it [AWP (*W* 61–62)]. So there is, besides the framework, this settled procedure for adjusting and expanding it, so that it can accommodate ever more entities ever more precisely and completely. This procedure persistently improves and extends the framework.

This method is in turn the precondition for a third crucial feature of modern science, its *industry* [*Betrieb*]. This is the way, within a shared practice and discipline, those experimental results are constantly applied back to the projected laws to modify them, thus setting up a new round of experiments, and so on. "This having-to-align-itself to its own results as the ways and means of a progressing procedure is the essence of research's character as industry" [AWP (*W* 63–64)]. As this industry spreads through academic disciplines the scholar is replaced by the researcher, participating in an institutionalized and communal enterprise.

The ground-plan built by method and industry is a cultural-historical product, the cumulative result of many generations of research. No individual possesses all of this structure "in mind." Instead we defer to a framework held in place by the understandings of scientists and others. But we feel that we share in this framework, and have rights in it: every part of it is there for us to understand too, if we take the appropriate steps. This world-plan is constantly improving in both its scope and its detail; this improvement indeed accelerates. And the framework is also increasingly accessible to individuals, through scientific education, and such technical advances as the web.

In identifying everything by reference to the framework, we live in the "age of the world picture," in which for the first time the world *becomes* a picture, such that "it first and only is an entity [*seiend ist*] insofar as it is enframed [*gestellt*] by representing-producing man" [AWP (*W* 67–68)]. So it is anachronistic to suppose that we have one world-picture and the ancient Greeks (for example) had another. "The basic event of the modern age is the conquest of the world as picture" [71]. Entities only are *as* they find place in the ground-plan we bring to them.

But what, let's ask, is the aim that makes science treat the world as picture and things as objects? The aim is said to be truth—that's what science says it wants. But Heidegger argues that it's something else, that comes to light only once early modern science has become technology. Not visible previously was what we now see was crucial to that science from the start: it is a way of controlling, it aims at control, by setting-in-place. IP 53: "from its beginning modern natural science is in its essence the technological assault on nature and its conquest." It's for this the ground-plan is built by method and industry. Technology is simply an extension of this ongoing effort, so that it is "the same" as science.

Placing things into science's framework confines them in a theory, a step to the full systematic and totalized mastery that now shows itself as the aim all along. Heidegger over and again stresses this aim behind science, e.g. in SR (QTE 167–68): "Science sets [*stellt*] the real. It sets it so that the real shows itself ... in the surveyable results of posited causes. The real thus becomes pursuable and surveyable in its results. The real is set secure [*sichergestellt*] in its objectness."[5]

This ur-aim at control is more overt in technology, where we adopt the imposing, demanding, intrusive relation to things that Heidegger calls "challenging" [*Herausfordern*]: "The revealing that rules in modern technology is a challenging which sets on nature the demand that it supply energy which *as such* can be extracted and stored" [QT (*BW* 320)]. And technology turns the "object" into "stand-by" [*Bestand*—which others have translated "standing-reserve" or "resource"], set there in place for use as needed: "Everywhere it is ordered [*bestellt*] to stand at order in place [*auf der Stelle zur Stelle zu stehen*], and indeed to stand itself orderable for a further ordering. What has been ordered so has its own standing. We call it the stand-by" [322]. Just as science sets everything within a theoretical framework in which it has a precisely defined place and relation to other things, so in technology everything has a role in the intricate network of equipment set in place for our purposes.

Heidegger illustrates this with the example of the Rhine already mentioned. He points out how the hydroelectric plant built on the river sets it into a network that reaches out through power cables and stations and into the electrical appliances in homes. Simultaneously the river is made to stand by for diverse other uses, in each case connected into a similar web laid out deliberately and calculatingly for human advantage. This includes, we must not forget, its use as a "scenic resource." Thus the hydroelectric plant serves as an emblem of our age's "mode of revealing," somewhat as the temple was of the Greeks', yet not thus as an artwork for a reason we'll see.

Although this frame is social—it is the way things are made to stand by for the whole society—each of us shares in it. I know that a thing would be fully usable by me too, if I were to step into the place the framework prepares. So I participate, if indirectly, in the control the framework subjects things to. More fundamentally, I share in the deep expectation that the world is there *to be* set in order and harnessed in this way. And this attitude infiltrates, necessarily, my relation to myself. My own life, my time and span, are there as resources to be put to maximal use—to be used wisely and well.

Now, as always, Heidegger thinks it is easy enough to say these things, but extremely hard to bring them into adequate view. We may notice this about ourselves, yet do so only at third hand, as it were: in the wake of our behavior, stepping back from it, we might agree that it has this character and purpose. But this isn't the way we need to "see" this, because it doesn't bring us down to the level in which we indeed project being this way. We don't experience where or how this insistence on enframing occurs in us, and so we have no inkling how we could *not* so insist. Even our assent to Heidegger's claim about enframing is just one more way of enframing our experience.

All of this is Heidegger's description-diagnosis of technology and *Gestell*. It has been obvious throughout that he has a negative view of them—but just what are his arguments? It may appear that his attack amounts only to depicting technology in various negative lights: as an "assault," as "controlling," and so on. Does he offer any clear reasons why technology's way of having a world is bad? Since many of the things he attributes to enframing may well seem to us to be good things—including individualism, humanism, the ideal of freedom, and rationality [e.g. AWP (*W* 70)]—we will need his reasons to be strong ones.

We've seen that his criticism is *not* what we might expect: that technology will lead to disasters such as by nuclear war or accident. "The threat to man does not come firstly from the potentially lethal machines and apparatus of technology. The authentic threat has already attacked man in his essence" [QT (*BW* 333)]. The worst is already happening to us, unawares. It happens to us not just as we use cars or computers or other such technological gear, but down at the bottom of our thinking all the time. It is our deepest "mindset" or project, and it's here that it does its crucial damage, Heidegger thinks, not out in its peripheral workings.

Gestell or enframing—the aim to "presence" things in theory and practice—is our guiding stance. It gives character to all our more particular projects and pursuits—settles how they'll be carried out, and what will count as success in them. So I think of my life as to-be-organized in just such a way: of my days and hours as

334 Technology and god

resources to be carefully deployed in service of personal or social ends. And I pursue each project from this same stance: when I garden I view the plants out of the developed sciences of biology, botany, and horticulture; deferring to this settled knowledge of their needs and uses, I see each as to-be-set in its best place in my garden-plan.

Heidegger's ultimate complaint against this basic stance is that it misrelates us to being; secondarily, it also misrelates us to things or entities. And it does so both epistemically and "functionally" (with respect to our own essence): enframing hides being from us, and also prevents us from standing in our proper (essential) relation to it.

Enframing hides being from us even though it brings all of science's accumulated knowledge into its view—and science now advanced by long exercise of those mathematical, methodical, and industrious traits. It hides being by preventing us from getting "beneath" its own enframing stance, to experience as an open question, how being shall be. It prevents this by its own seeming comprehensiveness, its full confidence in its claim to give the only right answers, which effectively cuts off the possibility of any alternative: I can't imagine any other way of letting those plants be for me. Enframing "drives out every other possibility of revealing" [QT (BW 332)]; it "blocks the shining and prevailing of truth" [333].

Enframing is particularly unable to step down to the level of being because its own aggressive "presencing" of entities is antithetical to the receptive attitude most conducive to that step. As we organize our lives and world with this calculating rationality, we bar experiences of any aspects other than those it licenses. We insist on bringing to things the whole framework of science and technology; we let them appear to us only in that light. "The ordering [Bestellen] belonging to en-framing sets [stellt] itself above the thing, leaves it, as thing, unsafeguarded, truthless" [Tu (QTE 46)]. So science makes "an attack [Angriff] on the actual, insofar as this is challenged to show itself within the perspective of the representing grip [Griffes]" [QB (P 304)]. But this aggressive slotting of each thing into this schema precludes its "showing itself from itself"—an experience of it we can only have by somehow stilling that deep enframing stance.

Due to the way I "enframe" the plants I garden with, I cut myself off from experiencing "earth"—i.e. the unavoidably hidden source from which they come to appearance for me. "Earth itself can only still show itself as the object of the attack arranged in the willing of man as unconditioned objectifying" [NW (W 191)]. By contrast the proper relation to earth has a religious aspect for Heidegger, though the gods themselves are distinct from it, as we'll shortly see.

Enframing's epistemic failure extends further: it involves a deep self-misunderstanding, which interprets us as at once too little and too much. On the one hand we interpret ourselves as the kind of thing enframing reveals to us: we interpret ourselves as stand-by— as one more resource available in the great framework set out by our science and control. (As we've seen, we even interpret our own life-time in this way.) But on the other hand we also interpret ourselves as accomplishing enframing. And in this regard we take ourselves as "lord[s] of the earth" [QT (BW 332)], since we project the framework that makes everything what it is. I have access to that framework's grasp and control; I feel I share in its authority over what is (which is more than I am, as given being).

These are the realist and idealist sides to Gestell's confidence in its ability to say being. On the one hand it has the sense of itself as penetrating fully into the thing itself, to lay bare its real character. But on the other hand it takes a responsibility for that theoretical and practical framework, which lets that real character "presence" for us. (Kant of course distinguished these aspects of the modern view, as an empirical realism set within a transcendental idealism.) But both of these, we've seen, mistake the true character of our relation to being.

Paradoxically, although technology has the point of control, it is not itself in our control. That is, this way of revealing, Gestell, is not chosen by us: "over unconcealment itself ... man does not have control" [QT (BW 323)]. We do not choose to have our world as a framework—and no founding thinker chose it to be so either. "Modern technology, as a revealing that orders, is thus no mere human doing" [324]. Technology arrives as the "destiny" of Western history, and its founding thinkers such as Nietzsche are not creative, but responsive to what that history is working towards.

Here we pass from the epistemic to the "functional" side of Heidegger's argument against enframing: *Gestell* not only conceals being and things, it also misrelates us to our own essence; indeed "the essence of the human is annihilated" [FC 13]. What is truly ours is to stand in a protecting and preserving stance towards being and towards things. We are "not ourselves" when we stand wrong emotively towards them, by our challenging and assaultive view of them.[6]

Heidegger interprets "nihilism" as the drift into *Gestell*: "Nihilism is the world-historical movement of the peoples of the earth who have been drawn into the power realm of the modern age" [NW (W 163–64)]. It is because Western history culminates in technology, as giving ultimate presence, that its age is "decisive and probably the most capable of enduring" [AWP (W 71)]. The danger is that "the racing of technology might install itself every-where" [QT (BW 340)]. The assumption that everything is really and just as it is in the latest, most potent science-technology may solidify its own grip on us, as our own grip on the world is better and better. Nor is this just a threat to the West, since "Western history ... stands in view of broadening out into world history" [NW (W 193)].

What should be our response to this threat? What are the concrete lessons of the critique of *Gestell* and technology? We must find, we'll see, a "saving power" within technology itself. We do so not by turning our backs on technology, but by finding our way through it to the truth of being, hidden within it. So "the essence of technology will be gotten over into its still concealed truth. This getting over is similar to what happens when, in the human realm, one gets over a pain" [Tu (QTE 39)].

2. The withdrawal and absence of gods

This critique of technology can be stated to a considerable extent in secular terms, but it also has a religious aspect that is crucial for Heidegger. One way to put what's wrong with our modern world of technological framing is that "the gods are absent." Indeed this may even be technology's ultimate ill. As we develop Heidegger's religious point now and in section 4, we'll see how it explains and clarifies so many other features of his later viewpoint as to have good claim to be its crux—the true pivot-point of his turning.

Gods' presence or absence in a world is crucial to how, in having this world, we stand towards being. We can only be in proper relation to being by giving place in our world to the divine. And we can only regain the divine, by healing our relation to being. LH (P 258): "But the holy [*Heilige*], which alone is the essential space of divinity [*Gottheit*] ... comes to shine only when being itself beforehand and after long preparation has been lighted and is experienced in its truth."

This religious element is absent in *Being and Time*. I say this despite Heidegger's rejection, in his 1947 "Letter on 'Humanism'," of Sartre's interpretation of *Being and Time* as an atheistic existentialism. He further denies there that the book was "indifferent" regarding "the holy" or "the divine." Nevertheless, it remains true that God or gods simply don't figure in the program of *Being and Time*, even in the book's larger plan, and this, together with the book's huge ambitiousness, suggests that the religious was not then philosophically important to him.

Heidegger's turn from *Being and Time* returns him to religion, but as necessary for an adequate relation to being, which remains primary for him. So religion—a relation to god or gods—is itself for the sake of that more basic relation, to being. This is a striking feature of Heidegger's later "theology," and it will have some surprising results. Because he does not identify the divine (or gods or god) with this being, the latter displaces divinity "at the top"—and not just at the top of his "ontology" but in his notion what we humans need most to mind. Divinity is not a first principle for Heidegger, and not what our ultimate insight-experience will be of. Nevertheless it is intimately related to that ultimate experience of being itself.

By this distinction Heidegger claims to leave behind metaphysics, since the latter is always an "ontotheology," in that it always interprets being in terms of a preeminent entity, God. In doing so metaphysics misses the "ontological difference"—it tries (hopelessly) to explain or understand being in terms of entities. So ND (N v4 209): "Because metaphysics, thinking entities as such, remains struck by being but thinks it towards and from entities, so must metaphysics as such say (*legein*) the *theion* in the sense of the highest entitive [*seiendes*] ground."[7]

The gods' status as secondary to being is the distinctive and indeed peculiar feature of Heidegger's "philosophy of religion." It recalls the Greek notion of the gods as subject to Fate. CP 287: "The utmost god needs be-ing."[8] Indeed the very divinity of gods is owing to a more ultimate "holiness" belonging to being. "The holy is not holy because it is divine; rather the divine is divine because in its way it is 'holy'" [AWH (EHP 82)]. And "neither humans nor gods by themselves can ever achieve an immediate relation to the holy" [90].

The crucial problem for Heidegger—and for our reading of him—concerns the precise nature of the relation of gods to being. We must settle in particular whether he is a realist or an idealist regarding the gods: does gods' dependence on being mean that they depend on our understanding of being? But I will defer this question until section 4, when we turn to Heidegger's idea how the gods might "return." We can say a lot about his conception of their absence, while leaving that basic question open.

This idea that gods are "away" from the world was important to Hölderlin, who powerfully influences Heidegger here. This is perhaps even what he most takes from Hölderlin: the view of modernity as an age of (properly) regretting the absence of gods. Many of Heidegger's treatments of "the gods" are couched within readings of Hölderlin.

We have some concrete questions for Heidegger here. Who are these absent gods? Are they all the gods that *have* been believed in, including the Judeo-Christian God? Then his reference would be retrospective—as Nietzsche's seems to be when he speaks of God as dead. Or is his notion instead prospective, so that the absent gods are new ones who will or might arrive? And is it significant that he usually (but not always) speaks of gods rather than God?

For now let's leave the notion of gods generic, as Heidegger himself very often does, speaking so often of "divinity" [*Gottheit*]. Again I'll see whether it can be specified further in section 4, regarding the "new gods." But it may be a feature of our age of absence that the gods remain indeterminate and obscure, and those questions unanswerable about them. So CP 308: "talk of 'gods' does not here mean the decided assertion on the being-at-hand of a plurality over against a singular, but rather means to point to the undecidability of the being of gods, whether one or many."

Even in this generic sense we can say some things about divinity: it has a certain abstract content—must have it, to play the role Heidegger assigns it. So first, the divine is something human-like to the extent of being intentional: it is something that means—and values. And as always for Heidegger I think this intentionality is crucially something that *aims*. But its intentionality is greater than our own, in kind not just degree, such that our appropriate stance towards its meanings (and aims) is submission and reception. In particular, divinity's meanings are such that we can't hope to grasp and master them by our own.

What matters most in our relation to gods is that we recognize such supra-human meanings. This is "the holy": how things have not just meaning but purposes higher than through us. But enframing, we've seen, precludes such meanings, since it requires that entities be precisely what they are when enframed within our science and technic. Gods are absent for us by our inability to recognize such meanings.

Moreover—of course—we need to "recognize" the holy in the right way, in the right kind of stance, and this is where we most fail. More important than the identity of these gods is—as always for Heidegger—our stance or attitude towards them. In particular, it's not enough to *believe* in gods, nor to *value* them; we need to "mean" them in some different way that really suits them.

Nietzsche saw this only partly in his idea that "God is dead." He sees that this is not just "a formula of unbelief" [NW (*W* 164)]. It's not—as he is commonly read—due to the scientific "will to truth" overturning all theological justifications for belief in God, and offering alternative, naturalistic explanations for that belief. "Unbelief in the sense of apostasy from the Christian doctrine of faith is ... never the essence or the ground of nihilism; rather it is always only a consequence of nihilism" [165].

If atheism is a belief [no gods] set in a system of beliefs by which we frame and control our world, then gods really are absent to it, but not in the way the atheist thinks. They would not be any the more present if that belief [no gods] were converted to the belief [gods]—not even if this new belief then ramified (worked its consequences) through all the rest of this new theist's beliefs. The real godlessness lies deeper, in how the world is projected by just such a "system of beliefs." It's not a matter of revising this frame-work, but of finding a religious dimension of experience lying quite apart from belief.

Rather than a matter of belief, Nietzsche thinks the death of God lies in a loss of values. But this still doesn't go deep enough, since the schema of "values" is one more expression of enframing. Real religiousness is a matter neither of believing in God, nor of giving God the very highest value. "The hardest blow against God is not that God is held to be unknowable, not that God's existence is proved to be unprovable, but rather that the God held to be actual is elevated to the highest value"; this blow comes from "believers and theologians" whose thinking and talking "is sheer blasphemy if it meddles in the theology of faith" [NW (*W* 194)].⁹

Godlessness is a feature of our very "framing" of the world by beliefs and values. We may think that the divine is most present in a theology that defines and proves it, and in the services and observances by which we make it part of our lives. But within *Gestell* these theoretical and practical dealings both push towards a control that is incompatible with true religiousness. They are efforts to enframe divinity, which is essentially not susceptible to such control. The absence of the gods lies in our inability to allow and find meanings higher than our own. Our deep commitment to enframe—to take things to be (truly) what they are in the frames of our beliefs and values—precludes such meanings. And it takes them away from other things in our world besides gods. When I garden in that way, with a will to enframe, the plants can have no "mystery": no meaning more than what we give them, in our scientific and horticultural slottings.

What we most need today is to notice—in the right way—this absence of the gods. We need to notice, that is, how our enframing stance precludes recognizing a certain kind of meaning. And this brings home to us that enframing stance, itself: this way we insist that everything takes its place in our scientific and technical frameworks. Living with gods' absence means living with a sense of the limits of *Gestell*—not simply of all that *hasn't yet* been brought into hand, but of what can never be gripped. Our hope lies in living more and more with a lack—which is a kind of descendent of *Being and Time*'s insistence on guilt.

So we push more deeply into the absence of gods, into nihilism, by becoming more aware of enframing itself, and the demands—and limits—it imposes on us. We plunge more deeply into *Gestell*, as it were. Since enframing is our understanding of being, we thereby come down to the level of being itself. And there, by this recognition of *Gestell*, we find the "saving power" within enframing or technology itself. Here Heidegger often quotes Hölderlin: "But where danger is, grows / The saving power also" [QT (BW 333)]. "It is precisely in enframing, … in this utmost danger that the innermost indestructible belongingness of man within the granting may come to appear, provided that we, for our part, begin to attend to the essence of technology" [337].

3. Beyond Nietzsche

Before proceeding to look at Heidegger's hopes for a return of divinity to our world, I want to turn aside to pull together some of the links to Nietzsche that I've been making all along. I focus on Heidegger's account of this relationship, and forgo developing my doubts about his reading of Nietzsche.

Heidegger shapes his later viewpoint in pointed contrast with Nietzsche, whom he considers of unique philosophical and cultural importance.[10] Nietzsche articulates the modern opening of being, which is the culmination of metaphysics, as it issues from the pre-Socratic start. So Nietzsche is the last in the line of great thinkers since that first beginning—as Heidegger aspires to be first in the line stemming from a new beginning.

Heidegger's reading of Nietzsche is especially relevant in this chapter, because their divergence has a crucial religious aspect. Heidegger thinks that Nietzsche leaves no room in the world for gods, as we need to have them. This is not just a matter of his doctrinal atheism, nor of his attack on Christianity. Nor does it reflect an absence of religious feeling: Heidegger sees Nietzsche's strong religious temperament.[11] But despite Nietzsche's poetic positings of gods—Dionysus in particular—his metaphysical stance projects a world lacking divinity.

Heidegger takes Nietzsche to give emblematic expression to the modern technological way of having a world. Thus he is a crucial aid to understanding modernity. "In Nietzsche's thought-route to the will to power, not only modern metaphysics but *Western* metaphysics as a whole is completed" [WPK (N v3 155); cf. M 341,

NW (*W* 189)]. Heidegger supports this with readings of what he counts Nietzsche's most important ideas, especially "will to power," "overman," and "eternal return": together these give the metaphysical statement of enframing, technology's distinctive way of letting entities be. We can learn what lies beneath or behind technology by examining these ideas. "To think through Nietzsche's metaphysics becomes a matter of reflecting on the situation and place of contemporary man" [NW (*W* 158)].

Heidegger is of course highly critical of this enframing he takes Nietzsche to state. But he credits Nietzsche himself with some resistance to it: although he expresses technology's stance, he also experiences something badly and generally wrong with it. Nietzsche proclaims the desolateness of modernity, warning that we are devolving inexorably towards nihilism. Heidegger takes over much of this attitude of alarm and horror over the modern age—this is where he most gets the stance of prophet crying against it, noted before. But he claims to be a truer prophet than Nietzsche, with a truer diagnosis: Nietzsche's analysis of the problem is just an ultimate manifestation of it, and "the intended overcoming is but the completion of nihilism" [NW (*W* 193)].[12]

So Nietzsche is not as free as he supposes, because he's not as psychologically astute: he hasn't brought his diagnosis down to the bottom of us and our nihilism. Nor indeed has he "created" his position through the special independence of will he seems to claim for himself. Technology has been destined as the culmination of the long metaphysics of presence, and Nietzsche is its mouthpiece not its inventor. "Nietzsche neither made nor chose his way himself, no more than any other thinker. He is *sent* on his way" [*WCT* 46].

Nietzsche's failure is his inability to get out of metaphysics. His strategy to escape it is to negate or reverse it—but this leaves him still within metaphysics. "As a mere countermovement it necessarily remains trapped, like everything anti-, in the essence of what it is attacking" [NW (*W* 162)].[13] Indeed, his reversal is really the most fully accomplished form of metaphysics, in which it best shows—because it best achieves—its underlying aim and character. Nietzsche's thought brings to ultimate fruition the project set in motion among the pre-Socratics, to bring the world to complete "presence." So he speaks "at the peak of the completion of Western philosophy" [AS (W 250)].

(a) Let's fill out this account by looking in turn at Heidegger's readings of "will to power," "overman," and "eternal return," beginning with the first. His claim that will to power is Nietzsche's metaphysics is well known, and in some quarters infamous.[14] Many have dismissed it out of hand on the ground that Nietzsche is a strong critic of metaphysics and constantly sets himself apart from it. But Heidegger is well aware of Nietzsche's dismissals of metaphysics; he thinks that Nietzsche doesn't see well enough just what metaphysics is. Heidegger tries to outdo him at his own game: he copies Nietzsche's use of "metaphysics" to label a traditional kind of philosophy that must be overcome—and argues that Nietzsche hasn't escaped it as he thought.

We must bear in mind here Heidegger's quite specific idea of metaphysics. Every metaphysics expresses a particular understanding of being, but misstates it as a claim about what entities universally are. So we can learn from it how being "shows itself" in the metaphysician's epoch, but we have to grasp this through and despite the metaphysician's own constant slippage back into points about entities. Metaphysics offers a theory of the whatness of entities, but in doing so it also gives—without quite seeing that it does so—a view of the stance or attitude to which entities appear as they are. It gives, indeed, the task to take this stance and to experience things through it.

This holds for Nietzsche too: he presents will to power as a broadest genus or kind to which all entities belong, and by which they are entities. He offers it as the essence of things—of animals and plants and even physical forces. But behind this is another idea that Nietzsche himself recognizes only partly and fleetingly. This is of will to power not as the genus of entities, but as the attitude or stance that lets them be—that lets them be what they really and most fully are. This is the way will to power really is about being: it states how that basic world-constituting works today, what its basic project now is. Will to power is our basic way of revealing, which underlies and guides all the ways things can appear. Nietzsche half sees that this is what he means about will to power, but within the grip of metaphysics he frames it as a thought about things.[15]

So Nietzsche articulates, with his idea of will to power, our current basic project of enframing or Gestell—of controlling entities by setting and fixing them in place within the frameworks perfected by our science and technology. When we "know" a thing so, both theoretically and practically, then it most fully *is*, by our modern way of having a world. Things are, by our achievement of such power over them. Nietzsche's idea also brings out well the dynamic and expanding character of this project. "Power is power only if and as long as it is enhancement of power and commands the increase in power" [NM (N v3 195)]. Our deep aim is continually to tighten our grip upon things, by refining the grid of our frameworks and fixing things into ever-narrower slots.

Despite our presumption that we're realists in our science and technology, the deep stance of enframing involves a subjectivist idealism. We claim for ourselves—in our scientific and technical frameworks—the right to let entities be: they are just as we so enframe them. And this is the prideful place that Nietzsche famously claims for humans, after the death of God: the only meaning there is in the world is what we ourselves put there.

Nietzsche's term for these meanings we impose on the world is "*values*." He thinks that all humans, as will to power, orient and steer themselves by values. Heidegger argues that this is really a narrower insight about just our modern way of steering, enframing. For Nietzsche thinks (according to Heidegger) that values involve a "reckoning" what to do, and so are not only representational but also quantitative [NW (*W* 170)]. Will to power posits its ends, and posits also a *degree* of value for each of these ends, allowing it to calculate how to maximize the value it achieves. But such calculating disposal of a field of posited values expresses enframing's effort to control the running of one's life—to make its pursuit scientific or technical.

Nietzsche holds that our task is to "revalue values," i.e. to formulate new values, and to do so on the basis of the adequate understanding we finally have of ourselves, as will to power. So will to power is "the principle of a new positing of value. It is new, because it is for the first time achieved knowingly out of the knowledge of its principle" [NW (*W* 173)]. But once again Heidegger objects that the diagnosis hasn't gone deep enough: we need to see that "having values," as an expression of enframing, is part of what's wrong.[16] In a better future, Heidegger suggests, we will not live by values. We will forgo the effort to so posit and quantify our aims.

(b) Heidegger interprets Nietzsche's "overman" as the individual who values on the basis of that finally adequate self-understanding. The human becomes overman by grasping himself as will to power, and putting this insight into effect in making new values for himself. "The human going out above the human-so-far takes the will to power, as the basic trait of entities, into his own willing and wills himself in the sense of the will to power" [NW (*W* 189)].

This advance has ontological implications: the overman is the one who most authoritatively says "what is." He plays the world-constituting role to the highest degree. "All entities *are* as what is posited [*gesetzte*] in this will" [NW (*W* 189)]. In positing entities—and especially their values—in the light of the self-understanding as will to power, the overman realizes to the fullest degree the aspiration to constitute being by our human subjectivity, which typifies the modern age. And more deeply still, he realizes the age-old project to understand being as presence.

A familiar way to think of Nietzsche's overman is that it's how he "puts man in place of God." But Heidegger labels this "crude," because it understates the nature of divinity. Nietzsche doesn't mean us to direct upon the overman the reverence felt towards gods. Instead he leaves the place for God empty, and opens up a new place for the overman, "another realm of another grounding of entities in their other being" [NW (W 190)]. Nevertheless, in the overman humanity claims an authority over being and entities, which it can't really have, and shouldn't properly seek. "The human is not the lord [Herr] of entities. The human is the shepherd [Hirt] of being" [LH (P 260)].

(c) Heidegger reads the idea of "eternal return" as the seat of Nietzsche's theology—or as what this becomes, in the absence of gods. We've already noticed Heidegger's claim that all metaphysics is ontotheology, and he holds this for Nietzsche too, despite the latter's insistence on the "death of God."

Heidegger offers several ways of distinguishing the ontological and theological aspects of metaphysics; it's not always clear just how he connects them.[17] Perhaps the guiding idea is that metaphysics' ontology is its account of the most *general* property of entities, what makes them all entities, whereas its theology is its account of the complete or perfect case of this property, in the entity that *most fully is*. Metaphysics includes a theology because it treats the being of entities—that essential property—as occurring in *degrees*. And it does this with a view to laying down *ends*—an end lodged in ontology itself that will serve as the proper judge of all our other aims. Our ultimate end is to more fully "be."

It has been the "destiny" of metaphysics to progressively drive god out of theology, and Nietzsche most fully achieves this. This does not eliminate, however, the theological arm to his metaphysics: he still has not only a theory about the being of entities generally, but a theory of the entity that *is* to the fullest degree, in a way that lets everything else be. This ultimate entity is not—as we might have expected—the overman, but rather what's expressed by "eternal return." This is the ultimately godless way, found by Nietzsche, of saying what most is.

Why is the overman not the perfection of being—not an entity
that is, completely? Very quickly, it is because he is becoming, and
not being. But "becoming" here does not mean simply "changing,"
since why would something changing not fully be? Rather, it means
that these entities-that-become are ontologically incomplete, that
they depend (to be what they are) on their relations to past and
future, as well as to other entities.[18] The overman, at any moment,
is always "en route," and what he is is dependent on what came to
be him-at-this-moment, and on what he is becoming. Moreover,
the overman is what he is only in relation to the context of other
entities—widening out to the whole world—in which he occurs.
So the overman falls short of the full "presence" required for full being.

Eternal return is the crux of Nietzsche's theology, because it gives
this completeness; it gives what there still can be, in this godless
world, of full presence, of full self-sufficiency. What it is that can be
fully, is only the whole world, *as it recurs*. For as long as this whole
world is itself "en route," it too has that same incompleteness. It is
only as coming back to itself in a circle that the whole world-
course can have ontological self-sufficiency, can be complete. This,
I think, is the key point that lies behind the way the eternal return
"permanentizes" the world of becoming: "Nietzsche's thought
thinks the constant constancy [*ständige Beständigung*] of the becoming
of what becomes in the one presence of the self-repeating of the
identical" [ERW (N v3 165)]. This is the ultimate "how" of will to
power.[19]

It would be out of place here to evaluate this account of
Nietzsche and his "theology." It might be doubted that Heidegger says
enough about Nietzsche's moves to introduce "new gods" himself,
after Christianity—in particular, of course, his Dionysus. But
whatever weight Nietzsche means to put on such a new god, it
seems Heidegger's point would still hold, that he does so not to
deny or temper the project of power and enframing, but to aid and
abet it. These new gods, as also the idea of eternal return, are models
for how we, as will to power, can best realize ourselves.

Let me sum up Heidegger's view of his difference from Nietzsche. They agree, he holds, that our age is the one in which will to power—the aim at control, *Gestell*—realizes itself, and makes values accordingly. But Nietzsche thinks this is all to the good: once we see that we are will to power, we discover how the prevailing values have hindered us, and experiment with new values that will advance us in this essence. So our insight into what we are can be a tool to freedom, diagnosing and giving us power over the social values that shaped us.

Heidegger draws a different lesson. He thinks he sees a sterility in will to power, exposed by the technological age—and kind of person—it has turned out to involve. We need to dig deeper to find the essence in us that can save us. It's not will to power, which is indeed an historical stage of the understanding of being. Rather it's the ability to understand and thereby "open" being at all—an ability that the technological understanding tends to conceal. So Heidegger makes, in this regard, a more radical diagnosis even than Nietzsche's (yet one whose lessons are, in another regard, quite conservative).

4. Gods' return

We've seen that Heidegger spends much more time telling us how to live with absent gods than what it might be like to have them with us again. He dwells much more on how we must recognize their absence than on how human life would be, lived in proper relation to them. Perhaps this is usual in the millenarianism he here echoes: the divine coming will change everything in ways we can only dimly anticipate. But it also belongs to his more general tendency to dwell in preliminaries.

This stress on a relation to absent gods has led some readers to think that this awaiting is the culmination to Heidegger's theology—the best relation to divinity he envisions. Yet I think he clearly views this "living with absence" as worthwhile especially for how it prepares for gods' return. Properly to recognize their absence from our lives we need to have some sense of what their presence would be. Moreover, Heidegger does sometimes describe the return. In *Contributions* the "last god" is a god to come: "The last god is not the end but the other beginning of immeasurable possibilities for our history. ... Preparation for the appearing of the last god is the utmost venture of the truth of be-ing, by virtue of which alone man succeeds in restoring entities" [CP 289].

Let's distinguish two questions: (1) What is the better relation to gods we are to aim at and prepare for? (2) How do we go about that preparing? I will start by pulling together some things we already know about (1), then discuss a puzzle that arises about (2), and then return to try to say more about (1).

Recall what has already emerged—and also some of the points we've left unresolved. Divinity is, by definition as it were, a source of meanings and ends greater than our own; it is a "higher intentionality." When we allow divinity in our world we recognize a domain of higher ends, the holy. Heidegger proposes that we need (ought) to have a world that includes such intentionality, and meanings, including ends, to which our own must defer.

Divinity is "higher" in a way that makes its meanings immune to enframing: they can't be ordered into our scientific and technical frameworks. Divinity's meanings can't be explained or controlled, and in order to allow them we must suspend the stance in which we insist on such control. So just as the arrival of enframing as our age's mode of being erased the possibility of such meanings, and expelled the holy from our world, so their return must involve a change in that mode of being—even though it is the deepest way we "let entities be."

Hence it is not enough, we've seen, to come to *believe* in gods. Belief is on the one hand too thin a relation, when what we need is a deep change in stance. Our world must be thoroughly charged and polarized by those higher meanings. But on the other hand belief is also too thick, inasmuch as it (now, typically) expresses the very stance of enframing we need to get out of. So we have to do both more and less than believe in gods. For both reasons Heidegger doesn't want to set up a new theology, a new theory about god, but rather to help reestablish a religious aspect in all our experience and practice.

Turning now to (2): given that "the goal" is this new stance different from *Gestell*, a certain dilemma, a catch-22, arises as to how we are to attain it. Heidegger is partly in the grip of this dilemma, and partly he notices it. The problem is that the attitude in which we would most naturally pursue this goal—that in which we pursue all our goals—expresses the very stance we need to overcome. The problem is, roughly, the old mystic's dilemma: can we really will our way out of willing?[20] Heidegger spoke just now of "preparing" for the god to appear, but he is persistently divided on the question whether we can do anything positive to bring it about. Any attempt or effort we make seems to pre-tune us to miss the divine.

We should notice how this issue—whether we can do anything to bring back the gods—depends strongly on a problem that we put off before (in section 2), and must now face: whether (and how) Heidegger is a realist or idealist regarding the gods. Are they, apart from our meaning or intending them? Or do they come to be only by our meaning them—including them in our world? If Heidegger is a realist regarding gods, then our positive effort would be insufficient this further way: initiative must come from a real source outside us. If he is instead an idealist, that positive effort faces the peculiar challenge to revere entities that only are by our own reverence.

Sometimes Heidegger seems to speak in that realist vein: the gods themselves must transmit the light of being to us. They do so, in particular, by giving poets the words for the new opening of being. Poets must wait for them to do so: "Only a ray of light that emanates again from the holy itself is strong enough. ... Therefore a higher one, who is nearer the holy and yet still remains beneath it, a god, must throw the kindling lightning into the poet's soul" [AWH (EHP 90)].

Also in this realist vein is a famous passage from the *Der Spiegel* interview [DS 107]: "Philosophy will be able to effect no immediate change in the state of the world. This is true not only of philosophy but of all purely human reflection and endeavor. Only a god can save us. I see the only possibility of a saving in thinking and poeming that prepares a readiness for the appearance of the god." Then: "We can not think them here, we can at best prepare the readiness to wait.'

However, I think we must read these realist passages to mean only an internal or empirical realism, set within a more ultimate idealism. Gods *are*, only in and for the opening of being to us. So "the god also is, when he is, an entity and stands as an entity within be-ing and its essence, which eventuates [*sich ereignet*] out of the worlding of world" [Tu (QTE 47)]. I think this deep idealism is a consequence of that most distinctive feature of Heidegger's "ontotheology," the way being replaces god at the center: his claim that being—being that only is by us—lies deeper than the gods. It lies deeper ontologically, as a "condition of their possibility."[21] In making gods secondary to being, he makes them secondary as well to our understanding of being, i.e. the world we open up by our meaning. "How few know that god awaits the grounding of the truth of be-ing and thus awaits man's leaping-into Da-sein. Instead it seems as if man must and would await god" [CP 293].[22]

This is the key starting-point from which we can resolve other puzzles, and generally clarify Heidegger's idea of the gods. Being is more ultimate than god, such that our ultimate (best) experience is not with god but with being. And indeed, this is the principal value in our experience of gods: that it helps us to experience being. It is to serve in just this way that Heidegger specifies the kind of gods, and experience of gods, we need. He models the gods so that our stance towards them will prepare us to encounter being.

A question arises here: why does Heidegger need both being and gods? He attacks the identification of being with god: such onto-theology elides (violates) the ontological difference by interpreting being as an entity. He gives being the ultimacy once assigned to god; it takes over much of the latter's role. Why does Heidegger not then give us a religion of being rather than of gods?

He needs gods for very roughly the reason religions have needed angels or saints—to mediate with the main thing, the principal divine. We need this reverence for gods because only so can we come into proper relation to being. Recognizing those higher meanings somehow fits us to live "in the truth of being," lets us realize our essence as "shepherds of being." And this is due to the strong similarity the gods bear to being. The gods are entities that are somehow congruent with being in a way that helps us into better relation to it ourselves.

So the gods are needed as models or stand-ins for being. They are entities towards which we stand in (roughly) the way we need to stand towards being. When we "have" gods as we should, we stand in an intentional attitude like the one that experiences being itself, in *Ereignis*. The gods stand in for being this way, by instantiating abstract traits of being; they are ontical concretions of the ontological. So they can be *reminders* of being, and can orient our life-stance on the vector that suits it to remember being as well.[23]

The principal point here is that a world with gods is a world whose meanings and ends we take to be set not by us but for us. We don't claim or aspire to create these meanings ourselves. Nor do we suppose that things' meanings would be set by the full scientific and technical grasp of them; they are not, in this way either, under our control. (We can't, by method and procedure, lay these meanings bare.) We take ourselves to be receiving these ends. And this angle of receptiveness is what we most need in order to notice being. By the stance we take towards gods—as entities in our world that also transcend and structure it—we model (or train ourselves for) the stance we are to take towards being.

Thus when Heidegger speaks of waiting for gods, he means waiting for a new understanding of being, opening a world in which gods "are there." However this god-idealism poses the challenge just mentioned: how can we acquire the attitude—call it reverence—needed to let gods be as we need them to be, when we realize that it's only this reverence that lets them be? (How can we make gods out of nothing?) This intensifies that earlier problem with "willing gods," that willing is enframing, which cuts us off from experience of gods. For both reasons, any effort to "come to revere" seems hopeless.

Certainly we cannot create or invent new gods. "Mortals dwell in that they await the divinities as divinities. ... They do not make their gods for themselves and do not do service to idols" [BDT (BW 352)].[24] How *could* god be something we know we make for ourselves? If we know we make it, it can't be a meaning greater than our own. Hence our dilemma: we want to have a kind of gods to whom we can stand in this proper relation, yet we can't have them by designing them, because by that we would have power over them.[25] (Compare with the old God's dilemma: he wants us to be good but doesn't want to make us good.)

Heidegger runs into this dilemma over and again. He wants to be doing something to help, he wants to show us what to do, but he is repeatedly brought up short by the thought that this very activity of planning and devising a strategy expresses the attitude of *Gestell*—is an effort to frame and control. And he is further stymied by the self-frustrating logic in the project to find gods for the sake of being. Once thinking reaches the (idealist) insight of the truth of being, how can it go back and devise gods to facilitate that insight? How can such strategized gods carry any conviction?

Heidegger's response to these problems is to delegate the work of making the new gods to poets. But the latter can't properly function with any such explicit purpose. Poets need to speak in an experience of being spoken through: they need to feel their words as emanating from a divine source that gives higher meanings to all the entities they name. They can't mean to make their gods. So their role, which the thinker sees, can't be transparent to poets themselves. They must proceed in a kind of "madness" which lies far apart from any planning or devising.[26]

However, there is a certain reason and insight behind this madness, working in poets themselves. When they "hear gods" they are not inventing out of nothing. Poets' words don't really come from gods, but they do come from something real, which the poets are especially receptive to. They come out of the "destiny of being"—out of the very large-scale and long-run logic of the history of being-as-presence. Poets are responsive to current developments broadly at work in the culture, and "hear" gods that suit their age's large-scale need, though of course they don't recognize this real source of their words.

It is this destiny that is ultimately responsible for new gods: "Whether the god lives or remains dead is not decided by the religiosity of men and even less by the theological aspirations of philosophy and natural science. Whether god is god eventuates [*sich ereignet*] from out of and within the constellation of be-ing" [Tu (QTE 49)]. Being, in its fatedness, determines our changing understanding of being, and whether this will make room for gods. And it determines, I think, just how poets will feel themselves as spoken through by gods.

The thinker, as we've seen, goes deeper than the poet, by seeing how that experience of the gods issues out of the destiny of being, as well as how it can lead to what is more important, an experience of the truth of being, in *Ereignis*. But this larger insight still leaves the thinker less to do than philosophers have usually claimed for themselves. He can improve understanding of our current technological opening of being—can show how this is the culmination of the original grasp of being as presence. He can show how this makes gods absent and so leaves us "not at home" in the world, despite our fullest scientific and technical control. But he can't show "the way out" because this very insight bars him from "making" the gods we need.

Indeed, it seems this insight might also prevent the thinker from genuinely revering these gods. For by it he sees through them, going deeper to their ground, in our understanding of being. It seems this god-idealism must preclude full faith or reverence for these gods—the whole-hearted relation to them Heidegger thinks we need. I think this is indeed his view: he himself can only stand in that relation (of faith or reverence) by giving up the stance of thinking, and becoming, for a time, a poet. These two attitudes don't fuse, but alternate. The thinker becomes poet to experience the world as divine, then returns to the stance by which he pushes past this divine aspect, to see the world's ground in being.

But now isn't it, on this story, intellectually irresponsible to believe in gods? Isn't this, according to my Heidegger, a matter of embracing lies? A first answer is that our relation to gods is not to be that of belief, insofar as the latter is a stance we take up within our enframing project. But more importantly, I think Heidegger holds that in revering gods we witness to a deeper truth. For it's important to him that although the gods (must be taken to) deliver the words that express higher-than-human meanings, they are not their ultimate source. They are "messengers" who bring these meanings from "the holy," i.e. from being. "The divinities [Göttlichen] are the beckoning messengers of the godhead [Gottheit]" [BDT (BW 351)].

And this, I think, is the real truth that lies beneath these ideal gods—the truth that makes faith in them not a through-and-through lie. These meanings do come from "something" greater outside us, albeit not an entity, nor personal or human-like. They come from being—or more precisely from the "destiny" of being, which is a kind of logic in the development of human clearings or openings of being. There are higher meanings, and we do need to receive and defer to them; the gods are helpful personifications of their real source.

So much for the question how we can "prepare" for new gods. Now let's turn back to (1) and try to bring this goal—the relation to gods we (should) want, the way we are to have them in our world—into (a very little) sharper focus. The key point, we've seen, is that we need gods so that we can live closer to the "truth of being," in contrast with the way enframing closes being off. So we must hope for a kind of gods, and a relation to gods, that will facilitate this *Ereignis*. We can read back from it the features of the gods Heidegger hopes there will be poets for.

First, some features of the Christian god will be dispensed with, because they express the enframing attitude inconsistent with true reverence. For example, Heidegger rejects this god's role of creating the world, since it models god on the human crafter, and so expresses the pragmatic, incipiently technological world-view. It also expresses a metaphysical emphasis on *causality*, as the key for scientific explanation. But this reduces gods and being to the "ordinary and familiar," as Heidegger says Christian dogma does: "[t]he cause–effect relationship is the most common, most crude, and closest [to us], which all human calculation and lostness to entities employs in order to clarify something, i.e. to shift into the clarity of the common and familiar" [CP 77].[27]

More broadly, Heidegger rejects the Christian god insofar as it has been identified and determined by metaphysics and theology. The god grasped by these enframing projects is not a god we can stand towards as we properly should:

> [*Causa sui* is] the suitable name for the god in philosophy. Man can neither pray nor sacrifice to this god. Before the *causa sui*, man can neither fall to his knees in awe nor can he play music and dance before this god. / The god-less thinking which must abandon the god of philosophy, god as *causa sui*, is thus perhaps closer to the divine god.
>
> [ID 72]

For the most part Heidegger seems to favor new divinity that is more a pagan pluralism than a Christian monotheism. He shares Hölderlin's and Nietzsche's nostalgia for the Greek gods.[28] Part of their appeal is precisely that they precede and are not affected by the metaphysics of Plato and Aristotle, in the way Heidegger thinks the Christian god has been; because of that metaphysical infusion, "it could be that Christianity itself represents a consequence and a form of nihilism" [NW (*W* 165)].[29]

Whereas the one God of monotheism rules all, and so epitomizes the maximal control sought by enframing, a plurality of gods can exemplify different ideals than such control. Their variety gives options to us—manifold ideal stances or attitudes to model ourselves after. So multiple gods project a value pluralism like Nietzsche's. But Heidegger doesn't want us to "choose" among these options by an act of calculating intelligence, nor by existentialism's "ground-less choice," but rather by following a thread to being: we discover which of the available ideals gives us the alignment—reverence— that carries us towards being, i.e. that lets us find the holy in the world.

The pagan character of the new religion also shows in the roles of "earth" and "nature" in it. Briefly, these introduce a second field of non-human meanings into the world. We've seen how Heidegger uses "earth" to refer to the layer of meaning artworks have by virtue of their materials: the particular stoniness of a sculpture, timbre of a clarinet, or sound of a poem. So there are meanings in the world not projected by intelligence. Heidegger also revives the Greek notion of "nature" as *phusis*, a pre-cognitive aiming and intending such as is found even in plants. The world we need has not just gods, but this deeper and pervasive directedness within things themselves. We could only be fully "at home" in a world in which the things around us have inner point or meaning, and not just a meaning conferred on them "from outside" by our-selves or gods.

The new gods' principal role, we've seen, is to deliver meanings and ends to our world that are "higher" than those it has from us. Heidegger sometimes says that these will take the form of "laws," which will need to be integrated with a different set of laws devised by us for social cohesion and functioning. The higher laws sent by the gods lack these social purposes. Instead they build into our everyday experience reminders of the attitude that will attune us to being—reminders that align us towards the special experience of *Ereignis*. The divine laws enable our world to "stand open to being," i.e. to be livable in a proper relation to being.

Summary

Heidegger treats technology as emblematic of the modern age; it reflects the stance of *Gestell* (enframing), which is the crux to our current understanding of being. This stance involves (has as its other side) that "gods are absent" for us. Heidegger's critique of the modern age, and his prescription of a way out, center here: he wants a route from technology back to gods.

His analysis and critique of technology are among his most influential views. The target is not our technological stuff itself, but that underlying stance that compels us to "enframe" all we encounter. We take everything to be just what it is (or will be) in its place in our framework, and strive, under all, to place things there. This framework is both our scientific system, and our technologically organized environment; these intermesh. By locating entities—theoretically or practically—within this framework, we fit them into the narrow place where we secure and control them. So we make them maximally "presences" to us, and culminate the great cultural project at presence initiated by the pre-Socratics.

But this consummation comes at a cost, which is the loss of a religious aspect to our world. Heidegger adopts Hölderlin's image of the gods as "absent" (not dead), and his attitude of hoping and waiting for their return. Our immediate challenge is to notice what we're missing: any independent and "higher" meaning in our world than what things have in our framework. This isn't just a matter of belief (that God doesn't exist) but of the kind of meaning things generally have: nothing means anything beyond that framework.

Heidegger thinks Nietzsche saw much of this in his account of nihilism, but fell short because he kept within enframing; indeed his idea of will to power is the prime metaphysical statement of enframing. So Nietzsche's offered way out of nihilism is for humans to make values for themselves, and to make their own enhancement (into the overman) their guiding value. Heidegger thinks this answer still belongs to the problem. We can't give ourselves the kind of values we really need, and indeed even the schema of "values" reflects the calculative enterprise of enframing.

Heidegger says little about what a "return" of gods would involve. Nor would it help, perhaps, to be told, because of the peculiar logic of this hope. We cannot engineer in ourselves the attitude in which there are gods for us again; we need to get away from "engineering" our projects this way. We need instead a more receptive stance, a kind of "releasement" that opens us to things. Heidegger verges here on a kind of quietism, while insisting that he doesn't mean a passivity. This receptivity prepares us both for gods' return, and for the unconcealment of being itself—though our attitude itself is still not sufficient. As he famously puts it, "only a god can save us."

Further reading

J. Young: *Heidegger's Later Philosophy*. Cambridge, UK: Cambridge University Press, 2002. [An engaging survey of themes in later Heidegger, especially technology and the gods.]

J. Caputo: *The Mystical Element in Heidegger's Thought*. Athens, OH: Ohio University Press, 1978. [An influential treatment of Heidegger's religious thinking.]

Ten

Heidegger's influences

Heidegger has been, on many reckonings, the most influential philosopher of (both in and from) the twentieth century. Due, however, to his sharp divisiveness, his influence has taken an unusually polarized form. He moves some to emulation and development, while others push off from him, away in directions partly favored by their being *not his*. His saying what he says persuades some to it, and some against it, both because of how he says it, and because he's Heidegger (and was a Nazi etc.).

This divide happens not just at a macro-level, separating camps of "friends and enemies," but also at the micro-level within many individual readers. Of course we do pick and choose what we take from any philosopher—almost nobody "swallows him whole." But Heidegger's readers tend to sustain sharper conflicts of respect and aversion, I think. This is exemplified in the way many of his most ardent disciples came to define themselves primarily *against* him.[1]

For reasons of space and optimism I'll focus on the positive and emulative effects—on some ways his ideas and views have spread. Since even this positive influence has been so wide and diverse, I can only survey it, and try to organize it under some general headings.[2] Obviously it's a further question whether this influence is "positive" in another sense: is a good and truth-promoting influence. But just as obviously it would be pointless to try to adjudicate that in these last few pages.

There's another question about this influence that deserves some address: did—or would—Heidegger approve of it? Would he judge that his "followers" were taking on views that were really his? We've seen his constant radicalizing—trying always to get a step further, and so keeping a step ahead; he was very ready to doubt that he was being understood, even by sympathetic hearers. The most famous case of this was his rejection of "existentialist" readings of *Being and Time*, in his "Letter on 'Humanism'." The common thrust of these disavowals is of course the usual: sight is always getting lost of *being*, the indispensable topic.

Heidegger would—and did—dislike the extent to which his ideas have been extracted from their relation to the question of being. In this light he may indeed seem not to have left much of a mark at all, inasmuch as there doesn't seem to have been the kind of renaissance of attention to being, an ontological revival, he seemed to want. But appearances are here deceiving. What we find when we attend to the different waves of his influence, I suggest, is in each case a stage or aspect of his own path towards being. Each of the main ways he tried to convey a sense of it—of how to find it—has spun off a group of other thinkers. These correspond roughly to the different "isms" Heidegger has operated through.

Before getting to these isms, however, we should note a kind of base-line influence Heidegger has, which is almost contentless. He conveys a passion for philosophy; he brings philosophical problems and concepts to life. This is what his lectures were so famous for, and we see the effect in his early students: Gadamer, Arendt, Marcuse, Jonas, Löwith, Levinas. The diversity of their later philosophical paths shows the great malleability of this basic effect, this philosophical energizing. And it operates through his writings as well.[3]

But of course usually Heidegger conveys more than just this neutral thrust: he passes on a particular philosophical stance, a conception of *how to do* philosophy. This conception is interwoven with several main lessons, his chief lines of influence. None of these lessons is uniquely taught by Heidegger, but he articulates them in forms that have been uncommonly persuasive. I'll illustrate these abstract lessons by associating each with a couple of prominent adherents, in whom Heidegger's influence can be pursued and evaluated. (Of course these philosophers underwent shifts in thinking themselves, and what I say about them won't hold true of them throughout.)

(a) The first lesson is, in brief, the notion of world: the idea that all of our particular beliefs, discoveries, experiences depend upon a certain background understanding of "a world"—and that the business of philosophy (at least part of it) is to uncover the secret logic or structure or goal in this deep understanding. This idea is conveyed in the first portion of *Being and Time*, but it is an ongoing presumption in Heidegger's later thinking too. It is, as it were, his first step to being.

Put so generally the point is quasi-Kantian, but Heidegger fills it out in several ways that make it more distinctively his. First, this world is not principally constituted by theories or beliefs or statements, but by (something like) our practical stance. So there's an anti-Cartesian conviction that it is not as "subjects" that we project the world. Second, this world is embodied in *language*, and is principally studied by exposing the ways we use words, and in particular certain privileged and founding uses. Third, this projected world has an *historical* character, and needs to be understood developmentally and in historical context. But fourth, despite this linguistic and historical complexity, there is still a deep unity in our projected world: it is organized bottom-up from a single principal character or aim, which permeates and explains all the rest.

This set of ideas is, I suggest, the first main line of Heidegger's influence. Others before him held all these ideas, but he conveyed them in forms, and as a package, that spread them widely. As the fourth point makes clear, the picture is more rationalist than empiricist, and I think this is an important part of its appeal. It gives philosophy a field of its own to study, with vast real-life significance. We don't get at this background understanding by piling up sociological or psychological facts, but by stepping somehow down or back to a meaning present in every one of our views and experiences. Philosophy's job is to take this step down.

This is, on the one hand, the *"phenomenological"* strand of Heidegger's influence. Much of European philosophy after him has been phenomenological in the broad sense of aiming to expose deep structures of human intentionality. Of course philosophers have taken this approach from Husserl as well as from Heidegger— some more one, some the other. But Heidegger's pragmatic and anti-Cartesian version has dominated. We may take Hubert Dreyfus as our sample here: within a generally hostile "analytic" environment, he shows the power of Heidegger's account of our practicality, and its fruitful potential as a method that can lead to further insights. His arguments against the feasibility of (a certain program in) artificial intelligence gave this phenomenology a voice in consequential debates, as did his ongoing argument with John Searle in the philosophy of mind. At the heart of Dreyfus' contribution is his phenomenology of "skilled coping," which he shows at the crux of Heidegger's break with Husserl.[4]

In a less hierarchical and more historical aspect, this line of Heidegger's influence can be called *"hermeneutic"*: philosophy's business is to show how to interpret human meaning. It's under this rubric that Hans-Georg Gadamer took over that set of ideas, and can serve as its clearest exponent. He develops the method by which that meaning needs to be studied, due to its non-subjective, linguistic, and historical character. He focuses on the situation in which one interprets a past text, and must exploit both what one shares from the tradition descending from the text, and also one's difference from it; interpreter and text reflect two "horizons," which overlap in a way that makes understanding possible. Indeed this understanding is not just of that historical text, but of oneself, in one's own historical place. This method is largely present in Heidegger's historical writing, but Gadamer forgoes the latter's step into ontology. His hermeneutics is done for its own sake—for the sake of the particular insights it gives of the tradition and our place in it.[5]

(b) The second main lesson many draw from Heidegger is the existentialist adjunct to his phenomenology: in brief, the idea that we're challenged to become a self through facing and making a groundless choice. This idea was expressed in the second portion of *Being and Time*, though Heidegger largely abandoned it after the turning. Again he was not original in it, but brought points from Kierkegaard (especially) into a conceptual order that has proven enormously compelling. The idea of humans as confronted with a deep lack or "nothing," and of authenticity or freedom as facing and "living in the light" of this lack, was absorbed by many philosophers—and many "civilians"—as the ultimate character of our human situation.

In France in the 1930s this line of influence ran importantly through Alexandre Kojeve, whose famous lectures (in Paris) on Hegel presented him in Heideggerianly existential fashion: we're called to heroically embrace our own finitude, overcoming the metaphysical effort to conceal the "becoming" of desire and its negativity. These lectures were attended by Lacan, Sartre, Merleau-Ponty, Bataille, and many others who absorbed this Heideggerian lesson through them—and then spread it by their own wide influence.

Jean-Paul Sartre can be our first example of this line of effect. Although there are important ways in which his phenomenology is more Husserlian—especially its Cartesian stress on consciousness—he turns it in an existential direction that borrows heavily from Heidegger in its overall shape, and even in the micro-structure of some arguments. The overall dichotomy between projection and thrownness, the temporal grounding of these, the stress on the limit-situation of "anguish" and the "nothing" this exposes, make much of *Being and Nothingness* (1943) a rewrite of Heidegger's book (along with the 1931 "What Is Metaphysics?"). Sartre very fruitfully extends this existential story, above all with his powerful account of our relations to others, as well as with his great talent for concrete illustrations.

A second instructive figure here is Emmanuel Levinas, who likewise absorbed a great deal of *Being and Time*'s existential structure, but who carried out a more insistent critique of it than Sartre. He links that book's failure to give us an ethics with Heidegger's later mistake about Nazism. Levinas tries to correct this fault by giving ultimacy to positive ("face-to-face") relations to individual others, in which their "mystery" shakes us out of our usual self-absorbed dealings. It's in these relations, not in solitude, that we need to face death, and it's here that we find our true temporality. These ideas amount to a reconfiguration of Heidegger's existentialism; *Time and the Other* (1947) gives a condensed statement of them.

(c) A third main line of influence lies in the lesson "against reason" that Heidegger promotes, partly in *Being and Time*'s anti-Cartesianism, but more decisively in his later diagnosis of rationality as an expression of technology and enframing. This suspicion against the usual methods of definition, statement, and argument, and the belief in a kind of "truth" that requires a more allusive, indirect, and "literary" approach, was a key element in a second wave of effect Heidegger had in France, on thinkers usually labeled "post-structuralists" and "deconstructionists."

It may be Jacques Derrida who took over the most of Heidegger's later thinking, and developed it. He explicitly rejects the Sartrean, existential lesson as subjectivistic and ahistorical. He absorbs instead Heidegger's idea of presence as the crux to the Western understanding of being—along with a suspicion against this basic project, and a will to diagnose and question it. Since this project lies so deep we can't escape it, but only raise it to attention by disrupting it; this is the method of *déconstruction*, a term rooted in Heidegger's *Destruktion* and *Abbau*. Derrida serves some analytic philosophers as a kind of reductio of Heidegger: with pupils like this, he must have been off track himself. But this is unjust to both. We saw that Heidegger's critique of "reason" wasn't indiscriminate; it prompted a revision not a dismissal of reason, leaving a method designed, for reasons, the better to secure the truth we should want. And so it is, mostly, for Derrida too—at least in his earlier years, and in his less self-indulgent moods. He works out the implications of that suspicion against presence, and conveys glimpses how human meaning might have a logic—of *différance*—that disappears each time we bring it to presence.[6]

Michel Foucault turns Heidegger's historical critique in a different direction; he melds it with Nietzsche's diagnosis of the power relations of social forces. This Nietzschean aspect is more evident in his work, and Heidegger is seldom mentioned; the empiricist focus on concrete social practices looks very unlike a "history of being." Yet there is a strong Heideggerian frame to those concrete studies: first in the presumption of an overall direction of the social process towards a completed control of individuals by something systemic (a control that paradoxically turns them into "subjects"), and second in the evident dissatisfaction with this development. So it's really less will to power than enframing that is at issue for Foucault; his accounts how "knowledge" belongs to the project of control mirrors Heidegger's analysis of science as deeply technological.[7]

(d) I think we can distinguish a fourth main line of influence which is more widespread but less philosophically articulated. Heidegger serves many as a pole or alternative to Nietzsche—as rejecting the latter's embrace of a godless, inherently meaningless world, and of the will to make ourselves (our power or growth) the only meaning for things. We've seen how Heidegger articulates, against this Nietzschean vision, a nostalgic hope that we will find a way back to a world with higher meanings than our own. So he stands for an alternative not just to Nietzsche, but to our modern secularism, and our scientific and technological relation to nature. This gives him special appeal in theology or religion,[8] of course, as well as in environmentalism.[9]

These seem to me the principal lines of influence Heidegger has had and will continue to have. Obviously the geographical center of this influence has been France, Germany, and Europe generally, but on all four of these points he has had many followers in the US and England as well. He has also been paid great attention in non-Western countries, especially Japan.[10]

We've seen how this influence reaches outside philosophy departments. Special features of his writing make it available and appealing to readers outside the discipline—help it address them in their own concerns, and not through that discipline (of structured argument). So his influence shows in such unexpected places as architectural theory.[11] But it extends especially into literary theory: he is a crucial figure in many literature departments, which (in the US) are often dissatisfied with philosophy departments' neglect or dismissal of him (and them). So there is the awkward circumstance that Heidegger's ideas are addressed in venues that don't interact with the main stream of philosophy.

Will this circumstance continue? Will Heidegger remain a thinker *non grata* in most analytic departments—will his standing even fall in Europe as analytic approaches make inroads there? I hope to have indicated the philosophical interest of his ideas, early and late, and their susceptibility to treatment in relatively rigorous fashion. So I can only be optimistic that that "main stream" of philosophy will develop ways to treat him in argument, that will let it absorb the value in his thinking, not spit it out.

Summary

Heidegger is strongly polarizing; his writing attracts and persuades some, but repels and dissuades others. To some he seems the most important philosopher of the twentieth century, to others not a philosopher at all—or a very poor one. Focusing on his positive influence, we can categorize his "followers" (each of whom also disagrees with Heidegger on many points) by certain abstract lessons they learn from him.

First is the lesson about the world: that all our concrete experience depends on the prior projection of a web of possibilities for experience to then instantiate. Heidegger insists that we project this world historically, linguistically, and practically (not in our beliefs). Followers of this line include phenomenologists like Dreyfus and hermeneuticists like Gadamer. A second lesson is the existential project to become a self by facing and making a groundless choice (this is an idea Heidegger himself gave up). Followers here include Sartre and Levinas, who redesign Heidegger's existential phenomenology. A third lesson is the critique of reason or rationality: the diagnosis of it as a device for control that distorts what it examines. It's the French "post-structuralists" who most famously follow him here, Derrida and Foucault foremost among them. A fourth lesson is the anti-Nietzschean, anti-humanistic nostalgia for a world with higher meanings than our own. Here Heidegger's influence extends outside philosophy into theology, environmentalism, and fields beyond.

Further reading

See in the bibliography representative works by Dreyfus, Gadamer, Sartre, Levinas, Derrida, and Foucault.

Glossary

The following are some of Heidegger's terms that I have tried to translate consistently, flagging exceptions by adding the German.

Sein	being
Seyn	be-ing
Seiendes	entity
Seiendheit	entitihood

Note: Given the great weight Heidegger puts on the ontological difference between *Sein* and *Seiendes*—given that it is even the main point of his thinking—I think it unwise to use the same word, "being," for both, hoping to disambiguate by articles and singular/plural. I think even the strategy of capitalizing "Being" in translating *Sein* tends to blur the difference. Rendering *Seiendes* by "entity" may go too far the other way, obscuring its relation to *Sein*, but I think this the better side to err on.

Anfang	beginning
anfänglich	incipient
Angst	anxiety
Anwesen	presencing
Anwesenheit	presence
Anwesendes	what presences; a presence; presences
Augenblick	moment
Aussage	assertion
ausweisen	(to) demonstrate
beweisen	(to) prove
Befindlichkeit	self-finding
Bestand	stand-by
Betrieb	industry

Brauch	usage
Dasein	[not translated; refers (roughly) to a human being, or else to the being of a human being]
Denken	thinking
Er-denken	en-thinking
Dichtung	poetry
Dichten	poeming
Dichter	poet
Eigentlichkeit	authenticity
Ekstase	ecstasis
Entbergung	revealing
entdecken	(to) uncover
Entschlossenheit	resoluteness
entwerfen	(to) project
Entwurf	projection
Ereignis	[not translated: refers to an event that "appropriates" in the sense of bringing something into its proper own]
Erkenntnis	knowledge
Erlebnis	lived-experience
erschliessen	(to) disclose
Erschlossenheit	disclosure
verschliessen	(to) close off
Fuge, Fug	jointing
Gegenwart	present
gegenwärtigen	(to) make present
Gelassenheit	releasement
Geschichtlichkeit	historicality
geschehen	(to) happen
Geschehen	happening
Geschick	destiny
Schicken	sending
Schicksal	fate
Gespräch	conversation
Gestell	enframing
stellen	(to) set
bestellen	(to) order
Griff	grip
greifen	(to) grasp
Begriff	concept
Angriff	attack
Herausfordern	challenging
Intentionalität	intentionality
Jemeinigkeit	mineness; in each case mineness

-können	ability-to
Seinkönnen	ability-to-be
das Man	[untranslated: refers to the common and shared comportment, carried out *as* common and shared, i.e. because "that's what one does"]
Mitteilung	communication
Möglichkeit	possibility
ermöglichen	(to) make possible
Nichtigkeit	nullity
Rede	talk
Gerede	chat
Schuld	guilt
Sorge	care
Besorgen	concern
Sprache	language
Stimmung	mood
Gestimmtsein	being-attuned
Technik	technology
unheimlich	uncanny
Unverborgenheit	unconcealment
Verborgenheit	concealment
Ursprung	origin
ursprünglich	originary
Verfallen	falling
Vergessenheit	oblivion
vergessen	(to) forget
Verhalten	comportment
Verstehen	understanding
verweisen	(to) assign
Verweisung	reference
vorhanden	at-hand
Vorhandenheit	at-handness
vorlaufen	(to) anticipate
Vorlaufen	anticipation
wählen	choose
Wahrheit	truth
Wahrung	securing
Bewahrung	preserving
Verwahren	safekeeping
Weg	path
unterwegs	underway
Welt	world
Weltlichkeit	worldhood
Umwelt	environment

werfen	(to) throw
Wurf	throw
Geworfenheit	thrownness
Wesen	essence
wesen	(to) essence
abwesen	(to) absence
anwesen	(to) presence
wirklich	actual
verwirklichen	(to) actualize
wohnen	(to) dwell
das Worumwillen	the for-which
Zeitlichkeit	temporality
Zeug	equipment
zuhanden	to-hand
Zuhandenheit	to-handness
zumeist	mostly
zunächst	firstly

Notes

Introduction

1 This closer attention to a few terms will also let us pay some attention to Heidegger's own German, and to some sample problems in translating it. Attention to translation is not pedantic but most germane, given Heidegger's own views about language.

2 The same point is at the opening of "Time and Being": don't expect philosophy to be "immediately intelligible," any more than painting, poetry, or physics [TB (OTB 1–2)].

3 BC 2: "We have to enter a stance whose achievement requires no special knowledge, neither scientific nor philosophical." It requires only "simple awakening" [Par 149].

4 Critchley [2008 39]: "Heidegger's work ... is motivated by a passion for absolute philosophical radicality."

5 Ryle, despite saying that Heidegger "shows himself to be a thinker of real importance by the immense subtlety and searchingness of his examination of consciousness ... ," and despite the value he clearly finds in BT, expresses the "personal opinion" that "qua First Philosophy Phenomenology is at present heading for bankruptcy and disaster and will end either in self-ruinous Subjectivism or in a windy mysticism" [1929 370]. See too Carnap's famous critique [1931] of Heidegger's 1929 discussion of "the Nothing" as a string of meaningless pseudostatements. Friedman [2000] examines this early "parting of the ways."

6 So, e.g., Philipse [1998 315]: "a desperate attempt by Heidegger to protect his highly questionable thought from criticism." Philipse details "eight characteristic rhetorical stratagems" by which Heidegger cleverly persuades many readers [311–17].

7 Consider the tone he strikes here, for example: "If a thinking question is not so simple and so outstanding as to determine the will and the style of thinking for centuries ... then it is best that it not be asked" [CP 15]. And here: "Thinking is not a means for knowing. Thinking draws furrows in the field of being" [EL (UL 70)].

8 Note Heidegger's apology for Nietzsche's histrionics: "Nietzsche, who was one of the quietest and shiest of men, ... endured the agony of having to scream"

[WCT 48]. Heidegger is presumably aware that he screams too, in his distinctive register.
9 See also the critique of "positivism" in CP 121.
10 So WCT sets out to give us "the distance needed for a run-up, by which one or another may succeed in the leap into thinking" [7].
11 IM 7: "it can never be determined objectively whether ... we are actually asking this question [why entities?], i.e. leaping, or whether we are caught in empty words." TB (OTB 6): "I mean think [being in the sense of presencing], not just re-speak and so act as if one understood the interpretation of being as presencing oneself."
12 Here we come to a key decision on translation. I will render Seiendes by "entity" (or "entities") rather than by the more usual "being" (or "beings"), because I think the latter tends to hide the ontological difference, given that Sein will also be translated by "being." (I think this is even so when Sein is translated by "Being," as Macquarrie and Robinson do for Being and Time—and I also think this capitalization has misleading connotations.)

One: Life and works

1 Notice how Heidegger treats in WPK (N v3 3f.) Nietzsche's apparent "personalizing" of his ideas.
2 Heidegger also makes links more privately between political positions and philosophy. See Friedman's account [2000] of the political undercurrent in his debate against Cassirer (and Carnap); Heidegger opposes their views as "liberal-democratic."
3 Hence Heidegger would perhaps not have cared that the principal text he used in his 1915 dissertation on Duns Scotus is now thought not to have been written by Scotus.
4 See, especially, Malpas 2006.
5 He wrote a philosophical account of this trip, translated as Sojourns [Soj].
6 On Heidegger's religious evolution, see: Caputo 2006, van Buren 2005.
7 Heidegger sets the third dialogue in FC in a Russian prisoner-of-war camp.
8 Jaspers later wrote that Heidegger "appeared to be a friend who betrayed one in one's absence" [quoted, Ott 1993 183].
9 See the account of their relationship in Ettinger 1995.
10 Arendt [1978 295]: "The rumor about Heidegger put it quite simply: Thinking has come to life again; the cultural traditions of the past, believed to be dead, are being made to speak, in the course of which it turns out that they propose things altogether different from the familiar, worn-out trivialities they had been presumed to say. There exists a teacher; one can perhaps learn to think."
11 So Löwith: "His lecture technique consisted in building up an edifice of ideas which he then proceeded to tear down, presenting the spellbound listeners with a riddle and then leaving them empty-handed" [quoted, Wolin 2001 34–35].
12 Gadamer [1994 11]: "It was almost life-threatening—and presented the organizer with nearly unsolvable problems—when Heidegger would announce one of his cryptic lectures. No lecture hall was large enough during the

1950s." See too Gadamer's account of the impact of his eyes [17] and voice [19].

13 Those that stirred the most attention were the attacks by Farias [1989] and Faye [2009]. See too Ott's very critical view [1993]. Habermas [1992] gives a thoughtful assessment. Young [1997] argues that Heidegger's philosophy is not implicated in fascism. A useful source on the Nazi question is Wolin 1993. Many relevant documents are in *GA* 16.

14 Marcuse: "from personal experience I can tell you that neither in his lectures, nor in his seminars, nor personally, was there ever any hint of his sympathies for Nazism" [quoted, Wolin 2001 157].

15 The 1934 lecture-course *LQ* argues that "the self" lies not in the "I" of an isolated individual, but in the "We" of the people/*Volk*: "We as Dasein fit ourselves in a proper way into belongingness to the *Volk*, we stand in the being of the *Volk*, we are this *Volk* itself" [50].

16 Two contrary cases should be noted, however. In a 1929 letter to a scholarship committee he advocates promoting "autochthonous forces and educators" and warns against a "growing Judaization" of German spiritual life. And in a 1933 report advocating against an academic promotion he mentions the candidate's link to "the Jew Fränkel." See details in Safranski [1998 ch. 14]; also Ott [1993 187ff.].

17 Jaspers' letter is in Wolin 1993.

18 At least once he altered a text from the Nazi period to render it more benign: in his 1953 publication of the 1935 lectures *Introduction to Metaphysics* he kept its infamous reference to "the inner truth and greatness of this [Nazi] movement," but added a parenthesis to make it refer to "the encounter between global technology and modern humanity."

19 We may question, of course, this effort to blame Nazism on something generic in the modern age, and also manifest in Russia and America. So Habermas asks, in his review of *IM* in 1953: "can the planned murder of millions of human beings ... be made understandable in terms of the history of being as a fateful going astray? Is this murder not the actual crime of those who, with full accountability, committed it?" [quoted, Wolin 1993 197]. See how in the 1944–45 *FC* 134ff. Heidegger shifts attention from "moral badness" [*moralischen Schlechtigkeit*] to a more pervasive "evil" [*Böse*] perhaps lodged in the will itself, and expressed in purportedly humane ideals as well.

Two: Early development

1 The texts I'll principally use: *Supplements* [S] (which gives English translations of several important very early texts), *Towards the Definition of Philosophy* [DP] (Heidegger's earliest lecture-course texts, from 1919), *Phenomenology of Intuition and Expression* [PIE] (a lecture-course from 1920), and *Phenomenology of Religious Life* [PR] (lecture-courses from 1920–21, and notes from 1918–19 for a course not given). The two dissertations are in *GA* 1, which collects other "early writings." Some later texts, in the few years just before *Being and Time*, I'll consider within the ambit of that book and reserve for later chapters; my

boundary is 1924, although this is almost arbitrary. See these secondary sources: Kisiel 1993; van Buren 1994, 2005; Crowe 2006.

2 I use "neo-Kantian" in a bare-bones sense: for the idea that our experience is of "phenomena" structured by our own *a priori* impositions (for Kant these are space and time and the categories), but without (contra Kant himself) positing any noumenon or thing-in-itself.

3 See Friedman 2000 on this early neo-Kantianism. Heidegger learned this principally through Rickert and Lask.

4 Polt says [2005 376] that these lectures in early 1919 mark Heidegger's "emergence as a thinker in his own right." And van Buren [1994 14]: 'the major rupture occurs around 1919." The 1919 lectures are in *DP*.

5 See, e.g., the critique of "philosophies of life" in KJ (P 13), of 1920; he has in mind Dilthey in particular.

Three: *Being and Time*: phenomenology

1 Although *Being and Time* so dominates this period of Heidegger's thought, there are several lecture-courses just before and after that are helpful in clarifying it. I'll particularly use the following: *Prolegomena to the History of the Concept of Time* [PH] (1925); *Basic Problems of Phenomenology* [BP] (1927); *The Metaphysical Foundations of Logic* [MF] (1928); and *The Basic Concepts of Metaphysics* [BCM] (1929–30). The 1924 lecture "The Concept of Time" [CT] gives remarkably succinct expression to many of BT's ideas. I'll flag some points on which these associated works are especially helpful.

2 This is "the fundamental question of philosophy" [BT g27], but it has today been "forgotten" and "trivialized" [g2]. (I cite *Being and Time* by the pagination of the original (German) edition, which is provided (in the margins) in both English translations.)

3 That Dasein is not a subject, and doesn't understand being by ideas—as we'll see—explains Heidegger's disavowal of any "subjectivizing" "idealism." But the logic of his position is still "idealist" in a broader sense: it makes being dependent on Dasein.

4 Of the other works of this period, PH and MF are especially useful as supplements to BT's account of the phenomenological method. See note 1.

5 Crowell [2005 49–50] lists ideas Heidegger took from Husserl, concluding "it is not too much to say that the shape of Heidegger's early philosophy is essentially Husserlian." Carman [2003 53–100] finds Heidegger disagreeing far more.

6 In lecture-courses before and after *Being and Time* Heidegger does introduce phenomenology as studying intentionality. So in PH [1925]: "*Intentio* literally means *directing-oneself-upon* [*Sich-richten-auf*]. Every lived-experience, every psychic comportment, directs itself upon something" [29]. And in BP [1927]: "Comportments have the structure of directing-oneself-upon, of being-directed-upon. Annexing a term from Scholasticism, phenomenology calls this structure *intentionality*" [58]. Critchley [2008] presents Heidegger as treating the *a priori* structure of intentionality.

7 Although Heidegger will deny that this meaning need be cognitive, he takes it to be something richer than what animals are capable of. See Carman's account of this [2003 46–52]; he points out Heidegger's denial that animals have the capacity to view *as*.

8 The idea is already in the 1924 CT [8]. See too PH 153 and BP 170.

9 As mentioned, we must hear "idealism" here *not* to imply that Dasein is a "subject" constituting being by its "ideas." The point of *Being and Time* is to show the *different* way in which Dasein "lets there be being."

10 "Entities *are*, independently of the experience, acquaintance, and grasp by which they are disclosed, uncovered, and determined. But being 'is' only in the understanding of [Dasein]" [BT g183]. And he later refers to the "dependence of being, not of entities, on the understanding of being, that is the dependence of reality, not the real, on care" [g212]. See the other passages Carman cites [2003 ch. 4]. Cerbone [2005] also defends a realist reading.

11 See the extended argument for this in Braver [2007 ch. 5].

12 Even to-hand equipment is independent of us in the sense that it can frustrate our expectations for it: we are prepared to discover that this thing, which we interpret as a (usable) hammer, is not really such. This realist loophole is built into the way we mean "hammer": we apply it with the understanding that this thing may turn out to need a different meaning (word). We know, implicitly, that our meaning is not authoritative, and that what the thing *is* depends also on something apart from us.

13 Husserl says [1973 20–21] that by the phenomenological *epochê* I acquire "my pure living, with all the pure subjective processes making this up, and everything meant in them, *purely as* meant in them: the universe of 'phenomena' in the (particular and also the wider) phenomenological sense."

14 Here I agree with Crowell [2005 60] rather than Carman [2003 82ff.].

15 BP 20: "The basic components of *a priori* knowledge constitute what we call *phenomenology.*"

16 In BP Heidegger initially [71] includes this level in intentionality: "Not only do *intentio* and *intentum* belong to the intentionality of perception but so also does *the understanding of the kind of being of what is intended in the intentum.*" But this is later overruled in the "more radical interpretation of intentionality" on 161ff. (although he later repeats that the understanding of being "belongs to" intentionality [175]).

17 PH 121: "Husserl is essentially taking account of my objections ... so that my critique today no longer applies in its full sharpness."

18 See Føllesdal's emphatic rejoinder [2000] to Dreyfus' reading of Husserl, that the latter held many of the views about an implicit background laid out by practical goals, that Dreyfus thinks distinguish Heidegger from Husserl. Føllesdal also calls into question whether Heidegger even saw *Being and Time* as subverting Husserl [257].

19 Marion [1996] examines BT's critique of Descartes and argues that the book is still strongly dependent on the Cartesian schema.

20 See Carman's treatment [2003 43–46] of Heidegger's doubts against the term; Carman thinks it can be kept if we understand intentionality as "a mode of interpretation," whose "conditions of the possibility" he takes Heidegger to be after.

21 See the defense of Husserl against Heidegger's charge by Smith [2003 146–56].

22 *Pace* Dreyfus, who interprets "trying" as involving an explicit means–end devising that occurs only when skillful coping is disrupted [1991 70]. But I think there is a way even the athlete "in the flow"—one of Dreyfus' paradigms for that coping—is indeed trying (to hit the ball with more or less top-spin, for example), only "without thinking."

23 PH treats this agreement between Husserl and Descartes: "What is here worked at a higher level of phenomenological analysis as pure consciousness is the field that Descartes glimpsed under the heading of *res cogitans*" [101]. It notes that Husserl asks "How can consciousness become the possible object of an absolute science?"—which is Descartes' question [107].

24 Dreyfus [esp. 1991] is well known for his powerful development of this point about a "background." See too Taylor 1993.

25 Okrent [2000], by contrast, denies that intentionality depends on consciousness even in a "horizonal" (rather than "focal") way.

26 So Dreyfus distinguishes [1991 33ff.] between Heidegger's "hermeneutics of everydayness"—which treats phenomena that are simply "undiscovered"—and his "hermeneutics of suspicion"—which treats phenomena that are "buried over" by our "not wanting to see the truth."

27 By contrast Kant "sees the impossibility of an ontical reduction of the 'I' to a substance," though he still "takes this 'I' as subject again," in attributing to it "the selfsameness and steadiness of something always already at-hand" [BT g319–20].

28 E.g. Dreyfus [1991 158ff.] and Crowell [2005 56].

29 BT g134: "the possibilities of disclosure by knowing reach far too short a way compared with the original disclosing by moods."

30 BCM 7: "we shall never have grasped [*begriffen*] these concepts [*Begriffe*] and their conceptual rigor unless we have first been *gripped* [*ergriffen*] by whatever they are supposed to grasp. The basic concern of philosophizing pertains to such being gripped, to awakening and planting it."

31 This is another topic that Dreyfus [1991 ch. 4] has particularly illuminated.

32 Heidegger approaches this point already in 1919: "When a situation of lived-experience is extinguished ... [t]he contents fall apart, they are not an empty lived-experience, but they are dissolved out of the specific unity of the situation" [DP 156 (these are student notes)].

33 MF 18: "philosophizing—and it especially—must always proceed through a rigorous conceptual knowing ... but this knowing is grasped in its genuine content only when in it the whole of existence is seized in the root sought by philosophy—in *freedom*."

34 Dreyfus says [1991 4] that Heidegger thinks we can only "point out" not "spell out" the background, i.e. point it out to those who already share it, not spell it out for any rational being.

35 And: "Every disclosure of being as the *transcendens* is *transcendental* knowledge. *Phenomenological truth (the disclosure of being) is veritas transcendentalis*" [g38].

36 Derrida [1993 29] remarks how this pursuit of "presuppositions" gives Heidegger "regions ... legitimately separated by pure, rigorous, and indivisible borders. An order is thus structured by *uncrossable* edges." He goes on to argue that *Being*

and Time "exceeds its own borders" [32], including its insistence on such bounded regions.

37 I go more fully into Heidegger's treatment of truth in Chapter 7.5.ii, but with respect to his later writings. See the extended treatment in Dahlstrom 2001.

38 Wrathall argues [2005 342ff.] that he doesn't reject this altogether, but rather claims (1) that this correspondence is not by a representation, and (2) that it presupposes unconcealing, a more basic and important kind of truth. My points run partly parallel.

39 BT g216: "According to this, the ideal content of judgment stands in a relation of agreement. This involves a connection between an ideal content of judgment and the real thing as that which is judged *about*."

40 Tugendhat [e.g. 1996] makes an influential criticism here: in interpreting uncovering as "truth," Heidegger really obliterates the notion because both correct and incorrect assertions count as uncovering. See the replies by Dahlstrom [2001 394–407], Carman [2003 258–63], and Wrathall [2011 34–39].

41 "What makes this very uncovering possible must necessarily be called 'true' in a still more originary sense" [BT g220].

Four: *Being and Time*: pragmatism

1 Other texts of the period that are especially helpful on this topic are PH and BP. See Chapter 3, note 1.

2 He doesn't accept the whole pragmatist program; see Blattner's argument that he lacks a pragmatist theory of truth [2000 236ff.]. But I agree with Okrent [1988] on the aptness of the term for his analysis of intentionality.

3 Here again I owe a large debt to Bert Dreyfus' great vivifying of this pragmatism—though Dreyfus also won't call it this.

4 He also proceeds this way in PH [160–67].

5 The hands are of special importance in our relation to equipment, and are often at the front of Heidegger's mind. He pays particular attention to them at BT g108–09, distinguishing how the hand uses gloves, from how it uses, e.g., hammers. As we'll see, this focus on the hand persists long after *Being and Time* (see, e.g., WCT 16). Derrida's essay [1987] on "Heidegger's hand" speaks of "the immense role the hand or the word *Hand* more or less directly plays in the whole Heideggerian conceptuality since *Sein und Zeit*" [176].

6 This must be distinguished from the sense of "object" in "intentional object," in which it means simply the "content" or *intentum* of an intending, what it's directed upon.

7 I offer a fuller account of this argument against "the Cartesian project" in epistemology in Richardson 1986.

8 Breakdowns already play this role in PH (1925), which speaks of "how things within the environing world become present in an emphatic sense, when an entity of the character of 'serving to' *breaks down* [*versagt*] in its serviceability, becomes unusable, is damaged" [188].

9 Note the way a different kind of "breakdown" illuminates in BP 172–73, which quotes Rilke's description of seeing rooms exposed in half-destroyed houses, and the privileged experience this gives of the lives lived there.

10 He presents it second in Chapter 5, but I think this is because it was already so well anticipated in Chapter 3. The priority of this dimension will be reinforced in Division II, in the account of temporality.

11 Compare the account of world in the 1929 EG (P 112).

12 I prefer the plainer "for-which" to Macquarrie and Robinson's "for-the-sake-of-which," though the latter may suggest the "*willen*" included in the German. I think that we can hear "for-which" in this heightened teleological way—and that Heidegger's ideas profit from less cumbersome terms.

13 Here a word on translating another of Heidegger's important telic expressions, *es geht um*. In this idiom the *geht um* is literally "goes about," as in "goes about making dinner," and I will translate it so in the hope that it can carry telic sense through enough contexts. Macquarrie and Robinson employ the different idiom "is an issue for." Notice that the um is shared with *umwillen* and *um-zu* (in-order-to).

14 BT g263: "understanding does not primarily mean: staring at a meaning, but understanding oneself in the ability-to-be, which reveals itself in projection."

15 Heidegger himself says near the start of §31 that "we have already come up against this originary understanding" [BT g143].

16 We should especially think of Kant's notion of being-affected, as one of our three basic cognitive stances, along with acting (practical) and mirroring (theoretical); it is the topic of the third Critique. Heidegger is operating with a comparable schema.

17 BCM 68: "Because we take moods from their outbreaks, they seem to be occurrences among others, and we overlook the peculiar and thorough being-attuned, the originary attunement of the whole Dasein as such."

18 Already in the 1924 CT: "It is in speaking [*Sprechen*] that humans' being-in-the-world mainly plays out" [8]. PH [261–72] develops at length the distinction between talk and language.

19 It deserves mention, however, that Heidegger re-opens this question near the end of §34, asking whether language is equipment, or has Dasein's being, or is neither [BT g166]. But he gives no overruling answer in the book. It should also be noted that he has a very different account of language in his later writings, after his "turn."

20 BT g168: "Talk that expresses itself is communication. Its tendency of being aims at bringing the hearer into participation [*Teilnahme*] in disclosed being towards what is talked about in the talk." BP 210: "In communication and through it, one Dasein enters with the other, the addressee, into the same being-relation to that about which the assertion is made."

21 As Carman well puts it, they "run orthogonally along different dimensions in the fabric of intelligibility" [2003 5].

22 I therefore largely agree with Carman's account of Heidegger's "social externalism"; see his defense of this [2003 146–54] against Wrathall's denial [in his 1999].

23 "Being-with-one-another in *das Man* is … an intent, ambiguous watching of one another, a secret and reciprocal listening-in. Under the mask of the

for-one-another an against-one-another plays" [BT g175]. Recall from Chapter 1 Heidegger's own careerism.

24 He already uses it in this way in the 1924 CT [8–9]. See also PH 244–48.

25 BT g169–70: "The dominance of the public interpretation has already decided the possibilities of having a mood, i.e. the basic way in which Dasein lets the world matter to it. *Das Man* prescribes the self-finding; it determines what and how one 'sees'."

26 Dreyfus [1991 7] says that Heidegger takes over Dilthey's point that the "meaning and organization of a culture" are basic—against a "methodological individualism." Compare Brandom's argument [2005] for "the ontological primacy of the social" [216].

Five: *Being and Time*: existentialism

1 The lecture-courses surrounding BT are scanty in their treatment of these ideas. But see PH, which analyzes anxiety as what falling flees [283–93], and begins accounts of death and guilt [307–19]. See too the treatment of freedom and self-choosing in MF [185ff.]. And CT gives an early preview of BT's treatment of these themes. See Chapter 3, note 1.

2 Poole [1998 51–53] is mockingly critical of Heidegger's heavy but unremarked borrowings: he "remorselessly ransacks Kierkegaard"; Poole cites especially the notions of anxiety, falling, *das Man*, and thrownness. In MF [190–91] Heidegger claims that Kierkegaard had "a completely different basic purpose, that also required different ways and means"; cf. also WCT 213.

3 If the pragmatism involves values, it is only the value of success in pursuit of whatever ends one might contingently have. This is uninteresting to Heidegger and to us.

4 Note Guignon's broader effort [e.g. 2000 85] to find Heidegger attributing a "narrative structure" to human situations. We'll return to this when we treat "historicality" in Chapter 6.2.

5 His argument runs parallel to Plato's partitioning of the soul and claims about the parts' proper balance (in the *Republic*).

6 See, again, Dreyfus' extensive treatment of this problem [1991 ch. 13], as well as that by Boedeker [2001].

7 Cf. Carman [2000 21]: "because it is rooted in discourse [*Rede*], interpretation is constantly subject to a kind of generic drift, since articulations and elaborations of meaning essentially move in the direction of common intelligibility."

8 Here the German plays on the affinity between *unzuhause* and *unheimlich*; I follow Macquarrie and Robinson in translating the latter as "uncanny," but it likewise literally means "not-at-home."

9 He proceeds the same way in PH 283–93; also WM (P 88).

10 Elsewhere Heidegger explores different attitudes with the same transcendental status, the same power to reveal deep structure: see the extended treatment of "profound boredom" in BCM 78–169, as well as its earlier discussion of "homesickness" [5].

11 Blattner puts it: "In anxiety the transparency of self-constitution breaks down, and I become aware of myself as a self-constituter" [2006 165].

12 Compare BCM 6 on "finitude" as the basic limitation in the human condition.
13 Another useful discussion is in PH, which sketches, two years earlier, much of the material in Division I; it makes only a very brief start on what will be Division II, and most of this is focused on death (307–19). It treats death as the crucial avenue to grasping Dasein's "whole," and thereby time. Also see CT 10–12. Heidegger returns to the topic in BCM 294–95.
14 Edwards [1979] is the best-known critic; many of his arguments are taken up and extended by Philipse [1998 352–74]. Their attacks express their outrage that Heidegger's views about death are taken at all seriously. But I think both miss the all-important phenomenological character of Heidegger's treatment of death—and the sense in which this makes death a "possibility."
15 Examples are Carman [2003 276ff.] and Blattner [e.g. 2006 145ff.].
16 Levinas opposes Heidegger just here, arguing that it's in proper notice of the death of others that we get the truth about death; see, e.g., his 1987.
17 PH 314 also makes this point that phenomenology "makes no decision about whether anything comes after death." See Derrida's treatment [1993 54ff.] of Heidegger's own decision to begin with a being-to-death prior to any question of immortality.
18 PH says that "this certainty, that I am myself in my going-to-die [Sterbenwerden], is the basic certainty of Dasein itself." Instead of cogito sum as our basic certainty, Heidegger offers sum moribundus [316–17]. "Only in dying can I to some extent say absolutely, 'I am'" [318].
19 Derrida [1993 62] says that "two meanings of possibility coexist" here: "the sense of the virtuality or of the imminence of the future," and "the sense of ability, of the possible as that of which I am capable."
20 We can understand "the possibility" I choose either (1) as the whole set of my roles (aims) with the ranking or priority I give them, or (2) as an individual role in this set. In the latter case the argument is trickier, because choice of one role is compatible with choosing many others as well (as a writer can also be a mother and a friend and a liberal).
21 BT g288: "Thus conscience manifests itself as an attestation belonging to Dasein's being, in which [conscience] calls Dasein itself before its ownmost ability-to-be."
22 BT g265: "In anticipating indefinitely certain death, Dasein opens itself to a constant threat arising out of its own there."
23 Compare the discussion of "selfhood" and "choosing itself" in MF 185–95.
24 "Resoluteness brings the self right into its current concernful being beside the to-hand, and pushes it into solicitous being with others" [BT g298].
25 We'll see on pp. 170–71, however, that Heidegger hints at a more positive consequence for my social relations: authenticity can make me "the conscience of others," i.e. relate me to them as defined by their own basic task of authenticity.
26 Already in CT: "Authenticity as the uttermost possibility of Dasein's being is the determination of being in which the aforementioned characters are what they are [das sind, was sie sind]" [10].
27 BCM 6: "In [becoming finite [Verendlichung]] ... there ultimately occurs an individuation [Vereinzelung] of man upon his Dasein."

28 MF 190: "In choosing itself Dasein authentically chooses precisely its being-with others." But this doesn't go very far.

29 See too the distinction between two positive forms of solicitude in BT g122: it can "leap in" and take away the other's "care" (helping with a practical need), or it can "leap ahead" "not in order to take away his 'care' but rather to give it back to him authentically as such for the first time." The latter "helps the other to become transparent to himself in his care and to become free for it."

30 See Sikka's [2006] analysis and critique of the Kantian elements in this strategy to ground ethics in the requirement to treat others "as Dasein."

31 See my 2004 for an account how Nietzsche thinks genealogy reveals different kinds of *selection* of values, and my 2009 for an account how this genealogy grounds his new idea of freedom.

Six: *Being and Time*: time and being

1 Dreyfus suggests [1991 38] that *Being and Time* waffles as to whether temporality lies at the "bottom" of Dasein, or phenomenology can always push deeper. So g26: "one is constantly compelled to face the possibility of disclosing an even more originary and more universal horizon." I agree that Heidegger was always prepared to think further and see better, but believe that he still wanted this book to tell a *complete* story, with no anticipated layers beneath the being it gets down to. BP gives an argument [325] that time is "the absolute earliest" condition for being; but it also allows [322] that "we can be quietly persuaded that there is also a faulty interpretation concealed within the temporal interpretation of being as such," without knowing just where.

2 See especially Blattner [1999] on this topic. CT is a remarkably concise anticipation (in 1924) of many of Heidegger's points. BP 227–330 is an extended treatment just after BT was published.

3 "Dasein does not fill up some at-hand track or stretch 'of life' with the phases of its momentary actualities, but rather stretches *itself* in such a way that its own being is constituted in advance as a stretching [*Erstreckung*]" [BT g374].

4 Blattner [1999 98ff.] argues that originary and authentic temporality are distinct. I agree that Heidegger sometimes has reason to distinguish them. But because he thinks of authenticity as both the becoming-explicit and the becoming-fully-itself of our originary or "deep" temporality, he also has reasons to identify them. That temporality "is what it is" when we're authentic.

5 "*The originary unity of the structure of care lies in temporality*" [BT g327]. Cf. Blattner [1999 122–26]. Heidegger's account stands in important relation to Kant's schematism, a connection I won't be able to pursue.

6 Already in CT: "*the basic phenomenon of time is the future*" [14].

7 See Blattner's very helpful discussion of this [1999 107f.].

8 Macquarrie and Robinson translate it "alongside," which I think too much connotes an at-hand relation.

9 He makes the point first about death, but brings in thrownness as well: "The mode of temporalizing by 'leaping-away' of the present is grounded in the essence of temporality, which is finite. Having been thrown into being-towards-death,

Dasein firstly and mostly flees before this thrownness, which has been more or less explicitly revealed" [BT g348].

10 BT g338: "That *present* which is held in authentic temporality and hence *authentic* itself, we call the '*moment*'." (Macquarrie and Robinson render *Augenblick* "moment of vision.")

11 This "now-time" more immediately levels off the "world-time" that Heidegger also analyzes in Chapter 6. This likewise views time as a sequence of nows, but understands these as dated, spanned, significant, and public, i.e. as meant by concern. See Blattner [1999] on world-time [ch. 3] and on the ordinary conception of time [ch. 4].

12 BP 308: "All arising and all genesis in the field of the ontological is not growth and unfolding but degeneration, since everything arising *arises*, that is, in a certain way runs *away*, removes itself from the superior force of the source."

13 Contrast Blattner [1999 287]: "this thrownness, this nullity, this inability to escape tradition and who we already are is what I am suggesting Heidegger might mean by 'birth'."

14 We find evidence of these in works just after BT: KP 65–80 treats Kant's schematism, and BP 231–56 examines Aristotle's "treatise on time," in *Physics* iv.10–14. And see the earlier IPR's account of Descartes.

15 Much later Heidegger criticizes how BT made historicity depend on Dasein: "In *Being and Time* historicity merely refers to Da-sein and not to the destiny of being. This cannot be explained from the historicity of Da-sein" [Z 184].

16 Already in BCM (1929–30) anxiety as existentiale gets replaced by boredom as "the basic mood of our contemporary Dasein" [160]. This involves a critique of the viewpoint of *Being and Time* itself.

17 Compare the proposal by Olafson [1987 134–50].

18 We can also find evidence in surrounding writings, especially the lecture-courses that came immediately after *Being and Time*. Some of these contain material surely intended to fill parts of the missing Division III. Especially useful are BP 227–330 and MF 196–211.

19 BP 228: "The ontological condition of the possibility of understanding being is temporality itself. Therefore we must be able to cull from it that by way of which we understand the like of being."

20 Another term that mediates between temporality and being is *Temporalität*, which Macquarrie and Robinson translate "Temporality"—with a capital "T" to distinguish it from *Zeitlichkeit*. This is "the way in which being and its modes and characteristics have their meaning determined originarily in terms of time" [BT g19]. Or: "It means temporality insofar as temporality itself is thematized as the condition of the possibility of the understanding of being" [BP 228; also 274]. So it is time or temporality *as* a condition for understanding being.

Seven: Heidegger's turning

1 See Philipse [1998 234] on the main later references to the turning, only four published by Heidegger: the 1947 "Letter on 'Humanism'," two other letters (1950 letter to Buchner, and 1962 to Richardson), and the 1949 talk "The

Turning" [Tu]. Also very relevant are "On the Essence of Truth" [ET] and "Time and Being" [TB]. See the accounts of the turning by Olafson [1987 153–60], Philipse [1998 233–46], Blattner [1999 277–310], and Braver [2007 257–341].

2 Braver [2007 261ff.] stresses this element in the turning. He notes Heidegger's own comment in FS 78: "there was not yet in *Being and Time* a genuine knowledge of the history of being, hence the awkwardness and, strictly speaking, the naivete of the 'ontological destruction'. Since then, this unavoidable naivete of the novice gave way to a knowing."

3 Heidegger sometimes denies such a logic, e.g. at Tu (QTE 39), but we'll see that he finds an overall aim or direction in this history, which each step advances; cf. TB 52.

4 CP 129 speaks of "that turning around in which entities are not grounded in terms of humans, but the human being is grounded from be-ing."

5 AS (W 279): "Every thinker is dependent, namely on the address of being. The extent of this dependence determines the freedom from misleading influences."

6 He aims to think "historically [*geschichtlich*]," not "historiographically [*historisch*]," where the latter involves calculating about the causes and effects of past events, and expresses the stance of technology [IP 52].

7 BC 6 puts it succinctly: "the remembrance of the inception can transport us into the essential."

8 But we must work to take them seriously, against our tendency to take up (e.g.) Greek words immediately into the common intelligibility of our own language [AS (W 252)].

9 QB (P 315) says that it's a matter of reattaining "the originary experiences of being in metaphysics by the dismantling [*Abbau*] of representations that have become familiar and empty."

10 TB (OTB 9): "Only the dismantling of these obscuring covers [over epochs]— that is what is meant by "destruction [*Destruktion*]"—procures for thinking an anticipatory insight into what then reveals itself as the destiny of being."

11 So "going back to what has historically been becomes a preview of what is yet to come, of what long approaches us" [FC 119].

12 ET (P 145): "The inceptive revealing of entities as a whole, the question about entities as such, and the beginning of Western history are the same and concurrent in a 'time' which, itself unmeasurable, first opens up the open, i.e. openness, for every measure."

13 A [EGT 114] speaks of "the uniqueness and oneness of *Hen*, the One that the early thinkers presumably beheld in the wealth of its simplicity, which has remained closed to those following."

14 The treatments of the pre-Socratics I will refer to: *Introduction to Metaphysic*, esp. ch. 4 [IM] (1935), *Basic Concepts*, pt. 2 [BC] (1941), *Parmenides* [Par] (1942–43), "Alêtheia (Heraclitus, Fragment B 16)" [A] (1943), "The Anaximander Saying" [AS] (1946), "Logos (Heraclitus, Fragment B 50)" [Lo] (1951), Lectures 5–11 in Part II of *What Is Called Thinking?* [WCT] (1951–52), "Moira (Parmenides VIII, 34–41)" [Mo] (1954). (The four essays are collected in *Early Greek Thinking*, though I cite AS from *Woodpaths*.)

15 WCT 236: "The Greeks do not represent 'essencing [wesen]', 'abiding [währen]' primarily as a mere duration. A quite different trait predominates in [these] for them, which is sometimes named by *para* and *apo*. Essencing is here-by, is pre-sencing [*an-wesen*] in conflict with ab-sencing [*ab-wesen*]." FC 101: "What presences in unconcealment—*paronta*—is that which is not away but rather essences [*west*] here in nearness."

16 ET (P 145) says that when "the first thinker" asks "what are entities," "unconcealment is experienced for the first time."

17 IM 145: "Parmenides shares Heraclitus's standpoint. And where should these two Greek thinkers, the founders of all thinking, stand if not in the being of entities?"

18 This sameness is not identity: "In sameness lies the relation of 'with', hence a mediation, a connection, a synthesis: the unification into a unity" [ID 25]; "the same [*Selbe*] is not the identical [*Gleiche*]" [ID 45]. Cf. FC 25–26, 56.

19 He is ready to believe that "the earliest still surpassed by far the latest" [AS (W 246)].

20 He makes the point with this etymology not just in AS but in WCT [189], this time regarding Parmenides' use of *chrê*, "it is necessary" (in Diels-Kranz 6). See too the great importance he gives to the hand at Par 80.

21 Par 84 says that *pragma* or action [*Handlung*] means "the unitary way that at any time things are at-hand and to-hand, i.e., are related to the hand, and that man, in his comportment, i.e. in his acting [*handelnde*] by the hand, is posited in relation to the at-hand."

22 Heidegger gives this same argument at WCT 198 (where he applies it to Parmenides) and at EC (P 213) and IM 131f. (where he applies it to the Greeks generally). This has some basis in the language. Liddell and Scott list three separate verbs for *legein*, with different roots, forms, and meanings: (1) to lay, (2) to pick out or gather, and (3) to say. At issue are (1) whether Heraclitus meant *logos* and *legein* with the first senses, and (2) Heidegger's further explications of "laying" and "gathering."

23 Lo (EGT 77): "Language would be: the gathering letting-lie-before of what presences in its presencing [*des Anwesenden in seinem Anwesen*]. In fact: the Greeks dwelt in this essence of language. But they never thought this essence of language, not even Heraclitus."

24 Einai is the infinitive of the Greek "to be," as *Sein* is of the German; similarly *eon* parallels *Seiendes* as the participle form.

25 Heidegger makes these links in his long discussion of Parmenides in WCT; his analysis of Diels-Kranz 6 shows how he fuses all three thinkers with one another.

26 Even at the start the duality is being forgotten: "At the beginning of Western thinking there occurs the unnoticed decline [*Wegfall*] of the duality" [Mo (EGT 87)].

27 Cf. Braver's account [2007 193ff.] of this history.

28 On Plato, see especially "Plato's Doctrine of Truth" [PD] (in P), *The Essence of Truth: On Plato's Cave Allegory and Theaetetus* [ETP], and *Parmenides* [Par].

29 In Plato *idea* gains "dominance over *alêtheia*," so that "[t]he essence of truth gives up its basic trait of unconcealment" [PD (P 176)].

30 "On the Essence and Concept of *Phusis* in Aristotle's *Physics* B, 1" [EC] (in P). See also *Aristotle's* Metaphysics *Theta 1–3* [AM].

31 "The whole of modern metaphysics, Nietzsche included, holds itself within the interpretation of entities and of truth initiated up by Descartes" [AWP (W 66)]. "The true, the *ens verum*, is since Descartes the *ens certum*: what knows itself in certainty, what presences in knowledge" [HC (*W* 111)].

32 See CP 352, PG 33.

33 See "Hegel's Concept of Experience" [HC] (in *W*), Identity and Difference [ID], and "Hegel and the Greeks" [HG] (in P).

34 "Hegel thinks about the matter of his thinking properly at the same time in a conversation with the previous history of thinking. Hegel is the first who can and must think in this way" [*ID* 43–44; cf. CP 149].

35 On these topics, see Taylor [2005] and Braver [2007 ch. 6].

36 Jonas [2001 252] points out how all the doings Heidegger attributes to being suggest that it's being treated as an entity.

37 WCT 79: "here there are neither members of the relation, nor the relation for itself." Cf. ID 31–33.

38 WCT 79: "Every philosophical, i.e. thinking doctrine of the human essence is *in itself already* a doctrine of the being of entities. Every doctrine of being is *in itself already* a doctrine of the human essence."

39 So he distinguishes [FC 72ff. (= DR (DT 63ff.))] between the transcendental "horizon," which gives us the world, and the deeper "region" [*Gegnet*] that lets us project any particular horizon. In genuine thinking one releases oneself into the region; this involves "getting oneself loose from transcendental representing [and] refraining from willing a horizon" [FC 92 (= DR (DT 79–80))], i.e. a suspension of one's transcendental projection of a world.

40 IM 219 describes the human as "*the site* … that being requires for its opening." Cf. FC 95 (= DR (DT 83)).

41 In CP metaphysics is philosophy "up to now," and the more adequate thinking of being will also be philosophy [e.g. 298]. Later, LH (P 276): "The thinking that is to come is no longer philosophy, because it thinks more originally than metaphysics, whose name says the same [as philosophy's]."

42 IWM (P 282): "So everything depends on this, that thinking become more thoughtful to its time. … Then the thinking that is set by entities as such and therefore represents and thereby illuminates, will be replaced by a thinking appropriated by being itself and therefore attending to being."

43 HC (*W* 116): "The entitihood [*Seiendheit*] of entities … is for us only one mode, even if a decisive one, of being which by no means must necessarily only appear as the presence of presences." Cf. IP 51.

44 See the suggestion at FC 42–43 that we can't "determine the essence of something without engaging in it"—and that this may even be so with "the essence of plants."

45 As the scientist says plaintively in the first of the *Fieldpath Conversations*, "I miss altogether a strict order of thought-progression" [FC 16].

46 Heidegger thinks of this as a disagreement with Nietzsche, who insists we must learn to give ourselves values. This reflects modernity's extreme alienation from being, since it precludes our waiting for it the right way.

47 EL (UL 71): "questioning is not the authentic behavior of thinking, but rather—hearing the address [Zusage] of that which should be put into question."

48 See Wrathall [2005 337] on the importance of the topic of "the essence of truth" between 1925 and 1945, but how Heidegger largely drops "truth" in favor of "unconcealment" after 1946. Two important essays on truth are in *Pathmarks*: "On the Essence of Truth" [ET], and "Plato's Doctrine of Truth" [PD].

49 I've been greatly helped here by Wrathall's account [2005] of unconcealment, which I follow (to an extent I won't try to specify).

50 Lafont [2000] asks this question many times [e.g. 157]. See, too, Tugendhat 1996.

51 ET (P 144): "If we translate *alêtheia* as 'unconcealment' rather than 'truth,' this translation is not merely 'more literal,' but it contains the directive to rethink the ordinary concept of truth in the sense of the correctness of assertion [*Aussage*] and to think it back to that still unconceived revealedness and revealing of entities."

52 So asks Philipse [1998 313], in the midst of a broader attack on Heidegger's "persuasive redefinition" of truth.

53 EP (BW 70): "it was inadequate and misleading to call *alêtheia* in the sense of the clearing, truth."

54 See again Wrathall 2005 on this privative logic of the notion.

55 PL (UL 127): "There is nothing else from which *Ereignis* still derives, from which it could be clarified." TB (OTB 19) calls it the "it" that "gives" being and time.

56 See Polt's analysis [2005] how *Ereignis* is variously used by Heidegger in 1919, in the *Beiträge* [CP] [1936–38], and in "Time and Being" [TB] [1962].

57 See Polt [2005 378] on the etymology of *Ereignis*; he points out that already in 1919 Heidegger heard *eigen* in *Ereignis*. (See Chapter 2.) Translators have tried to include this sense by building "own" or "appropriate" into their renderings.

Eight: Language and art

1 The principal references for this topic are the essays (dating from 1950–59) that Heidegger collected into *Underway to Language*. But the topic is so central that most of his later writings address it. See the discussion by Lafont [2000 ch. 2].

2 As we saw in Chapter 4.5, this was *Being and Time*'s view of language [*Sprache*], though it gave a deeper role to *Rede* or "talk."

3 BDT (BW 348): "Man behaves as though he were the shaper and master of language, whereas she remains the master [*Herrin*] of man. Perhaps it is before all else man's reversal of this mastery-relationship that drives his essence into alienation."

4 In the contemporary HE (EHP 56): "Only where there is language, is there world. ... Language is not a tool at our disposal, but that *Ereignis* which disposes the highest possibility of human being." FC 77 (= DR (DT 70)): "But is it really established that there is the nameless at all?"

5 Compare Taylor's way [2005] of developing language's constitutive work. See too the discussion in Lafont [2000 ch. 2].

6 I think this is Nietzsche's view, as I develop in my 2009; his genealogy of language involves a greater suspicion of it than Heidegger shows.

7 See Taylor [2005 447] on Heidegger's "Humboldtian" view of language as located in the speech community, not in the individual.

8 *Being and Time* seldom speaks of metaphysics; it usually applies the word to the tradition in scare-quotes, implying that it's not doing genuine metaphysics. This more favorable view becomes explicit soon after *Being and Time*, most notably in "What Is Metaphysics?," his inaugural (1929) lecture at Freiburg; metaphysics is our relation to being, what he calls us to: "Metaphysics is the basic happening in Dasein" [WM (P 96)]. But thereafter the word typically marks how the tradition has gone wrong, as in LH (P 245f.). Heidegger later explains that in WM he was using "metaphysics" in a sense not "strictly historical"; see how he handles this shift in his 1953 insertion in the 1935 text of *Introduction to Metaphysics* [IM 19–21]; so too in M [333, 342]. My principal sources on this topic are: WM, IM, IWM, and ID. See Thomson 2005.

9 Heidegger won't call it a "mistake," though it does involve "confusion" [IWM (P 281)].

10 The aspiration to transcend entities is built into the very term: "The name 'metaphysics' derives from the Greek *meta ta phusika*. This peculiar title was later interpreted as describing the questioning that extends *meta* – *trans* – 'over' entities as such" [WM (P 93)].

11 ID 58 puts the point both ways in succession: "Metaphysics thinks of entities as such, i.e. as a whole. Metaphysics thinks of the being of entities ... "

12 M 330–31; see also, e.g., IWM (P 287), ID 58ff. Cf. Thomson [2005 13–14]; as he well puts it, these ground entities respectively from the bottom up and from the top down.

13 This is clearest in Plato, metaphysics' inaugurator, whose Ideas are a special kind of entities, which do the work of constituting the genera giving (other) entities their identities. PD (P 181): "Since the interpretation of being as *idea*, thinking about the being of entities has been metaphysical."

14 Notice how Heidegger puts it in IWM (P 278): metaphysics does have roots reaching down into being, but instead of "turning toward the soil," its element, it "sends all sap and strength into the trunk and its branches," i.e. into treating entities.

15 PL (UL 115): "Since the Greeks, entities are experienced as presences. Insofar as language 'is', it belongs, each speaking that happens, to presences."

16 FC 113: "As long as one ascribes definitions [*Bedeutungen*] to words, one does not allow their meaning [*Deutung*] to come to word."

17 The worry is that "the rule of metaphysics may instead entrench itself, in the shape of modern technology ... " [ID 72].

18 Note too how in §42 the identification of Dasein's being as "care" is supported by quoting a Latin poem (giving a fable about *Cura*); there are further references to poetry in the supporting footnotes v and vi. In the 1927 lectures BP Heidegger says [171–72]: "Poetry is nothing but the elementary coming-to-word, i.e. the becoming-uncovered of existence as being-in-the-world." He follows this with a long (prose) passage from Rilke. Sluga [2005 104] says that Heidegger's friend Oskar Becke criticized his neglect of art in BT. As mentioned in Chapter 1, Heidegger was a dedicated reader of poetry and other literature from early on; cf. van Buren [1994 64].

19 Other sources I'll use on art and poetry: *Introduction to Metaphysics* [IM], "The Will to Power as Art" [WPA], *Elucidations of Hölderlin's Poetry* [EHP], *Hölderlin's Hymn "The Ister"* [HHI], "Why Poets?" [WP], and *Underway to Language* [UL]. See Young [2001] on this topic.

20 See Dreyfus' vivid account [2005 409–10] of the artwork as a (Kuhnian) *paradigm* articulating the (Geertzean) "style" of a culture.

21 So Young [2001 30] argues against Dreyfus' "Promethean" view that art creates the world.

22 Note the irony that the shoes Van Gogh paints are apparently not a peasant woman's but his own, so that much of the story Heidegger tells is false—though of course false in a sense he is not here interested in.

23 Young [2001] claims that in OA Heidegger allows only the social role to art ("the Greek paradigm"); he takes the Van Gogh passage as "an anomaly" [65; also 70]. Young argues [127] that after World War II Heidegger's aim shifted from saving society from nihilism to helping individuals overcome their alienation—but that in OA the focus is social.

24 But see Young's discussion [2001 147–62] of Heidegger's late interest in Cezanne, Klee, and Japanese art. And see Mitchell [2010] on his late interest in sculpture.

25 I dislike the usual translation of the verb *dichten* as "poetize" and hope that "(to) poem" can be heard as a verb meaning "(to) make (something into) a poem."

26 Young insists [2001 18] that Heidegger means also events like the Nuremberg rallies—any "cultural paradigm," as Dreyfus puts it—to count as art in this broad sense.

27 HE (EHP 60): "[poetry is the saying] whereby everything first steps into the open, which we then discuss and negotiate in everyday language."

28 See Gosetti-Ferencei's examination [2004] of Heidegger's reading of Hölderlin. Young [2001] also treats it extensively.

29 HHI 126: "no poet, especially not a poet of Hölderlin's rank, adopts 'concepts'."

30 Compare this with Nietzsche's famous account in "On Truth and Lie ... " of words as metaphors whose character as such has been "worn away."

31 GA 13 includes several short collections of poems from different periods of Heidegger's life; the longest set is "From the Experience of Thinking," translated in PLT.

32 See especially *Fieldpath Conversations* [FC], and its extract "Towards Discussion of Releasement ... " [DR].

33 Philipse [1998 78]: "comparing Aristotle's usage of Greek and Heidegger's usage of German, one will conclude that Heidegger would never have invented his highly original philosophical jargon had he not been inspired by Aristotle and, to a lesser extent, by Plato."

34 Young [2002 20] calls the later texts "a complementary mingling of both meditative and poetic thinking, a happy marriage between the two."

35 On the relation between these, see also White 1978 [ch. 7].

36 WP (W 206) speaks of the task "to bring the essence of both [thinking and poetry] into the most extreme discord in order to found their concord." Rem (EHP 126): "The unaccustomed opens itself and opens the open only in poeming (or, separated from it by an abyss and in its time, in 'thinking')."

37 *WCT* 128: "thinking and poeming are in themselves the initiating, essential, and therefore also the final speaking that language speaks through the human."
38 Young [2002 21] argues by contrast that philosophy plays the secondary role of "validating" ideas that first appear to Heidegger's "poetic vision."
39 Heidegger might acknowledge that he makes this judgment *only qua thinker*, and that the poet would similarly judge that divinity lies deeper. Since each is authoritative regarding his own domain [*HHI* 146], Heidegger might concede that these judgments are equally legitimate. He leaves off *IP* by raising the difficulty that "we, contemplating thinking and poeming as contemplators, already stand by thinking on one side of the relationship between thinking and poeming, such that everything to be said is one-sided in advance" [50].
40 *WCT* 186: "Parmenides' language is the language of a thinking, is this thinking itself. Therefore, it also speaks otherwise than the still older poetry of Homer."
41 Heidegger refers to a path or way in the titles of his two principal collections of essays, *Holzwege* [*Woodpaths*] and *Wegmarken* [*Pathmarks*]. Two of the three dialogues in *Feldweg Gespräche* [*Fieldpath Conversations*] are set on paths. The motto for his collected works is *Wege—nicht Werke* (Paths—not Works). He stresses that in reading him we must "pay attention to the path, less than to the content" [*ID* 23; cf. the opening of QT].
42 *M* 42 brings out another aspect of thinking's association with a path: it is always "on the way," so that, unlike poetry, "thinking of be-ing never dares to come to rest in a 'work'."

Nine: Technology and god

1 DL (*UL* 10): "Without this theological source I would never have arrived at the path of thinking. But source [*Herkunft*] always remains future [*Zukunft*]."
2 Some of the key places Heidegger treats technology are gathered, mostly from *W* and *GA* 7, in the collection QTE: "The Age of the World Picture" [AWP], "Nietzsche's Word: 'God Is Dead'" [NW], "The Question about Technology" [QT], "The Turning" [Tu], and "Science and Reflection" [SR]. Borgmann says [2005 424–25] that CP initiates Heidegger's thinking on technology; there the target is called "machination."
3 Borgmann [2005] argues that *Being and Time* depicts a handicraft stance different from technology, "a coherent pre-technological world" [422]. Yet technology seems just a completion of BT's world, not a perversion of it.
4 This ground-plan involves such definitions as: "Motion means change of place. No motion or direction of motion is superior to any other. ... Every force is defined according to, i.e. only is, its consequences in motion, i.e. again, in the magnitude of change of place in the unity of time" [AWP (*W* 60)].
5 In the first of the *Fieldpath Conversations* Heidegger has the scientist speak of "the feeling of domination [*Beherrschung*] that fuels scientific work" [FC 19]. Z 104–05 says that "the point [behind modern science] is *control* and *domination* of the processes of nature," an aim already evident in Descartes.
6 Braver [2007 339–40] recognizes that Heidegger still relies on "a minimal definition of man that remains the same across the epochs," but says that this

"has shrunk to the barest possible point of just the ability to experience or be aware of anything." But I think Heidegger gives it more structure: he builds into our essence several indications of our "proper" relation to being.

7 NW (*W* 190): "The place that, thought metaphysically, is proper to God, is the spot of the causal working and preserving of entities, as created." Again, see Thomson 2005 on ontotheology.

8 Jonas [2001 235ff.] brings out the huge difference this makes in Heidegger's theology, arguing it is a deep "paganism" that should make it unsavory to Christian theologians he thinks too enamored of it: "it seems to me that the Christian, and therefore the Christian theologian, must reject any such idea of fate and history as extending to the status of his own mandate" [246].

9 So Heidegger dismisses theological or doctrinal questions. CP 289: "The last god has its most unique uniqueness and stands outside that calculating determination meant by the titles 'mono-theism', 'pan-theism', and 'a-theism'."

10 Heidegger was preoccupied with Nietzsche beginning in 1935. The principal texts are those collected in the two-volume *Nietzsche*, *GA* 6.1 and 6.2 (most are translated in the four-volume *N*, whose page numbers I cite), as well as NW, IP, WCT, and WN. See Haar 1996 and Sluga 2005 on Heidegger's relation to Nietzsche.

11 They shared strong familial and childhood involvement in religion: Nietzsche's father and both grandfathers were Lutheran ministers; Heidegger's father was a sexton in the Catholic Church. Each was born within yards of his father's church.

12 NW (*W* 197): "Nietzsche, in the age when nihilism was beginning to be completed, experienced some traits of nihilism and at the same time interpreted them nihilistically and hence completely buried their essence. Nietzsche never recognized the *essence* of nihilism, like every other metaphysics before him." Thus Nietzsche is for him, as Sluga [2005 117] well puts it, "both a diagnostic and a symptomatic thinker."

13 FC 33: "Everything revolutionary remains fettered in opposition. Opposition though is servitude." Also LH (P 257). FC 122 gives a more divided assessment of Nietzsche.

14 He says that "Nietzsche's final philosophy ... can therefore be described as the metaphysics of the will to power" [NW (*W* 174)].

15 So Heidegger takes Nietzsche's expressions of realism about will to power, as well as his efforts to infer will to power from biology and psychology, as self-misunderstandings. Heidegger thus rules out the more naturalist and empiricist Nietzsche (and idea of will to power) I present in my 1996 and 2004.

16 LH (P 265): "precisely through the designation of something as 'a value' what is so valued is robbed of its worth." Also NW (*W* 193).

17 See Thomson's list [2005 16] of some contrast pairs, and the surrounding discussion.

18 I develop this reading of Nietzsche's notion of becoming in my 1996 [ch. 2].

19 WPK (N v3 156): "will to power in its *deepest* essence is nothing other than the constancy of becoming in presence."

20 See the discussion of this puzzle in FC, e.g.: "Against its will, by the willing of non-willing, willing entangles itself in itself and so loses precisely what it wills, namely non-willing" [33; also 48–50, 69].

21 Again Jonas [2001] brings out how alien this makes Heidegger to Christian theology: "where the gods are, God cannot be" [248].

22 CP 309: "'Gods' need philosophy, not as if they themselves must philosophize for the sake of their godding, but rather philosophy must be if 'gods' are again to come into decision." M 209: "gods and their godhead arise from out of the truth of be-ing."

23 Caputo [1978 38]: "for Heidegger the mystical relationship of God to the soul has become an implicit 'model' ... for the relationship of Being and thought."

24 HK (EHP 46): "the countrymen, too, may not try to make themselves a god by cunning, and thus eliminate by force the presumed deficiency."

25 In M [211 ff.] Heidegger describes such design as an "idolization" [Vergötterung] of certain things, such as nature or causality, by representing them as supra-human. But "gods who arise out of idolization lack godhead altogether" [213].

26 So poets "will in another manner than the intentional [vorsätzliche] self-assertion of the objectification of the world" [WP (W 239)].

27 M 212 says that "the Judeo-Christian God" is "the idolization of 'being-a-cause' as such, that is, the idolization of the ground of explanatory representation in general."

28 Caputo [2006 339]: "This god is a much more pagan-poetic god and much less Judeo-Christian, ethicoreligious God."

29 On the other hand there are some suggestions that Heidegger was covertly Christian after all, including his choice to be buried in a Catholic cemetery (though with a star not a cross on his stone).

Ten: Heidegger's influences

1 This often reflects, I think, the way these early students lived through the shock of his embrace of Nazism—this demanded choices of their own against the elements of his thinking they judged to explain that embrace. By contrast readers and students who came to Heidegger after the war, when that Nazism was well in the past, hadn't so strongly this motive to separate themselves.

2 Some useful secondary sources: Wolin 2001, Kleinberg 2005.

3 This diversity in his influencees seems a healthy sign, but we should bear in mind that Heidegger was less opposed to having "followers" than Nietzsche claimed to be. He doesn't much favor individuality among his students—their striking off to positions of their own. So Arendt experienced him as not just uninterested in her own ideas, but hostile to their very existence.

4 See, especially, Dreyfus' [1991], and the essays in his honor in Wrathall and Malpas 2000 (two volumes), with Dreyfus' replies.

5 See his chief work Truth and Method [1991], especially Part II's account of the hermeneutic method. Also see Gadamer's various accounts of Heidegger in his [1994].

6 See especially the essays collected in Margins of Philosophy [1972/1982].

7 See, e.g., The Order of Things [1966/1970]. Foucault said in a very late interview: "For me Heidegger has always been the essential philosopher. ... My whole philosophical development was determined by my reading of Heidegger."

8 On his influence in theology, see Caputo 2006.
9 For samples of his influence on environmentalism, see McWhorter and Stenstad 2009.
10 See Parkes 1987, which contains this assessment: "There is probably general agreement that among philosophers in the contemporary world Heidegger has left the greatest as well as the most continuous influence on philosophy in Japan" [Yuasa 1987 155].
11 Sharr [2007 2]: "a good deal of 'high' Western architecture—and architectural theory—from the latter half of the twentieth century owes a debt to Heidegger's influence."

Bibliography

Arendt, H. 1978. "Martin Heidegger at Eighty," in M. Murray (ed.), *Heidegger and Modern Philosophy*. New Haven: Yale University Press. First pub. in *New York Review of Books*, October 1971.

Blattner, W. 1999. *Heidegger's Temporal Idealism*. Cambridge, UK: Cambridge University Press.

——2000. "The Primacy of Practice and Assertoric Truth: Dewey and Heidegger," in M. Wrathall and J. Malpas (eds.), *Heidegger, Authenticity, and Modernity; Essays in Honor of Hubert L. Dreyfus*, Cambridge, MA: MIT Press, vol. 1.

——2006. *Heidegger's* Being and Time; *A Reader's Guide*. London: Continuum.

Boedeker, E. 2001. "Individual and Community in Early Heidegger: Situating *das Man*, the *Man*-self, and Self-ownership in Dasein's Ontological Structure," *Inquiry* 44: 63–99.

Borgmann, A. 2005. "Technology," in H. Dreyfus and M. Wrathall (eds.), *A Companion to Heidegger*, Oxford: Blackwell.

Brandom, R. 2005. "Heidegger's Categories in *Being and Time*," in H. Dreyfus and M. Wrathall (eds.), *A Companion to Heidegger*, Oxford: Blackwell. Orig. pub. in *The Monist* 66, no. 3 (1983): 387–409.

Braver, L. 2007. *A Thing of This World: A History of Continental Anti-Realism*. Evanston: Northwestern University Press.

Caputo, J. 1978. *The Mystical Element in Heidegger's Thought*. Athens, OH: Ohio University Press.

——2006. "Heidegger and Theology," in C. Guignon (ed.), *The Cambridge Companion to Heidegger*, 2nd Edition, Cambridge, UK: Cambridge University Press.

Carman, T. 2000. "Must We Be Inauthentic?," in M. Wrathall and J. Malpas (eds.), *Heidegger, Authenticity, and Modernity; Essays in Honor of Hubert L. Dreyfus*, Cambridge, MA: MIT Press, vol. 1.

——2003. *Heidegger's Analytic; Interpretation, Discourse, and Authenticity in* Being and Time. Cambridge, UK: Cambridge University Press.

Carnap, R. 1931. "Überwindung der Metaphysik durch logische Analyse der Sprache," in *Erkenntnis* 2 (1931). Tr. A. Pap, in A.J. Ayer (ed.), *Logical Positivism*,

Glencoe, IL: Free Press 1959; repr. in M. Murray (ed.), *Heidegger and Modern Philosophy; A Critical Reader*. New Haven: Yale University Press.

Cerbone, D. 2005. "Realism and Truth," in H. Dreyfus and M. Wrathall (eds.), *A Companion to Heidegger*, Oxford: Blackwell.

Critchley, S. 2008. "Heidegger for Beginners," in S. Levine (ed.), *On Heidegger's Being and Time*, London: Routledge.

Crowe, B. 2006. *Heidegger's Religious Origins*. Bloomington: Indiana University Press.

Crowell, S. 2001. *Husserl, Heidegger, and the Space of Meaning: Paths toward Transcendental Phenomenology*, Evanston: Northwestern University Press.

———2005. "Heidegger and Husserl: The Matter and Method of Philosophy," in H. Dreyfus and M. Wrathall (eds.), *A Companion to Heidegger*, Oxford: Blackwell.

Dahlstrom, D. 2001. *Heidegger's Concept of Truth*. Cambridge, UK: Cambridge University Press.

Derrida, J. 1982. *Margins of Philosophy*. Tr. A. Bass, Chicago: University of Chicago Press. Orig. pub. as *Marges de la philosophie*, Paris: Les Editions de Minuit, 1972.

———1987. "*Geschlechte* II: Heidegger's Hand." Tr. J. Leavey, in J. Sallis (ed.), *Deconstruction and Philosophy*, Chicago: University of Chicago Press. Orig. pub. as "La Main de Heidegger (*Geschlechte* II)" in *Psyche. Inventions de l'autre*, Paris: Editions Galilée, 1987.

———1993. *Aporias*. Tr. T. Dutoit, Stanford: Stanford University Press. Orig. pub. as "Apories: Mourir – s'attendre aux limites de la vérité" in *Le Passage des frontières: Autour du travail de Jacques Derrida*, Paris: Editions Galilée, 1993.

Dreyfus, H. 1991. *Being-in-the-World; A Commentary on Heidegger's* Being and Time, *Division I*. Cambridge, MA: MIT Press.

———2005. "Heidegger's Ontology of Art," in H. Dreyfus and M. Wrathall (eds.), *A Companion to Heidegger*, Oxford: Blackwell.

Dreyfus, H. and Hall, H. (eds.) 1992. *Heidegger: A Critical Reader*. Oxford: Blackwell.

Dreyfus, H. and Wrathall, M. (eds.) 2005. *A Companion to Heidegger*. Oxford: Blackwell.

Edwards, P. 1979. *Heidegger on Death: A Critical Evaluation*. Monist Monograph Nr. 1. La Salle, IL: The Hegeler Institute.

Ettinger, E. 1995. *Hannah Arendt/Martin Heidegger*. New Haven: Yale University Press.

Farias, V. 1989. *Heidegger and Nazism*. Philadelphia: Temple University Press.

Faye, E. 2009. *Heidegger: The Introduction of Nazism into Philosophy in Light of the Unpublished Seminars of 1933–1935*. Tr. M. Smith, New Haven: Yale University Press.

Føllesdal, D. 2000. "Absorbed Coping, Husserl, and Heidegger," in M. Wrathall and J. Malpas (eds.), *Heidegger, Authenticity, and Modernity; Essays in Honor of Hubert L. Dreyfus*, Cambridge, MA: MIT Press, vol. 1.

Foucault, M. 1970. *The Order of Things: An Archaeology of the Human Sciences*. New York: Random House. Orig. pub. as *Les Mots et les choses*, Paris: Editions Gallimard, 1966.

Friedman, M. 2000. *A Parting of the Ways: Carnap, Cassirer, and Heidegger*. Chicago: Open Court Publishing Co.

Gadamer, H.-G. 1991. *Truth and Method*. Tr. J. Weinsheimer and D.G. Marshall, New York: Crossroad, 1991. Orig. pub. as *Wahrheit und Methode*, Tübingen: Mohr (Siebeck), 1960.

——1994. *Heidegger's Ways*. Tr. J.W. Stanley, Albany: SUNY Press.

Gosetti-Ferencei, J. 2004. *Heidegger, Hölderlin, and the Subject of Poetic Language: Toward a New Poetics of Dasein*. New York: Fordham University Press.

Guignon, C. 2000. "Philosophy and Authenticity: Heidegger's Search for a Ground of Philosophizing," in M. Wrathall and J. Malpas (eds.), *Heidegger, Authenticity, and Modernity; Essays in Honor of Hubert L. Dreyfus*, Cambridge, MA: MIT Press, vol. 1.

——(ed.) 2006. *The Cambridge Companion to Heidegger*, 2nd Edition. Cambridge, UK: Cambridge University Press.

Haar, M. 1996. "Critical Remarks on the Heideggerian Reading of Nietzsche," in C. (ed.), *Critical Heidegger*, London: Routledge.

Habermas, J. 1992. "Work and *Weltanschauung*: The Heidegger Controversy from a German Perspective," in H. Dreyfus and H. Hall (eds.), *Heidegger: A Critical Reader*, Oxford: Blackwell.

Husserl, E. 1973. *Cartesian Meditations; An Introduction to Phenomenology*. Tr. D. Cairns, The Hague: Martinus Nijhoff. Orig. lectures presented in 1929. Orig. pub. in *Husserliana* 1, The Hague: Martinus Nijhoff, 1950.

Jonas, H. 2001. *The Phenomenon of Life; Toward a Philosophical Biology*. Repub. Evanston: Northwestern University Press. Orig. pub. New York: Harper & Row, 1966.

Kierkegaard, S. 1983. *The Sickness unto Death: A Christian Psychological Exposition for Upbuilding and Awakening*. Tr. H. and E. Hong, Princeton, Princeton University Press. Orig. pub. 1849.

——1992. *Concluding Unscientific Postscript to the Philosophical Fragments*. Tr. H. and E. Hong, Princeton: Princeton University Press. Orig. pub. 1846.

Kisiel, T. 1993. *The Genesis of Heidegger's* Being and Time. Berkeley: University of California Press.

Kleinberg, E. 2005. *Generation Existential: Heidegger's Philosophy in France, 1927–1961*. Ithaca: Cornell University Press.

Lafont, C. 2000. *Heidegger, Language, and World-Disclosure*. Tr. G. Harman, Cambridge, UK: Cambridge University Press.

Levinas, E. 1987. *Time and the Other*. Tr. R. Cohen, Pittsburgh: Duquesne University Press, 1987. Orig. pub. as "Le Temps et l'autre" in J. Wahl (ed.), *Le Choix, le monde, l'existence*, Grenoble: B. Arthaud, 1947.

Levine, S. (ed.) 2008. *On Heidegger's* Being and Time. London: Routledge.

Macann, C. (ed.) 1996. *Critical Heidegger*. London: Routledge.

McWhorter, L. and Stenstad, G. 2009. *Heidegger and the Earth: Essays in Environmental Philosophy*, 2nd Edition. Toronto: University of Toronto Press.

Malpas, J. 2006. *Heidegger's Topology: Being, Place, World*. Cambridge, MA: MIT Press.

Marion, J.-L. 1996. "Heidegger and Descartes." Tr. C. Macann in C. (ed.), *Critical Heidegger*, London: Routledge. Orig. pub. as "Heidegger et Descartes" in *Revue de Métaphysique et de Morale*, 1987.

Mitchell, A. 2010. *Heidegger Among the Sculptors*. Stanford: Stanford University Press.

Murray, M. (ed.) 1978. *Heidegger and Modern Philosophy; A Critical Reader*. New Haven: Yale University Press.

Nagel, T. 1986. *The View From Nowhere*. New York: Oxford University Press.

Okrent, M. 1988. *Heidegger's Pragmatism; Understanding, Being, and the Critique of Metaphysics*. Ithaca: Cornell University Press.

——2000. "Intending the Intender (Or, Why Heidegger Isn't Davidson)," in M. Wrathall and J. Malpas (eds.), *Heidegger, Authenticity, and Modernity; Essays in Honor of Hubert L. Dreyfus*, Cambridge, MA: MIT Press, vol. 1.

Olafson, F. 1987. *Heidegger and the Philosophy of Mind*. New Haven: Yale University Press.

Ott, H. 1993. *Martin Heidegger; A Political Life*. Tr. A. Blunden, New York: Basic Books.

Parkes, G. (ed.) 1987. *Heidegger and Asian Thought*. Honolulu: University of Hawaii Press.

Philipse, H. 1998. *Heidegger's Philosophy of Being; A Critical Interpretation*. Princeton: Princeton University Press.

Polt, R. 2005. "*Ereignis*," in H. Dreyfus and M. Wrathall (eds.), *A Companion to Heidegger*, Oxford: Blackwell.

Poole, R. 1998. "The Unknown Kierkegaard: Twentieth-Century Receptions," in A. Hannay and G.D. Marino (eds.), *The Cambridge Companion to Kierkegaard*, Cambridge, UK: Cambridge University Press.

Richardson, J. 1986. *Existential Epistemology; A Heideggerian Critique of the Cartesian Project*. Oxford: Oxford University Press.

——1996. *Nietzsche's System*. New York: Oxford University Press.

——2004. *Nietzsche's New Darwinism*. New York: Oxford University Press.

——2009. "Nietzsche's Freedoms," in K. Gemes and S. May (eds.), *Nietzsche on Freedom and Autonomy*, Oxford: Oxford University Press.

Ryle, G. 1929. Review of *Sein und Zeit*, in *Mind* 38 (July 1929): 355–70. Repr. in M. Murray (ed.), *Heidegger and Modern Philosophy; A Critical Reader*. New Haven: Yale University Press, 1978.

Safranski, R. 1998. *Martin Heidegger: Between Good and Evil*. Tr. E. Osers, Cambridge, MA: Harvard University Press.

Sartre, J.-P. 1993. *Being and Nothingness: An Essay of Phenomenological Ontology*. Tr. H. Barnes, New York: Washington Square Press. Orig. pub. 1943.

Sharr, A. 2007. *Heidegger for Architects*. London: Routledge.

Sheehan, T. (ed.) 1981. *Heidegger: The Man and the Thinker*. Chicago: Precedent Publishing.

Sikka, S. 2006. "Kantian Ethics in *Being and Time*," *Journal of Philosophical Research* 31: 309–34.

Sluga, H. 2005. "Heidegger's Nietzsche," in H. Dreyfus and M. Wrathall (eds.), *A Companion to Heidegger*, Oxford: Blackwell.

Smith, A. 2003. *Husserl and the Cartesian Meditations*. London: Routledge.

Taylor, C. 1993. "Engaged Agency and Background in Heidegger," in C. Guignon (ed.), *The Cambridge Companion to Heidegger*, 2nd Edition, Cambridge, UK: Cambridge University Press.

——2005. "Heidegger on Language," in H. Dreyfus and M. Wrathall (eds.), *A Companion to Heidegger*, Oxford: Blackwell.

Thomson, I. 2005. *Heidegger on Ontotheology: Technology and the Politics of Education.* Cambridge, UK: Cambridge University Press.

Tugendhat, E. 1996. "Heidegger's Idea of Truth." Tr. C. Macann in C. (ed.), *Critical Heidegger*, London: Routledge. Orig. pub. as "Heideggers Idee von Wahrheit" in O. Pöggeler (ed.), *Heidegger*, Berlin: De Gruyter, 1969.

van Buren, J. 1994. *The Young Heidegger; Rumor of the Hidden King.* Bloomington: Indiana University Press.

——2005. "The Earliest Heidegger: A New Field of Research," in H. Dreyfus and M. Wrathall (eds.), *A Companion to Heidegger*, Oxford: Blackwell.

White, D. 1978. *Heidegger and the Language of Poetry.* Lincoln: University of Nebraska Press.

Williams, B. 2002. *Truth and Truthfulness; An Essay in Genealogy.* Princeton: Princeton University Press.

Williams, J. 1977. *Martin Heidegger's Philosophy of Religion.* Waterloo, Ontario: Wilfrid Laurier University Press for the Canadian Corporation for Studies in Religion.

Wolin, R. (ed.) 1993. *The Heidegger Controversy: A Critical Reader.* Cambridge, MA: MIT Press.

——2001. *Heidegger's Children: Hannah Arendt, Karl Löwith, Hans Jonas, and Herbert Marcuse.* Princeton: Princeton University Press.

Wrathall, M. 1999. "Social Constraints on Conversational Content: Heidegger on *Rede* and *Gerede*," *Philosophical Topics* 27: 25–46. Repr. in M. Wrathall, *Heidegger and Unconcealment: Truth, Language, and History*, Cambridge, UK: Cambridge University Press.

——2005. "Unconcealment," in H. Dreyfus and M. Wrathall (eds.), *A Companion to Heidegger*, Oxford: Blackwell. Repr. in M. Wrathall, *Heidegger and Unconcealment: Truth, Language, and History*, Cambridge, UK: Cambridge University Press.

——2011. *Heidegger and Unconcealment: Truth, Language, and History.* Cambridge, UK: Cambridge University Press.

Wrathall, M. and Malpas, J. (eds.) 2000. *Heidegger, Authenticity, and Modernity; Essays in Honor of Hubert L. Dreyfus*, vols. 1 and 2. Cambridge, MA: MIT Press.

Young, J. 1997. *Heidegger, Philosophy, Nazism.* Cambridge, UK: Cambridge University Press.

——2001. *Heidegger's Philosophy of Art.* Cambridge, UK: Cambridge University Press.

——2002. *Heidegger's Later Philosophy.* Cambridge, UK: Cambridge University Press.

Yuasa, Y. 1987. "The Encounter of Modern Japanese Philosophy with Heidegger," in G. Parkes (ed.), *Heidegger and Asian Thought*, Honolulu: University of Hawaii Press.

Topic index

147–49; as possibility 146–47,
151–53, 160–61; see also
anticipation
destiny (Geschick) 192–93, 217,
232–33, 286, 355
disclosure (Erschlossenheit) 83, 100, 110
distantiality (Abständigkeit) 116

earth (Erd) 245, 305–6, 308–9, 317,
335, 358
ecstasis (Ekstase) 181, 190; of future
182–83, 188–89; of past 183–84,
188; of present 185–87
end-directedness 70, 88, 98–99
enframing (Gestell) 21, 210, 292,
326–28, 341, 345; argument
against 333–36; in science
328–31; in technology 327,
331–32
entity (Seiendes) 16, 57–58, 63, 80–82,
92–93, 100, 219–20, 230, 234–35,
240–42, 281, 289–90
equipment (Zeug) 92–93, 96–97,
100–101, 297; see also to-hand
Ereignis 51, 211, 242–43, 250,
269–73
essence (Wesen) 262, 265–66
everydayness (Alltäglichkeit) 69, 89,
144–45, 187
existence (Existenz) 61, 98, 111
existentialism 19, 124–25, 127, 129,
171–72, 176, 365–66

facticity (Faktizität) 111
falling (Verfallen) 112, 118, 130,
137–38, 185–89, 246–47;
deficiencies of 130–31; as
essential 132; as flight 138;
sources of 133–35
fate (Schicksal) 192–93; see also destiny
flight (Flucht) 133, 138–40; see also
falling
for-which (Worumwillen) 60–61, 102–5,
161, 312
forgetting (Vergessen) 188, 246–49
freedom (Freiheit) 163, 192–93
future (Zukunft) 182–83, 188

gods (Götter), God (Gott) 34, 52, 324–25,
357–59; as absent 338–41, 349–50;
and being 242, 289, 318, 338,
352–53; ideality of 351–52, 356;
for poets 318–19, 354–55
guilt (Schuld) 144, 153–59, 162–66,
184; see also conscience

hand 39, 92–93, 98, 223–24, 253
heritage (Erbe) 164, 193–94
historicality (Geschichtlichkei) 177,
190–93, 196–97, 207–8;
authentic h. 193–96
history of being 209–10, 213–15,
232–34
holy (Heilige) 337, 339–40

idealism 57–58, 63, 80, 199, 234,
236, 238–43, 345, 351–52
in-order-to (Um-zu) 100
intentionality 4, 48–49, 59–60, 178,
199; whether conscious 70–72; as
end-directed 60–61, 69–70, 88; as
mine 61, 128; studying i. 64–66,
74–78; not by substance 72–74
involvement (Bewandtnis) 100–101

knowing 89–90, 92; k.-how 99–101,
105, 135

language (Sprache) 20, 112–14,
119–20, 133, 135, 229, 276; as
constitutive 276–78, 281–83;
genuine uses of 285; Heidegger's l.
3–4, 211, 279, 311–13; as house
of being 278–79, 282, 286;
instrumental view of 280–81; as
point of view 283–84; see also
metaphysics, poeming, thinking
logos (word) 226–29

metaphysics 214, 233–36, 287–89,
315–16, 344, 347; language of
278–79, 288, 291–93, 304, 312;
views being as entity 289–90
mineness (Jemeinigkeit) 61, 93, 102, 128;
achieved in authenticity 161–64,

Name index

[Includes the names of philosophers, poets, and Nietzsche-scholars.]

Taylor & Francis

eBooks
FOR LIBRARIES

ORDER YOUR FREE 30 DAY INSTITUTIONAL TRIAL TODAY!

Over 23,000 eBook titles in the Humanities, Social Sciences, STM and Law from some of the world's leading imprints.

Choose from a range of subject packages or create your own!

Benefits for **you**

▶ Free MARC records
▶ COUNTER-compliant usage statistics
▶ Flexible purchase and pricing options

Benefits for your **user**

▶ Off-site, anytime access via Athens or referring URL
▶ Print or copy pages or chapters
▶ Full content search
▶ Bookmark, highlight and annotate text
▶ Access to thousands of pages of quality research at the click of a button

For more information, pricing enquiries or to order a free trial, contact your local online sales team.

UK and Rest of World: **online.sales@tandf.co.uk**

US, Canada and Latin America:
e-reference@taylorandfrancis.com

www.ebooksubscriptions.com

ALPSP Award for BEST eBOOK PUBLISHER 2009 Finalist

Taylor & Francis eBooks
Taylor & Francis Group

A flexible and dynamic resource for teaching, learning and research.

9780415350716